SAMUEL BECKETT

The Grove Centenary Edition

SAMUEL BECKETT
The Grove Centenary Edition

SAMUEL BECKETT

The Grove Centenary Edition

Volume IV

Poems, Short Fiction, Criticism

Paul Auster, Series Editor

Introduction by J. M. Coetzee

Grove Press
New York

Printed in the United States of America

FIRST GROVE PRESS EDITION

Design and textual supervision by Laura Lindgren

front cover illustration by Laura Lindgren, based on a photograph by David H. Davison

Library of Congress Cataloging-in-Publication Data

Beckett, Samuel, 1906–
    [Selections. 2006]
    Samuel Beckett : the Grove centenary edition / series editor, Paul Auster—1st ed.
      p. cm.
    Contents: v. 1. Novels. Murphy ; Watt ; Mercier and Camier / introduction by Colm Tóibín — v. 2. Novels. Molloy ; Malone dies ; The unnamable ; How it is / introduction by Salman Rushdie — v. 3. Dramatic works / introduction by Edward Albee — v. 4. Poems, short fiction, and criticism / introduction by J. M. Coetzee.
    ISBN-10: 0-8021-1820-8 ISBN-13: 978-0-8021-1820-2 (v. 4)
    ISBN-10: 0-8021-1831-3 ISBN-13: 978-0-8021-1831-8 (boxed set)
    I. Auster, Paul. 1947– II. Title.
    PR6003.E282A6 2006
    848'.81409—dc22   2005055078

Grove Press
an imprint of Grove/Atlantic, Inc.
841 Broadway
New York, NY 10003

DISTRIBUTED BY PUBLISHERS GROUP WEST
WWW.GROVEATLANTIC.COM

06 07 08 09 10 10 9 8 7 6 5 4 3 2 1

Poet, novelist, short-story writer, playwright, translator, and critic, Samuel Beckett created one of the most brilliant and enduring bodies of work in twentieth-century literature. In celebration of the one hundredth anniversary of his birth, the four volumes of this new edition bring together nearly every word Beckett published during his lifetime.

Nearly every word, but not all. Because these volumes are intended for English-language readers, and because Beckett wrote in both English and French, a number of untranslated French poems and short critical essays have not been included. Those with a knowledge of French can find them in *Collected Poems in English and French* and *Disjecta*, both available from Grove Press.

In the case of the poems, I was sorely tempted to translate them myself, but then I recalled a series of letters I exchanged with Beckett in the late seventies and early eighties. I was then in the process of putting together *The Random House Book of Twentieth-Century French Poetry*, a six-hundred-page anthology that contains the work of forty-eight poets. Beckett generously allowed me to use his translations of Apollinaire, Breton, and Eluard. When I broached the subject of including him as a *French* poet, however, he hesitated, claiming that he had neither the energy nor the inclination to revisit those old works from the late thirties. When I suggested that I translate them instead, he thought it over for a while, then said no. Only he could do the translations—and he didn't feel up to the task. So I let the matter drop.

With any other poet, I might have insisted more strenuously, but Samuel Beckett was and is a special case. Apart from some early collaborative efforts (notably with Richard Seaver on the stories "The End" and "The Expelled" and with Patrick Bowles on the novel *Molloy*), Beckett served as his own translator. But "translator" hardly does justice to the nature of the job he took upon himself. Beckett's renderings of his own work are never literal, word-by-word transcriptions. They are free, highly inventive adaptations of the original text—or, perhaps more accurately, "repatriations" from one language to the other, from one culture to the other. In effect, he wrote every work twice, and each version bears his own indelible mark, a style so distinctive that it resists all attempts at imitation. No matter how deft or skillful my translations might have been, they never would have come out sounding like Beckett.

This edition, then, does not constitute a Collected Works. Beckett scholars and astute bibliophiles will also note the omission of two posthumously published books, which the author blocked from appearing in print while he was alive: his first novel, *Dream of Fair to Middling Women*, completed in 1932 at age twenty-six (certain passages of which he later plundered and reworked into *More Pricks Than Kicks* and *Murphy*), and his first play, *Eleuthéria*, written in French in 1947. Both are available from other publishers (Arcade and Foxrock), but in my opinion they do not form an essential part of the Beckett canon.

What one will find between the covers of these four volumes are the works on which Samuel Beckett's reputation rests, everything that qualifies him as one of the great literary artists of our time, all the books and plays that will continue to be read and performed for generations to come. From the dazzling early essay on Proust to the revolutionary *Waiting for Godot*, from the uproarious prose of *Watt* to the austere minimalism of *How It Is*, from the poetic murmurs of *Texts for Nothing* to the tender, heartbreaking *Company*, from the mordant recollections of *Krapp's Last Tape* to the tragic feminine Mouth of *Not I*, everything is here: seven novels, thirty-two dramatic works, thirty poems, fifty-four stories, texts, and novellas, three pieces of criticism. Open anywhere and begin reading. It is an experience unequaled anywhere in the universe of words.

PAUL AUSTER

INTRODUCTION

1.

Most of the poems of Beckett's that we have belong to his earlier years: short, tightly constructed pieces, tending toward the cryptic, somewhat halting in their music. "Whoroscope" (1930), the most ambitious of them, is written in the uncompromising high Modernist manner of *The Waste Land*: it has to be decoded line by line rather than read.

After 1930 Beckett wrote poetry only occasionally, though one might argue that in their musicality and formal rigor the late fictions are prose poems of a kind. His most enduring contribution to poetic art is probably contained in his translations, particularly in the volume of Mexican poetry he translated into English in 1958 under the auspices of UNESCO.

2.

Ostentatious cleverness and ironic self-distancing also mark Beckett's first extended fiction, *Dream of Fair to Middling Women*, written 1931–32 and published posthumously. The story "Sedendo et quiescendo," extracted from *Dream*, shows Beckett following somewhat tentatively in the footsteps of James Joyce, whose experiments with language, later to appear as *Finnegans Wake*, seemed to promise a revolution in literature.

"A Case in a Thousand" (1934) stands oddly among the early stories. In its lack of verbal display, of self-interrogation, and of grotesquerie, it suggests what kind of writer Beckett might have become had he stayed in Ireland and been absorbed into the Irish literary establishment.

More Pricks Than Kicks is a set of loosely linked stories, written 1931–33, about the doings of Belacqua Shuah, an "indolent bourgeois poltroon" from Dublin, whose name calls to mind the slothful sinner encountered by Dante in Purgatory. This unlikely hero sets a substantial technical problem for his author: how to make a passive, self-absorbed figure the center of a lively action. Beckett solves—or circumvents—the problem by surrounding Belacqua with more energetic minor personages. The stories that result are of variable quality—the comedy is in places quite ponderous, and the young Beckett can be surprisingly clumsy at managing the business of self-conscious narration—but the intelligence behind them is distinctive, and they remain of interest for introducing a range of motifs—the mind/body split, vagrancy, the human body as an ill-designed and decrepit machine—and items—hats, boots, bicycles—that will become part of Beckett's stock in trade.

3.

Although *Watt*, written in English during the war years but published only in 1953, is a substantial presence in the Beckett canon, it can fairly be said that Beckett did not find himself as a writer until he switched to French and, in particular, until the years 1947–51, when in one of the great creative outpourings of modern times he wrote the prose fictions *Molloy*, *Malone Dies*, and *The Unnamable* ("the trilogy"), the play *Waiting for Godot*, and the thirteen *Texts for Nothing*.

These major works were preceded by four stories, also written in French, about one of which, "First Love," Beckett had his doubts. (He might also have queried the ending of "The End": usually a master of restraint, Beckett indulges here in an uncharacteristic dip into plangency.)

In these stories, in the novel *Mercier and Camier* (written in French in 1946), and in *Watt*, the outlines of the late-Beckettian world, and the procedures of Beckettian fiction generation, begin to become visible. It is a world of confined spaces or else bleak wastes, inhabited by asocial and indeed misanthropic monologuers helpless to terminate their monologue, tramps with failing bodies and never-sleeping minds condemned to a purgatorial treadmill on which they rehearse again and again the great themes of Western philosophy; and all of it will be presented in the distinctive prose that Beckett, using French models in the main, though with Jonathan Swift whispering ghostly in his ear, was in the process of perfecting for himself, lyrical and mordant in equal measures.

In *Texts for Nothing* (the French title *Textes pour rien* alludes to the orchestral conductor's initial beat over silence) we see Beckett trying to work himself out of the corner into which he had painted himself in *The Unnamable*: if "the Unnamable" is the verbal sign for whatever is left once every mark of identity has been stripped from the series of antecedent monologuers (Molloy, Malone, Mahood, Worm, and the rest of them), who/what comes when the Unnamable is stripped too, and who after that successor, and so forth; and—more important—does the fiction itself not degenerate into an increasingly mechanical stripping process?

The problem of how to concoct some verbal formula that will pin down and annihilate the unnamable residue of the self and thus at last achieve silence is formulated in the sixth of the *Texts*. By the eleventh text, that quest for finality—hopeless, as we know and Beckett knows—is in the process of being absorbed into a kind of verbal music, and the fierce comic anguish that accompanied it is in the process of being aestheticized too. Such is the solution that Beckett seems to arrive at, a makeshift solution if ever there was one, to the question of what to do next.

The next three decades will see Beckett, in his prose fictions, unable to move on—stalled, in fact, on the very question of what it means to move on, why one should move on, who it is that should do the moving on. A dribble of publications continues: brief quasi-musical compositions whose elements are phrases and sentences. *Ping* (1966) and *Lessness* (1969)—texts built up from repertoires of set phrases by combinatorial methods—represent the extreme of this tendency. Their music happens to be harsh; but as the fourth of the *Fizzles* of 1975 proves, Beckett's compositions can also be of haunting verbal beauty.

The narrative premise of *The Unnamable*, and of *How It Is* (1961), is held on to in these short fictions: a creature constituted of a voice attached, for reasons unknown, to some kind of body enclosed in a space more or less reminiscent of Dante's Hell, is condemned for a certain length of time to speak, to try to make sense of things. It is a situation well described by Heidegger's term *Geworfenheit*: being thrown without explanation into an existence governed by obscure rules. *The Unnamable* was sustained by its dark comic energy. But by the late 1960s that comic energy, with its power to surprise, had reduced itself to a relentless, arid self-laceration. *The Lost Ones* (1970) is hell to read and was perhaps hell to write too.

Then, with *Company* (1980), *Ill Seen Ill Said* (1981), and *Worstward Ho* (1983), we emerge miraculously into clearer water. The prose is suddenly more expansive, even, by Beckettian standards, genial. Whereas in the preceding fictions the interrogation of the trapped, *geworfen* self had had a mechanical quality, as though it were accepted from the beginning that the questioning was futile, there is in these late pieces a sense that individual existence is a genuine mystery worth exploring. The quality of thought and of language remains as philosophically scrupulous as ever, but there is a new element of the personal, even the autobiographical: the memories that float into the mind of the speaker clearly come from the early childhood of Samuel Beckett himself, and these are treated with a certain wonder and tenderness even though—like images from early silent film—they flicker and vanish on the screen of the inner eye. The key Beckettian word *on*, which had earlier had a quality of grinding hopelessness to it ("I can't go on, I'll go on") begins to take on a new meaning: the meaning, if not of hope, then at least of courage.

The spirit of these last writings, optimistic yet humorously skeptical about what can be achieved, is well captured in a 1983 letter of Beckett's: "The long crooked straight is laborious but not without excitement. While still 'young' I began to seek consolation in the thought that then if ever, i.e. now, the true words at last, from the mind in ruins. To this illusion I continue to cling."

4.

Beckett's book on Proust, written when he was in his twenties, is not easy to pigeonhole. It is a work of advocacy or appreciation of a new and controversial master rather than a work of literary criticism. It is certainly not an introduction to Proust, for it assumes a ready familiarity with *A la recherche* and deploys dismayingly abstruse philosophical terminology, language that Beckett would in retrospect dismiss as merely flashy.

Does the book represent a move by Beckett to claim Proust as a father figure? The idea may seem tempting; yet Beckett, a writer who concerned himself neither with the psyche and its obscurer reaches nor with the anatomizing of society, is in no obvious sense one of Proust's progeny. When he touches on love and desire, very much at the heart of Proust's opus, Beckett reveals more of his own distinctively sour views than he does of Proust's.

What Beckett really admires in Proust is his brave sense of vocation and his belief in the kind of truth that art tells. "[Proust's] explanations are experimental and not demonstrative," Beckett writes. "He explains [the problems he addresses] in order that they may appear as they are— inexplicable." This is a moment of fine disdain for any science of psychology, and perhaps for the powers of language itself to explain the world.

The *Three Dialogues*, philosophical dialogues in the pristine sense of the term, belong to the postwar years, when Beckett had a firmer grasp of his talent and his calling. They enounce concisely his paradoxical fidelity to an art at the end of the line, an art that does not know why it exists, does not know to what it should address itself, and has nothing to say—a plight that is properly comical rather than tragic.

5.

Though it is not a label he would have accepted, Beckett can justly be called a philosophical writer, one whose works can be read as a series of sustained skeptical raids on Descartes and the philosophy of the subject that Descartes founded. In his suspicion of Cartesian axiomatics Beckett aligns himself with Nietzsche and Heidegger, and with his younger contemporary Jacques Derrida. The satiric interrogation to which he subjects the Cartesian cogito (I am thinking, therefore I must exist) is so close in spirit to Derrida's program for exposing the metaphysical assumptions behind Western thought that we must speak, if not of Beckett's direct influence on Derrida, then of a striking case of sympathetic vibration.

Starting out as an uneasy Joycean and an even more uneasy Proustian, Beckett eventually settled on philosophical comedy as the medium for his uniquely anguished, arrogant, self-doubting, scrupulous temperament.

In the popular mind his name is associated with the mysterious Godot who may or may not come but for whom we wait anyhow, passing the time as best we can. In this he seemed to define the mood of an age. But his range is wider than that, and his achievement far greater. Beckett was an artist possessed by a vision of life without consolation or dignity or promise of grace, in the face of which our only duty—inexplicable and futile, but a duty nonetheless—is not to lie to ourselves. It was a vision to which he gave expression in language of a virile strength and intellectual subtlety that marks him as one of the great prose stylists of the twentieth century.

J. M. COETZEE

POEMS

Whoroscope

What's that?
An egg?
By the brothers Boot it stinks fresh.
Give it to Gillot.

Galileo how are you
and his consecutive thirds!
The vile old Copernican lead-swinging son of a sutler!
We're moving he said we're off—Porca Madonna!
the way a boatswain would be, or a sack-of-potatoey charging Pretender.
That's not moving, that's *moving*.   10

What's that?
A little green fry or a mushroomy one?
Two lashed ovaries with prostisciutto?
How long did she womb it, the feathery one?
Three days and four nights?
Give it to Gillot.

Faulhaber, Beeckman and Peter the Red,
come now in the cloudy avalanche or Gassendi's sun-red crystally cloud
and I'll pebble you all your hen-and-a-half ones
or I'll pebble a lens under the quilt in the midst of day.   20

To think he was my own brother, Peter the Bruiser,
and not a syllogism out of him
no more than if Pa were still in it.
Hey! pass over those coppers,
sweet millèd sweat of my burning liver!
Them were the days I sat in the hot-cupboard throwing Jesuits out of
                                                    the skylight.

Who's that? Hals?
Let him wait.

My squinty doaty!
I hid and you sook.   30
And Francine my precious fruit of a house-and-parlour foetus!
What an exfoliation!
Her little grey flayed epidermis and scarlet tonsils!
My one child
scourged by a fever to stagnant murky blood—
blood!
Oh Harvey belovèd
how shall the red and white, the many in the few,
(dear bloodswirling Harvey)
eddy through that cracked beater?   40
And the fourth Henry came to the crypt of the arrow.

What's that?
How long?
Sit on it.

A wind of evil flung my despair of ease
against the sharp spires of the one
lady:
not once or twice but. . . .
(Kip of Christ hatch it!)
in one sun's drowning   50
(Jesuitasters please copy).
So on with the silk hose over the knitted, and the morbid leather—
what am I saying! the gentle canvas—
and away to Ancona on the bright Adriatic,
and farewell for a space to the yellow key of the Rosicrucians.
They don't know what the master of them that do did,
that the nose is touched by the kiss of all foul and sweet air,
and the drums, and the throne of the fæcal inlet,
and the eyes by its zig-zags.
So we drink Him and eat Him   60
and the watery Beaune and the stale cubes of Hovis
because He can jig
as near or as far from His Jigging Self
and as sad or lively as the chalice or the tray asks.
How's that, Antonio?

In the name of Bacon will you chicken me up that egg.
Shall I swallow cave-phantoms?

Anna Maria!
She reads Moses and says her love is crucified.
Leider! Leider! she bloomed and withered,   70
a pale abusive parakeet in a mainstreet window.

No I believe every word of it I assure you.
Fallor, ergo sum!
The coy old frôleur!
He tolle'd and legge'd
and he buttoned on his redemptorist waistcoat.
No matter, let it pass.
I'm a bold boy I know
so I'm not my son
(even if I were a concierge)   80
nor Joachim my father's
but the chip of a perfect block that's neither old nor new,
the lonely petal of a great high bright rose.

Are you ripe at last,
my slim pale double-breasted turd?
How rich she smells,
this abortion of a fledgling!
I will eat it with a fish fork.
White and yolk and feathers.
Then I will rise and move moving   90
toward Rahab of the snows,
the murdering matinal pope-confessed amazon,
Christina the ripper.
Oh Weulles spare the blood of a Frank
who has climbed the bitter steps,
(René du Perron. . . . !)
and grant me my second
starless inscrutable hour.

NOTES
René Descartes, Seigneur du Perron, liked his omelette made of eggs hatched
from eight to ten days; shorter or longer under the hen and the result, he says,
is disgusting.

He kept his own birthday to himself so that no astrologer could cast his nativity.

The shuttle of a ripening egg combs the warp of his days.

p. 3,   l. 3   In 1640 the brothers Boot refuted Aristotle in Dublin.

       4   Descartes passed on the easier problems in analytical geometry to his valet Gillot.

   5–10   Refer to his contempt for Galileo Jr. (whom he confused with the more musical Galileo Sr.), and to his expedient sophistry concerning the movement of the earth.

     17   He solved problems submitted by these mathematicians.

p. 4,   l. 21–26   The attempt at swindling on the part of his elder brother Pierre de la Bretaillière— The money he received as a soldier.

     27   Franz Hals.

  29–30   As a child he played with a little cross-eyed girl.

  31–35   His daughter died of scarlet fever at the age of six.

  37–40   Honoured Harvey for his discovery of the circulation of the blood, but would not admit that he had explained the motion of the heart.

     41   The heart of Henri iv was received at the Jesuit college of La Flèche while Descartes was still a student there.

p. 5,   l. 45–53   His visions and pilgrimage to Loretto.

  56–65   His Eucharistic sophistry, in reply to the Jansenist Antoine Arnauld, who challenged him to reconcile his doctrine of matter with the doctrine of transubstantiation.

     68   Schurmann, the Dutch blue-stocking, a pious pupil of Voët, the adversary of Descartes.

p. 6,   l. 73–76   Saint Augustine has a revelation in the shrubbery and reads Saint Paul.

  77–83   He proves God by exhaustion.

  91–93   Christina, queen of Sweden. At Stockholm, in November, she required Descartes, who had remained in bed till midday all his life, to be with her at five o'clock in the morning.

     94   Weulles, a Peripatetic Dutch physician at the Swedish court, and an enemy of Descartes.

Home Olga

J might be made sit up for a jade of hope (and exile, don't you know)
And Jesus and Jesuits juggernauted in the haemorrhoidal isle,
Modo et forma anal maiden, giggling to death in stomacho.
E for the erythrite of love and silence and the sweet noo style,
Swoops and loops of love and silence in the eye of the sun and view of
                                the mew,
Juvante Jah and a Jain or two and the tip of a friendly yiddophile.
O for an opal of faith and cunning winking adieu, adieu, adieu.
Yesterday shall be tomorrow, riddle me that my rapparee.
Che sarà sarà che fu, there's more than Homer knows how to spew,
Exempli gratia: ecce himself and the pickthank agnus—e.o.o.e.

Gnome

Spend the years of learning squandering
Courage for the years of wandering
Through a world politely turning
From the loutishness of learning.

The Vulture

dragging his hunger through the sky
of my skull shell of sky and earth

stooping to the prone who must
soon take up their life and walk

mocked by a tissue that may not serve
till hunger earth and sky be offal

Enueg I

Exeo in a spasm
tired of my darling's red sputum
from the Portobello Private Nursing Home
its secret things
and toil to the crest of the surge of the steep perilous bridge
and lapse down blankly under the scream of the hoarding
round the bright stiff banner of the hoarding
into a black west
throttled with clouds.

Above the mansions the algum-trees
the mountains
my skull sullenly
clot of anger
skewered aloft strangled in the cang of the wind
bites like a dog against its chastisement.

I trundle along rapidly now on my ruined feet
flush with the livid canal;
at Parnell Bridge a dying barge

carrying a cargo of nails and timber
rocks itself softly in the foaming cloister of the lock;
on the far bank a gang of down and outs would seem to be mending

a beam.

Then for miles only wind
and the weals creeping alongside on the water
and the world opening up to the south
across a travesty of champaign to the mountains
and the stillborn evening turning a filthy green
manuring the night fungus
and the mind annulled
wrecked in wind.

I splashed past a little wearish old man,
Democritus,
scuttling along between a crutch and a stick,
his stump caught up horribly, like a claw, under his breech, smoking.
Then because a field on the left went up in a sudden blaze
of shouting and urgent whistling and scarlet and blue ganzies
I stopped and climbed the bank to see the game.
A child fidgeting at the gate called up:
"Would we be let in Mister?"
"Certainly" I said "you would."
 But, afraid, he set off down the road.
"Well" I called after him "why wouldn't you go on in?"
"Oh" he said, knowingly,
"I was in that field before and I got put out."
 So on,
 derelict,
 as from a bush of gorse on fire in the mountain after dark,
 or, in Sumatra, the jungle hymen,
 the still flagrant rafflesia.

Next:
a lamentable family of grey verminous hens,
perishing out in the sunk field,
trembling, half asleep, against the closed door of a shed,
with no means of roosting.
The great mushy toadstool,
green-black,
oozing up after me,
soaking up the tattered sky like an ink of pestilence,
in my skull the wind going fetid,
the water . . .

Next:
on the hill down from the Fox and Geese into Chapelizod
a small malevolent goat, exiled on the road,
remotely pucking the gate of his field;
the Isolde Stores a great perturbation of sweaty heroes,
in their Sunday best,
come hastening down for a pint of nepenthe or moly or half and half
from watching the hurlers above in Kilmainham.

Blotches of doomed yellow in the pit of the Liffey;
the fingers of the ladders hooked over the parapet,
soliciting;
a slush of vigilant gulls in the grey spew of the sewer.

Ah the banner
the banner of meat bleeding
on the silk of the seas and the arctic flowers
that do not exist.

Enueg II

world world world world
and the face grave
cloud against the evening

de morituris nihil nisi

and the face crumbling shyly
too late to darken the sky
blushing away into the evening
shuddering away like a gaffe

veronica mundi
veronica munda
give us a wipe for the love of Jesus

sweating like Judas
tired of dying
tired of policemen
feet in marmalade
perspiring profusely

heart in marmalade
smoke more fruit
the old heart the old heart
breaking outside congress
doch I assure thee
lying on O'Connell Bridge
goggling at the tulips of the evening
the green tulips
shining round the corner like an anthrax
shining on Guinness's barges

the overtone the face
too late to brighten the sky
doch doch I assure thee

Alba

before morning you shall be here
and Dante and the Logos and all strata and mysteries
and the branded moon
beyond the white plane of music
that you shall establish here before morning

       grave suave singing silk
       stoop to the black firmament of areca
       rain on the bamboos flower of smoke alley of willows

who though you stoop with fingers of compassion
to endorse the dust
shall not add to your bounty
whose beauty shall be a sheet before me
a statement of itself drawn across the tempest of emblems
so that there is no sun and no unveiling
and no host
only I and then the sheet
and bulk dead

Dortmunder

In the magic the Homer dusk
past the red spire of sanctuary
I null she royal hulk
hasten to the violet lamp to the thin K'in music of the bawd.
She stands before me in the bright stall
sustaining the jade splinters
the scarred signaculum of purity quiet
the eyes the eyes black till the plagal east
shall resolve the long night phrase.
Then, as a scroll, folded,
and the glory of her dissolution enlarged
in me, Habbakuk, mard of all sinners.
Schopenhauer is dead, the bawd
puts her lute away.

Sanies I

all the livelong way this day of sweet showers from Portrane on the
                                                                    seashore
Donabate sad swans of Turvey Swords
pounding along in three ratios like a sonata
like a Ritter with pommelled scrotum atra cura on the step
Botticelli from the fork down pestling the transmission
tires bleeding voiding zeep the highway
all heaven in the sphincter
the sphincter

müüüüüüüde now
potwalloping now through the promenaders
this trusty all-steel this super-real
bound for home like a good boy
where I was born with a pop with the green of the larches
ah to be back in the caul now with no trusts
no fingers no spoilt love
belting along in the meantime clutching the bike
the billows of the nubile the cere wrack
pot-valiant caulless waisted in rags hatless
for mamma papa chicken and ham
warm Grave too say the word

happy days snap the stem shed a tear
this day Spy Wedsday seven pentades past
oh the larches the pain drawn like a cork
the glans he took the day off up hill and down dale
with a ponderous fawn from the Liverpool London and Globe
back the shadows lengthen the sycomores are sobbing
to roly-poly oh to me a spanking boy
buckets of fizz childbed is thirsty work
for the midwife he is gory
for the proud parent he washes down a gob of gladness
for footsore Achates also he pants his pleasure
sparkling beestings for me
tired now hair ebbing gums ebbing ebbing home
good as gold now in the prime after a brief prodigality
yea and suave
suave urbane beyond good and evil
biding my time without rancour you may take your oath
distraught half-crooked courting the sneers of these fauns these smart
                                                             nymphs
clipped like a pederast as to one trouser-end
sucking in my bloated lantern behind a Wild Woodbine
cinched to death in a filthy slicker
flinging the proud Swift forward breasting the swell of Stürmers
I see main verb at last
her whom alone in the accusative
I have dismounted to love
gliding towards me dauntless nautch-girl on the face of the waters
dauntless daughter of desires in the old black and flamingo
get along with you now take the six the seven the eight or the little
                                                 single-decker
take a bus for all I care walk cadge a lift
home to the cob of your web in Holles Street
and let the tiger go on smiling
in our hearts that funds ways home

Sanies II

there was a happy land
the American Bar
in Rue Mouffetard
there were red eggs there
I have a dirty I say henorrhoids
coming from the bath
the steam the delight the sherbet
the chagrin of the old skinnymalinks
slouching happy body
loose in my stinking old suit
sailing slouching up to Puvis the gauntlet of tulips
lash lash me with yaller tulips I will let down
my stinking old trousers
my love she sewed up the pockets alive the live-oh she did she said that
was better

spotless then within the brown rags gliding
frescoward free up the fjord of dyed eggs and thongbells
I disappear don't you know into the local
the mackerel are at billiards there they are crying the scores
the Barfrau makes a big impression with her mighty bottom
Dante and blissful Beatrice are there
prior to Vita Nuova

the balls splash no luck comrade
Gracieuse is there Belle-Belle down the drain
booted Percinet with his cobalt jowl
they are necking gobble-gobble
suck is not suck that alters
lo Alighieri has got off au revoir to all that
I break down quite in a titter of despite
hark
upon the saloon a terrible hush
a shiver convulses Madame de la Motte
it courses it peals down her collops
the great bottom foams into stillness
quick quick the cavaletto supplejacks for mumbo-jumbo
vivas puellas mortui incurrrrrsant boves
oh subito subito ere she recover the cang bamboo for bastinado
a bitter moon fessade la mode
oh Becky spare me I have done thee no wrong spare me damn thee
spare me good Becky
call off thine adders Becky I will compensate thee in full
Lord have mercy upon
Christ have mercy upon us

Lord have mercy upon us

Serena I

without the grand old British Museum
Thales and the Aretino
on the bosom of the Regent's Park the phlox
crackles under the thunder
scarlet beauty in our world dead fish adrift
all things full of gods
pressed down and bleeding
a weaver-bird is tangerine the harpy is past caring
the condor likewise in his mangy boa
they stare out across monkey-hill the elephants
Ireland
the light creeps down their old home canyon
sucks me aloof to that old reliable
the burning btm of George the drill
ah across the way a adder
broaches her rat
white as snow
in her dazzling oven strom of peristalsis
limae labor

ah father father that art in heaven

I find me taking the Crystal Palace
for the Blessed Isles from Primrose Hill
alas I must be that kind of person
hence in Ken Wood who shall find me
my breath held in the midst of thickets
none but the most quarried lovers

I surprise me moved by the many a funnel hinged
for the obeisance to Tower Bridge
the viper's curtsy to and from the City
till in the dusk a lighter
blind with pride
tosses aside the scarf of the bascules
then in the grey hold of the ambulance
throbbing on the brink ebb of sighs
then I hug me below among the canaille
until a guttersnipe blast his cernèd eyes
demanding 'ave I done with the Mirror
I stump off in a fearful rage under Married Men's Quarters
Bloody Tower
and afar off at all speed screw me up Wren's giant bully
and curse the day caged panting on the platform
under the flaring urn
I was not born Defoe

but in Ken Wood
who shall find me

my brother the fly
the common housefly
sidling out of darkness into light

fastens on his place in the sun
whets his six legs
revels in his planes his poisers
it is the autumn of his life
he could not serve typhoid and mammon

Serena II

this clonic earth

see-saw she is blurred in sleep
she is fat half dead the rest is free-wheeling
part the black shag the pelt
is ashen woad
snarl and howl in the wood wake all the birds
hound the harlots out of the ferns
this damfool twilight threshing in the brake
bleating to be bloodied
this crapulent hush
tear its heart out

in her dreams she trembles again
way back in the dark old days panting
in the claws of the Pins in the stress of her hour
the bag writhes she thinks she is dying
the light fails it is time to lie down
Clew Bay vat of xanthic flowers
Croagh Patrick waned Hindu to spite a pilgrim
she is ready she has lain down above all the islands of glory
straining now this Sabbath evening of garlands
with a yo-heave-ho of able-bodied swans
out from the doomed land their reefs of tresses

in a hag she drops her young
the whales in Blacksod Bay are dancing
the asphodels come running the flags after
she thinks she is dying she is ashamed

she took me up on to a watershed
whence like the rubrics of a childhood
behold Meath shining through a chink in the hills
posses of larches there is no going back on
a rout of tracks and streams fleeing to the sea
kindergartens of steeples and then the harbour
like a woman making to cover her breasts
and left me

with whatever trust of panic we went
out with so much shall we return
there shall be no loss of panic between a man and his dog
bitch though he be

sodden packet of Churchman
muzzling the cairn
it is worse than dream
the light randy slut can't be easy
this clonic earth
all these phantoms shuddering out of focus
it is useless to close the eyes
all the chords of the earth broken like a woman pianist's
the toads abroad again on their rounds
sidling up to their snares
the fairy-tales of Meath ended
so say your prayers now and go to bed
your prayers before the lamps start to sing behind the larches
here at these knees of stone
then to bye-bye on the bones

Serena III

fix this pothook of beauty on this palette
you never know it might be final

or leave her she is paradise and then
plush hymens on your eyeballs

or on Butt Bridge blush for shame
the mixed declension of those mammae
cock up thy moon thine and thine only
up up up to the star of evening
swoon upon the arch-gasometer
on Misery Hill brand-new carnation
swoon upon the little purple
house of prayer
something heart of Mary
the Bull and Pool Beg that will never meet
not in this world

whereas dart away through the cavorting scapes
bucket o'er Victoria Bridge that's the idea
slow down slink down the Ringsend Road
Irishtown Sandymount puzzle find the Hell Fire

the Merrion Flats scored with a thrillion sigmas
Jesus Christ Son of God Saviour His Finger
girls taken strippin that's the idea
on the Bootersgrad breakwind and water
the tide making the dun gulls in a panic
the sands quicken in your hot heart
hide yourself not in the Rock keep on the move
keep on the move

Malacoda

thrice he came
the undertaker's man
impassible behind his scutal bowler
to measure
is he not paid to measure
this incorruptible in the vestibule
this malebranca knee-deep in the lilies
Malacoda knee-deep in the lilies
Malacoda for all the expert awe
that felts his perineum mutes his signal
sighing up through the heavy air
must it be it must be it must be
find the weeds engage them in the garden
hear she may see she need not

to coffin
with assistant ungulata
find the weeds engage their attention
hear she must see she need not

to cover
to be sure cover cover all over

your targe allow me hold your sulphur
divine dogday glass set fair
stay Scarmilion stay stay
lay this Huysum on the box
mind the imago it is he
hear she must see she must
all aboard all souls
half-mast aye aye

nay

Da Tagte Es

redeem the surrogate goodbyes
the sheet astream in your hand
who have no more for the land
and the glass unmisted above your eyes

Echo's Bones

asylum under my tread all this day
their muffled revels as the flesh falls
breaking without fear or favour wind
the gantelope of sense and nonsense run
taken by the maggots for what they are

Cascando

1.

why not merely the despaired of
occasion of
wordshed

is it not better abort than be barren

the hours after you are gone are so leaden
they will always start dragging too soon
the grapples clawing blindly the bed of want
bringing up the bones the old loves
sockets filled once with eyes like yours
all always is it better too soon than never
the black want splashing their faces
saying again nine days never floated the loved
nor nine months
nor nine lives

2.

saying again
if you do not teach me I shall not learn
saying again there is a last
even of last times
last times of begging
last times of loving
of knowing not knowing pretending
a last even of last times of saying
if you do not love me I shall not be loved
if I do not love you I shall not love

the churn of stale words in the heart again
love love love thud of the old plunger
pestling the unalterable
whey of words

terrified again
of not loving
of loving and not you
of being loved and not by you
of knowing not knowing pretending
pretending

I and all the others that will love you
if they love you

3.

unless they love you

Ooftish

offer it up plank it down
Golgotha was only the potegg
cancer angina it is all one to us
cough up your T.B. don't be stingy
no trifle is too trifling not even a thrombus
anything venereal is especially welcome
that old toga in the mothballs
don't be sentimental you won't be wanting it again
send it along we'll put it in the pot with the rest
with your love requited and unrequited
the things taken too late the things taken too soon
the spirit aching bullock's scrotum
you won't cure it you won't endure it
it is you it equals you any fool has to pity you
so parcel up the whole issue and send it along
the whole misery diagnosed undiagnosed misdiagnosed
get your friends to do the same we'll make use of it
we'll make sense of it we'll put it in the pot with the rest
it all boils down to blood of lamb

they come
different and the same
with each it is different and the same
with each the absence of love is different
with each the absence of love is the same

Dieppe

again the last ebb
the dead shingle
the turning then the steps
towards the lights of old

Saint-Lô

Vire will wind in other shadows
unborn through the bright ways tremble
and the old mind ghost-forsaken
sink into its havoc

my way is in the sand flowing
between the shingle and the dune
the summer rain rains on my life
on me my life harrying fleeing
to its beginning to its end

my peace is there in the receding mist
when I may cease from treading these long shifting thresholds
and live the space of a door
that opens and shuts

what would I do without this world faceless incurious
where to be lasts but an instant where every instant
spills in the void the ignorance of having been
without this wave where in the end
body and shadow together are engulfed
what would I do without this silence where the murmurs die
the pantings the frenzies towards succour towards love
without this sky that soars
above its ballast dust

what would I do what I did yesterday and the day before
peering out of my deadlight looking for another
wandering like me eddying far from all the living
in a convulsive space
among the voices voiceless
that throng my hiddenness

I would like my love to die
and the rain to be raining on the graveyard
and on me walking the streets
mourning her who thought she loved me

dread nay

head fast
in out as dead
till rending
long still
faint stir
unseal the eye
till still again
seal again

head sphere
ashen smooth
one eye
no hint when to
then glare
cyclop no
one side
eerily

on face
of out spread
vast in
the highmost
snow white
sheeting all
asylum head
sole blot

faster than where
in hellice eyes
stream till
frozen to
jaws rail
gnaw gnash
teeth with stork
clack chatter

come through
no sense and gone
while eye
shocked wide
with white
still to bare
stir dread
nay to nought

sudden in
ashen smooth
aghast
glittering rent
till sudden
smooth again
stir so past
never been

at ray
in latibule
long dark
stir of dread
till breach
long sealed
dark again
still again

so ere
long still
long nought
rent so
so stir
long past
head fast
in out as dead

Something There

something there
where
out there
out where
outside
what
the head what else
something there somewhere outside
the head

at the faint sound so brief
it is gone and the whole globe
not yet bare
the eye
opens wide
wide
till in the end
nothing more
shutters it again

so the odd time
out there

somewhere out there
like as if
as if
something
not life
necessarily

Roundelay

on all that strand
at end of day
steps sole sound
long sole sound
until unbidden stay
then no sound
on all that strand
long no sound
until unbidden go
steps sole sound
long sole sound
on all that strand
at end of day

thither

thither
a far cry
for one
so little
fair daffodils
march then

then there
then there

then thence
daffodils
again
march then
again
a far cry
again
for one
so little

away dream all away

What Is the Word

folly—
folly for to—
for to—
what is the word—
folly from this—
all this—
folly from all this—
given—
folly given all this—
seeing—
folly seeing all this—
this—
what is the word—
this this—
this this here—
all this this here—
folly given all this—
seeing—
folly seeing all this this here—
for to—
what is the word—
see—

glimpse—
seem to glimpse—
need to seem to glimpse—
folly for to need to seem to glimpse—
what—
what is the word—
and where—
folly for to need to seem to glimpse what where—
where—
what is the word—
there—
over there—
away over there—
afar—
afar away over there—
afaint—
afaint afar away over there what—
what—
what is the word—
seeing all this—
all this this—
all this this here—
folly for to see what—
glimpse—
seem to glimpse—
need to seem to glimpse—
afaint afar away over there what—
folly for to need to seem to glimpse afaint afar away over there what—
what—
what is the word—

what is the word

SHORT FICTION

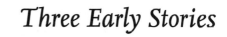
Three Early Stories

Assumption

He could have shouted and could not. The buffoon in the loft swung steadily on his stick and the organist sat dreaming with his hands in his pockets. He spoke little, and then almost huskily, with the low-voiced timidity of a man who shrinks from argument, who can reply confidently to Pawn to King's fourth, but whose faculties are frozen into bewildered suspension by Pawn to Rook's third, of the unhappy listener who will not face a clash with the vulgar, uncultivated, terribly clear and personal ideas of the unread intelligenzia. He indeed was not such a man, but his voice was of such a man; and occasionally, when he chanced to be interested in a discussion whose noisy violence would have been proof against most resonant interruption of the beautifully banal kind, he would exercise his remarkable faculty of whispering the turmoil down. This whispering down, like all explosive feats of the kind, was as the apogee of a Vimy Light's parabola, commanding undeserved attention because of its sudden brilliance. The actual imposition of silence by an agent that drifted off itself into silence a few tables away was merely the easy climax of a long series of subtle preparations: all but imperceptible twitches of impatience, smiles artistically suppressed, a swift affection of uninterested detachment, all finely produced and thrown into the heat of the conflict, so that the most fiercely oblivious combatant could not fail to be neatly and intolerably irritated. Then, when his work had been done and an angry lull was imminent, he whispered. As with all artists, this casting of an effect in the teeth of his audience was the least difficult part of his business; he had been working hard for the last half-hour, and no one had seen him; that long chain of inspired gesture had been absorbed unconsciously by every being within the wide orbit of his control, and accepted as normal and spontaneous. To avoid the expansion of the commonplace is not enough; the highest art reduces significance in order to obtain that inexplicable bombshell perfection. Before no supreme manifestation of Beauty do we proceed comfortably up a staircase of sensation, and sit down mildly on the topmost stair to digest our gratification: such is the pleasure of Prettiness. We are taken up bodily and pitched breathless on the peak of a sheer crag: which is the pain of Beauty. Just as the creative artist must be partly illusionist, our whispering prestidigitator was partly artist. A member of the Browning Society would say that he played on the souls of men as on an instrument; a unanimist, that he imposed his personality on a group. But we must be careful not to imply that the least apostolic fervour coloured what was at its worst the purely utilitarian contrivance of a man who wished to gain himself a hearing, and at its best an amused experiment in applied psychology.

In the silence of his room he was afraid, afraid of that wild rebellious surge that aspired violently towards realization in sound. He felt its implacable caged resentment, its longing to be released in one splendid drunken scream and fused with the cosmic discord. Its struggle for divinity was as real as his own, and as futile. He wondered if the Power which, having denied him the conscious completion of the meanest mongrel, bade him forget his fine imperfection beside it in the gutter, ever trembled at the force of his revolt. Meanwhile that flesh-locked sea of silence achieved a miserable consummation in driblets of sound, as each failing leaf saps the painful vigour of a tree in a cruelly windless autumn. The process was absurd, extravagantly absurd, like boiling an egg over a bonfire. But in his case it was not a willful extravagance; he felt compassion as well as fear; he dreaded lest his prisoner should escape, he longed that it might escape; it tore at his throat and he choked it back in dread and sorrow. Fear breeds fear: he began to have a horror of unexpected pain, of sleep, of anything that might remove the involuntary inhibition. He drugged himself that he might sleep heavily, silently; he scarcely left his room, scarcely spoke, thus denying even that rare transmutation to the rising tossing soundlessness that seemed now to rend his whole being with the violence of its effort. He felt he was losing, playing into the hands of the enemy by the very severity of his restrictions. By damming the stream of whispers he had raised the level of the flood, and he knew the day would come when it could no longer be denied. Still he was silent, in silence listening for the first murmur of the torrent that must destroy him. At this moment the Woman came to him. . . .

He was listening in the dusk when she came, listening so intently that he did not hear her enter. From the door she spoke to him, and he winced at the regularity of her clear, steady speech. It was the usual story, vulgarly told: admiration for his genius, sympathy with his suffering, only a woman could understand. . . . He clenched his hands in a fury against the enormous impertinence of women, their noisy intrusive curious enthusiasm, like the spontaneous expression of admiration bursting from American hearts before Michelangelo's tomb in Santa Croce. The voice droned on, wavered, stopped. He sketched a tired gesture of acceptation, and prepared to withdraw once more within that terrifying silent immobility. She turned on the light and advanced carelessly into the room. An irruption of demons would not have scattered his intentness so utterly. She sat down before him at the table, and leaned forward with her jaws in the cups of her hands. He looked at her venomously, and was struck in spite of himself by the extraordinary pallor of her lips, of which the lower protruded slightly and curled upwards contemptuously to compress the upper, resulting in a faintly undershot local sensuality which went strangely with the extreme cold purity stretching sadly from the low broad brow to the closed nostrils. He thought of George Meredith and recovered something of his calm. The eyes were so deeply set as to be almost cavernous; the light falling on the cheekbones threw them back into a misty shadow. In daylight they were strange, almost repulsive, deriving a pitiless penetration from the rim of white showing naturally above the green-flecked pupil. Now as she leaned forward beneath the light, they were pools of obscurity. She wore a close-fitting hat of faded green felt: he thought he had never seen such charming shabbiness. . . . When at last she went away he felt that something had gone out from him, something he could not spare, but still less could grudge, something of the desire to live, something of the unreasonable tenacity with which he shrank from dissolution. So each evening, in contemplation and absorption of this woman, he lost a part of his essential animality: so that the water rose, terrifying him. Still he fought on all day, hopelessly, mechanically, only relaxing with twilight, to listen for her coming to loosen yet another stone in the clumsy dam set up and sustained by him, frightened and corruptible. Until at last, for the first time, he was unconditioned by the Satanic dimensional Trinity, he was released, achieved, the blue flower, Vega, GOD. . . . After a timeless parenthesis he found himself alone in his room, spent with ecstasy, torn by the bitter loathing of that which he had condemned to the humanity of silence. Thus each night he died and was God, each night revived and was torn, torn and battered with increasing grievousness, so that he hungered to be irretrievably engulfed in the light of eternity, one with the birdless cloudless colourless skies, in infinite fulfillment.

Then it happened. While the woman was contemplating the face that she had overlaid with death, she was swept aside by a great storm of sound, shaking the very house with its prolonged, triumphant vehemence, climbing in a dizzy, bubbling scale, until, dispersed, it fused into the breath of the forest and the throbbing cry of the sea.

They found her caressing his wild dead hair.

Sedendo et Quiescendo

Down you get now and step around. Two hours menopause. Drag your coffin my lord. Half a day and I'll be with. HIER! The bright beer goes like water through the nearsighted Frank-fort porter. In Perpignan exiled dream-Dantes screaming in the planetrees and freezing the sun with peacock feathers and at last at least a rudimentary black swan with the bloodbeak and HIC! for the bladderjerk of the little Catalan postman. Oh who can hold a fire in his hand by thinking on the frosty Caucasus. Here oh here oh art thou pale with weariness. I hope yes after a continental third-class insomnia among the reluctantly military philologists asleep and armed as to nasals and dentals. Laughter. Ten Pfenigs in such a dainty slot gives the la I am bound to concede and releases the appropriate tonic for the waning lust-affair. Moderate strength rings the bell. I don't believe it. Così fan tutte with the magic flute. Even in the Xmas holidays. Half a day and I'll be in.

Up to time then after this little railway-station rectification she advanced up the railway-platform like a Gozzi-Epstein, being careful not to lose the platform ticket that yet ten Pfenigs cost had, insisting on the Garden of Eden in Mammy's furcoat, scarcely suggesting within the mild aphrodisiac of cheap loose black leather Russian boots legs that even flexed nervously in black stockings stretched to the absolute limit of intensity and viewed from a certain very special Blickpunkt against a very special quality of hard light during a period of oestruation were not alas reasonably exciting. The truly tremendous bowl of the hips (frequent and easy) breaking out and away from the waistroot (she won't need no Lupercus) like a burdocked bulb of Ruffino and the two great melons of the buttocks received an almost Rhineline from the dark peltsheath. Sheath within sheath and the missing sword. Not forgetting this was the suit he had bought for next to nothing from a lefthanded indivisible individual, with a charitable desire to justify his fatigue he forced his right hand down past the craggy coxa (almost a woman's basin in these trousers) into the glairy gallant depths and fished up a fifty. A cigarette quick for the cheekbones and the ticket handy there in the breast of my reefer and the heavy valise to snatch him skilfully detached and extenuated into the loveglue and a smoke after that was nearly as good as in the Maison du Café.

"At last!"

"Beloved!"

"Taxi!" Vie de taxi. Je t'adore à l'égal.

Carry your coffin my lord. Männer. Moving east to the segregation of the sexes. Ausgang on the right. Rule of the road. Lady on right arm. Nonsens unique. Astuce. All the same sleep on right side. Gentle reader don't overlook will you the fact that he celebrated the signing of the armistice with a pubic lanugo and

BELACQUA

we'll call him and no indolent virgin is his sister (indolent virgin!) and he doesn't much care whether he plays the tinkle-tinkle of a fourhander or not but he won't facing the keyboard observe the rule of the road (a megalomaniac you see with his head in his thighs as a general rule) so we ask you to humour what of course naturally looks merely like so much intestinal incohesion, remember he belongs to the costermonger times of a pale and ardent generation, pray that he'll let a few sighs out of him ere it's too late and speedy promotion from the Godbirds. And the lady that even in this very short and public space of time and notwithstanding that fur has no conductive properties of the appropriate kind worth speaking of has succeeded in transmitting certain unexpectedly stimulating sensations to her young visitor, what shall we call her. What name would you suggest? I'm rather inclined myself to think

SMERALDINA-RIMA

and anything that comes in handy for short. He handed her into the cab
of the Wagen with its charming deep Bluepoint zoster and spoke an
address confidently to the chauffeur who but a moment previously had
thought to light a cigarette and who now naturally was in no humour to
start his engine and set off but was not slow to yield to the promising
accent of the young tourist whose heavy fibre case he hoisted vigorously
on board on his left beside him and clipping the yet intact Ova between
his rubbery helix and hypertrophied mastoid process gratified in his dia-
logue doubtless his nearest colleagues with what no doubt was a passion-
ate Hessian epigram, set his machine angrily in motion, suffering with a
kind of hopeless interest the refracted deportment of his clients. Down
the cobbled avenue then of bitter Xmas trees, trembling in many and
many a shadowy stasis between tram and sidewalk, the superb Wagen ran
towards the spire that eliminates in impeccable imperial alignment the
now dim height of Hercules and the meagre cascade sullen and aban-
doned dropping, what there was of it and because it bloody well had to,
down the choked channel of Hohenzollern rocaille, snowclad, upon the
castle. Blocus sentimental. Belacqua took her hand and drew it down
upon the skirted, nearly the thighjoy through the fingers, and all the
same he enquires:

"Where did you get the hat?" A glaucous helmethat.

"Do you like it?"

"Very nice do you?"

"Oh I don't know do you?" Snotgasp of reliefhilarity in honour of pri-
vate joke.

"It goes with the ring." He turned over the hand and looked at the
warts. Two dwindling warts in the shadow of the Mount of Venus. Warts
in the valley of the shadow of.

"Your warts are better." Ostentatiously he dropped his mouth upon
the place. She squeezed the Giudecca of her palm against the centre
of distribution, nailing his cheekbones with thumb and index. In the
rue Delambre with a silk handkerchief did he not staunch the vomit-
dribble of a littérateur deaddrunk and cornuted what's more into the

bargain on Pernod and Pickmeup? How often had he not denied all
knowledge of Hernani? Poor Hamlet rolling his belly waxes and tapers
the spike of his navelthread for the red waistcoat. The beadlust. By no
thinking shall he consume that enterprise, by no new thoughts shall he
be altogether released from the postulate of his undertaking. Fast in
the black sand.

Let me off the tutti chords now and tell me frankly shutting your eyes
like Rouletabille what you think of my erotic sostenutino, Crémieux hold
your saliva and you Curtius, I have a note somewhere on Anteros I believe,
in fact I seem to remember I once wrote a poem (Nth. Gt. George's St.
diphthong Captain Duncan if you please) on him or to him cogged from
the lecherous laypriest's Magic Ode and if I don't forget I'll have the
good taste to use the little duckydiver as a kind of contrapuntal com-
pensation do you comprehend me and in deference to your Pisan pen-
chants for literary stress and strain. Well really you know and in spite
of the haricot skull and a tendency to use up any odds and ends of pig-
ment that might possibly be left over she was the living spit he thought
of Madonna Lucrezia del Fede. Ne suis-je point pâle? Suis-je belle? Cer-
tainly pale and belle my pale belle Braut with a winter skin like an old
sail in the wind. The root and the source between and behind the little
athletic or esthetic bit of a birdnose was indeed I assure you a constant
source of delight and astonishment, when his solitude was not peopled
and justified and beautified and even his sociability by a cold in the head,
to his forefinger pad and nail, rubbing and plumbing and boring it just
as for many years he polished his glasses (ecstasy of attrition!) or suf-
fered the shakes and gracenote strangulations and enthrottlements of
the Winkelmusik of Szopen or Pichon or Chopinek or Chopinetto or
whoever it was embraced her heartily as sure as my name is Fred, dying
all his life (thank you Mr. Auber) on a sickroom talent (thank you Mr.
Field) and a Kleinmeister's Leidenschaftsucherei (thank you Mr. Beckett),
or crossed the Seine or the Tolka or the Pegnitz or the Fulda as the case
might be and it never for one single solitary instant occurring to me that
he was on all such and similar occasions (which we are sorry to say lack

of space obliges us regretfully to exclude from this chronicle) indulging in and pandering to the vilest and basest excesses of sublimation of a certain kind. The wretched little wet rag of an upperlip, pugnozzling up and back in a kind of a duck or a cobra sneer to the nostrils, was happily to some extent mollified and compensated by the full firm undershot priapism of underlip and chin, a signal recovery to say the least and a reaffirmation of the promise of sentimental vehemence already so gothically declamatory in the wedgehead of the strapping girl. From time to time she literally only had to lift off her casco to be a birdface and to have put Mr. John Kissmearse and Orchids in mind of his Perpetually Succourful Lady as she positively must have appeared on two probationary occasions: *primo*, pinned, there's no other word for it, to her loggia by the shining sage-femme: *secundo*, confined, by Thermidor, in the interests of her armpits, to her bathroom, shamed in mind, yes, and yet—grieving for the doomed olives. Well I must say and no offence intended, that class of egoterminal immaculate quackery and dupery gives me the sick properly. No, whatever she was she wasn't that kind. I suppose I'm entitled to say she looked like a parrot in a Pieta, a pietra serena parrot. On occasions that is. Not in the helmet of salvation I need hardly point out. By Jove when I look back and think how chaste was the passion of mutual attraction that juxtaposed those two young people in the first instance. It's out of the question to give you any idea of the reverence with which they—how shall I say?—*clave* the one to the other in an ecstasy and an agony of mystical adhesion. Yessir! An ecstasy and an agony! A sentimental coagulam, sir, that biggers descruption. Don't I know for a positive fact that the unhappy Belacqua (Bollocky, though it's hardly the time or the place for that, to his friends) separated from his sweet Vega by two channels and 29 hours third-class if he went over Ostend, tossing and turning and tightening the slender white cords of his nervi nervorum with the frogs' and the corncrakes' Chinese chromatism, muting the long fever of the midos and the dolas in a scorching a piacere, inscribed to his darling blue flower some of the finest Night of May hiccupsobs that ever left a fox's paw sneering and rotting in a snaptrap. For example:

At last I find in my confusèd soul,
Dark with the dark flame of the cypresses,
The certitude that I cannot be whole,
Consummate, finally achieved, unless
I be consumed and fused in the white heat
Of her sad finite essence, so that none
Shall sever us who are at last complete,
Eternally, irrevocably one,
One with the birdless cloudless colourless skies,
One with the bright purity of the fire
Of which we are and for which we must die
A strange exalted death and be entire,
Like two merged stars, intolerably bright,
Conjoined in One and in the Infinite!

Lilly Neary has a lovely Gee and her poor Paddy got his B.A. and by the holy fly I wouldn't recommend you to ask me what class of a tree they were under when he put his hand on her and enjoyed that. The thighjoy through the fingers. What does she want for her thighbeauty? A bitch-melba arid a long long come before breakfast, toast and. Keycold Lucrece the chaste and the castaway in the cruel tights and Christ the useful cul-mination, footpounds through the fingers. No, more—more?—other than that to my bright agenesia. No no don't admire that. No but I thought per-haps honeysuckle round the cradle, custard and nutmeg on my grave, and the Eingang? Then he reddied his nose with the hand that came off her. Christ that was fine too. I wouldn't look at your Haus Albrecht Dürer, Adam Kraft my iron buck virgin. No smoking in the torture-chamber. Not really you don't mean to tell me well well! Now the thin little sandy the others do the streets but I go and dien in the, furchtbar, all of a sudden with tears, now I must go and dien in the, the others do the streets but I go and dien in the, furchtbar, find a hotel, take a Wagen, no?, aufwieder-sehen, write, to hell with you, strive for your stout little hoffentlich ball-bearing bastardpimp, I'll spend the night in the station without the Benedictina, my old bald darling, you slip in and dien, your room stinks of spunksweat, I won't kiss your playful hand, dass heisst spielen, my dolorific nymphae and a tic douleureux in my imperforate hymen, what's the Deutsch for randy, my dirty little hungry bony vulture of a whorchen away up first floor Burgwards over the stream, I'll send you a Schein when I have a Schwips. No f—— smoking in the f—— Folterzimmer. I had to ask her sister and she closed me the vowel. I wonder did I do well to leave my notes at home, in 39 under the east wind, weind please. Well then when he'd picked his nose for a little bit and the thighs there Gott sei dank up he rose didn't he and left her playing there against the oak before the ash oh don't infuriate me don't bother me, let me pay let me buy you was, eat my little Augen Celeryice, didn't he, and wandered uphill and downdale like the cat and the mouse in business together or the Marienkind. No no I *won't* say everything, I *won't* tell you everything. No but surely now you see what he am? See! Heiliger Brahmaputra! A hedgecreeper! A peeping Tom in bicycle clips! I once said that otherwise. Well then up he rose and apprehended without passion round and about the weekend brushwood foothill copulations. Yes indeed of course you're right it'd be hard for you to understand my meaning, you see he led a fairly small fleshy maiden I might have said Jungfrau into the wood I might have said Wald and creeped and peeped at the Sabbath fornications instead of. Oh did I do right to leave my notes at home! So then after another little bit he came back through the leaves and stood looking with his tongue in his cheek instead of.

J'aime et je veux pââlir. Livid rapture of a Zurbaran St. Onan. Schwindsucht and pollution in a tunnel in de Thebaid. Strange exalted death! Plus précieuse que la vie, the dirty dog! But right enough all the same what more miserable than the miserable being who commiserates not himself, caesura, with a new grief grieves not for his grief, is not worn by a double sorrow, drowns not in ken of shore. Who said that? Turned he hath the audacious soul, turned he hath and turned again upon back sides and belly, like Miss Florence on the mattress while Virgil and Sordello, yet all was painful. As an herpetic spider (do you recognize the style?) hath he consumed away. He dared to grow wild with his shadowy love and he daily watered by daily littles the ground under his face and beerbibbing did not lay siege to his spirit and he was continent and he was not sustenant and many of his months have since run out with him the pestilent person to take him from behind his crooked back and set him before his ulcerous gob in the boiling over of his fornications and in chambering and wantonness and in deafness and death and bitter and blind bawling against the honey what honey bloody well you know the honey and in canvassing and getting and weltering in filth and scratching off the scabies of lust. All on a mild scale of course, don't be misled, Paterson's Camp Coffee is the Best, perhaps I let my pen run away with me, don't for a moment imagine Bollocky's down the drain, of course he's got a bit wasted that was bound to happen and his feet have gone to bits and his bitch of a heart knocks hell out of his bosom three or four nights a week and to make a long story short Lucy and Jude are kept going pretty well from dawn to dark with his shingles and his graphospasmus and his weeping eczema and his general condition, but for all that we'll all agree I feel sure that there's a long call from feeling a bit slack and run down to lying senseless in a deathsweat. Here we are. Out we get. Step around. Thank you. You put on the light. Up we go. Out of step. Randygasp of ruthilarity in honour of private joke. Here we are. There they are. Hello. Great to be here. Grand to be here. Same old Wohnung. Wonderful to be here, Prosit. God bless. Lav on the left. Won't be a sec. Mind the bike. Mind the skis. Beschissenes Dasein beschissenes Dasein Augenblick bitte beschissenes Dasein Augenblickchen bitte beschissenes.

A Case in a Thousand

Surgeon Bor operated with the utmost success on a boy called Bray who had been brought to him suffering from tubercular glands in the neck, since when the boy showed an unfathomable tendency to sink, and did in fact begin to sink. Surgeon Bor shrugged his shoulders without rancour and called in his physician, Dr. Nye, young but most eminent.

Dr. Nye belonged to the sad men, but not to the extent of accepting, in the blank way the most of them do, this condition as natural and proper. He looked upon it as a disorder. He stood still before the window of his consulting-room, his right hand opening and closing the jigger button of his jacket, his left hand playing with the small change in his trouser pocket. He felt the afternoon light, glistening now between showers, like a high frequency shampoo on his face. Children throughout the locality had been waiting angrily for the rain to stop, so that they might go out to play. Without warning a proposition sprang up in his mind: Myself I cannot save. He sat down on the couch, still tossed from the last patient. After a while he lay down on it. The distant furious crying of a child, the light fading and then the rain again, his heart that knocked and misfired for no reason known to the medical profession, these and a compound of minor disturbances began to exhaust his mind and senses. In the absence of the feet of some other person, he thought, the meditative life has little to recommend it. His distress was interrupted by Surgeon Bor, on the telephone.

Dr. Nye found a rightsided empyema. He stood with Surgeon Bor at the end window of the long ward and looked out. Canal, bridge, lock and bright hoarding composed the scene. Three groups had gathered, one on the bridge and one on either bank, to watch a barge pass through the lock. Detached from the far group, paying no heed to the manoeuvre, holding up an umbrella as though oblivious of the fine interval, a large woman stood looking up at the hospital.

"Mrs. Bray," said Surgeon Bor.

Sister came up to tell Surgeon Bor he was wanted.

"Tell Dr. Nye the Mother Bray saga," he said and went away.

Already the barge was working clear of the dock. The group on the bridge had crossed over to the other parapet, with the result, most pleasing to Dr. Nye, that where formerly he had seen their faces, now he enjoyed a clear view of their buttocks, male and female. The groups on the banks had passed out of sight under the bridge. Mrs. Bray's umbrella was still open, but reposing now on her hat and bosom, so that both her arms were free to dangle. Thus partially eclipsed she kept watch. Dr. Nye watched the long line of buttocks, sister watched Dr. Nye.

"She would come first thing in the morning," said sister, "and stay all day till she was put out last thing. Not saying anything, only watching the boy. The same when the doctor came, she wouldn't say anything, only watch his face. Then the other patients began to complain and the nurses said she was upsetting the ward. So we had to tell her she could only have an hour in the morning and another in the evening. So there she stands now the best part of the day, watching the window and waiting for it to be time to come up."

Dr. Nye did not feel there was anything he wanted particularly to say in reply to all this.

"God knows she was quiet enough," said sister, "and no trouble, only she got on the nurses' nerves some way."

Dr. Nye mumbled something smart about her no doubt being widowed and he her only child.

"Well, then, she's married," said sister, "and has a family down in Tuam."

"Then it is as I feared," said Dr. Nye. "The woman is my old nurse."

"Oh, doctor," said sister, "what a coincident!"

The barge had passed on its way, the fine interval was drawing to an end, the buttocks had dispersed, only Mrs. Bray had suffered no change. The handle of the umbrella, carved in bog-oak to represent a bird, rose and fell. Dr. Nye planted himself before her. Sister called out to the nurses to come and look. "It's his old nanny," she cried.

Mrs. Bray, when she learned who he was and who he had been, lowered, as though in deference, her umbrella. He was troubled to find that of the woman whom as baby and small boy he had adored, nothing remained but the strawberry mottle of the nose and the breath smelling heavily of clove and peppermint. He took her arm and they walked up and down, to and fro between the bridge and her station. The conversation turned first on her son. "He has turned the corner," said Dr. Nye, but did not make it clear in what direction. Then it passed to the good old days. "Yes," said Mrs. Bray, "you were always in a great hurry to grow up so's you could marry me," but did not disclose the trauma at the root of this attachment. On the bridge they parted, Dr. Nye to visit an old schoolfellow professionally, Mrs. Bray to move over to the hospital steps, for it was nearly her time.

A nurse let a loud giggle. "Did you see him kiss her?" she said. "Why wouldn't he kiss her?" said sister, "and she his old nanny."

The boy developed an empyema on the left side, so now he had two, and they put a screen round his bed. One good result of this was that the mother could be with him all day. She neither spoke to him nor touched him; it was not even certain that she saw him, though she kept her face turned steadfastly in his direction. She made no attempt to draw Dr. Nye when he came, but was content to watch his face, and this not so much in order to learn what he was thinking as in the hope of recognizing him as the creature she had once cared. There was always something he wanted to ask her with reference to the good old days, but he felt it was neither the time nor the place, and this feeling grew steadily stronger. One day, when he had made an end of his examination, instead of departing without comment as he always had done, he sat down on the edge of the bed.

The point had been reached when he must decide whether to operate at once or hold his hand a little longer. It was a decision that lay outside the scope of his science, because from the strictly pathological point of view there was as much to be urged on the one side as there was on the other. Nevertheless it had to be made, and at once, and by him. He took hold of the boy's wrist, stretched himself all along the edge of the bed and entered the kind of therapeutic trance that he reserved for such happily rare dilemmas.

Mrs. Bray, noting the expression, at once aghast and rapt, that overcame his face, was moved in a number of ways: to trouble, at such dissolution of feature; to gratification that at last she saw him as she could remember him; to shame, as the memory grew defined; to embarrassment, as though she were intruding on a privacy or a face asleep. She forced herself to look at her son instead. Then, very sensibly, she closed her eyes altogether.

Sister peeped round the corner of the screen and surveyed the tableau. As soon as it began to show signs of coming to life she advanced with great heartiness, craving loudly to be of service. She received no encouragement, not the slightest. She went, having seen what she had seen.

Little by little Dr. Nye reintegrated his pathological outlook. He sat up on the bed, without releasing the boy's wrist however. He stood up and laid the hand gently on the breastbone. Exasperated by the inaptness of this arrangement he looked sharply at Mrs. Bray, whose mild and baffled gaze, as though she had seen nothing, had resumed operations. No doubt it was his duty to make known to her the decision that had been reached, but he really could not bear another moment of her presence. If only he had a box of peppermint creams to leave with her. Mrs. Bray again closed her eyes as she felt the imposition too pregnant for words of his hand on the crown of her hat (which nothing could ever induce her to leave off), the rapid flutter of his fingers down her cheek, the ineffable chuck to her dewlap. Feeling nothing further, she opened them. She was alone. She turned her face towards her son.

Surgeon Bor operated, the boy's lung collapsed and he died. Mrs. Bray suddenly found her tongue and thanked Dr. Nye for all he had done. Dr.

Nye tried hard to recapture the sensation which as a medical student he had experienced when a baby died under his hand, just as he had it nicely spitted for a lumbar puncture. He succeeded up to a point. The blush gathered together like a wave in his entrails, sweeping aloft and breaking in his heart—this much at least he was permitted to re-enact. He realized that she had quite done thanking him, also that he could not hope to reproduce that profound blush in her honour, yet somehow he did not seem able to get away from her. So they remained together for a time in silence, making great efforts to speak their minds. Then they gave it up and parted.

Dr. Nye took a short holiday at the seaside, towards the end of which he received a letter from Surgeon Bor, with a postscript to the effect that Mrs. Bray was back at her old games. Dr. Nye had supposed her back in Tuam. He took the first train up to town and went straight to the hospital.

"What do you mean," he said to Surgeon Bor, "back at her old games?"

Surgeon Bor turned to sister.

"Has she come on duty yet?" he said.

Sister looked at her watch.

"She should be due any minute now," she said.

They went up to the long ward and stood at the end window. There was no sign of Mrs. Bray. But before long she came into view, carrying the umbrella and a shooting-stick. This she opened and plunged into the earth of the towing-path. Then she sat down and cocked up her face at the hospital.

"Ever since the funeral," said sister.

Dr. Nye set out on his rounds. At one o'clock the news came through that Mrs. Bray, having eaten an orange, was walking up and down between the bridge and the stick; a little later, that she was again in position; finally, about lighting-up time, that she was making ready to go. Dr. Nye dropped what he was doing, happily nothing very important, and hastened out to intercept her. On the bridge they met face to face. They moved into a recess in the parapet out of the noise, they leaned out over the water.

"There's something I've been wanting to ask you," he said, looking at the water where it flowed out of the shadow of the bridge.

She replied, also looking down at the water:

"I wonder would that be the same thing I've been wanting to tell you ever since that time you stretched out on his bed."

There was a silence, she waiting for him to ask, he for her to tell.

"Can't you go on?" he said.

Thereupon she related a matter connected with his earliest years, so trivial and intimate that it need not be enlarged on here, but from the elucidation of which Dr. Nye, that sad man, expected great things.

"Thank you very much," he said, "that was what I was wondering."

They watched the water flowing out of the shadow a little longer, then she said she must be going. Dr. Nye took a box out of his pocket.

"I brought you a few peppermint creams," he said.

So they parted, Mrs. Bray to go and pack up her things and the dead boy's things, Dr. Nye to carry out Wassermann's test on an old schoolfellow.

More Pricks Than Kicks

Dante and the Lobster

It was morning and Belacqua was stuck in the first of the canti in the moon. He was so bogged that he could move neither backward nor forward. Blissful Beatrice was there, Dante also, and she explained the spots on the moon to him. She shewed him in the first place where he was at fault, then she put up her own explanation. She had it from God, therefore he could rely on its being accurate in every particular. All he had to do was to follow her step by step. Part one, the refutation, was plain sailing. She made her point clearly, she said what she had to say without fuss or loss of time. But part two, the demonstration, was so dense that Belacqua could not make head or tail of it. The disproof, the reproof, that was patent. But then came the proof, a rapid shorthand of the real facts, and Belacqua was bogged indeed. Bored also, impatient to get on to Piccarda. Still he pored over the enigma, he would not concede himself conquered, he would understand at least the meanings of the words, the order in which they were spoken and the nature of the satisfaction that they conferred on the misinformed poet, so that when they were ended he was refreshed and could raise his heavy head, intending to return thanks and make formal retraction of his old opinion.

He was still running his brain against this impenetrable passage when he heard midday strike. At once he switched his mind off its task. He scooped his fingers under the book and shovelled it back till it lay wholly on his palms. The *Divine Comedy* face upward on the lectern of his palms. Thus disposed he raised it under his nose and there he slammed it shut. He held it aloft for a time, squinting at it angrily, pressing the boards inwards with the heels of his hands. Then he laid it aside.

He leaned back in his chair to feel his mind subside and the itch of this mean quodlibet die down. Nothing could be done until his mind got better and was still, which gradually it did and was. Then he ventured to consider what he had to do next. There was always something that one had to do next. Three large obligations presented themselves. First lunch, then the lobster, then the Italian lesson. That would do to be going on with. After the Italian lesson he had no very clear idea. No doubt some niggling curriculum had been drawn up by someone for the late after-noon and evening, but he did not know what. In any case it did not mat-ter. What did matter was: one, lunch; two, the lobster; three, the Italian lesson. That was more than enough to be going on with.

Lunch, to come off at all, was a very nice affair. If his lunch was to be enjoyable, and it could be very enjoyable indeed, he must be left in abso-lute tranquillity to prepare it. But if he were disturbed now, if some brisk tattler were to come bouncing in now big with a big idea or a petition, he might just as well not eat at all, for the food would turn to bitterness on his palate, or, worse again, taste of nothing. He must be left strictly alone, he must have complete quiet and privacy, to prepare the food for his lunch.

The first thing to do was to lock the door. Now nobody could come at him. He deployed an old *Herald* and smoothed it out on the table. The rather handsome face of McCabe the assassin stared up at him. Then he lit the gas-ring and unhooked the square flat toaster, asbestos grill, from its nail and set it precisely on the flame. He found he had to lower the flame. Toast must not on any account be done too rapidly. For bread to be toasted as it ought, through and through, it must be done on a mild steady flame. Otherwise you only charred the outside and left the pith as sodden as before. If there was one thing he abominated more than another it was to feel his teeth meet in a bathos of pith and dough. And it was so easy to do the thing properly. So, he thought, having regulated the flow and adjusted the grill, by the time I have the bread cut that will be just right. Now the long barrel-loaf came out of its biscuit-tin and had its end evened off on the face of McCabe. Two inexorable drives with the bread-saw and a pair of neat rounds of raw bread, the main elements of his meal, lay before him, awaiting his pleasure. The stump of the loaf went back into prison, the crumbs, as though there were no such thing as a sparrow in the wide world, were swept in a fever away, and the slices snatched up and carried to the grill. All these preliminaries were very hasty and impersonal.

It was now that real skill began to be required, it was at this point that the average person began to make a hash of the entire proceedings. He laid his cheek against the soft of the bread, it was spongy and warm, alive. But he would very soon take that plush feel off it, by God but he would very quickly take that fat white look off its face. He lowered the gas a suspicion and plaqued one flabby slab plump down on the glowing fabric, but very pat and precise, so that the whole resembled the Japanese flag. Then on top, there not being room for the two to do evenly side by side, and if you did not do them evenly you might just as well save yourself the trouble of doing them at all, the other round was set to warm. When the first candidate was done, which was only when it was black through and through, it changed places with its comrade, so that now it in its turn lay on top, done to a dead end, black and smoking, waiting till as much could be said of the other.

For the tiller of the field the thing was simple, he had it from his mother. The spots were Cain with his truss of thorns, dispossessed, cursed from the earth, fugitive and vagabond. The moon was that countenance fallen and branded, seared with the first stigma of God's pity, that an outcast might not die quickly. It was a mix-up in the mind of the tiller, but that did not matter. It had been good enough for his mother, it was good enough for him.

Belacqua on his knees before the flame, poring over the grill, controlled every phase of the broiling. It took time, but if a thing was worth

doing at all it was worth doing well, that was a true saying. Long before
the end the room was full of smoke and the reek of burning. He switched
off the gas, when all that human care and skill could do had been done,
and restored the toaster to its nail. This was an act of dilapidation, for it
seared a great weal in the paper. This was hooliganism pure and simple.
What the hell did he care? Was it his wall? The same hopeless paper had
been there fifty years. It was livid with age. It could not be disimproved.

Next a thick paste of Savora, salt and Cayenne on each round, well
worked in while the pores were still open with the heat. No butter, God
forbid, just a good foment of mustard and salt and pepper on each round.
Butter was a blunder, it made the toast soggy. Buttered toast was all right
for Senior Fellows and Salvationists, for such as had nothing but false
teeth in their heads. It was no good at all to a fairly strong young rose like
Belacqua. This meal that he was at such pains to make ready, he would
devour it with a sense of rapture and victory, it would be like smiting the
sledded Polacks on the ice. He would snap at it with closed eyes, he would
gnash it into a pulp, he would vanquish it utterly with his fangs. Then
the anguish of pungency, the pang of the spices, as each mouthful died,
scorching his palate, bringing tears.

But he was not yet all set, there was yet much to be done. He had burnt
his offering, he had not fully dressed it. Yes, he had put the horse behind
the tumbrel.

He clapped the toasted rounds together, he brought them smartly
together like cymbals, they clave the one to the other on the viscid salve
of Savora. Then he wrapped them up for the time being in any old sheet
of paper. Then he made himself ready for the road.

Now the great thing was to avoid being accosted. To be stopped at this
stage and have conversational nuisance committed all over him would
be a disaster. His whole being was straining forward towards the joy in
store. If he were accosted now he might just as well fling his lunch into
the gutter and walk straight back home. Sometimes his hunger, more of
mind, I need scarcely say, than of body, for this meal amounted to such
a frenzy that he would not have hesitated to strike any man rash enough
to buttonhole and baulk him, he would have shouldered him out of his

path without ceremony. Woe betide the meddler who crossed him when his mind was really set on this meal.

He threaded his way rapidly, his head bowed, through a familiar labyrinth of lanes and suddenly dived into a little family grocery. In the shop they were not surprised. Most days, about this hour, he shot in off the street in this way.

The slab of cheese was prepared. Separated since morning from the piece, it was only waiting for Belacqua to call and take it. Gorgonzola cheese. He knew a man who came from Gorgonzola, his name was Angelo. He had been born in Nice but all his youth had been spent in Gorgonzola. He knew where to look for it. Every day it was there, in the same corner, waiting to be called for. They were very decent obliging people.

He looked sceptically at the cut of cheese. He turned it over on its back to see was the other side any better. The other side was worse. They had laid it better side up, they had practised that little deception. Who shall blame them? He rubbed it. It was sweating. That was something. He stooped and smelt it. A faint fragrance of corruption. What good was that? He didn't want fragrance, he wasn't a bloody gourmet, he wanted a good stench. What he wanted was a good green stenching rotten lump of Gorgonzola cheese, alive, and by God he would have it.

He looked fiercely at the grocer.

"What's that?" he demanded.

The grocer writhed.

"Well?" demanded Belacqua, he was without fear when roused, "is that the best you can do?"

"In the length and breadth of Dublin" said the grocer "you won't find a rottener bit this minute."

Belacqua was furious. The impudent dogsbody, for two pins he would assault him.

"It won't do" he cried "do you hear me, it won't do at all. I won't have it." He ground his teeth.

The grocer, instead of simply washing his hands like Pilate, flung out his arms in a wild crucified gesture of supplication. Sullenly Belacqua undid his packet and slipped the cadaverous tablet of cheese between the hard cold black boards of the toast. He stumped to the door where he whirled round however.

"You heard me?" he cried.

"Sir" said the grocer. This was not a question, nor yet an expression of acquiescence. The tone in which it was let fall made it quite impossible to know what was in the man's mind. It was a most ingenious riposte.

"I tell you" said Belacqua with great heat "this won't do at all. If you can't do better than this" he raised the hand that held the packet "I shall be obliged to go for my cheese elsewhere. Do you mark me?"

"Sir" said the grocer.

He came to the threshold of his store and watched the indignant customer hobble away. Belacqua had a spavined gait, his feet were in ruins, he suffered with them almost continuously. Even in the night they took no rest, or next to none. For then the cramps took over from the corns and hammer-toes, and carried on. So that he would press the fringes of his feet desperately against the end-rail of the bed or, better again, reach down with his hand and drag them up and back towards the instep. Skill and patience could disperse the pain, but there it was, complicating his night's rest.

The grocer, without closing his eyes or taking them off the receding figure, blew his nose in the skirt of his apron. Being a warm-hearted human man he felt sympathy and pity for this queer customer who always looked ill and dejected. But at the same time he was a small tradesman, don't forget that, with a small tradesman's sense of personal dignity and what was what. Thruppence, he cast it up, thruppence worth of cheese per day, one and a tanner per week. No, he would fawn on no man for that, no, not on the best in the land. He had his pride.

Stumbling along by devious ways towards the lowly public where he was expected, in the sense that the entry of his grotesque person would provoke no comment or laughter, Belacqua gradually got the upper hand of his choler. Now that lunch was as good as a *fait accompli*, because the incontinent bosthoons of his own class, itching to pass on a big idea or inflict an appointment, were seldom at large in this shabby quarter of the

city, he was free to consider items two and three, the lobster and the les-
son, in closer detail.

At a quarter to three he was due at the school. Say five to three. The
public closed, the fishmonger reopened, at half-past two. Assuming then
that his lousy old bitch of an aunt had given her order in good time that
morning, with strict injunctions that it should be ready and waiting so
that her blackguard boy should on no account be delayed when he called
for it first thing in the afternoon, it would be time enough if he left the
public as it closed, he could remain on till the last moment. Benissimo.
He had half-a-crown. That was two pints of draught anyway and per-
haps a bottle to wind up with. Their bottled stout was particularly excel-
lent and well up. And he would still be left with enough coppers to buy
a *Herald* and take a tram if he felt tired or was pinched for time. Always
assuming, of course, that the lobster was all ready to be handed over.
God damn these tradesmen, he thought, you can never rely on them.
He had not done an exercise but that did not matter. His Professor-
essa was so charming and remarkable. Signorina Adriana Ottolenghi!
He did not believe it possible for a woman to be more intelligent or bet-
ter informed than the little Ottolenghi. So he had set her on a pedes-
tal in his mind, apart from other women. She had said last day that they
would read *Il Cinque Maggio* together. But she would not mind if he told
her, as he proposed to, in Italian, he would frame a shining phrase on his
way from the public, that he would prefer to postpone the *Cinque Maggio*
to another occasion. Manzoni was an old woman, Napoleon was another.
Napoleone di mezza calzetta, fa l'amore a Giacominetta. Why did he think
of Manzoni as an old woman? Why did he do him that injustice? Pel-
lico was another. They were all old maids, suffragettes. He must ask his
Signorina where he could have received that impression, that the 19th
century in Italy was full of old hens trying to cluck like Pindar. Carducci
was another. Also about the spots on the moon. If she could not tell him
there and then she would make it up, only too gladly, against the next
time. Everything was all set now and in order. Bating, of course, the lob-
ster, which had to remain an incalculable factor. He must just hope for

the best. And expect the worst, he thought gaily, diving into the public, as usual.

Belacqua drew near to the school, quite happy, for all had gone swimmingly. The lunch had been a notable success, it would abide as a standard in his mind. Indeed he could not imagine its ever being superseded. And such a pale soapy piece of cheese to prove so strong! He must only conclude that he had been abusing himself all these years in relating the strength of cheese directly to its greenness. We live and learn, that was a true saying. Also his teeth and jaws had been in heaven, splinters of vanquished toast spraying forth at each gnash. It was like eating glass. His mouth burned and ached with the exploit. Then the food had been further spiced by the intelligence, transmitted in a low tragic voice across the counter by Oliver the improver, that the Malahide murderer's petition for mercy, signed by half the land, having been rejected, the man must swing at dawn in Mountjoy and nothing could save him. Ellis the hangman was even now on his way. Belacqua, tearing at the sandwich and swilling the precious stout, pondered on McCabe in his cell.

The lobster was ready after all, the man handed it over instanter, and with such a pleasant smile. Really a little bit of courtesy and goodwill went a long way in this world. A smile and a cheerful word from a common working-man and the face of the world was brightened. And it was so easy, a mere question of muscular control.

"Lepping" he said cheerfully, handing it over.

"Lepping?" said Belacqua. What on earth was that?

"Lepping fresh, sir" said the man, "fresh in this morning."

Now Belacqua, on the analogy of mackerel and other fish that he had heard described as lepping fresh when they had been taken but an hour or two previously, supposed the man to mean that the lobster had very recently been killed.

Signorina Adriana Ottolenghi was waiting in the little front room off the hall, which Belacqua was naturally inclined to think of rather as the vestibule. That was her room, the Italian room. On the same side, but at the back, was the French room. God knows where the German room was. Who cared about the German room anyway?

He hung up his coat and hat, laid the long knobby brown-paper parcel on the hall-table, and went prestly in to the Ottolenghi.

After about half-an-hour of this and that obiter, she complimented him on his grasp of the language.

"You make rapid progress" she said in her ruined voice.

There subsisted as much of the Ottolenghi as might be expected to of the person of a lady of a certain age who had found being young and beautiful and pure more of a bore than anything else.

Belacqua, dissembling his great pleasure, laid open the moon enigma.

"Yes" she said "I know the passage. It is a famous teaser. Off-hand I cannot tell you, but I will look it up when I get home."

The sweet creature! She would look it up in her big Dante when she got home. What a woman!

"It occurred to me" she said "apropos of I don't know what, that you might do worse than make up Dante's rare movements of compassion in Hell. That used to be" her past tenses were always sorrowful "a favourite question."

He assumed an expression of profundity.

"In that connexion" he said "I recall one superb pun anyway: *'qui vive la pietà quando è ben morta . . .'* "

She said nothing.

"Is it not a great phrase?" he gushed.

She said nothing.

"Now" he said like a fool "I wonder how you could translate that?"

Still she said nothing. Then:

"Do you think" she murmured "it is absolutely necessary to translate it?"

Sounds as of conflict were borne in from the hall. Then silence. A knuckle tambourined on the door, it flew open and lo it was Mlle. Glain, the French instructress, clutching her cat, her eyes out on stalks, in a state of the greatest agitation.

"Oh" she gasped "forgive me. I intrude, but what was in the bag?"

"The bag?" said the Ottolenghi.

Mlle. Glain took a French step forward.

"The parcel" she buried her face in the cat "the parcel in the hall."

Belacqua spoke up composedly.

"Mine" he said, "a fish."

He did not know the French for lobster. Fish would do very well. Fish had been good enough for Jesus Christ, Son of God, Saviour. It was good enough for Mlle. Glain.

"Oh" said Mlle. Glain, inexpressibly relieved, "I caught him in the nick of time." She administered a tap to the cat. "He would have tore it to flitters."

Belacqua began to feel a little anxious.

"Did he actually get at it?" he said.

"No no" said Mlle. Glain "I caught him just in time. But I did not know" with a blue-stocking snigger "what it might be, so I thought I had better come and ask."

Base prying bitch.

The Ottolenghi was faintly amused.

"Puisqu'il n'y a pas de mal . . ." she said with great fatigue and elegance.

"Heureusement" it was clear at once that Mlle. Glain was devout "heureusement."

Chastening the cat with little skelps she took herself off. The grey hairs of her maidenhead screamed at Belacqua. A devout, virginal blue-stocking, honing after a penny's worth of scandal.

"Where were we?" said Belacqua.

But Neapolitan patience has its limits.

"Where are we ever?" cried the Ottolenghi "where we were, as we were."

Belacqua drew near to the house of his aunt. Let us call it Winter, that dusk may fall now and a moon rise. At the corner of the street a horse was down and a man sat on its head. I know, thought Belacqua, that that is considered the right thing to do. But why? A lamplighter flew by on his bike, tilting with his pole at the standards, jousting a little yellow light into the evening. A poorly dressed couple stood in the bay of a pretentious gateway, she sagging against the railings, her head lowered, he standing facing her. He stood up close to her, his hands dangled by his sides. Where we were, thought Belacqua, as we were. He walked on gripping his parcel. Why not piety and pity both, even down below? Why not mercy and Godliness together? A little mercy in the stress of sacrifice, a little mercy to rejoice against judgement. He thought of Jonah and the gourd and the pity of a jealous God on Nineveh. And poor McCabe, he would get it in the neck at dawn. What was he doing now, how was he feeling? He would relish one more meal, one more night.

His aunt was in the garden, tending whatever flowers die at that time of year. She embraced him and together they went down into the bowels of the earth, into the kitchen in the basement. She took the parcel and undid it and abruptly the lobster was on the table, on the oilcloth, discovered.

"They assured me it was fresh" said Belacqua.

Suddenly he saw the creature move, this neuter creature. Definitely it changed its position. His hand flew to his mouth.

"Christ!" he said "it's alive."

His aunt looked at the lobster. It moved again. It made a faint nervous act of life on the oilcloth. They stood above it, looking down on it, exposed cruciform on the oilcloth. It shuddered again. Belacqua felt he would be sick.

"My God" he whined "it's alive, what'll we do?"

The aunt simply had to laugh. She bustled off to the pantry to fetch her smart apron, leaving him goggling down at the lobster, and came back with it on and her sleeves rolled up, all business.

"Well" she said "it is to be hoped so, indeed."

"All this time" muttered Belacqua. Then, suddenly aware of her hideous equipment: "What are you going to do?" he cried.

"Boil the beast" she said, "what else?"

"But it's not dead" protested Belacqua "you can't boil it like that."

She looked at him in astonishment. Had he taken leave of his senses?

"Have sense" she said sharply, "lobsters are always boiled alive. They must be." She caught up the lobster and laid it on its back. It trembled. "They feel nothing" she said.

In the depths of the sea it had crept into the cruel pot. For hours, in the midst of its enemies, it had breathed secretly. It had survived the Frenchwoman's cat and his witless clutch. Now it was going alive into scalding water. It had to. Take into the air my quiet breath.

Belacqua looked at the old parchment of her face, grey in the dim kitchen.

"You make a fuss" she said angrily "and upset me and then lash into it for your dinner."

She lifted the lobster clear of the table. It had about thirty seconds to live.

Well, thought Belacqua, it's a quick death, God help us all.

It is not.

Fingal

The last girl he went with, before a memorable fit of laughing incapacitated him from gallantry for some time, was pretty, hot and witty, in that order. So one fine Spring morning he brought her out into the country, to the Hill of Feltrim in the country. They turned east off the road from Dublin to Malahide short of the Castle woods and soon it came into view, not much more than a burrow, the ruin of a mill on the top, choked lairs of furze and brambles passim on its gentle slopes. It was a landmark for miles around on account of the high ruin. The Hill of the Wolves.

They had not been very long on the top before he began to feel a very sad animal indeed. But she was to all appearance in high spirits, enjoying the warm sun and the prospect.

"The Dublin mountains" she said "don't they look lovely, so dreamy."

Now Belacqua was looking intently in the opposite direction, across the estuary.

"It's the east wind" he said.

She began to admire this and that, the ridge of Lambay Island rising out of the brown woods of the Castle, Ireland's Eye like a shark, and the ridiculous little hills far away to the north, what were they?

"The Naul" said Belacqua. "Is it possible you didn't know the Naul?" This in the shocked tone of the travelled spinster: "You don't say you were in Milan (to rime with villain) and never saw the Cena?" "Can it be possible that you passed through Chambéry and never called on Mme. de Warens?"

"North Dublin" she said "I don't know at all. So flat and dull, all roads leading to Drogheda."

"Fingal dull!" he said. "Winnie you astonish me."

They considered Fingal for a time together in silence. Its coast eaten away with creeks and marshes, tesserae of small fields, patches of wood springing up like a weed, the line of hills too low to close the view.

"When it's a magic land" he sighed "like Saône-et-Loire."

"That means nothing to me" said Winnie.

"Oh yes" he said, "bons vins et Lamartine, a champaign land for the sad and serious, not a bloody little toy Kindergarten like Wicklow."

You make great play with your short stay abroad, thought Winnie.

"You and your sad and serious" she said. "Will you never come off it?"

"Well" he said "I'll give you Alphonse."

She replied that he could keep him. Things were beginning to blow up nasty.

"What's that on your face?" she said sharply.

"Impetigo" said Belacqua. He had felt it coming with a terrible itch in the night and in the morning it was there. Soon it would be a scab.

"And you kiss me" she exclaimed "with that on your face."

"I forgot" he said. "I get so excited you know."

She spittled on her handkerchief and wiped her mouth. Belacqua lay humbly beside her, expecting her to get up and leave him. But instead she said:

"What is it anyway? What does it come from?"

"Dirt" said Belacqua, "you see it on slum children."

A long awkward silence followed these words.

"Don't pick it darling" she said unexpectedly at last, "you'll make it worse."

This came to Belacqua like a drink of water to drink in a dungeon. Her goodwill must have meant something to him. He returned to Fingal to cover his confusion.

"I often come to this hill" he said "to have a view of Fingal, and each time I see it more as a back-land, a land of sanctuary, a land that you don't have to dress up to, that you can walk on in a lounge suit, smoking a cigar." What a geyser, she thought. "And where much has been suffered in secret, especially by women."

"This is all a dream" she said. "I see nothing but three acres and cows. You can't have Cincinnatus without a furrow."

Now it was she who was sulky and he who was happy.

"Oh Winnie" he made a vague clutch at her sincerities, for she was all anyway on the grass, "you look very Roman this minute."

"He loves me" she said, in earnest jest.

"Only pout" he begged, "be Roman, and we'll go on across the estuary."

"And then . . . ?"

And then! Winnie take thought!

"I see" he said "you take thought. Shall we execute a contract?"

"No need" she said.

He was as wax in her hands, she twisted him this way and that. But now their moods were in accordance, things were somehow very pleasant all of a sudden. She gazed long at the area of contention and he willed her not to speak, to remain there with her grave face, a quiet puella in a blurred world. But she spoke (who shall silence them, at last?), saying that she saw nothing but the grey fields of serfs and the ramparts of ex-favourites. Saw! They were all the same when it came to the pinch—clods. If she closed her eyes she might see something. He would drop the subject, he would not try to communicate Fingal, he would lock it up in his mind. So much the better.

"Look" he pointed.

She looked, blinking for the focus.

"The big red building" he said "across the water, with the towers."

At last she thought she saw what he meant.

"Far away" she said "with the round tower?"

"Do you know what that is" he said "because my heart's right there."

Well, she thought, you lay your cards on the table.

"No" she said, "it looks like a bread factory to me."

"The Portrane Lunatic Asylum" he said.

"Oh" she said "I know a doctor there."

Thus, she having a friend, he his heart, in Portrane, they agreed to make for there.

They followed the estuary all the way round, admiring the theories of swans and the coots, over the dunes and past the Martello tower, so that they came on Portrane from the south and the sea instead of like a vehicle by the railway bridge and the horrible red chapel of Donabate. The place was as full of towers as Dun Laoghaire of steeples: two Martello, the red ones of the asylum, a water-tower and the round. Trespassing unawares, for the notice-board was further on towards the coastguard station, they climbed the rising ground to this latter. They followed the grass margin of a ploughed field till they came to where a bicycle was lying, half hidden in the rank grass. Belacqua, who could on no account resist a bicycle, thought what an extraordinary place to come across one. The owner was out in the field, scarifying the dry furrows with a fork.

"Is this right for the tower?" cried Belacqua.

The man turned his head.

"Can we get up to the tower?" cried Belacqua.

The man straightened up and pointed.

"Fire ahead" he said.

"Over the wall?" cried Belacqua. There was no need for him to shout. A conversational tone would have been heard across the quiet field. But he was so anxious to make himself clear, he so dreaded the thought of having to repeat himself, that he not merely raised his voice, but put on a flat accent that astonished Winnie.

"Don't be an eejit" she said, "if it's straight on it's over the wall."

But the man seemed pleased that the wall had been mentioned, or perhaps he was just glad of an opportunity to leave his work, for he dropped his fork and came lumbering over to where they were standing. There was nothing at all noteworthy about his appearance. He said that their way lay straight ahead, yes, over the wall, and then the tower was on top of the field, or else they could go back till they came to the road and go

along it till they came to the Banks and follow up the Banks. The Banks?
Was this fellow one of the more harmless lunatics? Belacqua asked was
the tower an old one, as though it required a Dr. Petrie to see that it was
not. The man said it had been built for relief in the year of the Famine,
so he had heard, by a Mrs. Somebody whose name he misremembered in
honour of her husband.

"Well Winnie" said Belacqua, "over the wall or follow up the Banks?"

"There's a rare view of Lambay from the top" said the man.

Winnie was in favour of the wall, she thought that it would be more
direct now that they had come so far. The man began to work this out.
Belacqua had no one but himself to blame if they never got away from
this machine.

"But I would like to see the Banks" he said.

"If we went on now" said Winnie "now that we have come so far, and
followed the Banks *down*, how would that be?"

They agreed, Belacqua and the man, that it needed a woman to think
these things out. Suddenly there was a tie between them.

The tower began well; that was the funeral meats. But from the door
up it was all relief and no honour; that was the marriage tables.

They had not been long on the top before Belacqua was a sad animal
again. They sat on the grass with their faces to the sea and the asylum was
all below and behind them.

"Right enough" said Winnie "I never saw Lambay look so close."

Belacqua could see the man scraping away at his furrow and felt a
sudden longing to be down there in the clay, lending a hand. He checked
the explanation of this that was beginning and looked at the soft chord
of yellow on the slope, gorse and ragwort juxtaposed.

"The lovely ruins" said Winnie "there on the left, covered with ivy." Of
a church and, two small fields further on, a square bawnless tower.

"That" said Belacqua "is where I have sursum corda."

"Then hadn't we better be getting on" said Winnie, quick as lightning.

"This absurd tower" he said, now that he had been told, "is before the
asylum, and they are before the tower." He didn't say! "The crenels on the
wall I find as moving . . ."

Now the loonies poured out into the sun, the better behaved left to their own devices, the others in herds in charge of warders. The whistle blew and the herd stopped; again, and it proceeded.

"As moving" he said "and moving in the same way, as the colour of the brick in the old mill at Feltrim."

Who shall silence them, at last?

"It's pinked" continued Belacqua, "and as a little fat overfed boy I sat on the floor with a hammer and a pinking-iron, scalloping the edge of a red cloth."

"What ails you?" asked Winnie.

He had allowed himself to get run down, but he scoffed at the idea of a sequitur from his body to his mind.

"I must be getting old and tired" he said "when I find the nature outside me compensating for the nature inside me, like Jean-Jacques sprawling in a bed of saxifrages."

"Appearing to compensate" she said. She was not sure what she meant by this, but it sounded well.

"And then" he said "I want very much to be back in the caul, on my back in the dark for ever."

"A short ever" she said "and working day and night."

The beastly punctilio of women.

"Damn it" he said "you know what I mean. No shaving or haggling or cold or hugger-mugger, no"—he cast about for a term of ample connotation—"no night-sweats."

Below in the playground on their right some of the milder patients were kicking a football. Others were lounging about, alone and in knots, taking their ease in the sun. The head of one appeared over the wall, the hands on the wall, the cheek on the hands. Another, he must have been a very tame one, came halfway up the slope, disappeared into a hollow, emerged after a moment and went back the way he had come. Another, his back turned to them, stood fumbling at the wall that divided the grounds of the asylum from the field where they were. One of the gangs was walking round and round the playground. Below on the other hand a long line of workmen's dwellings, in the gardens children playing and crying. Abstract the asylum and there was little left of Portrane but ruins.

Winnie remarked that the lunatics seemed very sane and well-behaved to her. Belacqua agreed, but he thought that the head over the wall told a tale. Landscapes were of interest to Belacqua only in so far as they furnished him with a pretext for a long face.

Suddenly the owner of the bicycle was running towards them up the hill, grasping the fork. He came barging over the wall, through the chord of yellow and pounding along the crest of the slope. Belacqua rose feebly to his feet. This maniac, with the strength of ten men at least, who should withstand him? He would beat him into a puddle with his fork and violate Winnie. But he bore away as he drew near, for a moment they could hear his panting, and plunged on over the shoulder of the rise. Gathering speed on the down grade, he darted through the gate in the wall and disappeared round a corner of the building. Belacqua looked at Winnie, whom he found staring down at where the man had as it were gone to ground, and then away at the distant point where he had watched him scraping his furrows and been envious. The nickel of the bike sparkled in the sun.

The next thing was Winnie waving and halloing. Belacqua turned and saw a man walking smartly towards them up the slope from the asylum.

"Dr. Sholto" said Winnie.

Dr. Sholto was some years younger than Belacqua, a pale dark man with a brow. He was delighted—how would he say?—at so unexpected a pleasure, honoured he was sure to make the acquaintance of any friend of Miss Coates. Now they would do him the favour to adjourn . . . ? This meant drink. But Belacqua, having other fish to fry, sighed and improvised a long courteous statement to the effect that there was a point in connexion with the church which he was most anxious to check at first hand, so that if he might accept on behalf of Miss Coates, who was surely tired after her long walk from Malahide . . .

"Malahide!" ejaculated Dr. Sholto.

. . . and be himself excused, they could all three meet at the main entrance of the asylum in, say, an hour. How would that be? Dr. Sholto demurred politely. Winnie thought hard and said nothing.

"I'll go down by the Banks" said Belacqua agreeably "and follow the road round. Au revoir."

They stood for a moment watching him depart. When he ventured to look back they were gone. He changed his course and came to where the bicycle lay in the grass. It was a fine light machine, with red tires and wooden rims. He ran down the margin to the road and it bounded alongside under his hand. He mounted and they flew down the hill and round the corner till they came at length to the stile that led into the field where the church was. The machine was a treat to ride, on his right hand the sea was foaming among the rocks, the sands ahead were another yellow again, beyond them in the distance the cottages of Rush were bright white, Belacqua's sadness fell from him like a shift. He carried the bicycle into the field and laid it down on the grass. He hastened on foot, without so much as a glance at the church, across the fields, over a wall and a ditch, and stood before the poor wooden door of the tower. The locked appearance of this did not deter him. He gave it a kick, it swung open and he went in.

Meantime Dr. Sholto, in his pleasantly appointed sanctum, improved the occasion with Miss Winifred Coates. Thus they were all met together in Portrane, Winnie, Belacqua, his heart and Dr. Sholto, and paired off to the satisfaction of all parties. Surely it is in such little adjustments that the benevolence of the First Cause appears beyond dispute. Winnie kept her eye on the time and arrived punctually with her friend at the main entrance. There was no sign of her other friend.

"Late" said Winnie "as usual."

In respect of Belacqua Sholto felt nothing but rancour.

"Pah" he said, "he'll be sandpapering a tomb."

A stout block of an old man in shirt sleeves and slippers was leaning against the wall of the field. Winnie still sees, as vividly as when then they met her anxious gaze for the first time, his great purple face and white moustaches. Had he seen a stranger about, a pale fat man in a black leather coat.

"No miss" he said.

"Well" said Winnie, settling herself on the wall, to Sholto, "I suppose he's about somewhere."

A land of sanctuary, he had said, where much had been suffered secretly. Yes, the last ditch.

"You stay here" said Sholto, madness and evil in his heart, "and I'll take a look in the church."

The old man had been showing signs of excitement.

"Is it an escape?" he enquired hopefully.

"No no" said Winnie, "just a friend."

But he was off, he was unsluiced.

"I was born on Lambay" he said, by way of opening to an endless story of a recapture in which he had distinguished himself, "and I've worked here man and boy."

"In that case" said Winnie "maybe you can tell me what the ruins are."

"That's the church" he said, pointing to the near one, it had just absorbed Sholto, "and that" pointing to the far one " 's the tower."

"Yes" said Winnie "but what tower, what was it?"

"The best I know" he said "is some Lady Something had it."

This was news indeed.

"Then before that again" it all came back to him with a rush "you might have heard tell of Dane Swift, he kep a"—he checked the word and then let it come regardless—"he kep a motte in it."

"A moth?" exclaimed Winnie.

"A motte" he said "of the name of Stella."

Winnie stared out across the grey field. No sign of Sholto, nor of Belacqua, only this puce mass up against her and a tale of a motte and a star. What was a motte?

"You mean" she said "that he lived there with a woman?"

"He kep her there" said the old man, he had read it in an old *Telegraph* and he would adhere to it, "and came down from Dublin."

Little fat Presto, he would set out early in the morning, fresh and fasting, and walk like camomile.

Sholto appeared on the stile in the crenellated wall, waving blankly. Winnie began to feel that she had made a mess of it.

"God knows" she said to Sholto when he came up "where he is."

"You can't hang around here all night" he said. "Let me drive you home, I have to go up to Dublin anyhow."

"I can't leave him" wailed Winnie.

"But he's not here, damn it" said Sholto, "if he was he'd be here."

The old man, who knew his Sholto, stepped into the breach with a tender of his services: he would keep his eyes open.

"Now" said Sholto, "he can't expect you to wait here for ever."

A young man on a bicycle came slowly round the corner from the Donabate direction, saluted the group and was turning into the drive of the asylum.

"Tom" cried Sholto.

Tom dismounted. Sholto gave a brief satirical description of Belacqua's person.

"You didn't see that on the road" he said "did you?"

"I passed the felly of it on a bike" said Tom, pleased to be of use, "at Ross's gate, going like flames."

"On a BIKE!" cried Winnie. "But he hadn't a bike."

"Tom" said Sholto "get out the car, look sharp now, and run her down here."

"But it can't have been him" Winnie was furious for several reasons, "I tell you he had no bike."

"Whoever it is" said Sholto, master of the situation, "we'll pass him before he gets to the main road."

But Sholto had underestimated the speed of his man, who was safe in Taylor's public-house in Swords, drinking in a way that Mr. Taylor did not like, before they were well on their way.

Ding-Dong

My sometime friend Belacqua enlivened the last phase of his solipsism, before he toed the line and began to relish the world, with the belief that the best thing he had to do was to move constantly from place to place. He did not know how this conclusion had been gained, but that it was not thanks to his preferring one place to another he felt sure. He was pleased to think that he could give what he called the Furies the slip by merely setting himself in motion. But as for sites, one was as good as another, because they all disappeared as soon as he came to rest in them. The mere act of rising and going, irrespective of whence and whither, did him good. That was so. He was sorry that he did not enjoy the means to indulge this humour as he would have wished, on a large scale, on land and sea. Hither and thither on land and sea! He could not afford that, for he was poor. But in a small way he did what he could. From the ingle to the window, from the nursery to the bedroom, even from one quarter of the town to another, and back, these little acts of motion he was in a fair way of making, and they certainly did do him some good as a rule. It was the old story of the salad days, torment in the terms and in the intervals a measure of ease.

Being by nature however sinfully indolent, bogged in indolence, asking nothing better than to stay put at the good pleasure of what he called the Furies, he was at times tempted to wonder whether the remedy were not rather more disagreeable than the complaint. But he could only suppose that it was not, seeing that he continued to have recourse to it, in a small way it is true, but nevertheless for years he continued to have recourse to it, and to return thanks for the little good it did him.

The simplest form of this exercise was boomerang, out and back; nay, it was the only one that he could afford for many years. Thus it is clear that his contrivance did not proceed from any discrimination between different points in space, since he returned directly, if we except an occasional pause for refreshment, to his point of departure, and truly no less recruited in spirit than if the interval had been whiled away abroad in the most highly reputed cities.

I know all this because he told me. We were Pylades and Orestes for a period, flattened down to something very genteel; but the relation abode and was highly confidential while it lasted. I have witnessed every stage of the exercise. I have been there when he set out, springing up and hastening away without as much as by your leave, impelled by some force that he did not care to gainsay. I have had glimpses of him enjoying his little trajectory. I have been there again when he returned, transfigured and transformed. It was very nearly the reverse of the author of the Imitation's "glad going out and sad coming in."

He was at pains to make it clear to me, and to all those to whom he exposed his manoeuvre, that it was in no way cognate with the popular act of brute labour, digging and such like, exploited to disperse the dumps, an antidote depending for its efficaciousness on mere physical exhaustion, and for which he expressed the greatest contempt. He did not fatigue himself, he said; on the contrary. He lived a Beethoven pause, he said, whatever he meant by that. In his anxiety to explain himself he was liable to come to grief. Nay, this anxiety in itself, or so at least it seemed to me, constituted a break-down in the self-sufficiency which he never wearied of arrogating to himself, a sorry collapse of my little internus homo, and alone sufficient to give him away as inept ape of his own shadow. But he wriggled out of everything by pleading that he had been drunk at the time, or that he was an incoherent person and content to remain so, and so on. He was an impossible person in the end. I gave him up in the end because he was not *serious*.

One day, in a positive geyser of confidence, he gave me an account of one of these "moving pauses." He had a strong weakness for oxymoron. In the same way he over-indulged in gin and tonic-water.

Not the least charm of this pure blank movement, this "gress" or "gression," was its aptness to receive, with or without the approval of the subject, in all their integrity the faint inscriptions of the outer world. Exempt from destination, it had not to shun the unforeseen nor turn aside from the agreeable odds and ends of vaudeville that are liable to crop up. This sensitiveness was not the least charm of this roaming that began by being blank, not the least charm of this pure act the alacrity with which it welcomed defilement. But very nearly the least.

Emerging, on the particular evening in question, from the underground convenience in the maw of College Street, with a vague impression that he had come from following the sunset up the Liffey till all the colour had been harried from the sky, all the tulips and aerugo expunged, he squatted, not that he had too much drink taken but simply that for the moment there were no grounds for his favouring one direction rather than another, against Tommy Moore's plinth. Yet he durst not dally. Was it not from brooding shill I, shall I, dilly, dally, that he had come out? Now the summons to move on was a subpoena. Yet he found he could not, any more than Buridan's ass, move to right or left, backward or forward. Why this was he could not make out at all. Nor was it the moment for self-examination. He had experienced little or no trouble coming back from the Park Gate along the north quay, he had taken the Bridge and Westmoreland Street in his stride, and now he suddenly found himself good for nothing but to loll against the plinth of this bull-necked bard, and wait for a sign.

There were signs on all hands. There was the big Bovril sign to begin with, flaring beyond the Green. But it was useless. Faith, Hope and—what was it?—Love, Eden missed, every ebb derided, all the tides ebbing from the shingle of Ego Maximus, little me. Itself it went nowhere, only round and round, like the spheres, but mutely. It could not dislodge him now, it could only put ideas into his head. Was it not from sitting still among his ideas, other people's ideas, that he had come away? What would he not give now to get on the move again! Away from ideas!

Turning aside from this and other no less futile emblems, his attention was arrested by a wheel-chair being pushed rapidly under the arcade of the Bank, in the direction of Dame Street. It moved in and out of sight behind the bars of the columns. This was the blind paralytic who sat all day near to the corner of Fleet Street, and in bad weather under the shelter of the arcade, the same being wheeled home to his home in the Coombe. It was past his time and there was a bitter look on his face. He would give his chairman a piece of his mind when he got him to himself. This chairman, hireling or poor relation, came every evening a little before the dark, unfastened from the beggar's neck and breast the placard announcing his distress, tucked him up snugly in his coverings and wheeled him home to his supper. He was well advised to be assiduous, for this beggar was a power in the Coombe. In the morning it was his duty to shave his man and wheel him, according to the weather, to one or other of his pitches. So it went, day after day.

This was a star the horizon adorning if you like, and Belacqua made off at all speed in the opposite direction. Down Pearse Street, that is to say, long straight Pearse Street, its vast Barrack of Glencullen granite, its home of tragedy restored and enlarged, its coal merchants and Florentine Fire Brigade Station, its two Cervi saloons, ice-cream and fried fish, its dairies, garages and monumental sculptors, and implicit behind the whole length of its southern frontage the College. Perpetuis futuris temporibus duraturum. It was to be hoped so, indeed.

It was a most pleasant street, despite its name, to be abroad in, full as it always was with shabby substance and honest-to-God coming and going. All day the roadway was a tumult of buses, red and blue and silver. By one of these a little girl was run down, just as Belacqua drew near to the railway viaduct. She had been to the Hibernian Dairies for milk and bread and then she had plunged out into the roadway, she was in such a childish fever to get back in record time with her treasure to the tenement in Mark Street where she lived. The good milk was all over the road and the loaf, which had sustained no injury, was sitting up against the kerb, for all the world as though a pair of hands had taken it up and set it down there. The queue standing for the Palace Cinema was torn between conflicting desires: to keep their places and to see the excitement. They craned their necks and called out to know the worst, but they stood firm. Only one girl, debauched in appearance and swathed in a black blanket, fell out near the sting of the queue and secured the loaf. With the loaf under her blanket she sidled unchallenged down Mark Street and turned into Mark Lane. When she got back to the queue her place had been taken of course. But her sally had not cost her more than a couple of yards.

Belacqua turned left into Lombard Street, the street of the sanitary engineers, and entered a public-house. Here he was known, in the sense that his grotesque exterior had long ceased to alienate the curates and make them giggle, and to the extent that he was served with his drink without having to call for it. This did not always seem a privilege. He was tolerated, what was more, and let alone by the rough but kindly habitués of the house, recruited for the most part from among dockers, railway-men and vague joxers on the dole. Here also art and love, scrabbling in dispute or staggering home, were barred, or, perhaps better, unknown. The aesthetes and the impotent were far away.

These circumstances combined to make of this place a very grateful refuge for Belacqua, who never omitted, when he found himself in its neighbourhood with the price of a drink about him, to pay it a visit.

When I enquired how he squared such visits with his anxiety to keep on the move and his distress at finding himself brought to a standstill, as when he had come out of the underground in the mouth of College Street, he replied that he did not. "Surely" he said "my resolution has the right to break down." I supposed so indeed. "Or" he said "if you pre-fer, I make the raid in two hops instead of non-stop. From what" he cried "does that disqualify me, I should very much like to know." I has-tened to assure him that he had a perfect right to suit himself in what, after all, was a manoeuvre of his own contriving, and that the raid, to adopt his own term, lost nothing by being made in easy stages. "Easy!" he exclaimed, "how easy?"

But notice the double response, like two holes to a burrow.

Sitting in this crapulent den, drinking his drink, he gradually ceased to see its furnishings with pleasure, the bottles, representing centuries of loving research, the stools, the counter, the powerful screws, the shining phalanx of the pulls of the beer-engines, all cunningly devised and elaborated to further the relations between purveyor and consumer in this domain. The bottles drawn and emptied in a twinkling, the casks responding to the slightest pressure on their joysticks, the weary proletarians at rest on arse and elbow, the cash register that never complains, the graceful curates flying from customer to customer, all this made up a spectacle in which Belacqua was used to take delight and chose to see a pleasant instance of machinery decently subservient to appetite. A great major symphony of supply and demand, effect and cause, fulcrate on the middle C of the counter and waxing, as it proceeded, in the charming harmonics of blasphemy and broken glass and all the aliquots of fatigue and ebriety. So that he would say that the only place where he could come to anchor and be happy was a low public-house, and that all the wearisome tactics of gress and dud Beethoven would be done away with if only he could spend his life in such a place. But as they closed at ten, and as residence and good faith were viewed as incompatible, and as in any case he had not the means to consecrate his life to stasis, even in the meanest bar, he supposed he must be content to indulge this whim from time to time, and return thanks for such sporadic mercy.

All this and much more he laboured to make clear. He seemed to derive considerable satisfaction from his failure to do so.

But on this particular occasion the cat failed to jump, with the result that he became as despondent as though he were sitting at home in his own great armchair, as anxious to get on the move and quite as hard put to it to do so. Why this was he could not make out. Whether the trituration of the child in Pearse Street had upset him without his knowing it, or whether (and he put forward this alternative with a truly insufferable complacency) he had come to some parting of the ways, he did not know at all. All he could say was that the objects in which he was used to find such recreation and repose lost gradually their hold upon him, he became insensible to them little by little, the old itch and algos crept back into his mind. He had come briskly all the way from Tommy Moore, and now he suddenly found himself sitting paralysed and grieving in a pub of all places, good for nothing but to stare at his spoiling porter, and wait for a sign.

To this day he does not know what caused him to look up, but look up he did. Feeling the impulse to do this strong upon him, he forced his eyes away from the glass of dying porter and was rewarded by seeing a hatless woman advancing slowly towards him up the body of the bar. No sooner had she come in than he must have become aware of her. That was surely very curious in the first instance. She seemed to be hawking some ware or other, but what it was he could not see, except that it was not studs or laces or matches or lavender or any of the usual articles. Not that it was unusual to find a woman in that public-house, for they came and went freely, slaking their thirst and beguiling their sorrows with no less freedom than their men-folk. Indeed it was always a pleasure to see them, their advances were always most friendly and honourable, Belacqua had many a delightful recollection of their commerce.

Hence there was no earthly reason why he should see in the advancing figure of this mysterious pedlar anything untoward, or in the nature of the sign in default of which he was clamped to his stool till closing-time. Yet the impulse to do so was so strong that he yielded to it, and as she drew nearer, having met with more rebuffs than pence in her endeavours to dispose of her wares, whatever they were, it became clear to him that his instinct had not played him false, in so far at least as she was a woman of very remarkable presence indeed.

Her speech was that of a woman of the people, but of a gentlewoman of the people. Her gown had served its time, but yet contrived to be respectable. He noticed with a pang that she sported about her neck the insidious little mock fur so prevalent in tony slumland. The one deplorable feature of her get up, as apprehended by Belacqua in his hasty survey, was the footwear—the cruel strait outsizes of the suffragette or welfare worker. But he did not doubt for a moment that they had been a gift, or picked up in the pop for a song. She was of more than average height and well in flesh. She might be past middle-age. But her face, ah her face, was what Belacqua had rather refer to as her countenance, it was so full of light. This she lifted up upon him and no error. Brimful of light and serene, serenissime, it bore no trace of suffering, and in this alone it might be said to be a notable face. Yet like tormented faces that he had seen, like the face in the National Gallery in Merrion Square by the Master of Tired Eyes, it seemed to have come a long way and subtend an infinitely narrow angle of affliction, as eyes focus a star. The features were null, only luminous, impassive and secure, petrified in radiance, or words to that effect, for the reader is requested to take notice that this sweet style is Belacqua's. An act of expression, he said, a wreathing or wrinkling, could only have had the effect of a dimmer on a headlight. The implications of this triumphant figure, the just and the unjust, etc., are better forgone.

At long last she addressed herself to Belacqua.

"Seats in heaven" she said in a white voice "tuppence apiece, four fer a tanner."

"No" said Belacqua. It was the first syllable to come to his lips. It had not been his intention to deny her.

"The best of seats" she said "again I'm sold out. Tuppence apiece the best of seats, four fer a tanner."

This was unforeseen with a vengeance, if not exactly vaudeville. Belacqua was embarrassed in the last degree, but transported also. He felt the sweat coming in the small of his back, above his Montrouge belt.

"Have you got them on you?" he mumbled.

"Heaven goes round" she said, whirling her arm, "and round and round and round and round and round."

"Yes" said Belacqua "round and round."

"Rowan" she said, dropping the d's and getting more of a spin into the slogan, "rowan an' rowan an' rowan."

Belacqua scarcely knew where to look. Unable to blush he came out in this beastly sweat. Nothing of the kind had ever happened to him before. He was altogether disarmed, unsaddled and miserable. The eyes of them all, the dockers, the railwaymen and, most terrible of all, the joxers, were upon him. His tail drooped. This female dog of a pixy with her tiresome Ptolemy, he was at her mercy.

"No" he said "no thank you, no not this evening thank you."

"Again I'm sold out" she said "an' buked out, four fer a tanner."

"On whose authority . . ." began Belacqua, like a Scholar.

"For yer frien' " she said "yer da, yer ma an' yer motte, four fer a tanner." The voice ceased, but the face did not abate.

"How do I know" piped Belacqua "you're not sellin' me a pup?"

"Heaven goes rowan an' rowan . . ."

"Rot you" said Belacqua "I'll take two. How much is that?"

"Four dee" she said.

Belacqua gave her a sixpence.

"Gobbless yer honour" she said, in the same white voice from which she had not departed. She made to go.

"Here" cried Belacqua "you owe me twopence." He had not even the good grace to say tuppence.

"Arragowan" she said "make it four cantcher, yer frien', yer da, yer ma an' yer motte."

Belacqua could not bicker. He had not the strength of mind for that. He turned away.

"Jesus" she said distinctly "and his sweet mother preserve yer honour."

"Amen" said Belacqua, into his dead porter.

Now the woman went away and her countenance lighted her to her room in Townsend Street.

But Belacqua tarried a little to listen to the music. Then he also departed, but for Railway Street, beyond the river.

A Wet Night

Hark, it is the season of festivity and goodwill. Shopping is in full swing, the streets are thronged with revellers, the Corporation has offered a prize for the best-dressed window, Hyam's trousers are down again.

Mistinguett would do away with chalets of necessity. She does not think them necessary. Not so Belacqua. Emerging happy body from the hot bowels of McLouglin's he looked up and admired the fitness of Moore's bull neck, not a whit too short, with all due respect to the critics. Bright and cheery above the strom of the Green, as though coached by the Star of Bethlehem, the Bovril sign danced and danced through its seven phases.

The lemon of faith jaundiced, annunciating the series, was in a fungus of hopeless green reduced to shingles and abolished. Whereupon the light went out, in homage to the slain. A sly ooze of gules, carmine of solicitation, lifting the skirts of green that the prophecy might be fulfilled, shocking Gabriel into cherry, flooded the sign. But the long skirts came rattling down, darkness covered their shame, the cycle was at an end. *Da capo.*

Bovril into Salome, thought Belacqua, and Tommy Moore there with his head on his shoulders. Doubt, Despair and Scrounging, shall I hitch my bath-chair to the greatest of these? Across the way, beneath the arcade, the blind paralytic was in position, he was well tucked up in his coverings, he was lashing into his dinner like any proletarian. Soon his man would come and wheel him home. No one had ever seen him come or go, he was there one minute and gone the next. He went and returned. When you scrounge you must go and return, that was the first great article of Christian scrounging. No man could settle down to scrounge properly in a foreign land. The Wanderjahre were a sleep and a forgetting, the proud dead point. You came back wise and staked your beat in some sheltered place, pennies trickled in, you were looked up to in a tenement.

Belacqua had been proffered a sign, Bovril had made him a sign.

Whither next? To what licensed premises? To where the porter was well up, first; and the solitary shawly like a cloud of latter rain in a waste of poets and politicians, second; and he neither knew nor was known, third. A lowly house dear to shawlies where the porter was up and he could keep himself to himself on a high stool with a high round and feign to be immersed in the Moscow notes of the *Twilight Herald*. These were very piquant.

Of the two houses that appealed spontaneously to these exigencies the one, situate in Merrion Row, was a home from home for jarveys. As some folk from hens, so Belacqua shrank from jarveys. Rough, gritty, almost verminous men. From Moore to Merrion Row, moreover, was a perilous way, beset at this hour with poets and peasants and politicians. The other lay in Lincoln Place, he might go gently by Pearse Street, there was nothing to stop him. Long straight Pearse Street, it permitted of a simple cantilena in his mind, its footway peopled with the tranquil and detached in fatigue, its highway dehumanised in a tumult of buses. Trams were monsters, moaning along beneath the wild gesture of the trolley. But buses were pleasant, tires and glass and clash and no more. Then to pass by the Queens, home of tragedy, was charming at that hour, to pass between the old theatre and the long line of the poor and lowly queued up for thruppence worth of pictures. For there Florence would slip into the song, the Piazza della Signoria and the No. 1 tram and the Feast of St. John, when they lit the torches of resin on the towers and the children, while the rockets at nightfall above the Cascine were still flagrant in their memory, opened the little cages to the glutted cicadae after their long confinement and stayed out with their young parents long after their usual

bedtime. Then slowly in his mind down the sinister Uffizi to the para-
pets of Arno, and so on and so forth. This pleasure was dispensed by
the Fire Station opposite which seemed to have been copied here and
there from the Palazzo Vecchio. In deference to Savonarola? Ha! Ha! At
all events it was as good a way as any other to consume the Homer hour,
darkness filling the streets and so on, and a better than most in virtue of
his great thirst towards the lowly house that would snatch him in off the
street through the door of its grocery department if by good fortune that
were still open.

Painfully then under the College ramparts, past the smart taxis, he
set off, clearing his mind for its song. The Fire Station worked without
a hitch and all was going as well as could be expected considering what
the evening held in pickle for him when the blow fell. He was run plump
into by one Chas, a highbrow bromide of French nationality with a dia-
bolical countenance compound of Skeat's and Paganini's and a mind like
a tattered concordance. It was Chas who would not or could not leave
well alone, Belacqua being rapt in his burning feet and the line of the
song in his head.

"*Halte-là*" piped the pirate, "whither so gay?"

In the lee of the Monumental Showroom Belacqua was obliged to
pause and face this machine. It carried butter and eggs from the Hiber-
nian Dairy. Belacqua however was not to be drawn.

"Ramble" he said vaguely "in the twilight."

"Just a song" said Chas "at twilight. No?"

Belacqua tormented his hands in the gloom. Had he been blocked on
his way and violated in the murmur of his mind to listen to this clock-
work Bartlett? Apparently.

"How's the world" he said nevertheless, in spite of everything, "and
what's the news of the great world?"

"Fair" said Chas, cautiously, "fair to meedling. The poem moves,
eppure."

If he mentions *ars longa*, Belacqua made this covenant with himself,
he will have occasion to regret it.

"*Limae labor*" said Chas "*et mora.*"

"Well" said Belacqua, casting off with clean hands, "see you again."

"But shortly, I thrrust" cried Chas, "casa Frica, dis collied night. No?"

"Alas" said Belacqua, well adrift.

Behold the Frica, she visits talent in the Service Flats. In she lands, singing Havelock Ellis in a deep voice, frankly itching to work that which is not seemly. Open upon her concave breast as on a lectern lies Portigliotti's *Penombre Claustrali*, bound in tawed caul. In her talons earnestly she grasps Sade's 120 *Days* and the *Anterotica* of Aliosha G. Brignole-Sale, unopened, bound in shagreened caul. A septic pudding hoodwinks her, a stodgy turban of pain it laps her horse face. The eyehole is clogged with the bulbus, the round pale globe goggles exposed. Solitary meditation has furnished her with nostrils of generous bore. The mouth champs an invisible bit, foam gathers at the bitter commissures. The crateriform brisket, lipped with sills of paunch, cowers ironically behind a maternity tunic. Keyholes have wrung the unfriendly withers, the osseous rump screams behind the hobble-skirt. Wastes of woad worsted advertise the pasterns. Aïe!

This in its absinthe whinny had bidden Belacqua and, what is more, the Alba, to backstairs, claret cup and the intelligentsia. The Alba, Belacqua's current one and only, had much pleasure in accepting for her scarlet gown and broad pale bored face. The belle of the ball. Aïe!

But seldom one without two and scarcely had Chas been shed than lo from out the Grosvenor sprang the homespun Poet wiping his mouth and a little saprophile of an anonymous politico-ploughboy setting him off. The Poet sucked his teeth over this unexpected pleasure. The golden eastern lay of his bullet head was muted by no covering. Beneath the Wally Whitmaneen of his Donegal tweeds a body was to be presumed. He gave the impression of having lost a harrow and found a figure of speech. Belacqua was numbed.

"Drink" decreed the Poet in a voice of thunder.

Belacqua slunk at his heels into the Grosvenor, the gimlet eyes of the saprophile probed his loins.

"Now" exulted the Poet, as though he had just brought an army across the Beresina, "give it a name and knock it back."

"Pardon me" stuttered Belacqua "just a moment, will you be so kind." He waddled out of the bar and into the street and up it at all speed and into the lowly public through the groceries door like a bit of dirt into a Hoover. This was a rude thing to do. When intimidated he was rude beyond measure, not timidly insolent like Stendhal's Comte de Thaler, but finally rude on the sly. Timidly insolent when, as by Chas, exasperated; finally rude on the sly when intimidated, outrageously rude behind the back of his oppressor. This was one of his little peculiarities.

He bought a paper of a charming little sloven, no but a truly exquisite little page, a freelance clearly, he would not menace him, he skipped in on his miry bare feet with only three or four under his oxter for sale. Belacqua gave him a thruppenny bit and a cigarette picture. He sat to himself on a stool in the central leaf of the main triptych, his feet on a round so high that his knees topped the curb of the counter (admirable posture for man with weak bladder and tendency to ptosis of viscera), drank despondent porter (but he dared not budge) and devoured the paper.

"A woman" he read with a thrill "is either: a short-below-the-waist, a big-hip, a sway-back, a big-abdomen or an average. If the bust be too cogently controlled, then shall fat roll from scapula to scapula. If it be made passable and slight, then shall the diaphragm bulge and be unsightly. Why not therefore invest *chez* a reputable corset-builder in the brassière-cum-corset décolleté, made from the finest Broches, Coutils and Elastics, centuple stitched in wearing parts, fitted with immovable spiral steels? It bestows stupendous diaphragm and hip support, it enhances the sleeveless backless neckless evening gown . . ."

O Love! O Fire! but would the scarlet gown lack all these parts? Was she a short-below or a sway-back? She had no waist, nor did she deign to sway. She was not to be classified. Not to be corseted. Not woman of flesh.

The face on the curate faded away and Grock's appeared in its stead.

"Say that again" said the red gash in the white putty.

Belacqua said it all and much more.

"*Nisscht mööööööglich*" moaned Grock, and was gone.

Now Belacqua began to worry lest the worst should come to the worst and the scarlet gown be backless after all. Not that he had any doubts as to the back thus bared being a sight for sore eyes. The omoplates would be well defined, they would have a fine free ball-and-socket motion. In repose they would be the blades of an anchor, the delicate furrow of the spine its stem. His mind pored over this back that inspired him with awe. He saw it as a flower-de-luce, a spatulate leaf with segments angled back, like the wings of a butterfly sucking a blossom, from their common hinge. Then, fetching from further afield, as an obelisk, a cross-potent, pain and death, still death, a bird crucified on a wall. This flesh and bones swathed in scarlet, this heart of washed flesh draped in scarlet. . . .

Unable to bear any longer his doubt as to the rig of the gown he passed through the counter and got her house on the telephone.

"Dressing" said the maid, the Venerilla, his friend and bawd to be, "and spitting blood."

No, she could not be got down, she had been up in her room cursing and swearing for the past hour.

"I'm afeared of me gizzard" said the voice "to go near her."

"Is it closed at the back?" demanded Belacqua "or is it open?"

"Is what?"

"The gown" cried Belacqua, "what else? Is it closed?"

The Venerilla requested him to hold on while she called it to the eye of the mind. The objurgations of this ineffable member were clearly audible.

"Would it be the red one?" she said, after countless ages.

"The scarlet bloody gown of course" he cried out of his torment, "do you not know?"

"Hold on now. . . . It buttons . . ."

"Buttons? What buttons?"

"It buttons ups behind, sir, with the help of God."

"Say it again" implored Belacqua, "over and over again."

"Amn't I after saying" groaned the Venerilla "it buttons ups on her."

"Praise be to God" said Belacqua "and his blissful Mother."

Calm now and sullen the Alba, dressed insidiously up to the nines, bides her time in the sunken kitchen, paying no heed to her fool and foil who has made bold to lay open Belacqua's distress. She is in pain, her brandy is

at hand, mulling in the big glass on the range. Behind her frontage aban-
doned in elegance, sagging in its elegance and clouded in its native sor-
row, a more anxious rite than sumptuous meditation is in progress. For
her mind is at prayer-stool before a perhaps futile purpose, she is loading
the spring of her mind for a perhaps unimportant undertaking. Letting
her outside rip pro tem she is screwing herself up and up, she is wind-
ing up the weights of her mind, to being the belle of the ball, banquet or
party. Any less beautiful girl would have contemned such tactics and con-
sidered this class of absorption at the service of so simple an occasion
unwarranted and, what was worse, a sad give away. Here am I, a less boun-
tiful one would have argued, the belle, and there is the ball; let these two
items be brought together and the thing is done. Are we then to insinuate,
with such a simplist, that the Alba questioned the virtue of her appear-
ance. Indeed and indeed we are not. She had merely to unleash her eyes,
she had merely to unhood them, as well she knew, and she might have
mercy on whom she would. There was no difficulty about that. But what
she did question, balefully, as though she knew the answer in advance,
was the fitness of a distinction hers for the asking, of a palm that she
had merely to open her eyes and assume. That the simplicity of the gest
turned her in the first place against it, relegating it among the multitude
of things that were not her *genre*, is indisputable. But this was only a min-
ute aspect of her position. It is with the disparagement attaching in the
thought of Belacqua, and in hers tending to, to the quality of the exploit
that she now wrestles. It is with its no doubt unworthiness that she now
has to do. Sullen and still, aware of the brandy at hand but not thirsting
for it, she cranks herself up to a reality of preference, slowly but surely
she gilds her option, she exalts it into realms of choice. She will do this
thing, she will be belle of the ball, gladly, gravely and carefully, *humili-
ter, fideliter, simpliciter*, and not merely because she might just as well. Is
she, she a woman of the world, she who knows, to halt between two opin-
ions, founder in a strait of two wills, hang in suspense and be the more
killed? She who *knows*? So far from such nonsense she will soon chafe to
be off. And now she dare, until it be time, the clock strike, delegate a por-
tion of her attention with instructions to reorganise her features, hands,

shoulders, back, outside in a word, the inside having been spiked. At once she thirsts for the Hennessy. She sings to herself, for her own pleasure, stressing all the words that cry for stress, like Dan the first to warble without fear or favour:

> No me jodas en el suelo
> Como si fuera una perra,
> Que con esos cojonazos
> Me echas en el coño tierra.

The Polar Bear, a big old brilliant lecher, was already on his way, speeding along the dark dripping country roads in a crass honest slob of a clangorous bus, engaging with the effervescent distinction of a Renaissance cardinal in rather languid tongue-play an acquaintance of long standing, a Jesuit with little or no nonsense about him.

"The *Lebensbahn*" he was saying, for he never used the English word when the foreign pleased him better, "of the Galilean is the tragi-comedy of the solipsism that will not capitulate. The humilities and *retro me's* and quaffs of sir-reverence are on a par with the hey presto's, arrogance and egoism. He is the first great self-contained playboy. The cryptic abasement before the woman taken red-handed is as great a piece of megalomaniacal impertinence as his interference in the affairs of his boy-friend Lazarus. He opens the series of slick suicides, as opposed to the serious Empedoclean variety. He has to answer for the wretched Nemo and his *coratés*, bleeding in paroxysms of *dépit* on an unimpressed public."

He coughed up a plump cud of mucus, spun it round the avid bowl of his palate and stowed it away for future degustation.

The S.J. with little or no nonsense had just enough strength to voice his fatigue.

"If you knew" he said "how you bore me with your twice two is four."

The P.B. failed to get him.

"You bore me" drawled the S.J. "worse than an infant prodigy." He paused to recruit his energies. "In his hairless voice" he proceeded "preferring the druggist Borodin to Mozart."

"By all accounts" retorted the P.B. "your sweet Mozart was a *Hexenmeister* in the pilch."

That was a nasty one, let him make what he liked of that one.

"Our Lord———"

"Speak for yourself" said the P.B., nettled beyond endurance.

"Our Lord was not."

"You forget" said the PB., "he got it all over at procreation."

"When you grow up to be a big boy" said the Jesuit "and can understand the humility that is beyond masochism, come and talk to me again. Not cis-, ultra-masochistic. Beyond pain and service."

"But precisely" exclaimed the P.B., "he did not serve, the late lamented. What else am I saying? A valet does not have big ideas. He let down the central agency."

"The humility" murmured the janizary "of a love too great for skivvying and too real to need the tonic of urtication."

The infant prodigy sneered at this comfortable variety.

"You make things pleasant for yourselves" he sneered, "I must say."

"The best reason" said the S.J. "that can be given for believing is that it is more amusing. Disbelief" said the soldier of Christ, making ready to arise "is a bore. We do not count our change. We simply cannot bear to be bored."

"Say that from the pulpit" said the P.B. "and you'll be drummed into the wilderness."

The S.J. laughed profusely. Was it possible to conceive a more artless impostor of a mathematician than this fellow!

"Would you" he begged, putting his greatcoat on, "would you, my dear good fellow, have the kindness to bear in mind that I am not a Parish Priest."

"I won't forget" said the P.B. "that you don't scavenge. Your love is too great for the slops."

"Egg-sactly" said the S.J. "But they are excellent men. A shade on the assiduous side, a shade too anxious to strike a rate. Otherwise . . ." He rose. "Observe" he said, "I desire to get down. I pull this cord and the bus stops and lets me down."

The P.B. observed.

"In just such a Gehenna of links" said this remarkable man, with one foot on the pavement, "I forged my vocation."

With which words he was gone and the burden of his fare had fallen on the P.B.

Chas's girl was a Shetland Shawly. He had promised to pick her up on his way to Casa Frica and now, cinched beyond reproach in his double-breasted smoking, he subdued his impatience to catch a tram in order to explain the world to a group of students.

"The difference, if I may say so————"

"Oh" cried the students, *una voce*, "oh please!"

"The difference, then, I say, between Bergson and Einstein, the essential difference, is as between philosopher and sociolog."

"Oh!" cried the students.

"Yes" said Chas, casting up what was the longest divulgation he could place before the tram, which had hove into view, would draw abreast.

"And if it is the smart thing now to speak of Bergson as a cod"—he edged away—"it is that we move from the Object"—he made a plunge for the tram—"and the Idea to SENSE"—he cried from the step—"AND REASON."

"Sense" echoed the students "and reason!"

The difficulty was to know what exactly he meant by *sense*.

"He must mean *senses*" said a first, "smell, don't you know, and so on."

"Nay" said a second, "he must mean *common sense*."

"I think" said a third "he must mean *instinct*, intuition, don't you know, and that kind of thing."

A fourth longed to know what Object there was in Bergson, a fifth what a sociolog was, a sixth what either had to do with the world.

"We must ask him" said a seventh, "that is all. We must not confuse ourselves with inexpert speculation. Then we shall see who is right."

"We must ask him" cried the students, "then we shall see. . . ."

On which understanding, that the first to see him again would be sure and ask him, they went their not so very different ways.

·   ·   ·

The hair of the homespun Poet, so closely was it cropped, did not lend itself kindly to any striking effects of dressing. Here again, in his plumping for the austerity of a rat's back, he proclaimed himself in reaction to the nineties. But the little that there was to do he had done, with a lotion that he had he had given alertness to the stubble. Also he had changed his tie and turned his collar. And now, though alone and unobserved, he paced up and down. He was making up his piece, *d'occasion* perhaps in both senses, whose main features he had recently established riding home on his bike from the Yellow House. He would deliver it when his hostess came with her petition, he would not hum and haw like an amateur pianist nor yet as good as spit in her eye like a professional one. No he would arise and say, not declaim, state gravely, with the penetrating Middle West gravity that is like an ogleful of tears:

CALVARY BY NIGHT

the water
the waste of water
in the womb of water
an pansy leaps.

rocket of bloom flare flower of night wilt for me
on the breasts of the water it has closed it has made
an act of floral presence on the water
the tranquil act of its cycle on the waste
from the spouting forth
to the re-enwombing
untroubled bow of petaline sweet-smellingness
kingfisher abated
drowned for me
lamb of insustenance mine

till the clamour of a blue bloom
beat on the walls of the womb of
the waste of
the water

Resolved to put across this strong composition and cause something of a flutter he was anxious that there should be no flaw in the mode of presentation adopted by him as most worthy of his aquatic manner. In fact he had to have it pat in order not to have to say it pat, in order to give the impression that in the travail of its exteriorisation he was being torn asunder. Taking his cue from the equilibrist, who encaptures us by failing once, twice, three times, and then, in a regular lather of volition, bringing it off, he deemed that this little turn, if it were to conquer the salon, required stress to be laid not so much on the content of the performance as on the spiritual evisceration of the performer. Hence he paced to and fro, making a habit of the words and effects of *Calvary by Night*.

The Frica combed her hair, back and back she raked her purple tresses till to close her eyes became a problem. The effect was throttled gazelle, more appropriate to evening wear than her workaday foal at foot. Belacqua's Ruby, in her earlier campaigns, had favoured the same taut Sabine coiffure, till Mrs. Tough, by dint of protesting that it made her little bird-face look like a sucked lozenge, had induced her to fluff things a bit and crimp them. Unavailingly alas! for nimbed she was altogether too big dolly that opens and shuts its eyes. Nor indeed was lozenge, sucked or buck, by any means the most ignoble office that face of woman might discharge. For here at hand, saving us our fare to Derbyshire, we have the Frica, looking something horrid.

Throttled gazelle gives no idea. Her features, as though the hand of an unattractive ravisher were knotted in her chevelure, were set at half-cock and locked in a rictus. She had frowned to pencil her eyebrows, so now she had four. The dazzled iris was domed in a white agony of entreaty, the upper lip writhed back in a snarl to the untented nostrils. Would she bite her tongue off, that was the interesting question. The nutcracker chin betrayed a patent clot of thyroid gristle. It was impossible to set aside the awful suspicion that her flattened mammae, in sympathy with this tormented eructation of countenance, had put forth cutwaters and were rowelling her corsage. But the face was beyond appeal, a flagrant seat of injury. She had merely to arrange her hands so that the palm and fingers of the one touched the palm and fingers of the other and hold them thus joined before the breast with a slight upward inclination to look like a briefless martyress in rut.

Nevertheless the arty Countess of Parabimbi, backing through the press, would dangle into the mauve presence of the crone-mother, Caleken Frica's holiest thing alive, and

"My dear" she would positively be obliged to ejaculate, "never have I seen your Caleken *quite* so striking! Simply Sistine!"

What would her Ladyship be pleased to mean? The Cumaean Sibyl on a bearing-rein, sniffing the breeze for the Grimm Brothers? Oh, her Ladyship did not care to be so infernal finical and nice, that would be like working out how many pebbles in Tom Thumb's pocket. It was just a vague impression, it was merely that she looked, with that strange limy hobnailed texture of complexion, so *frescosa*, from the waist up, my dear, with that distempered cobalt modesty-piece, a positive gem of ravished Quattrocento, a positive jewel, my dear, of sweaty Big Tom. Whereupon the vidual virgin, well aware after these many years that all things in heaven, the earth and the waters were as they were taken, would vow to cherish as long as she was spared the learned praise of such an expert.

"Maaaccche!" bleats the Parabimbi.

This may be premature. We have set it down too soon, perhaps. Still, let it bloody well stand.

To return to the Frica, there is the bell at long last, pealing down her Fallopian pipettes, galvanising her away from the mirror as though her navel had been pressed in annunciation.

The Student, whose name we shall never know, was the first to arrive. A foul little brute he was, with a brow.

"Oh Lawdee!" he gushed, his big brown eyes looking della Robbia babies at the Frica, "don't tell me I'm the first!"

"Don't distress yourself" said Caleken, who could smell a poet against the wind, "only by a short gaffe."

Hard on the heels of the Poet came a gaggle of nondescripts, then a public botanist, then a Galway Gael, then the Shetland Shawly with her Chas. Him the Student, mindful of his pledge, accosted.

"In what sense"—he would have it out of him or perish—"did you use *sense* when you said . . . ?"

"He said that?" exclaimed the botanist.

"Chas" said Caleken, as though she were announcing the name of a winner.

"Adsum" admitted Chas.

A plum of phlegm burst in the vestibule.

"What I want to know" complained the Student, "what we all want to know, is in what sense he was using *sense* when he said . . ."

The Gael, in the heart of a cabbage of nondescripts, was bungling Duke Street's thought for the day to the crone.

"Owen . . ." he began again, when a nameless ignoramus, anxious to come into the picture as early on in the proceedings as possible, said rashly:

"What Owen?"

"Good evening" squalled the Polar Bear, "good evening good evening. Wat a night, Madame" he addressed himself vehemently, out of sheer politeness, directly to his hostess, "God *wat* a night!"

The crone was as fond of the P.B. as though she had bought him in Clery's toy fair.

"And you so far to come!" She wished she could dandle him on her knee. He was a shabby man and often moody. "Too good of you to come" she hushabied, "too good of you."

The Man of Law, his face a blaze of acne, was next, escorting the Parabimbi and three tarts dressed for the backstairs.

"I met him" whispered Chas "zigzagging down Pearse Street, Brunswick Street, you know, that was."

"En route?" ventured Caleken. She was a bit above herself with all the excitement.

"Hem?"

"On his way here?"

"Well" said Chas, "I regret, my dear Miss Frica, that he did not make it abso*lu*tely clear if he comes or not."

The Gael said to the P.B. in an injured voice:

"Here's a man wants to know what Owen."

"Not possible" said the P.B., "you astonish me."

"Is it of the sweet mouth?" said a sandy son of Ham.

Now the prong of the P.B.'s judgement was keen and bright.

"That *emmerdeur*" he jeered, "the strange sweet mouth!"

The Parabimbi jumped.

"You said?" she said.

Caleken emerged from the ruck, she came to the fore.

"What can be keeping the girls" she said. It was not exactly a question.

"And your sister" enquired the botanist, "your charming sister, where can she be this evening now I wonder."

The Beldam sprang into the breach.

"Unfortunately" she said, in ringing tones and with great precipitation, "in bed, unwell. A great disappointment to us all."

"Nothing of moment, Madam" said the Man of Law "let us hope?"

"Thank you, no. Happily not. A slight indisposition. Poor little Dande-lion!" The Beldam heaved a heavy sigh.

The P.B. exchanged a look of intelligence with the Gael.

"What girls?" he said.

Caleken expanded her lungs:

"Pansy"—the Poet had a palpitation, why had he not brought his nux vomica?—"Lilly Neary, Olga, Elliseva, Bride Maria, Alga, Ariana, tall Tib, slender Sib, Alma Beatrix, Alba—" They were really too numerous, she could not go through the entire list. She staunched her mouth.

"Alba!" ejaculated the P.B., "Alba! She!"

"And why" interposed the Countess of Parabimbi "why not Alba, who-ever she may be, rather than, say, the Wife of Bath?"

A nondescript appeared in their midst, he panted the glad tidings. The girls had arrived.

"They are gurrls" said the botanist "beyond question. But are they *the* gurrls?"

"Now I hope we can start" said the younger Frica, and, the elder being aware of no let or hindrance, up on to the estrade smartly she stepped and unveiled the refreshments. Turning her back on the high dumb-waiter,

with a great winged gesture of lapidated piety, she instituted the follow-
ing selection:

"Cup! Squash! Cocoa! Force! Julienne! Pan Kail! Cock-a-Leekie! Hul-
luah! Apfelmus! Isinglass! Ching-Ching!"

A terrible silence fell on the assembly.

"Great cry" said Chas "and little wool."

The more famished faithful stormed the platform.

Two banned novelists, a bibliomaniac and his mistress, a paleographer,
a violist d'amore with his instrument in a bag, a popular parodist with his
sister and six daughters, a still more popular Professor of Bullscrit and
Comparative Ovoidology, the saprophile the better for drink, a communist
painter and decorator fresh back from the Moscow reserves, a merchant
prince, two grave Jews, a rising strumpet, three more poets with Lauras to
match, a disaffected cicisbeo, a chorus of playwrights, the inevitable envoy
of the Fourth Estate, a phalanx of Grafton Street Stürmers and Jemmy
Higgins arrived now in a body. No sooner had they been absorbed than
the Parabimbi, very much the lone bird on this occasion in the absence
of her husband the Count who had been unable to escort her on account
of his being buggered if he would, got in her attributions of the Frica for
which, as has been shown, the Beldam was so profoundly beholden.

"Maaaacche!" said the Countess of Parabimbi, "I do but constate."

She held the saucer under her chin like a communion-card. She low-
ered the cup into its socket without a sound.

"Excellent" she said, "most excellent Force."

The crone smiled from the teeth outward.

"So glad" she said, "so glad."

The Professor of Bullscrit and Comparative Ovoidology was nowhere
to be seen. But that was not his vocation, he was not a little boy. His func-
tion was to be heard. He was widely and distinctly heard.

"When the immortal Byron" he bombled "was about to leave Ravenna,
to sail in search of some distant shore where a hero's death might end
his immortal spleen . . ."

"Ravenna!" exclaimed the Countess, memory tugging at her carefully
cultivated heart-strings, "did I hear someone say Ravenna?"

"Allow me" said the rising strumpet: "a sandwich: egg, tomato, cucumber."

"Did you know" blundered the Man of Law "that the Swedes have no fewer than seventy varieties of Smoerrbroed?"

The voice of the arithmomaniac was heard:

"The arc" he said, stooping to all in the great plainness of his words, "is longer than its chord."

"Madam knows Ravenna?" said the paleographer.

"Do I know Ravenna!" exclaimed the Parabimbi. "Sure I know Ravenna. A sweet and noble city."

"You know of course" said the Man of Law "that Dante died there."

"Right" said the Parabimbi, "so he did."

"You know of course" said the Professor "that his tomb is in the Piazza Byron. I did his epitaph in the eye into blank heroics."

"You knew of course" said the paleographer "that under Belisarius . . ."

"My dear" said the Parabimbi to the Beldam, "how well it goes. What a happy party and how at home they all seem. I declare" she declared "I envy you your flair for making people feel at their ease."

The Beldam disclaimed faintly any such faculty. It was Caleken's party reelly, it was Caleken who had arranged everything reelly. She personally had had very little to do with the arrangements. She just sat there and looked exhausted. She was just a weary old Norn.

"To my thinking" boomed the Professor, begging the question as usual, "the greatest triumph of the human mind was the calculation of Neptune from the observed vagaries of the orbit of Uranus."

"And yours" said the P.B. That was an apple of gold and a picture of silver if you like.

The Parabimbi waxed stiff.

"What's that?" she cried, "what's that he says?"

A still more terrible silence fell on the assembly. The saprophile had slapped the communist painter and decorator.

The Frica, supported by Mr. Higgins, pounced on the disturbance.

"Go" she said to the saprophile "and let there be no scene."

Mr. Higgins, who kicked up his heels in the scrum for the Rangers, made short work of the nuisance. The Frica turned on the poor P. and D.

"It is not my intention" she said "to tolerate hooligans in this house."

"He called me a bloody Bolshy" protested the glorious Komsomolet, "and he a labour man himself."

"Let there be no more of it" said the Frica, "let there be no more of it." She was very optative. "I beg of you." She stepped back fleetly to the altar.

"You heard what she said" said the Gael.

"Let there be no more of it" said the native speaker.

"I beg of you" said the P.B.

But now she cometh that all this may disdain, Alba, dauntless daughter of desires. Entering just on the turn of the hush, advancing like a midinette to pay her ironical respects to the Beldam, she fired the thorns under every pot. Turning her scarlet back on the crass crackling of the Parabimbi she mounted the estrade and there, silent and still before the elements of refreshment, in profile to the assistance, cast her gravitational nets.

The rising strumpet studied how to do it. The sister of the parodist passed on to such as were curious what little she and her dear nieces knew of the Alba who was much spoken of in certain virtuous circles to which they had access, though to be sure how much of what they heard was true and how much mere idle gossip they were really not in a position to determine. However, for what it was worth, it appeared . . .

The Gael, the native speaker, a space-writer and the violist d'amore got together as though by magic.

"Well" invited the space-writer.

"Pret-ty good" said the Gael.

"Ex-quisite" said the violist d'amore.

The native speaker said nothing.

"Well" insisted the space-writer, "Larry?"

Larry tore his eyes away from the estrade and said, drawing his palms slowly up the flanks of his kilt:

"Jaysus!"

"Meaning to say?" said the space-writer.

Larry turned his wild gaze back on the estrade.

"You don't happen to know" he said finally "does she?"

"They all do" said the violist d'amore.

"Like hell they do" groaned the Gael, *ricordandosi del tempo felice.*

"What I want to know" said the Student, "what we all are most anxious to know . . ."

"Some do abstain" said the space-writer, "our friend here is right, through bashfulness from venery. It is a pity, but there you are."

Great wits will jump and Jemmy Higgins and the P.B. converged on the estrade.

"You look pale" said the Frica "and ill, my pet."

The Alba raised her big head from the board, looked longly at the Frica, closed her eyes and intoned:

> Woe and Pain, Pain and Woe,
> Are my lot, night and noon . . .

Caleken fell back.

"Keep them off" said the Alba.

"Keep them off!" echoed Caleken, "keep them off?"

"We go through this world" observed the Alba "like sunbeams through cracks in cucumbers."

Caleken was not so sure about the sunbeams.

"Take a little cup" she urged, "it will do you good. Or a Ching-Ching."

"Keep them off" said the Alba, "off off off off."

But the P.B. and Higgins were on the estrade, they hemmed her in.

"So be it" said the Alba, "let it run over by all means."

Phew! The Frica was unspeakably relieved.

Half-past nine. The guests, led by the rising strumpet and declining cicisbeo, began to scatter through the house. The Frica let them go. In due course she would visit the alcoves, she would round them up for the party proper to begin. Had not Chas promised a piece of old French? Had not the Poet written a poem specially? She had peeped into the bag in the hall and seen the viol d'amore. So they would have a little music.

. . .

Half-past nine. It was raining bitterly when Belacqua, keyed up to take his bearings, issued forth into the unintelligible world of Lincoln Place. But he had bought a bottle, it was like a breast in the pocket of his reefer. He set off unsteadily by the Dental Hospital. As a child he had dreaded its façade, its sheets of blood-red glass. Now they were black, which was worse again, he having put aside a childish thing or two. Feeling suddenly white and clammy he leaned against the iron wicket set in the College wall and looked at Johnston, Mooney and O'Brien's clocks. Something to ten by the whirligig and he disinclined to stand, let alone walk. And the daggers of rain. He raised his hands and held them before his face, so close that even in the dark he could see the lines. They smelt bad. He carried them on to his forehead, the fingers sank in his wet hair, the heels crushed torrents of indigo out of his eyeballs, the rabbet of his nape took the cornice, it wrung the baby anthrax that he always wore just above his collar, he intensified the pressure and the pangs, they were a guarantee of identity.

The next thing was his hands dragged roughly down from his eyes, which he opened on the vast crimson face of an ogre. For a moment it was still, plush gargoyle, then it moved, it was convulsed. This, he thought, is the face of some person talking. It was. It was that part of a Civic Guard pouring abuse upon him. Belacqua closed his eyes, there was no other way of ceasing to see it. Subduing a great desire to visit the pavement he catted, with undemonstrative abundance, all over the boots and trouser-ends of the Guard, in return for which incontinence he received such a dunch on the breast that he fell hip and thigh into the outskirts of his own offal. He had no feeling of hurt either to his person or to his *amour propre*, only a very amiable weakness and an impatience to be on the move. It must have gone ten. He bore no animosity towards the Guard, although now he began to hear what he was saying. He knelt before him in the filth, he heard all the odious words he was saying in the recreation of his duty, and bore him not the slightest ill-will. He reached up for a purchase on his gleaming cape and hoisted himself to his feet. The apology he made when stable for what had occurred was profusely rejected. He furnished his name and address, whence he came and whither he went, and why, his occupation and immediate business, and why. It distressed him to learn that for two pins the Guard would frog-march him to the Station, but he appreciated the officer's dilemma.

"Wipe them boots" said the Guard.

Belacqua was only too happy, it was the least he could do. Contriving two loose swabs of the *Twilight Herald* he stooped and cleaned the boots and trouser-ends to the best of his ability. A magnificent and enormous pair of boots emerged. He rose, clutching the fouled swabs, and looked up timidly at the Guard, who seemed rather at a loss as how best to press home his advantage.

"I trust, Sergeant," said Belacqua, in a murmur pitched to melt the hardest heart, "that you can see your way to overlooking my misdemeanour."

Justice and mercy had doubtless joined their ancient issue in the conscience of the Guard, for he said nothing. Belacqua tendered his right hand, innocent of any more mercantile commodity than that "gentle peace" recommended by the immortal Shakespeare, having first wiped it clean on his sleeve. This member the Dogberry, after a brief converse with his incorruptible heart, was kind enough to invest with the office of a cuspidor. Belacqua strangled a shrug and moved away in a tentative manner.

"Hold on there" said the Guard.

Belacqua halted, but in a very irritating way, as though he had just remembered something. The Guard, who had much more of the lion than of the fox, kept him standing until inside his helmet the throbbing of his Leix and Offaly head became more than he could endure. He then decided to conclude his handling of this small affair of public order.

"Move on" he said.

Belacqua walked away, holding tightly on to the swabs, which he rightly interpreted as litter. Once safely round the corner of Kildare Street he let them fall. Then, after a few paces forward, he halted, turned, hastened back to where they were fidgeting on the pavement and threw them into an area. Now he felt extraordinarily light and limber and *haeres caeli*. He followed briskly through the mizzle the way he had chosen, exalted, fashioning intricate festoons of words. It occurred to him, and he took great pleasure in working out this little figure, that the locus of his fall from

the vague grace of the drink had intersected with that of his rise there-
unto at its most agreeable point. That was beyond a doubt what had hap-
pened. Sometimes the drink-line looped the loop like an eight and if you
had got what you were looking for on the way up you got it again on the
way down. The bum-less eight of the drink-figure. You did not end up
where you started, but coming down you met yourself going up. Some-
times, as now, you were glad; more times you were sorry and hastened on
to your new home.

Suddenly walking through the rain was not enough, stepping out
smartly, buttoned up to the chin, in the cold and the wet, was an inad-
equate thing to be doing. He stopped on the crown of Baggot Street bridge,
took off his reefer, laid it on the parapet and sat down beside it. The
Guard was forgotten. Stooping forward then where he sat and flexing his
leg until the knee was against his ear and the heel caught on the parapet
(admirable posture) he took off his boot and laid it beside the reefer. Then
he let down that leg and did the same with the other. Next, resolved to get
full value from the bitter nor'-wester that was blowing, he slewed himself
right round. His feet dangled over the canal and he saw, lurching across
the remote hump of Leeson Street bridge, trams like hiccups-o'-the-wisp.
Distant lights on a dirty night, how he loved them, the dirty low-church
Protestant! He felt very chilly. He took off his jacket and belt and laid
them with the other garments on the parapet. He unbuttoned the top of
his filthy old trousers and coaxed out his German shirt. He bundled the
skirt of the shirt under the fringe of his pullover and rolled them up
clockwise together until they were hooped fast across his thorax. The rain
beat against his chest and belly and trickled down. It was even more agree-
able than he had anticipated, but very cold. It was now, beating his bosom
thus bared to the mean storm vaguely with marble palms, that he took
leave of himself and felt wretched and sorry for what he had done. He had
done wrong, he realized that, and he was heartily sorry. He sat on, drum-
ming his stockinged heels sadly against the stone, wondering whence on
earth could comfort spring, when suddenly the thought of the bottle he
had bought pierced his gloomy condition like a beacon. It was there at
hand in his pocket, a breast of Bisquit in the pocket of his reefer. He

dried himself as best he might with his cambric pochette and adjusted his clothes. When everything was back in place, the reefer buttoned up as before, the boots laced and not a hole skipped, then, but not a moment before, he permitted himself to drink the bottle at a single gulp. The effect of this was to send what is called a glow of warmth what is called coursing through his veins. He squelched off down the street at a trot, resolved to make it, in so far as he had the power to do so, a non-stop run to Casa Frica. Jogging along with his elbows well up he prayed that his appearance might not provoke too much comment.

His mind, in the ups and downs of the past hour, had not had leisure to dwell upon the sufferings in store for it. Even the Alba's scarlet gown— for the qualified assurance of the Venerilla, that it buttoned up *with the help of God*, had not been of a nature to purge it altogether of misgiving— had ceased to be a burden. But now, when the Frica came pattering out of the mauve salon to intercept him in the vestibule and with her presence shocked him into something worse than sobriety, the full seriousness of his position came to him with the force of an abstract calamity.

"There you are" she whinnied "at long last."

"Here" he said rudely "I float."

She recoiled with bursting eyes and clapped a hand to her teeth. Was it possible that he had been courting damp death and damnation or something of the kind? The wet dripped off him as he stood aghast before her and gathered in a little pool at his feet. How dilated her nostrils were!

"You must get out of those wet things" said the Frica, she must hurry now and put the lens in the keyhole, "this very moment. But the dear boy is drenched to the . . . skin!" There was no nonsense about the Frica. When she meant skin she said skin. "Every stitch" she gloated "must come off at once, this very instant."

From the taut cock of the face viewed as a whole, and in particular from the horripilating detail of the upper-lip writhing up and away in a kind of a duck or a cobra sneer to the quivering snout, he derived the impression that something had inflamed her. And right enough a condition of the highest mettle and fettle had followed hard upon her asinine dumfusion. For here indeed was an unexpected little bit of excitement! In a moment she would break into a caper. Belacqua thought it might be as well to take this disposition in time.

"No" he said composedly, "if I might have a towel . . ."

"A towel!" The scoff was so shocked that she was obliged to blow her nose better late than never.

"It would take off the rough wet" he said.

The rough wet! But how too utterly absurd to speak of the rough wet when it was clear to be seen that he was soaked through and through.

"To the skin!" she cried.

"No" he said, "if I might just have a towel . . ."

Caleken, though deeply chagrined as may well be imagined, knew her man well enough to realize that his determination to accept no more final comfort at her hands than the loan of a towel was unalterable. Also in the salon her absence was beginning to make itself heard, the mice were beginning to enjoy themselves. So off she pattered with a sour look— goose, thought Belacqua, flying barefoot from McCabe—and was back in no time with a hairy towel of great size and a hand-towel.

"You'll get your death" she said, with the adenoidal asperity that he knew so well, and left him. Rejoining her guests she felt that all this had happened to her before, by hearsay or in a dream.

Chas, conversing in low tones with the Shawly, was waiting in some trepidation to be called on for his contribution. This was the famous occasion when Chas, as though he had taken leave of his senses or begun to be irked by his brand new *toga virilis*, concluded an unexceptionable recitation with the quatrain:

> Toutes êtes, serez ou fûtes,
> De fait ou de volonté, putes,
> Et qui bien vous chercheroit
> Toutes putes vous trouveroit.

The Alba, whom in order to rescue Belacqua we were obliged to abandon just as with characteristic impetuosity she swallowed the pill, opened her campaign by sending Mr. Higgins and the P.B. flying, there is no other word for it, about their business. Upon which, not deigning to have any share in the sinister kiss-me-Charley hugger-mugger that had spread like wildfire throughout the building, till it raged from attic to basement, under the aegis of the rising strumpet and the casual cicisbeo, she proceeded in her own quiet and inimitable style to captivate all those who had curbed their instinct to join in the vile necking expressly in order to see what they could make of this pale little person so self-possessed and urbane in the best sense in the scarlet costume. So that, from the point of view of her Maker and in the absence of Belacqua, she was quite a power for good that evening in Casa Frica.

It had not occurred to her, fond as she was of that shabby hero in her own rather stealthy and sinuous fashion, to miss him or think of him at all unless possibly as a rather acute spectator whose eyes behind his glasses upon her and vernier of appraisement going like mad might have slightly spiced her fun. Among the many whom the implacable Frica had hounded from the joys of sense she had marked down for her own one of the grave Jews, him with the bile-tinged conjunctivae, and the merchant prince. She addressed herself to the Jew, but too slackly, as to an insipid dish, and was repulsed. Scarcely had she reloaded and trained her charms more nicely upon this interesting miscreant, of whom she proposed, her mind full of hands rubbing, to make a most salutary example, than the Frica, still smarting under her frustration, announced in a venomous tone of voice that Monsieur Jean du Chas, too well known to the Dublin that mattered for the most talentuous nonesuch that he was to require any introduction, had kindly consented to set the ball a-rolling. Notwithstanding the satisfaction that would have accrued to the Alba had Chas died the death without further delay, she made no attempt to restrain her merriment, in which of course she was uproariously seconded by the P.B., when he came out with the iniquitous apothegm quoted above, and the less so as she observed how bitter-sweetly the paleographer and Parabimbi, who had been surprised by the Frica being slightly naughty together, dissociated themselves from the applause that greeted his descent from the estrade.

This, roughly speaking, was the position when Belacqua framed him-self in the doorway.

Surveying him as he stood bedraggled under the lintel, clutching his enormous glasses (a precautionary measure that he never neglected when there was the least danger of his *appearing* embarrassed, appearing in italics because he was always embarrassed), bothered seriously in his mind by a neat little point that had arisen out of nowhere in the vesti-bule, waiting no doubt for some kind friend to lead him to a seat, the Alba thought she had never seen anybody, man or woman, look quite such a sovereign booby. Seeking to be God, she thought, in the slavish arrogance of a piffling evil.

"Like something" she said to her neighbour the P.B. "that a dog would bring in."

The P.B. played up, he overbade.

"Like something" he said "that, on reflection, he would not."

He cackled and snuffled over his sottish mot as though it were his own.

In an unsubduable movement of misericord the Alba started out of her chair.

"Niño" she called, without shame or ceremony.

The distant call came to Belacqua like a pint of Perrier to drink in a dungeon. He stumbled towards it.

"Move up in the bed" she ordered the P.B. "and make room."

Everybody in the row had to move up one. Like the totem chorus, thought the Alba with complacency, in *Rose Marie*. Belacqua came down on the end seat thus freed like a sack of potatoes. Observe, now at last they are juxtaposed. His next difficulty was how to get her on his other side, for he could not bear on any account to be on a person's right hand, without finding himself stuck up against the P.B. as a result. Though it scarcely required an expert statistician to realize that the desired order could only be established by his changing places with the P.B., leaving the Alba where she was, yet he wasted much valuable time, in a fever of notes of exclamation, failing to understand that of the six ways in which they could arrange themselves only one satisfied his conditions. He sat not looking, his head sunk, plucking vaguely at his filthy old trousers. When she placed her hand on his sleeve he roused himself and looked at her. To her disgust he was shedding tears.

"At it again" she said.

The Parabimbi could bear it no longer. Clutching and clawing and craning her neck all over the suffocating paleographer she demanded in a general way:

"What's that? Who's that? Is that *promessi?*"

"I was amazed" said a voice, "truly amazed, to find Sheffield more hilly than Rome."

Belacqua made a stupendous effort to acknowledge the cordial greeting of the P.B., but could not. He longed to subside on the floor and pillow his head on the slight madder thigh of his one and only.

"The bicuspid" from the Ovoidologist "monotheistic fiction ripped by the sophists, Christ and Plato, from the violated matrix of pure reason."

Who shall silence them, at last? Who shall circumcise their lips from speaking, at last?

The Frica insisted that she trod the estrade.

"Maestro Gormely" she said "will now play."

Maestro Gormely executed Scarlatti's Capriccio, without the least aid or accompaniment, on the viol d'amore. This met with no success to speak of.

"Plato!" sneered the P.B. "Did I hear the word Plato? That dirty little Borstal Boehme!" That was a sockdologer for someone if you like.

"Mr. Larry O'Murcahaodha"—the Frica pronounced it as though he were a connexion of Hiawatha— "will now sing."

Mr. Larry O'Murcahaodha tore a greater quantity than seemed fair of his native speech-material to flat tatters.

"I can't bear it" said Belacqua, "I can't bear it."

The Frica threw the Poet into the breach. She informed the assistance that it was privileged.

"I think I am accurate in saying" she presented her teeth for the lie "one of his most recent compositions."

"Vinegar" moaned Belacqua "on nitre."

"Don't you try" said with forced heartiness the Alba, who began to fear for her wretched adorer, "to put across the Mrs. Gummidge before the coverture on me."

He had no desire, oh none, to put across the Mrs. Gummidge at any stage of her experience or anything whatever on her or anyone else. His distress was profound and unaffected. He had abandoned all hope of getting her where he wanted her, he could neither be on her left hand nor at her feet. His only remaining concern, before his soul heaved anchor, was to get some kind friend to scotch a wolf that he could not hold off by the ears very much longer. He leaned across to the Polar Bear.

"I wonder" he said "could you possibly—"

"Motus!" screamed the bibliomaniac, from the back row.

The P.B. turned a little yellow, as well he might.

"Let the man say his lines" he hissed "can't you?"

Belacqua said in a loud despairing voice, falling back into position, a foreign word that he would understand.

"What is it?" whispered the Alba.

Belacqua was green, he did the King of Brobdingnag in a quick dumb crambo.

"Curse you" said the Alba, "what is it?"

"Let the man say his lines" he mumbled, "why won't you let the man say his lines?"

An outburst of applause unprecedented in the annals of the mauve salon suggested that he might have done so at last.

"Now" said the Alba.

Belacqua helped himself to a deep breath of the rank ambience and then, with the precipitation of one exhibiting a tongue-teaser, rattled off the borrowed quodlibet as follows:

"When with indifference I remember my past sorrow, my mind has indifference, my memory has sorrow. The mind, upon the indifference which is in it, is indifferent; yet the memory, upon the sorrow which is in it, is not sad."

"Again" she said, "slower."

He was getting on nicely with the repeat when the Alba had a sudden idea and stopped him.

"See me home" she said.

"Have you got it" said Belacqua, "because I haven't."

She covered his hand with her hand.

"What I want to know" said the Student.

"Will you?" she said.

"I see" said the Man of Law agreeably to Chas "by the paper that sailors are painting the Eiffel Tower with no fewer than forty tons of yellow."

The Frica, returning from having seen off the premises some renegade with a thin tale of a train to catch, made as though to regain the estrade. Her face was suffused with indignation.

"Quick" said Belacqua, "before it starts."

The Frica came plunging after them, torrents of spleen gushed out of her. Belacqua held the street-door open for the Alba, who seemed half inclined to do the polite, to precede him.

"The lady first" he said.

He insisted on their taking a taxi to her home. They found nothing to say on the way. *Je t'adore à l'égal.* . . .

"Can you pay this man" he said when they arrived "because I spent my last on a bottle?"

She took money out of her bag and gave it to him and he paid the man off. They stood on the asphalt in front of the gate, face to face. The rain had almost ceased,

"Well" he said, wondering might he hazard a quick baisemain before he went. He released the gesture but she shrank away and unlatched the gate.

Tire la chevillette, la bobinette cherra.

Pardon these French expressions, but the creature dreams in French.

"Come in" she said, "there's a fire and a bottle."

He went in. She would sit in a chair and he would sit on the floor at last and her thigh against his baby anthrax would be better than a foment. For the rest, the bottle, some natural tears and in what hair he had left her high-frequency fingers.

Nisscht mööööööglich. . . .

. . .

Now it began to rain again upon the earth beneath and greatly incommoded Christmas traffic of every kind by continuing to do so without remission for a matter of thirty-six hours. A divine creature, native of Leipzig, to whom Belacqua, round about the following Epiphany, had occasion to quote the rainfall for December as cooked in the Dublin University Fellows' Garden, ejaculated:

"Himmisacrakrüzıdırkenjesusmariaundjosefundblütigeskrcuz!"

Like that, all in one word. The things people come out with sometimes!

But the wind had dropped, as it so often does in Dublin when all the respectable men and women whom it delights to annoy have gone to bed, and the rain fell in a uniform untroubled manner. It fell upon the bay, the littoral, the mountains and the plains, and notably upon the Central Bog it fell with a rather desolate uniformity.

So that when Belacqua that uneasy creature came out of Casa Alba in the small hours of the morning it was a case of darkness visible and no mistake. The street-lamps were all extinguished, as were the moon and stars. He stood out well in the midst of the tramlines, inspected every available inch of the firmament and satisfied his mind that it was quite black. He struck a match and looked at his watch. It had stopped. Patience, a public clock would oblige.

His feet pained him so much that he took off his perfectly good boots and threw them away, with best wishes to some early bird for a Merry Christmas. Then he set off to paddle the whole way home, his toes rejoicing in their freedom. But this small gain in the matter of ease was very quickly more than revoked by such a belly-ache as he had never known. This doubled him up more and more till finally he was creeping along with his poor trunk parallel to the horizon. When he came to the bridge over the canal, not Baggot Street, not Leeson Street, but another nearer the sea, he gave in and disposed himself in the knee-and-elbow position on the pavement. Gradually the pain got better.

What was that? He shook off his glasses and stooped his head to see. That was his hands. Now who would have thought that! He began to try would they work, clenching them and unclenching, keeping them moving for the wonder of his weak eyes. Finally he opened them in unison, finger by finger together, till there they were, wide open, face upward, rancid, an inch from his squint, which however slowly righted itself as he began to lose interest in them as a spectacle. Scarcely had he made to employ them on his face than a voice, slightly more in sorrow than in anger this time, enjoined him to move on, which, the pain being so much better, he was only too happy to do.

Love and Lethe

The Toughs, consisting of Mr. and Mrs. and their one and only Ruby, lived in a small house in Irishtown. When dinner, which they took in the middle of the day, was ended, Mr. Tough went to his room to lie down and Mrs. Tough and Ruby to the kitchen for a cup of coffee and a chat. The mother was low-sized, pale and plump, admirably preserved though well past the change. She poured the right amount of water into the saucepan and set it to boil.

"What time is he coming?" she said.

"He said about three" said Ruby.

"With car?" said Mrs. Tough.

"He hoped with car" answered Ruby.

Mrs. Tough hoped so most devoutly, for she had an idea that she might be invited to join the party. Though she would rather have died than stand in the way of her daughter, yet she saw no reason why, if she kept herself to herself in the dicky, there should be any objection to her joining in the fun. She shook the beans into the little mill and ground them violently into powder. Ruby, who was neurasthenic on top of everything else, plugged her ears. Mrs. Tough, taking a seat at the deal table against the water would be boiling, looked out of the window at the perfect weather.

"Where are you going?" she said. She had the natural curiosity of a mother in what concerns her child.

"Don't ask me" answered Ruby, who was inclined to resent all these questions.

He to whom they referred, who had hopes of calling at three with a car, was the doomed Belacqua and no other.

The water boiling, Mrs. Tough rose and added the coffee, reduced the flame, stirred thoroughly and left to simmer. Though it seems a strange way to prepare coffee, yet it was justified by the event.

"Let me put you up some tea" implored Mrs. Tough. She could not bear to be idle.

"Ah no" said Ruby "no thanks really."

It struck the half-hour in the hall. It was half-past two, that zero hour, in Irishtown.

"Half-two!" ejaculated Mrs. Tough, who had no idea it was so late.

Ruby was glad that it was not earlier. The aroma of coffee pervaded the kitchen. She would have just nice time to dream over her coffee. But she knew that this was quite out of the question with her mother wanting to talk, bursting with questions and suggestions. So when the coffee was dispensed and her mother had settled down for the comfortable chat that went with it she unexpectedly said:

"I think, mother, if you don't mind, I'll take mine with me to the lav, I don't feel very well."

Mrs. Tough was used to the whims of Ruby and took them philosophically usually. But this latest fancy was really a little bit too unheard of. Coffee in the lav! What would father say when he heard? However.

"And the rosiner" said Mrs. Tough, "will you have that in the lav too?"

Reader, a rosiner is a drop of the hard.

Ruby rose and took a gulp of coffee to make room.

"I'll have a gloria" she said.

Reader, a gloria is coffee laced with brandy.

Mrs. Tough poured into the proffered cup a smaller portion of brandy than in the ordinary way she would have allowed, and Ruby left the room.

We know something of Belacqua, but Ruby Tough is a stranger to these pages. Anxious that those who read this incredible adventure shall not pooh-pooh it as unintelligible we avail ourselves now of this lull, what time Belacqua is on his way, Mrs. Tough broods in the kitchen and Ruby dreams over her gloria, to enlarge a little on the latter lady.

For a long period, on account of the beauty of her person and perhaps also, though in lesser degree, the distinction of her mind, Ruby had been the occasion of much wine-shed; but now, in the thirty-third or -fourth year of her age, she was so no longer. Those who are in the least curious to know what she looked like at the time in which we have chosen to cull her we venture to refer to the Magdalene[1] in the Perugino Pietà in the National Gallery of Dublin, always bearing in mind that the hair of our heroine is black and not ginger. Further than this hint we need not allow her outside to detain us, seeing that Belacqua was scarcely ever aware of it.

The facts of life had reduced her temper, naturally romantic and idealistic in the highest degree, to an almost atomic despair. Her sentimental experience had indeed been unfortunate. Requiring of love, as a younger and more appetising woman, that it should unite or fix her as firmly and as finally as the sun of a binary in respect of its partner, she had come to avoid it more and more as she found, with increasing disappointment and disgust, its effect at each successive manifestation, for she had been in great demand, to be of quite a different order. The result of this erotic frustration was, firstly, to make her eschew the experience entirely; secondly, to recommend her itch for syzygy to more ideal measures, among which she found music and malt the most efficacious; and finally, to send her caterwauling to the alcove for whatever shabby joys it could afford. These however, *embarras de richesse* as long as she remained the scornful maiden, were naturally less at pains to solicit one whose sense of proportion had been acquired to the great detriment of her allurements. The grapes of love, set aside as abject in the days of hot blood, turned sour as soon as she discovered a zest for them. As formerly she had recoiled into herself because she would not, so now she did because she could not,

---

1. This figure, owing to the glittering vitrine behind which the canvas cowers, can only be apprehended in sections. Patience, however, and a retentive memory have been known to elicit a total statement approximating to the intention of the painter.

except that in her retreat the hope that used to solace her was dead. She saw her life as a series of staircase jests.

Belacqua, paying pious suit to the hem of her garment and gutting his raptures with great complacency at a safe remove, represented precisely the ineffable long-distance paramour to whom as a homesick meteorite abounding in IT she had sacrificed her innumerable gallants. And now, the metal of stars smothered in earth, the IT run dry and the gallants departed, he appeared, like the agent of an ironical Fortune, to put her in mind of what she had missed and rowel her sorrow for what she was missing. Yet she tolerated him in the hope that sooner or later, in a fit of ebriety or of common or garden incontinence, he would so far forget himself as to take her in his arms.

Join to all this the fact that she had long been suffering from an incurable disorder and been assured positively by no fewer than fifteen doctors, ten of whom were atheists, acting independently, that she need not look forward to her life being much further prolonged, and we feel confident that even the most captious reader must acknowledge, not merely the extreme wretchedness of Ruby's situation, but also the verisimilitude of what we hope to relate in the not too distant future. For we assume the irresponsibility of Belacqua, his faculty for acting with insufficient motivation, to have been so far evinced in previous misadventures as to be no longer a matter for surprise. In respect of this apparent gratuity of conduct he may perhaps with some colour of justice be likened to the laws of nature. A mental home was the place for him.

He cultivated Ruby, for whom at no time did he much care, and made careful love in the terms he thought best calculated to prime her for the part she was to play on his behalf, the gist of which, as he revealed when he deemed her ripe, provided that she should connive at his felo de se, which he much regretted he could not commit on his own bottom. How he had formed this resolution to destroy himself we are quite unable to discover. The simplest course, when the motives of any deed are found subliminal to the point of defying expression, is to call that deed *ex nihilo* and have done. Which we beg leave to follow in the present instance.

The normal woman of sense asks "what?" in preference to "why?" (this is very deep), but poor Ruby had always been deficient in that exquisite quality, so that no sooner had Belacqua opened his project than she applied for his reasons. Now though he had none, as we have seen, that he could offer, yet he had armed himself so well at this point, forewarned by the study he had made of his cats-paw's mind, that he was able to pelt her there and then with the best that diligent enquiry could provide: Greek and Roman reasons, Sturm und Drang reasons, reasons metaphysical, aesthetic, erotic, anterotic and chemical, Empedocles of Agrigentum and John of the Cross reasons, in short all but the true reasons, which did not exist, at least not for the purposes of conversation. Ruby, flattened by this torrent of incentive, was obliged to admit that this was not, as she had inclined to suspect, a greenhorn yielding to the spur of a momentary pique, but an adult desperado of fixed and even noble purpose, and from this concession passed to a state almost of joy. She was done in any case, and here was a chance to end with a fairly beautiful bang. So the thing was arranged, the needful measures taken, the date fixed in the spring of the year and a site nearby selected, Venice in October having been rejected as alas impracticable. Now the fateful day had come and Ruby, in the posture of Philosopher Square behind Molly Seagrim's arras, sat winding herself up, while Belacqua, in a swagger sports roadster chartered at untold gold by the hour, trod on the gas for Irishtown.

So fiercely indeed did he do this, though so far from being insured against third-party risks he was not even the holder of a driving-licence, that he scored a wake of objurgation as he sped through the traffic. The better-class pedestrians and cyclists turned and stared after him. "These stream-lined Juggernauts" they said, shaking their heads, "are a positive menace." Civic Guards at various points of the city and suburbs took his number. In Pearse Street he smote off the wheel of a growler as cleanly as Peter Malchus's ear after the agony, but did not stop. Further on, in some lowly street or other, the little children playing beds and ball and other games were scattered like chaff. But before the terrible humped Victoria Bridge, its implacable bisection, in a sudden panic at his own temerity he stopped the car, got out and pushed her across with the help of a bystander. Then he drove quietly on through the afternoon and came in due course without further mishap to the house of his accomplice.

Mrs. Tough flung open wide the door. She was all over Belacqua, with his big pallid gob much abused with imagined debauches.

"Ruby" she sang, in a third, like a cuckoo, "Rubee! Rubee!"

But would she ever change her tune, that was the question.

Ruby dangled down the stairs, with the marks of her teeth in her nether lip where she could persuade no bee to sting her any more.

"Get on your bonnet and shawl" said Belacqua roughly "and we'll be going."

Mrs. Tough recoiled aghast. This was the first time she had ever heard such a tone turned on her Ruby. But Ruby got into a coat like a lamb and seemed not to mind. It became only too clear to Mrs. Tough that she was not going to be invited.

"May I offer you a little refreshment" she said in an icy voice to Belacqua "before you go?" She could not bear to be idle.

Ruby thought she had never heard anything quite so absurd. Refreshment *before* they went! It was if and when they returned that they would be in need of refreshment.

"Really, mother" she said, "can't you see we must be off."

Belacqua chimed in with a heavy lunch at the Bailey. The truth was not in him.

"Off where?" said Mrs. Tough.

"Off" cried Ruby, "just off."

What a strange mood she is in to be sure, thought Mrs. Tough. However. At least they could not prevent her from going as far as the gate.

"Where did you raise the car?" she said.

If you had seen the car you would agree that this was the most natural question.

Belacqua mentioned a firm of motor engineers.

"Oh indeed" said Mrs. Tough.

Mr. Tough crept to the window and peeped out from behind the curtain. He had worked himself to the bone for his family and he could only afford a safety-bicycle. A bitter look stole over his cyanosis.

Belacqua got in a gear at last, he had no very clear idea himself which, after much clutch-burning, and they shot forward in Hollywood style. Mrs. Tough might have been waving to Lot for all the response she received. Was the cut-out by way of being their spokesman? Ruby's parting gird, "Expect us when you see us," echoed in her ears. On the stairs she met Mr. Tough descending. They passed.

"There is something about that young man" called down Mrs. Tough "that I can't relish."

"Pup" called up Mr. Tough.

They increased the gap between them.

"Ruby is very strange" cried down Mrs. Tough.

"Slut" cried up Mr. Tough.

Though he might be only able to afford a safety-bicycle he was nevertheless a man of few words. There are better things, he thought, going to the bottle, there are better things in this stenching world than Blue Birds.

The pup and slut drove on and on and there was dead silence between them. Not a syllable did they exchange until the car was safely stowed at the foot of a high mountain. But when Ruby saw Belacqua open the dicky and produce a bag she thought well to break a silence that was becoming a little awkward.

"What have you got" she said "in the maternity-bag?"

"Socrates" replied Belacqua "the son of his mother, and the hemlocks."

"No" she said, "codding aside, what?"

Belacqua let fly a finger for each item.

"The revolver and balls, the veronal, the bottle and glasses, *and* the notice."

Ruby could not repress a shiver.

"In the name of God" she said "what notice?"

"The one that we are fled" replied Belacqua, and not another word would he say though she begged him to tell her. The notice was his own idea and he was proud of it. When the time came she would have to subscribe to it whether she liked it or not. He would keep it as a little surprise for her.

They ascended the mountain in silence. Wisps of snipe and whatever it is of grouse squirted out of the heather on all sides, while the number of hares, brooding in their forms, that they started and sent bounding away, was a credit to the gamekeeper. They plunged on and up through the deep ling and whortleberry. Ruby was sweating. A high mesh wire fence, flung like a shingles round the mountain, obstructed their passage.

"What are all the trusses for?" panted Ruby.

Right along on either hand as far as they could see there were fasces of bracken attached to the wire. Belacqua racked his brains for an explanation. In the end he had to give it up.

"God I don't know at all" he exclaimed.

It certainly was the most astounding thing.

Ladies first. Ruby scaled the fence. Belacqua, holding gallantly back with the bag in his hand, enjoyed a glimpse of her legs' sincerity. It was the first time he had had occasion to take stock of those parts of her and certainly he had seen worse. They pushed on and soon the summit, complete with fairy rath, came into view, howbeit still at a considerable distance.

Ruby tripped and fell, but on her face. Belacqua's strong arms were at hand to raise her up.

"Not hurt" he kindly enquired.

"This foul old skirt gets in my way" she said angrily.

"It *is* an encumbrance" agreed Belacqua, "off with it."

This struck Ruby as being such a good suggestion that she acted upon it without further ado and stood revealed as one of those ladies who have no use for a petticoat. Belacqua folded the skirt over his arm, there being no room for it in the bag, and Ruby, greatly eased, stormed the summit in her knickers.

Belacqua, who was in the lead, halted all of a sudden, clapped his hands, spun round and told Ruby he had got it. He was keenly conscious of her standing knee-deep in the ling before him, grateful for a breather and not bothering to ask what.

"They tie those bundles to the wire" he said "so that the grouse will see them."

Still she did not understand.

"And not fly against the fence and hurt themselves."

Now she understood. The calm way she took it distressed Belacqua. It was to be hoped that the notice would have better success than this splendid divulgation. Now the ling was up to her garters, she seemed to be sinking in the heath as in a quicksand. Could it be that she was giving at the knees? "Spirits of this mountain" murmured the heart of Belacqua "keep me steadfast."

Now since parking the car they had not seen a living soul.

The first thing they had to do of course when they got to the top was admire the view, with special reference to Dun Laoghaire framed to perfection in the shoulders of Three Rock and Kilmashogue, the long arms of the harbour like an entreaty in the blue sea. Young priests were singing in a wood on the hillside. They heard them and they saw the smoke of their fire. To the west in the valley a plantation of larches nearly brought tears to the eyes of Belacqua, till raising those unruly members to the slopes of Glendoo, mottled like a leopard, that lay beyond, he thought of Synge and recovered his spirits. Wicklow, full of breasts with pimples, he refused to consider. Ruby agreed. The city and the plains to the north meant nothing to either of them in the mood they were in. A human turd lay within the rath.

Like fantoccini controlled by a single wire they flung themselves down on the western slope of heath. From now on till the end there is something very *secco* and Punch Judy about their proceedings, Ruby looking more bawdy Magdalene than ever, Belacqua like a super out of the Harlot's Progress. He kept putting off opening the bag.

"I thought of bringing the gramophone" he said "and Ravel's *Pavane*. Then—"

"Then you thought again" said Ruby. She had a most irritating habit of interrupting.

"Oh yes" said Belacqua, "the usual pale cast."

Notice the literary man.

"S'pity" said Ruby, "it might have made things easier."

Happy Infanta! Painted by Velásquez and then no more pensums!

"If you would put back your skirt" said Belacqua violently, "now that you have done walking, you would make things easier for me."

How difficult things were becoming, to be sure. The least thing might upset the apple-cart at this juncture.

Ruby pricked up her ears. Was this a declaration at last? In case it might be she would not oblige him.

"I prefer it off" she said.

Belacqua, staring fiercely at the larches, sulked for a space.

"Well" he grumbled at last, "shall we have a little drink to start off?"

Ruby was agreeable. He opened the bag as little as possible, put in his hand, snatched out the bottle, then the glasses and shut it quick.

"Fifteen year old" he said complacently, "on tick."

All the money he owed for one thing or another. If he did not pull it off now once and for all he would be broke.

"God" he exclaimed, executing a kind of passionate tick-tack through his pockets, "I forgot the screw."

"Pah" said Ruby, "what odds. Knock its head off, shoot its neck off."

But the screw turned up as it always does and they had a long drink.

"Length without breath" gasped Belacqua "that's the idea, Hiawatha at Dublin bar."

They had another.

"That makes four doubles" said Ruby "and they say there's eight in a bottle."

Belacqua held up the bottle. In that case there was something wrong with her statement.

"Never two without three" he said.

They had another.

"O Death in Life" vociferated Belacqua, "the days that are no more."

He fell on the bag and ripped out the notice for her inspection. Painted roughly in white on an old number-plate she beheld:

TEMPORARILY SANE

IK-6996 had been erased to make room for this inscription. It was a palimpsest.

Ruby, pot-valiant, let a loud scoff.

"It won't do" she said, "it won't do at all."

It was a disappointment to hear her say this. Poor Belacqua. Sadly he held the plate out at arm's length.

"You don't like it" he said.

"Bad" said Ruby "very bad."

"I don't mean the way it's presented" said Belacqua, "I mean the idea."

It was all the same what he meant.

"If I had a paddle" she said "I'd bury it, idea and all."

Belacqua laid the offensive object face downward in the heather. Now there was nothing left in the bag but the firearm, the ammunition and the veronal.

The light began to die, there was no time to be lost.

"Will you be shot" said Belacqua "or poisoned? If the former, have you any preference? The heart? The temple? If the latter" passing over the bag, "help yourself."

Ruby passed it back.

"Load" she ordained.

"Chevaliers d'industrie" said Belacqua, inserting the ball, "nearly all blow their brains out. Kreuger proved the rule."

"We don't exactly die together darling" drawled Ruby "or do we?"

"Alas" sighed Belacqua "what can you expect? But a couple of minutes" with a bounteous brandish of the revolver, "the time it takes to boil an egg, what is that to eternity?"

"Still" said Ruby "it would have been rather nice to pass out together."

"The problem of precedence" said Belacqua, as from a rostrum, "always arises, even as between the Pope and Napoleon."

" 'The Pope the puke' " quoted Ruby " 'he bleached her soul . . .' "

"But perhaps you don't know that story" said Belacqua, ignoring the irrelevance.

"I do not" said Ruby "and I have no wish to."

"Well" said Belacqua "in that case I will merely say that they solved it in a strictly spatial manner."

"Then why not we?" said Ruby.

The gas seems to be escaping somewhere.

"We" said Belacqua "like twins—"

"Are gone astray" sneered Ruby.

"Are slaves of the sand-glass. There is not room for us to run out arm in arm."

"As though there were only the one in the world" said Ruby. "Pah!"

"We happen to pine in the same one" said Belacqua, "that is the difficulty."

"Well, it's a minor point" said Ruby "and by all means ladies first."

"Please yourself" said Belacqua, "I'm the better shot."

But Ruby, instead of expanding her bosom or holding up her head to be blown off, helped herself to a drink. Belacqua fell into a passion.

"Damn it" he cried "didn't we settle all these things weeks ago? Did we or did we not?"

"A settlement was reached" said Ruby, "certainly."

"Then why all this bloody talk?"

Ruby drank her drink.

"And leave us a drop in the bottle" he snarled, "I'll need it when you're gone."

That indescribable sensation, compound of exasperation and relief, relaxing, the better to grieve, the coenaesthesis of the consultant when he finds the surgeon out, now burst inside Belacqua. He felt suddenly hot within. The bitch was backing out.

Though whiskey as a rule helped Ruby to feel starry, yet somehow on this occasion it failed to effect her in that way, which is scarcely surprising if we reflect what a very special occasion it was. Now to her amazement the revolver went off, harmlessly luckily, and the bullet fell *in terram* nobody knows where. But for fully a minute she thought she was shot. An appalling silence, in the core of which their eyes met, succeeded the detonation.

"The finger of God" whispered Belacqua.

Who shall judge of his conduct at this crux? Is it to be condemned as wholly despicable? Is it not possible that he was gallantly trying to spare the young woman embarrassment? Was it tact or concupiscence or the white feather or an accident or what? We state the facts. We do not presume to determine their significance.

"Digitus Dei" he said "for once."

That remark rather gives him away, does it not?

When the first shock of surprise had passed and the silence spent its fury a great turmoil of life-blood sprang up in the breasts of our two young felons, so that they came together in inevitable nuptial. With the utmost reverence at our command, moving away on tiptoe from where they lie in the ling, we mention this in a low voice.

It will quite possibly be his boast in years to come, when Ruby is dead and he an old optimist, that at least on this occasion, if never before nor since, he achieved what he set out to do; *car*, in the words of one competent to sing of the matter, *l'Amour et la Mort*—caesura—*n'est qu'une mesme chose*.

May their night be full of music at all events.

Walking Out

One fateful fine Spring evening he paused, not so much in order to rest as to have the scene soak through him, out in the middle of the late Boss Croker's Gallops, where no horses were to be seen any more. Pretty Polly that great-hearted mare was buried in the vicinity. To stroll over this expanse in fine weather, these acres of bright green grass, was almost as good as to cross the race-course of Chantilly with one's face towards the Castle. Leaning now on his stick, between Leopardstown down the hill to the north and the heights of Two Rock and Three Rock to the south, Belacqua regretted the horses of the good old days, for they would have given to the landscape something that the legions of sheep and lambs could not give. These latter were springing into the world every minute, the grass was spangled with scarlet afterbirths, the larks were singing, the hedges were breaking, the sun was shining, the sky was Mary's cloak, the daisies were there, everything was in order. Only the cuckoo was wanting. It was one of those Spring evenings when it is a matter of some difficulty to keep God out of one's meditations.

Belacqua leaned all his spare weight on the stick and took in the scene, in a sightless passionate kind of way, and his Kerry Blue bitch sat on the emerald floor beside him. She was getting old now, she could not be bothered hunting any more. She could tree a cat, that was no bother, but beyond that she did not care to go. So she just remained seated, knowing perfectly well that there were no cats in Croker's Gallops, and did not care very much what happened. The bleating of the lambs excited her slightly.

My God, it occurred to Belacqua, I must be past my best when I find myself preferring this time of year to the late Autumn.

This vivid thought, quite irrefutable as he recognized at once, did not so distress him that he was unable to move on. Past the worst of his best, there was nothing so very terrible in that, on the contrary. Soon he might hope to be creeping about in a rock-garden with tears in his eyes. Indeed proof, if proof he needed, that he was rather elated than distressed, appears in his taking his weight off the stick and moving forward; for the effect of a real dereliction was always to cast him up high and dry and unable to stir. The bitch walked behind. She was hot and bored.

Slowly he raised his eyes till they were levelled at his destination. Tom Wood, it graced like a comb a low hill in the distance. There he had assignation, but only in the sense that an angler has with the fish in a river. He had been there so often that he knew all its ins and outs, yet he could not have given a name to its timber. Oak, he supposed vaguely, or elm, but even had he looked he would not have been any wiser. This country lad, he could not tell an oak from an elm. Larches however he knew, from having climbed them as a little fat boy, and a young plantation of these, of a very poignant reseda, caught his eye now on the hillside. Poignant and assuasive at once, the effect it had upon him as he advanced was prodigious.

He thought if only his wife would consent to take a cicisbeo how pleasant everything would be all round. She knew how he loved her and yet she would not hear of his getting her a cicisbeo. He was merely betrothed, but already he thought of his fiancée as his wife, an anticipation that young men undertaking this change of condition might be well advised to imitate. Time and again he had urged her to establish their married life on this solid basis of a cuckoldry. She understood and appreciated his sentiment, she acknowledged that his argument was sound, and yet she would not or could not bring herself to act accordingly. He was not a bad-looking young fellow, a kind of cretinous Tom Jones. She would kill his affection with her nonsense before the wedding bells, that would be the end of it.

Turning this and cognate anxieties over and over in his mind he came at length to the southern limit of the Gallops and the by-road that he had to cross to get into the next list of fields. Thus, large tracts of champaign, hedges and ditches and blessed grass and daisies, then the deep weal of road, again and again, until he would come to the wood. The wall was too high for the bitch at her time of life, so he helped her across with a vigorous heave on the grey hunkers. This gave him pleasure if he had stopped to analyse it. But himself, he made short work of the obstacle, thinking: what a splendid thing it is when all is said and done to be young and vigorous.

In the ditch on the far side of the road a strange equipage was installed: an old high-wheeled cart, hung with rags. Belacqua looked round for something in the nature of a team, the crazy yoke could scarcely have fallen from the sky, but nothing in the least resembling a draught-beast was to be seen, not even a cow. Squatting under the cart a complete down-and-out was very busy with something or other. The sun beamed down on this as though it were a new-born lamb. Belacqua took in the whole outfit at a glance and felt, the wretched bourgeois, a paroxysm of shame for his capon belly. The bitch, in a very remote manner, stepped up to the cart and sniffed at the rags.

"Cmowathat!" vociferated the vagabond.

Now Belacqua could see what he was doing. He was mending a pot or a pan. He beat his tool against the vessel in his anxiety. But the bitch made herself at home.

"Wettin me throusers" said the vagabond mildly "wuss 'n meself."

So that was his trousers!

This privacy which he had always assumed to be inalienable, this ultimate prerogative of the Christian man, had now been violated by somebody's pet. Yet he might have been calling a score, his voice was so devoid of rancour. But Belacqua was embarrassed in the last degree.

"Good evening" he piped in fear and trembling, "lovely evening."

A smile proof against all adversity transformed the sad face of the man under the cart. He was most handsome with his thick, if unkempt, black hair and moustache.

"Game ball" he said.

After that further comment was impossible. The question of apology or compensation simply did not arise. The instinctive nobility of this splendid creature for whom private life, his joys and chagrins at evening under the cart, was not acquired, as Belacqua one day if he were lucky might acquire his, but antecedent, disarmed all the pot-hooks and hangers of civility. Belacqua made an inarticulate flourish with his stick and passed down the road out of the life of this tinker, this real man at last.

But he had not gone far, he had not yet turned aside into the next zone of field, before he heard cries behind him and the taratantara of hooves. This was none other than his dearest Lucy, his betrothed, astride her magnificent jennet. Reining in she splashed past him in a positive tornado of caracoling. When her mount had calmed down and her own panting somewhat abated she explained to the astonished and, be it said, somewhat vexed Belacqua how she came to be there.

"Oh, I called round and they told me you were gone out."

Belacqua caressed the soft jowl of the jennet. Poor beast, it had been ridden into a lather. It looked at him with a very white eye. It would tolerate his familiarities since of such was its servitude, but it hoped, before it died, to bite a man.

"So I didn't know what to do, so what do you think?"

Belacqua could not imagine. There seemed to be nothing to do under the circumstances but make the best of it.

"I got up on the roof and did the Sister Ann."

"No!" exclaimed Belacqua. This was pleasant.

"Yes, and I found you in the end, all alone in the Gallops."

This was charming. Belacqua came over to her leg.

"Darling!" she ejaculated.

"Well" he said "well well well."

"So I skited round by the road" she was overcome by the success of her little manoeuvre "and here I am."

She had rounded him up, she had cut him off, it was nearly as good as catching an ocean greyhound on the pictures. He kissed her flexed knee.

"Brava!"

To think that somebody needed him in this way! He could not but be touched.

In face and figure Lucy was entrancing, her entire person was quite perfect. For example, she was as dark as jet and of a paleness that never altered, and her thick short hair went back like a pennon from her fan-light forehead. But it would be waste of time to itemise her. Truly there was no fault or flaw in the young woman. Yet we feel we must say before we let her be, her poor body that must wither, that her nether limbs, from where they began even unto where they ended, would have done credit to a Signorelli page. Let us put it this way, that through her riding-breeches they came through. What more can be said for a woman's legs, thighs included? Or is all this merely ridiculous?

Belacqua wondered, when the first rapture at having been spied from afar had worn off, what the hell she wanted. But it appeared that she did not want anything in particular, she just wanted to be with him. This was a falsehood of course, she did want something in particular. However.

"Listen my dear Lucy" he said with a kind of final franchise "I know you won't mind if I can't spend this evening with my"—it took him some time to find a term of endearment to cover the facts—"my Fünklein."

But she pulled a very bitter face. The lizard of hers, he seemed to be making a habit of giving her the go-by, very soon if he did not watch out she would have no use for him.

"I have the chinks" he complained and apologized. "God help me, I'm no fit company for anyone let alone lovely Lucy."

Indeed she was better than lovely, with its suggestion of the Nobel Yeats, with her jet of hair and her pale set face, the whipcord knee and the hard bust sweating a little inside the black jersey.

Now it is her turn to go on.

Does he really imagine, she wondered, that it is his company I want, which seems to me at this stage about as futile an article as a pen-wiper. Let the ink clot on the nib, let the wine, to put it another way, scour the lees.

He spoke, as she knew he was bound to, if only she held her pose long enough.

"I went out to walk it off."

"Walk *what* off?" cried Lucy. She was sick and tired of his moods.

"Oh I don't know" he said, "our old friend, the devil's bath."

He drew designs with his devil's finger on the jennet's coat, wondering how to put it.

"Then I thought" he said at last "that the best thing to do was to go to the wood for a little sursum corda."

This was another falsehood, because the wood had been in his thoughts all day. He told it with a kind of miserable conviction.

"Corda is good" said Lucy.

As she uttered these words with one of her smart smiles the truth, or something that seemed very like it, struck her with such violence that she nearly fell out of the saddle. But she recovered herself and Belacqua, back at the bridle courting disaster, saw nothing.

"I know" he said sadly "you don't believe in these private experiences, women don't I know as a rule. And if you distrust them now——"

He stopped, and it was obvious, even to the jennet, that he had gone too far.

What was the bitch doing all this time? She was sitting in the ditch, listening.

The sun seemed to be sinking in the south, for the group was now wholly in the shadow of the high hedge on Lucy's left, though to be sure on her right the Gallops were still shining. Though the larks had gone to bed and the rooks were going there was no loss of pastoral clamour, for the lambs cried more loudly as the light fell and dogs began to bark in the distance. The cuckoo however was still in abeyance. Belacqua stepped back into the ditch and stood irresolute beside his pet, the jennet drooped its head and closed its eyes, Lucy sat very still on its back staring straight before her, they all seemed to be listening, the woman, the bitch, the jennet and the man. The vagabond could see them between adjoining spokes of his wheel, by moving his head into the right position he was far enough away to frame the whole group in a sector of his wheel.

Lucy, resolved to put her terrible surmise to the proof, had very soon shamed her lover into making terms, for of course he was as wax in her hands[1] when it came to a course of action. It was arranged that they should meet at the gate that led off the lane into the wood, he going his way across country direct and she, because it was out of the question to negotiate walls and dikes with the jennet, her devious one by road. What adverse fate forbad them at this point to fund their ways? The group broke up and soon the vagabond, peering out through his sector, saw only the grey of the road with its green hem.

Lucy jogged along briskly. We may mention that the effect of this motion was usually to exhilarate her, but it did not do so now, so stunned was she by the sudden vision of Belacqua that damned him, were it true, as her mate, her partner in life's journey. If what she dreaded were true her heart was broken, to say nothing of her engagement. But could it? This young man of good family, so honourable to her certain knowledge in all his dealings, so spiritual, a Varsity man too, could he be such a creepy-crawly? It seemed inconceivable that she should have been so blinded to his real nature as to let her love, born in a spasm more than a year ago in the Portrush Palais de Danse, increase steadily from day to day till now it amounted to something like a morbid passion. Yet at the same time she was forced to admit how perfectly the horrible diagnosis which had just been revealed to her fitted in with certain aspects of his behaviour that she had never been able to fathom: all his baby talk, for example, of her living with him like a music while being the wife in body of another; all his fugues into "sursum corda" and "private experience," from the inception of their romance, when he used to leave her in the evening and prowl among the sandhills, until now, the very eve of their nuptials, a time that she would always think of, whatever its upshot, as throttled in a pinetum.

There even now a pretty little German girl subsided, with a "wie heimlich!" on the bed of needles alongside her Harold's Cross Tanzherr.

The way screwed uphill between hedges of red may. Lucy, anxious to be the first to arrive, kept the jennet at the trot, digging in her knees and timing the rise and fall of the difficult motion to a nicety. Yet her

---

1. Cp. *Fingal*.

engrossment was so profound that she might have had privet on either hand for all she knew or cared, so that the blossom, fading now in a most beautiful effect as the shadows lengthened, was quite lost on the unhappy horsewoman. She saw nothing of the wood, the root of all the mischief, that loomed directly at some little distance before her, its outposts of timber serried enough to make a palisade, but not so closely as to screen the secret things beyond them. She was spared the high plume of smoke waxing and waning, like a Lied, fume of signs, against the dark green of the pines.

Belacqua saw these things, the trees, the plume of smoke, the may, dead lambs also lying in the hedgetops, all the emblems of the spring of the year. He would. And Lucy, groping in a sudden chaos of mind, saw nothing. Poor little Lucy! The more she struggled to eject the idea that possessed her ever since those careless words: "Corda is good," the more it seemed to prevail to the exclusion of all others. The derogation of her gentle Belacqua from one whom she had loved in all the shadows and tangles of his conduct to a trite spy of the vilest description was not to be set aside by a girl of her mettle merely on account of its being a great shock to her sentimental system. The two Belacquas, the old and dear enigma and now this patent cad, played cruel battledore with her mind. But she would decide between them before she slept, how she did not know, she had laid no plan, but somehow she would do it. Whatever loathing the truth might beget within her, was it not better to be sure than sorry?

Now it was definitely dusk.

A superb silent limousine, a Daimler no doubt, driven by a drunken lord, swept without warning round a bend in the narrow round and struck the jennet a fearful blow in the sternum. Lucy came a sickening cropper backwards down the rampant hind-quarters, the base of her spine, then of her skull, hit the ground a double welt, the jennet fell on top of her, the wheels of the car jolted over what was left of the jennet, who expired there and then in the twilight, *sans jeter un cri*. Lucy however was not so fortunate, being crippled for life and her beauty dreadfully marred.

Now it is Belacqua's turn to carry on.

He arrived in due course at the rendezvous, expecting to find Lucy there before him, for he had loitered on the way to marvel at the evening effects. He climbed the gate and sat down on the grass to await her arrival, but of course she did not turn up.

"Damn it" he said at last to the bitch "does she expect me to wait here all night?"

He gave her five more minutes, then he rose and walked up the hill till he came to the skirts of the wood. There he turned and combed the darkling landscape with his weak eye. Just as she but a short time back had stood on the housetop and looked for him eagerly and found him, so he did now standing on the hilltop in respect of her, with this difference however, that his eagerness was so slight that he was rather relieved than otherwise when he could see no sign of her. Gradually indeed he ceased to look for her and looked at the scene instead.

It was at this moment that he heard with a pang, rattling away in the distance, crex-crex, crex-crex, crex-crex, the first corncrake of the season. With a pang, because he had not yet heard the cuckoo. He could not help feeling that there must be something wrong somewhere when a man who had been listening day after day for the cuckoo suddenly heard the corncrake instead. The velvet third of the former bird, with its promise of happiness, was denied him, and the death-rattle of one that he had never seen proposed in its place. It was a good thing for Belacqua that he set no store by omens. He tethered the bitch to a tree, switched on his pineal eye and entered the wood.

With all the delays that he had been put to on Lucy's account he was long past his usual time and it was very dark in the wood. He drew blank in all the usual coverts and was just about to give it up as a bad job and wend his way home when he suddenly spied a flutter and a gleam of white in a hollow. This was Fräulein and friend. Belacqua came up on them cautiously from behind and watched for a short time. But for once, whatever was the matter with him, he seemed to find but little zest in the performance, so little indeed that he surprised himself not looking at all but staring vacantly into the shadows, alive to nothing but the weight and darkness and silence of the wood bearing down on top of him. It was all very submarine and oppressive.

He roused himself finally and moved away on tiptoe over the moss that would not betray him. He would go home and sit with Lucy and play the gramophone and see how he felt then. But he stumbled against a rotten bough growing close to the ground, it snapped off with a loud report and he fell forward on his face. Then almost before he knew what had happened, he was running in and out through the trees with the infuriated Tanzherr pounding along behind in hot pursuit.

Any advantage that familiarity with the ground may have conferred on Belacqua was liberally outweighed by the condition of his feet that were so raw with one thing and another that even to walk was painful, while to run was torture. As he neared the point where he had tethered the bitch and entered the wood he realized that he was being overhauled fast and that there was nothing for it but to turn and give battle. Shortening his grasp of the stick and slackening his pace as he ran clear of the trees he stopped abruptly, turned and with both hands thrust the sharp ferrule at the hypogastrium of his pursuer. This blow, however well conceived, was prematurely delivered. The Tanzherr saw it on its way, jazzed neatly out of the line, skidded round, lowered his head, charged, crashed into his quarry and bore him to the ground.

Now a fierce struggle ensued. Belacqua, fighting like a woman, kicking, clawing, tearing and biting, put up a gallant resistance. But his strength was as little as his speed and he was soon obliged to cry mercy. Whereupon the victor, holding him cruelly by the nape face downward, administered a brutal verberation with the stick. The bitch, to do her justice, strained at her tether. The Fräulein, wraith-like in the gloom in her flimsy white frock, came to the edge of the wood and watched, rapt, clutching her bosom, valour towards men being an emblem of ability towards women.

Belacqua's screams grew fainter and fainter and at length the Tanzherr, his fury appeased, desisted, launched a parting kick and swaggered off with his girly under his brawny arm.

How long he lay there, half insensible, he never knew. It was black night when he crept painfully to the bitch and released her. Nor has he ever been able to understand how he reached home, crawling rather than climbing over the various hedges and ditches, leaving the bitch to follow as best she could. So much for his youth and vigour.

But *tempus edax*, for now he is happily married to Lucy and the question of cicisbei does not arise. They sit up to all hours playing the gramophone, *An die Musik* is a great favourite with them both, he finds in her big eyes better worlds than this, they never allude to the old days when she had hopes of a place in the sun.

What a Misfortune

Belacqua was so happy married to the crippled Lucy that he tended to be sorry for himself when she died, which she did on the eve of the second anniversary of her terrible accident,[1] after two years of great physical suffering borne with such fortitude as only women seem able to command, having passed from the cruellest extremes of hope and despair that ever sundered human heart to their merciful resolution, some months before her decease, in a tranquillity of acquiescence that was the admiration of her friends and no small comfort to Belacqua himself.

Her death came therefore as a timely release and the widower, to the unutterable disgust of the deceased's acquaintance, wore none of the proper appearances of grief. He could produce no tears on his own account, having as a young man exhausted that source of solace through overindulgence; nor was he sensible of the least need or inclination to do so on hers, his small stock of pity being devoted entirely to the living, by which is not meant this or that particular unfortunate, but the nameless multitude of the current quick, life, we dare almost say, in the abstract. This impersonal pity was damned in many quarters as an intolerable supererogation and in some few as a positive sin against God and Society. But Belacqua could not help it, for he was alive to no other kind

---

1. Cp. *Walking Out.*

than this: final, uniform and continuous, unaffected by circumstance, assigned without discrimination to all the undead, without works. The public, taking cognisance of it only as callousness in respect of this or that wretched individual, had no use for it; but its private advantages were obviously very great.

All the hags and faggots, male and female, that he had ever seen or heard of, inarticulate with the delicious mucus of sympathy, disposed in due course of that secretion, when its flavour had been quite exhausted, *viva sputa* and by letter post, through the emunctory of his bereavement. He felt as though he had been sprayed from head to foot with human civet and would never again be clean or smell sweet, i.e. of himself, whose odours he snuffed up at all times with particular complacency. These however began to reassert themselves as time ran out and the spittle of the hags, while Lucy's grave subsided, grew green and even began to promise daisies, was introverted upon their own sores and those more recent of their nearest and dearest. Restored to these dearworthy effluvia, lapped in this pungent cocoon as the froghopper in its foam, Belacqua would walk in his garden and play with the snapdragons. To kneel before them in the dust and the clay of the ground and throttle them gently till their tongues protruded, at that indigo hour when the only barking (to consider but a single pastoral motiv) to be heard was that which could be scarcely heard, released so far away under the mountains that it came as a pang of sound of just the right severity, was the recreation he found best suited to his melancholy at this season and most satisfying to that fairy tale need of his nature whose crises seemed to correspond with those of his precious ipsissimosity, if such a beautiful word may be said to exist. It pleased his fancy to think of himself as a kind of easy-going Saint George at the Court of Mildendo.

The snapdragons were beginning to die of their own accord and Belacqua to feel more and more the lack of those windows on to better worlds that Lucy's big black eyes had been, when he woke up one fine afternoon to find himself madly in love with a *girl of substance*—a divine frenzy, you understand, none of your lewd passions. This lady he served at his earliest convenience with a tender of his hand and fortune which, however inconsiderable, had a certain air of distinction, being unearned. First she said *no*, then *oh no*, then *oh really*, then *but really*, then, in ringing tones, *yes sweetheart.*

When we say a girl of substance we mean that her promissory wad, to judge by her father's bearing in general and in particular by his respiration after song, was, so to speak, short-dated. To deny that Belacqua was alive to this circumstance would be to present him as an even greater imbecile than he was when it came to seeing the obvious; whereas to suggest that it was implied, however slightly, in his brusque obsession with the beneficiary to be, would constitute such obloquy as we do not much care to deal in. Let us therefore put forth a minimum of charity and observe in a casual way, with eyes cast down and head averted until the phase has ceased to vibrate, that he happened to conceive one of his Olympian fancies for a fairly young person with expectations. We can't straddle the fence nicer than that.

Her name it was Thelma bboggs, younger daughter of Mr. and Mrs. Otto Olaf bboggs. She was not beautiful in the sense that Lucy was; nor could she be said to transcend beauty, as the Alba seemed to do; nor yet to have slammed her life and person in its face, as Ruby perhaps had. She brought neither the old men running nor the young men to a standstill. To be quite plain she was and always had been so definitely not beautiful that once she was seen she was with difficulty forgotten, which is more than can be said for, say, the Venus Callipyge. Her trouble was to get herself seen in the first instance. But what she did have, as Belacqua never wearied of asserting to himself, was a most cherharming personality, together with intense appeal, as he repudiated with no less insistence, from the strictly sexual standpoint.

Otto Olaf had made his money in toilet requisites and necessaries. His hobby, since retiring from active participation in the affairs of the splendid firm that was his life-work, brain-child, labour of love and the rest, was choice furniture. He was said to have the finest and most comprehensive collection of choice furniture in North Great George's Street, from which lousy locality, notwithstanding the prayers of his wife and first-born for a home of their own very own in Foxrock, he refused coarsely to remove. The fondest memories of his boyhood, beguiled as a plumber's improver; the most copious sweats and triumphs of his prime, both in business and (with a surly look at Mrs. bboggs) the office and affairs of love, from the vernal equinox, in his self-made sanitary phrase, to the summer solstice of his life; all the ups and downs of a strenuous career, instituted in the meanest household fixture and closing now in the glories of Hepplewhites and bombé commodes, were bound up in good old grand old North Great George's Street, in consideration of which he had pleasure in referring his wife and first-born to that portion of himself which he never desired any person to kick nor volunteered to kiss in another.

The one ground lay under Mr. bboggs's contempt for Belacqua and Thelma's consent to be his bride: he was a poet. A poet is indeed a very nubile creature, dowered, don't you know, with the love of love, like La Rochefoucauld's woman from her second passion on. So nubile that the women, God bless them, can't resist them, God help them. Except of course those intended merely for breeding and innocent of soul, who prefer, as less likely to upset them, the more balanced and punctual raptures of a chartered accountant or a publisher's reader. Now Thelma, however much she left to be desired, was not a brood-maiden. She had at least the anagram of a good face, while as for soul, sparkling or still as preferred, it was her speciality. Which explains how Belacqua had merely to hold out against *no* and its derivatives to have her fly in the end, as a swallow to its eave or a long losing jenny down the whirlpool of a pocket, into his keycold embrace.

Mr. bboggs, on the other hand, was of Coleridge's opinion that every literary man ought to have an illiterate profession. Indeed he seemed to go a step further than Coleridge when he asserted, to the embarrassment of Mrs. bboggs and Thelma, the satisfaction of his elder daughter Una, for whom an ape had already been set aside in hell, and the alarm of Belacqua, that when he looked round and saw what they called a poet allowing his bilge to interfere with his business he developed a *Beltschmerz* of such intensity that he was obliged to leave the room. The poet present, observing that Mr. bboggs remained seated, plucked up courage to exclaim:

"*Beltschmerz*, Mr. bboggs sir, did I hear you say?"

Mr. bboggs threw back his head until it seemed as though his dewlap must burst and sang, in the slight sweet tenor that never failed to electrify those that heard it for the first time:

> "He wore a belt
> Whenever he felt
> A pain in his tiddlypush,
> A chemical vest
> To cover his chest
> When cannoning off the cush."

Belacqua said in a grieved tone to Mrs. bboggs, appreciation being most penetrating when oblique:

"I never knew Mr. bboggs had such a voice."

This endowment Mr. bboggs, when the dewlap, like a bagful of ferrets, had settled down after a brief convulsion, proceeded to demean further:

> "He took qui*nine* . . ."

"Otto" cried Mrs. bboggs. "Enough."

"As clear as a bell" said Belacqua "and I was never told."

"Yes" said Mr. bboggs, "a real quality voice." He closed his eyes and was back in the bathrooms of his beginnings. "A trifle fine" he conceded.

"Fine how are you!" cried Belacqua. "A real three dimensional organ, Mr. bboggs sir, I give you my word and honour."

Mrs. bboggs had a lover in the Land Commission, so much so in fact that certain ill-intentioned ladies of her acquaintance lost no occasion to insist on the remarkable disparity, in respect not only of physique but of temperament, between Mr. bboggs and Thelma: he so sanguine, so bland and solid in every way, which properties, observe, were no less truly to be predicated of his Una; and she such a black wisp of a creature. A most extraordinary anomaly, to put it mildly, and one that could scarcely be ignored by any friend of the family.

The presumptive cuckoo, if not exactly one of those dapper little bureaucrats that give the impression of having come into the world dressed by

Austin Reed, presented some of the better-known differentiae: the dimpled chin, the bright brown doggy eyes that were so appealing, the unrippled surface of vast white brow whose area was at least double that of the nether face, and anchored there for all eternity the sodden cowlick that looked as though it were secreting macassar to discharge into his eye. With his high heels he attained to five foot five, his nose was long and straight and his shoes a size and a half too large to bear it out. A plug of moustache cowered at his nostrils like a frightened animal before its lair, at the least sign of danger it would scurry up into an antrum. He expelled his words with gentle discrimination, as a pastry-cook squirts icing upon a cake. He had a dirty mind, great assurance and ability towards women, and a cap for every joke, ancient and modern. He drank just a little in public for the sake of sociability, but made up for it in private. His name was Walter Draffin.

The horns of Otto Olaf sat easily upon him. He knew all there was to be known about Walter Draffin and treated him with special consideration. Any man who saved him trouble, as Walter had for so many years, could rely on his esteem. Thus the treacherous bureaucrat was made free of the house in North Great George's Street where, as formerly he had abused that privilege in the bed of his host, so now he did out of his decanter. Indeed he was subject to such vertiginous satisfactions in his elevated position on Saint Augustine's ladder, the deeds of shame with Mrs. bboggs beyond recall in the abyss, that the power to tell himself when would desert him completely.

Bridie bboggs was nothing at all, neither as wife, as Otto Olaf had been careful to ascertain before he made her one, nor as mistress, which suited Walter's taste for moderation in all things. Unless some small positive value be allowed her in right of the fascination which she seemed to exert over her domestic staff, whose obstinacy in the employment of a mistress neutral to the point of idiocy moved such others as were better equipped and worse served to expressions of admiration that were not free of malice, no doubt.

The elder daughter was very dull. Think of holy Juliana of Norwich, to her aspect add a dash of souring, to her tissue half a hundredweight of adipose, abstract the charity and prayers, spray in vain with opopanax and assafoetida, and behold a radiant Una after a Hammam and a face massage. But withal she rejoiced in one accomplishment for which Belacqua had no words to express his respect, namely, an ability to play from memory, given the opening bar, any Mozart sonata whatsoever, with a xylophonic precision and an even-handed mezzo forte that scorned to observe the least distinction between those notes that were significant and those that were not. Belacqua, anxious to improve his position with Una, who held him and all that pertained to him in the greatest abhorrence, would control these feats, choking with admiration, in Augener's edition; which trouble, however, he very soon learned to spare himself.

A little bird whispered when to Walter Draffin who, with his right hand thus released, drew from his pocket a card and read, printed in silver on an azure ground:

Mr. and Mrs. Otto Olaf bboggs
request the pleasure of
Mr. Walter Draffin's
Company
at the marriage of their daughter
THELMA
with
MR. BELACQUA SHUAH
at the Church of Saint Tamar
Glasnevin
on Saturday, 1st August,
at 2:30 P.M.
and afterwards
at 55 North Great George's Street

55 North Great George's Street   R.S.V.P.

How like an epitaph it read, with the terrible sigh in the end-pause of each line. And yet, thought Walter, quenching the conceit as he did so, one might have expected a little enjambment in an invitation to such an occasion. Ha! He drew back his head from the card in order that he might see it as a whole. A typical Bridie bboggs production. What did it remind him of? A Church of Ireland Sunday School certificate of good conduct and regular attendance? No. They had his in the old home locked up in the family Bible, marking the place where Lamentations ended and Ezekiel began. Then perhaps the menu of an Old Boys Reunion Dinner, incorporating the School colours? No. Walter heaved a heavy sigh. He knew it reminded him of something, but what that something was, over and above Bridie and her sense of style, he could not discover. No doubt it would come back to him when he was least expecting it. But his little enjambment joke was pretty hot. He slaked it a second time. The only thing he did not like about it was its slight recondity, so few people knowing what an enjambment was. For example, it could not be expected to convulse a snug. Well, he must just put it into his book.

Under separate cover by the same post he received a note from Mrs. bboggs: "Dear Walter, Both Otto and I are most anxious that you, as such an old friend of the family, should propose the health of the happy couple. We do hope, dear Walter, and I feel confident, that you will." To which he hastened to reply: "Dear Bridie, Of course I shall be most happy and honoured to perform."

Dear Otto Olaf! Wrapped up in his tables and chairs and allowing himself to be duped, as he knew, by Walter and, as he thought, by Belacqua. Let Mr. Draffin, who had been of service, drink his whiskey; and Thelma, that by-product of a love-encounter, bestow herself on whom she pleased. Let there be a circus wedding by all means, his house invaded and his furniture wrecked. The days that came after would be of better rest. Dear Otto Olaf!

Belacqua prepared to negotiate a loan sufficient to meet his obligations, which fell heavily on a man of his modest condition. There was the ring (Lucy's redeemed), the endless fees relative to the ceremony, duties to vicar, verger, organist, officiating clergymen and bell-ringers, the big bridal bouquet, the little nosegays for the maids, new linen and other indispensable household effects, to say nothing at all of the price of a quick honeymoon, which fiasco, touring Connemara in a borrowed car, he had no intention of allowing to run away with more than a week or ten days.

His best man helped him to work it out over a bottle.

"I do not propose—" said Belacqua, when the average of their independent estimates had been augmented by ten pounds for overhead expenses.

"Overhead!" cackled the best man. "Very good!"

Belacqua shrank in a most terrifying manner.

"Either I misunderstand you" he said "or you forget yourself."

"Beg pardon" said the best man, "beg pardon, beg pardon. No offence."

Belacqua came back into the picture at his own convenience.

"I do not propose" he resumed "to affront you with a gift on this delicate occasion."

The best man bridled and squirmed at the mere suggestion.

"But" Belacqua made haste to extenuate this refinement of feeling "if you would care to have the original manuscript of my *Hypothalamion*, corrected, autographed, dated, inscribed and half-bound in time-coloured skivers, you are more than welcome."

Capper Quin, for so we must call him, known to his admirers as Hairy, he was so glabrous, and to the ladies as Tiny, he was so enormous, was not merely a bachelor, and thus qualified to attend Belacqua without violence to etiquette, but also one of the coming writers, which accounts for his alacrity to hold the hat of a member of the Cuttings Association. He now choked with gratification.

"Oh" he gasped "really I . . . really you . . ." and broke down. To construct a sentence with subject, predicate and object Hairy required a pencil and a sheet of paper.

"Capper" said Belacqua, "say no more. I'll have it made up for you."

When Hairy had quite done panting his pleasure he held up his hand.

"Well" said Belacqua.

"Thyme-coloured" said Hairy, and broke down.

"Well" said Belacqua.

"Sage-green" said Hairy. "Am I right?"

In the dead silence that followed this suggestion Hairy received the impression that his patron's spirit had left its prison, on ticket of leave at all events, and was already casting about for something light and hey nonny that would serve to cover his own departure when Belacqua made answer, in a voice blistered with emotion:

"Ouayseau bleheu, couleurre du temps,
    Vole à mouay, promptement."

and bust into tears.

Hairy rose and trode with penetrating softness to the door. Tact, he thought, tact, tact, the need for tact at a time like this.

"Study our duties" sobbed Belacqua "and call me not later than twelve."

The bboggses were gathered together in conclave.

"Thelma" said Una with asperity "let us kindly have your attention."

For Thelma's thoughts, truant to the complicated manoeuvres required of a snow-white bride, had flown on the usual wings to Galway, Gate of Connaught and dream of stone, and more precisely to the Church of Saint Nicolas whither Belacqua projected, if it were not closed when they arrived, to repair without delay and kneel, with her on his right hand at last for a pleasant change, and invoke, in pursuance of a vow of long standing, the spirits of Crusoe and Columbus, who had knelt there before him. Then no doubt, as they returned by the harbour to integrate their room in the Great Southern, she would see the sun sink in the sea. How was it possible to give them her attention with such a prospect opening up before her? Oh well is thee, and happy shalt thou be.

Otto Olaf sang a little song. Mrs. bboggs just sat, a big blank beldam, scarcely alive. Una struck the table sharply with a big pencil. When some measure of order had been restored, some little show of attention, she said, consulting her list:

"We have only five maids: the Clegg twins and the Purefoy triplets."

This statement was not disputed. It seemed to Otto Olaf that five was a very respectable haul. It would have been considered so in his day.

"But we need nine" cried Una.

By good fortune a thought now presented itself to Mrs. bboggs.

"My dear" she said, "would not seven be ample?" For two pins Una would have walked out of the conference.

"I think not" she said.

The idea! As though it were the wind-up of the football season.

"However" she added "it is not my wedding."

The ironical tone conveyed to this concession provoked Thelma to side with her mother for once. At no time indeed was this an easy matter, Mrs. bboggs being almost as non-partisan as Pope Celestine the fifth. Dante would probably have disliked her on this account.

"I am all in favour" said Thelma "of as few as is decent."

"It's a very distinguished quorum" said Otto Olaf, "more so even than nine."

"As head maid" said Una "I protest."

Again Mrs. bboggs came to the rescue. She had never been in such form.

"Then that leaves one" she said.

"What about Ena Nash?" said Thelma.

"Impossible" said Una. "She reeks."

"Then the McGillycuddy woman" said Otto Olaf.

Mrs. bboggs sat up.

"I know of no McGillycuddy woman" said Una. "Mother, do you know of any McGillycuddy woman?"

No, Mrs. bboggs was completely in the dark. She and Una therefore began to wait indignantly for an explanation.

"Sorry" said Otto Olaf, "no offence."

"But who is the woman?" cried mother and daughter together.

"I spoke without thinking" said Otto Olaf.

Mrs. bboggs was utterly nonplussed. How was it possible to name a woman without thinking? The thing was psychologically impossible. With mouth ajar and nostrils dilated she goggled psychological impossibilities at the offender.

"Hell roast the pair of you" he said in a sudden pet, "I was only joking."

Mrs. bboggs, though still entirely at a loss, made up her mind in a flash to accept this explanation. Una was not in the least amused. In fact she was sorely tempted to wash her hands of the whole affair.

"I propose Alba Perdue" she said. It was really more a nomination than a proposal.

"That is her last word" observed Otto Olaf.

Alba Perdue, it may be remembered, was the nice little girl in *A Wet Night*. Thelma, whom Belacqua had favoured with his version of that half-remembered love, could hardly dissemble her great satisfaction. When the turmoil of her blood had sufficiently abated she pronounced, in a voice just loud enough to be heard, this most depreciative hyperbole.

"I second that."

Now it was Otto Olaf's turn to make enquiries.

"I understand" said Una who, unlike her father, could give a plain answer to a plain question, "correct me, Thelma, if I am wrong, an old flame of the groom."

"Then she won't act" said the simple Otto Olaf.

Even Mrs. bboggs could not refrain from joining in the outburst of merriment that greeted this fatuity. Una in particular seemed certain to do herself an injury. She trembled and perspired in a most fearful manner.

"Oh my God!" she panted, "won't act!"

But Nature takes care of her own and a loud rending noise was heard. Una stopped laughing and remained perfectly still. Her bodice had laid down its life to save hers.

Belacqua was so quiescent during the fortnight that preceded the ceremony that it almost seemed as though he were to suffer a complete metamorphosis. He had left all the arrangements to the discretion of Capper Quin, saying: "Here is the money, do the best you can."

But before being overtaken by this inertia, which proceeded partly from fatigue and partly no doubt from the need for self-purification, he had been kept busy in a number of ways: finding a usurer, redeeming the ring, and searching among the hags for two to tally with Mr. and Mrs. bboggs in the interest of the nuptial jamboree. In the prosecution of this last duty Belacqua was called upon to sustain every kind of abusive denial and suffer Lucy's posthumous temperature to be thrown in his face, as though she were a bottle of white Burgundy. Until finally a female cousin, so remote as to be scarcely credible, and a kind of moot Struldbrug, to whom Belacqua's father had used to refer as "dear old Jimmy the Duck," agreed to rise to the occasion. Hermione Näutzsche and James

Skyrm were the names of these two deadbeats. Belacqua had not laid eyes
on either of them since he was an infant prodigy.

Except for a short daily visit from Thelma, swallowed as being all in
the game, Belacqua's retreat was undisturbed. The wedding gifts flowed
in, not upon him, for he was friendless, but upon her, and she encour-
aged him day by day with the bulletin of their development.

She arrived one afternoon in a state of some excitement. Belacqua
raised himself in the bed to be kissed, which he was with such unexpected
voracity that he went weak before the end. Poor fellow, he had not been
giving due attention to his meals.

"Your present is got" she said.

To Belacqua, who had been setting aside a portion of each day for
polyglot splendours, this phrase came as a great shock. Perhaps the pres-
ent would make him amends.

"It came this morning" she said.

"At what time exactly?" said Belacqua, easing his nerves in the usual
sneer. "That is most important."

"What devil" said Thelma, her gaiety all gone, "makes you so beastly?"

Ah, if he only knew.

"But it so happens" she said "that I can tell you."

Belacqua thought for a bit and then plumped for saying nothing.

"Because" she proceeded "the first thing I did was to set it."

The hideous truth dawned on his mind.

"Not a clock" he implored, "don't say a grandfather clock."

"The grandfather and mother" she did say "of a period clock."

He turned his face to the wall. He who of late years and with the
approval of Lucy would not tolerate a chronometer of any kind in the
house, for whom the local publication of the hours was six of the best on
the brain every hour, and even the sun's shadow a torment, now to have
this time-fuse deafen the rest of his days. It was enough to make him
break off the engagement.

Long after she had gone he tossed and turned until the thought, like
God appearing to a soul in hell, that he could always spike the monster's

escapement and turn its death's-head to the wall, came in the morning with the canticle of the ring-doves. Then he slept.

What time Capper Quin was here, there and everywhere, attending to the interests of his principal. Conscious of his own shortcomings in a matter so far removed from the integrities of self-expression, he engaged, on the basis of a modest inverted commission, to aid him in his work, one Sproule, a lately axed jobber to a firm in the City, whose winning manner and familiarity with the shopping centres north of the river were beyond rubies. Bright and early on the fateful Saturday they met to buy the bouquets, the big one for the bride and the seven nosegays.

"Mrs. bboggs" said Hairy, "ought we?"

"Ought we what?" said Sproule.

"I thought maybe a bloom" said Hairy.

"Superfoetation" said Sproule.

He led the way to a florist's off Mary Street. The proprietress, having just discovered among her stock an antirrhinum with the rudiment of a fifth stamen, was highly delighted.

"Oh, Mr. Sproule sir" she exclaimed, "would you believe it . . ."

"Good morning" said Sproule. "One large orchid and seven of your best ox-eyes."

Now Capper Quin, however unsuited to strike a bargain, was endowed with a sense of fitness, and one so exquisite indeed that he could make himself clear in its defence.

"On behalf of my client" he said "I must insist on two orchids."

"By all means" said Sproule. "Make it three, make it a dozen."

"Two" repeated Hairy.

"Two large orchids" said Sproule "and seven of your best ox-eyes."

As though by magic wand the nine blooms appeared in her hand.

"Four lots" said Sproule, "one, two, three and one with orchids." Rapidly he equated addresses and consignments on a sheet of paper. "So" he said, "first thing."

She now mentioned a sum that caused the buyer great amusement. He appealed to Hairy.

"Mr. Quin" he said, "do I wake or sleep?"

She not merely made good her figures but mentioned that she had to live. Sproule could not see the connexion. He pinched his cheek to make sure he was not in Nassau Street.

"My dear madam" he said, "we do not have to live in Nassau Street."

This thrust so weakened his adversary that she suffered him to place specie in her hand.

"Take this" he said, in a eucharistic voice, "or leave it."

The cold alloy in her hot palm, conjoined with the depression and the urge to live, determined the issue in Sproule's favour. Upon which the combatants shook hands with great heartiness. How could there be any question of rancour when both were fully satisfied of having obtained the victory?

Sproule, his duties at an end, received his commission in the Oval bar, where nothing would do him but that Hairy should toast his employer in gin and peppermint.

"Happy dawg" said Sproule. He had come unscathed through the Great War.

The hyperaesthesia of Hairy was so great that the mere fact of standing on licensed ground, without the least reference to its liberties, was of force sufficient to exhilarate him. Now therefore, under the influence of his situation, he dilated with splendid incoherence on the contradiction involved in the idea of a happy Belacqua and on the impertinence of desiring that he should derogate into such an anomaly.

"Fornication" he vociferated "before the Shekinah."

This observation was accompanied and graced by a spasm of such passionate repugnance that it was no less an act of charity on the part of the ex-jobber, who was familiar with Boy Scouts and their ways and knew that he might never pass that way again, to substitute his empty glass for the bumper of his agitated companion.

In the bright street a bitter-sweet sorrow entered into Sproule, sweet at parting, bitter at the knowledge that his services were no longer required.

"Farewell" he said, flinging out his dreadful hand, "may luck rise with you on the way."

But Hairy was too full, too overcome by the fumes of his position, to shake, let alone reply. He stepped, as upon an Underground escalator, into the stream of pedestrians and was gone. Sproule raised his sad eyes to the sky and saw the day, its outstanding hours that could not be numbered, in the form of a beautiful Girl Guide galante, reclining among the clouds. She beckoned to him with her second finger, like one preparing a certificate in pianoforte, Junior Grade, at the Leinster School of Music. Closing his mind softly on this delicious vision, feeling it in his mind like a sponge of toilet vinegar on a fever, he advanced into the Oval towards it.

Whom should Hairy meet on the crest of the Metal Bridge but Walter Draffin, fresh from his effeminate ablutions and as spruce and keen as a new-ground hatchet in his miniature tails and stripes. The sun shone bright upon him, his languorous poll, for he carried his topper crown downward in his hand. The two gentlemen were on speaking terms.

"This is where I stand" said the little creature, with a sigh that made Hairy look nervously round for prisons and palaces, "and watch the Liffey swim."

"Blue-eyed cats" quoted the colossal Capper, for no other reason than that the phrase had been running in his mind and now here was a chance to discharge it on a wit, "are always deaf."

Walter smiled, he felt greatly pleased, he held up his little face to the kindly sun like a child to be kissed.

"The burrowing tucutucu" he answered "is occasionally blind, but the mole is *never* sober."

The mole is never sober. A profound mot. Hairy, having tried all he knew to say as much, hung his head, a gallant loser, consoled by the certitude that Walter would take the will for the deed. Poor Hairy, there was a great deal he understood, but he could not make this known in the absence of a battery of writing materials.

"That unspeakable invite" exclaimed Walter, "of all things to be destitute of enjambment!"

He was confirmed in his initial misgiving by Hairy's having clearly no idea what he was talking about. There was nothing for it but to put it into his book. Walter's book was a long time in coming out because he refused to regard it as anything more than a mere dump for whatever he could not get off his chest in the ordinary way.

"So off you go" he said "to attend your happy client, and I to buy myself a buttonhole."

This, ensuing so soon upon mole and enjambment, brought Hairy's brain to the boil, and out of his mouth came the one word "rose" like a big bubble.

"Blood-red and newly born" said Walter "to aromatic pain. Eh?"

Hairy, with a sudden feeling that he was wasting his client's time and his own precarious energies on a kind of rubber Stalin, took his departure with a more than boorish abruptness, leaving Walter to enjoy the great central agency and hang out as it were his cowlick to air or dry. A passing humorist dropped a penny into the empty hat, it fell on the rich wadding without a sound, and so the joke was lost.

In Parliament Street a funeral passed and Hairy did not uncover. Many of the chief mourners, consoling themselves in no small measure with the reverence expressed by every section of the community, noticed with rage in their hearts that he did not, though to be sure they made no allusion to it at the time. Let this be a lesson to young men, strangers perhaps to sorrow, to uncover whenever a funeral passes, less in act of respect towards the defunct than in sympathetic acknowledgment of the survivors. One of these fine days Hairy will observe, from where he sits bearing up bravely behind the hearse in a family knot, a labourer let go of his pick with one hand, or gay dandy snatch both his out of his pockets, in a gesture of more value and comfort than a ton of lilies. Take the case of Belacqua, who ever since the commitment of his Lucy wears a hat, contrary to his inclination, on the off chance of his encountering a cortège.

The best man had received instructions to collect in Molesworth Street the Morgan, fast but noisy, lent for the period of the high time journey by a friend of the bboggses. Needless to say some eejit had parked it so far up towards the arty end that luckless Hairy, coming from the west upon the stand after the usual Duke Street complications, hastening along the shady southern pavement because he felt there was not a moment to lose, was almost in despair of ever finding the solitary hind-wheel that he had been advised to look out for. He was much relieved to espy it at last, last but one or two in the row, but embarrassed also to remark a group made up of small boys, loafers and the official stand attendant gathered round and passing judgement on the strange machine's design and performance. He kept his head none the less and examined the car, as he had been strictly enjoined to do, for any hymeneal insignia that might have been annexed, doubtless with the very best intentions, to its body, such as a boot, an inscription or other shameful badge. Satisfied that there were none, he hoisted his vast frame on board the light weight which thereupon reduced the expert comment of the bystanders, if we except the attendant who was most grave and attentive, to jeers and laughter, by rocking like a cockle-shell. Hairy, wondering what on earth to do next, sat blushing and hopeless at the controls. The general provisions for starting a motor engine were familiar to him, and these in every imaginable combination he fruitlessly applied to that, exceptional presumably, fitted to the Morgan. The boys were most anxious to push, the loafers to give a tow, while the attendant could not be deterred from flooding the carburettor and swinging the engine, which started most perversely and unexpectedly with a backfire that broke the obliging fellow's arm. Hairy was so pressed for time that he hardened his heart to the consistence of an Uebermensch's, roared his engine and found himself abruptly, in a paroxysm of plunges and saccades, cutting the corner of Kildare Street under the prow of a bus, which happily did no more than remove the back number-plate and thus provide, not merely a neat instance of poetic justice, but the winged attendant with the nucleus of compensation.

All these little encounters and contretemps take place in a Dublin flooded with sunshine.

Belacqua had passed an excellent night, as he always did when he condescended to assign precise value to the content of his mind, no matter whether that were joy or sorrow, and did not awake when Hairy stalled the machine beneath his window on the cruel stroke of midday. Much liquor in secret the previous evening may have contributed to this torpor, but scarcely if at all, for many and many a time when footless, and simply because the forces in his mind would not resolve, he had tossed and turned like the Florence of Sordello, and found all postures painful.

He opened his burning eyes on Hairy, rose, bathed, shaved and decked himself out, all in silence and without the least assistance. They plunged the packed bag in the well of the Morgan. Belacqua stood before the pier-glass.

"It's a small thing, Hairy" he said, and his voice, after so long silence, grated on his ear, "separates lovers."

"Not mountain chain" said Hairy.

"No, nor city ramparts" said Belacqua.

Hairy made a lunge of condolence at his companion, he simply could not help it, and was repulsed.

"Am I all right behind?" asked Belacqua.

"You know what it is" said Hairy, asserting thus and with a clarity quite unusual in him his independence and intolerance of all posterior aspects, "you perish in your own plenty."

Belacqua pressed apart his lips with his forefinger.

"If what I love" he said "were only in Australia."

Capper the faithful companion simply faded away, at least for the purposes of conversation.

"Whereas what I am on the look out for" said Belacqua, pursuing it would almost seem his train of thought, "is nowhere as far as I can see."

"Vobiscum" whispered Capper. "Am I right?"

A cloud obscured the sun, the room grew dark, the light ebbed from the pier-glass and Belacqua, feeling his eyes moist, turned away from the blurred image of himself.

"Remember" he said, "true of me now who have ceased to Charleston: *Dum vivit aut bibit aut minxit.* Take a note of it now."

The Quaker's get!

Then driving through the City it occurred to him that an empty buttonhole would be the haporth of tar and no error. So he entered a flower-shop and came out with a purple tassel of veronica, fixed in the wrong lapel. Hairy stared. What startled him was not so much the breach of etiquette as the foolhardiness of getting married in a turned suit.

A pestilential hotel was their next stop. Hairy changed his clothes and looked more mangy king of beasts than ever. Belacqua lunched frugally on stout and scallions, scarcely the meal, one would have thought, for a man about to be married for the second time. However.

At the Church of Saint Tamar, pointed almost to the point of indecency, the maids, attired in glove-tight gossamer and sporting the awful ox-eyes, having just been joined by Mrs. bboggs, who had chosen gauze and a bunch of omphalodes in her bosom, and Walter, very shaky and exalted, were massed in the porch when Morgante and Morgutte, to adopt the venomous reference of Una, not arm in arm but in single file, came forward. All but Walter were taken quite aback by the bridegroom's breath. Mrs. bboggs buried her face (poor little Thelma!) in the omphalodes, the Cleggs turned scarlet in unison, the Purefoys crowded into a shade, while Una was only restrained by her hatred of anything in the nature of sacrilege from spitting it out. Miss Perdue found the smell rather refreshing. The cad and his faithful companion advanced to the chancel and took up their stand beside the gate, the latter to the right and a little to the rear, holding a hat in each hand.

The south pews were plentifully furnished with members and adherents of the bboggs clan, while those to the north were empty save for two grotesques, seated far apart: Jimmy the Duck Skyrm, an aged cretin, outrageous in pepper and salt, Lavallière and pull-over, gnashing his teeth without ceasing at invisible spaghetti; and Hermione Näutzsche, a powerfully built nymphomaniac panting in black and mauve between shipped crutches. Her missing sexual hemisphere, despite a keen look out all her life long, had somehow never entered her orbit, and now, bursting as she was with chalk at every joint, she had no great hopes of being rounded off in that interesting sense. Little does she dream what a flurry she has set up in the spirits of Skyrm, as he gobbles and mumbles the air at the precise remove of enchantment behind her.

"Ecce" hissed Hairy, according to plan, and Belacqua's heart made a hopeless dash against the wall of its box, the church suddenly cruciform cage, the bulldogs of heaven holding the chancel, the procession about to give tongue in the porch, the transepts culs-de-sac. The organist darted into his loft like an assassin and set in motion the various forces that could be relied on to mature in a merry peal all in good time. Thelma, looking very striking and illegitimate in grey and green pieds de poule, split skirt and piqué insertions of negress pink, swept up the aisle on the right arm of Otto Olaf, in whose head since leaving 55 a snatch had been churning and did not now desert him:

> Drink little at a time,
> Put water in your wine,
> Miss your glass when you can,
> And go off the first man.

Wise old Otto Olaf! He died in the end of clot and left his cellar to the cuckoo.

The maids, terminating in the curious deltoid formation of the Alba, Mrs. bboggs and Walter, took their speed from the bride and their demeanour from the head maid, with the result that their advance was at once rapid and sullen, for Una had become aware of an uncontrollable and ill-placed dehiscence in the stuff of her gossamer. The dread lest this should come to a head as she braced herself to receive her foul little sister's gloves and bouquet, over and above an habitual misanthropy aggravated by the occasion, had made her, and hence her team of maids, appear as cross as two sticks. Always excepting the Alba who, bating the old pain in the core of her vitals that seemed to be a permanent part of her existence, could scarcely have been more diverted had she been the bride herself instead of the odd maid out. Also with Walter so close on her heels she was kept busy.

Without going so far as to say that Belacqua felt God or Thelma the sum of the Apostolic series, still there was in some indeterminate way communicated to the solemnisation a kind or sort of mystical radiance that Joseph Smith would have found touching. Belacqua passed the ring like a mouse belling the cat, with a quick prayer all his own that the marriage knuckle of his love might so swell against the token and pledge as to spare her the pain of ever reading, inscribed on its inner periphery: *Mens mea Lucia lucescit luce tua.* His state of mind was so tense and complex at this stage (not to be wondered at when we consider all that he had gone through: the bereavement, obliging him to wear a hat at all seasons;

the sweet and fierce pain of his passion for Miss bboggs; the long retreat in bed that had landed him in a nice marasmus; the stout and scallions; and now the sense of being cauterized with an outward and visible sign) that it might be likened to that of his dear departed Lucy listening pale and agog for the second incidence of

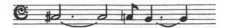

in the first movement of the Unbuttoned Symphony. Say what you will, you can't keep a dead mind down.

Talking of cats, Thelma remained throughout the service feline and inscrutable and was not at all incommoded by the famous viticultural passage which so abashed, or perhaps better angered, Belacqua that his platter face went from its native dingy to scarlet and back again through livid. Should he then avail himself of the first . . . opportunity to sulphurate his bride and thus make sure? No, that would be doing the dirty on man's innocency. And make sure of what? Olives? The absurdity of the figure and all its harmonics like muscae volitantes provoked him to a copious scoff that would have put the kibosh on the sacrament altogether had it not been for the coolness and skill of the priest who covered as with a hand this coarseness with a collect.

Talking of hands, Thelma's right, as it danced through the find-the-lady sleights recommended in the liturgy, had quite bewitched the chancel. The curate swore he had never seen anything like it outside the Musée Rodin, it reminded the clerk of a Dürer cartoon and the priest of his incumbency, and it indicted Belacqua, tempest of stifled groans at having to produce anti-clockwise eyes and gestures for so long at a stretch, with Maupassant's scorching phrase: *phylloxera of the spirit.*

At length they had consented together beyond all possibility of cavil, the dearly beloved had for ever after held their peace and then let their cry come with a rush, and Otto Olaf's rendering of:

> Be present, awful Father!
> To give away this bride

had so moved the Sidneian heart of Skyrm that he transferred himself, for better for worse, into the pew where Hermione sat as on a thwart, and there, under cover of a kinsman's seasonable emotion, rooted and snuffled his way into her affections with a suilline avidity that can only have seemed horrible to any decent person not conversant with the phenomenon of crystallisation. The vestry was over, its signatures, duties and busses, and Mrs. bboggs was back in 55, whipping the muslin off the Delikatessen, almost before the organist had regained control of his instrument. The Alba went with Walter in a taxi, Otto Olaf and Morgutte took a tram, the two grotesques never knew how they got there, while as for the maids, all but Una who wisely huddled on a cloak and cadged a lift, why they just floated on foot like brownies through the garish thoroughfares.

These are the little things that are so important.

To say that the drawing-room was thronged would be to put it mildly. It was stiff with guests. Otto Olaf found himself in that most painful of all possible positions, constrained to see his furniture, his loved ones, suffer and know himself helpless to relieve them.

There was something so bright and meaty about the assembly, something so whorled in its disposition with the procession loosely coiled in the midst waiting to move off, that Walter was slowly but surely put in mind of a Benozzo fresco and said so in his high-smelling voice to the Alba.

"Ass and all" she replied, with indescribable bitterness.

Una stamped her foot like a sheep and like sheep all present turned scared faces towards her. She had somehow contrived to consolidate and shore up her gossamer, but now she had fresh grounds for complaint, namely, that the newly married couple, who should have been first home and in position for congratulations, had actually not yet turned up. Thus the action was brought to a dead halt. In its present headless condition the procession could not uncoil itself out through the door as arranged, and it was obvious that until the procession uncoiled itself there could be no relief for the congestion of casual ladies and gentlemen of which it was, so to speak, the mainspring. But let the truant pair appear and take their station and lo the press, as though by magic, would tick off merrily to its stand-up lunch. In the meantime, what a waste of good saliva!

"Raise me up Mr. Quin" cried Una, in her anger throwing caution to the winds.

Hairy looked wildly at the bust of his partner, for so she was in pursuance of the regulations, they together forming—to vary the figure slightly—the fourth link of this nuptial hawser, in the immediate rear, that is, of Mrs. bboggs and Skyrm, who in their turn surveyed the massive flitches of Hermione, sagging and flagging in her crutches as in a quicksand, and poor Otto Olaf, trembling in every limb—looked wildly at it for a point of purchase at once effective and respectful, some form of nelson that would not be too familiar, though for what purpose she desired to be raised he did not pause to enquire.

But before he could begin to make a mess of it in his flushing blushing panting ponderous way a great perturbation, dominated by the voice of Belacqua raised in abuse, made itself heard in the vestibule. This was they at last, but escorted by a pukkah Civic Guard of the highest rank compatible with duty and the stricken car-park attendant, as pale as a stone and clutching in his whole hand the damning number-plate.

Otto Olaf inserted his elbow in the eye of Hermione's crutch and released a dig. Having thus gained her attention he said, in a ruined whisper: "My right lung is very weak."

Hermione let a little pipe of terror.

"But my left lung" he vociferated "is as sound as a bell."

"I suppose" said Mrs. bboggs to James Skyrm, whose facial paddles had begun to churn the air so fiercely that she feared lest he were meditating some gallant act on behalf of his kinswoman, "I presume and I take it that Mr. bboggs may do and say what he likes in his own home."

James, on the matter being presented to him in this light, toed the line at once.

The tilted kepi of the attendant, its green band and gilt harp, and the clang beneath in black and white of his riotous hair and brow, so ravished Walter that he merely had to close his eyes to be back in Pisa. The powers of evocation of this Italianate Irishman were simply immense, and if his *Dream of Fair to Middling Women*, held up in the *limae labor* stage for the past ten or fifteen years, ever reaches the public, and Walter says it is bound to, we ought all be sure to get it and have a look at it anyway.

Belacqua reviled his captor and accuser with the utmost ferocity. Otto Olaf, then Capper, broke their ranks, the former to make a peace at all hazard, the latter, with bursting heart, a clean breast. The attendant was very soon browbeaten into admission that his injury had resulted, not from the ordinary exercise of his functions, not yet from any act of solicited assistance, but purely and simply from his own excessive zeal, rooted beyond a shadow of a doubt in greed.

A whip-round was made, and a small sum, on no account to be regarded as anything in the nature of an indemnity, subscribed charitably for his relief. This closed the incident.

"My heart bleeds for him" said Walter.

"Not at all" said the Alba, "is he not insured?"

She had a sudden idea.

"See me home" she said to Walter.

Walter explained how he had been let in for a health, upon which, if the offer were still open, he would be more than happy to see her home. They would go one of the long ways round that he adored.

"I make no promises" said the Alba.

The lunch was a great disappointment to all and sundry—a few firkins of molasses and husks off the ice. Belacqua closed his eyes and saw, clearer than ever before, a beer-engine. The sweets were doled out and then Thelma refused to cut the cake. She was a very strange girl. Pressed hard by Una and Bridie she appealed to her husband. Her husband! His advice to her, quite frankly, when after great difficulty he discovered what she was talking about, was that it might be rather more gracious to cut the brute since all seemed so set on her doing so. Warming to his subject he urged her to hold out just a little longer, soon it would be all over. What had begun as a hurried and rather furtive aside now developed into a regular tête-à-tête, and when at length Thelma turned to do the gracious thing she found the cake in bits. It had been dressed with orange blossoms. What few of these had escaped the onivomaniacs she gathered up and hid in her bosom. These she would lock up in the furthest recesses of a casket and cherish as long as she drew breath, these and her own two orchids and Belacqua's veronica, which spire of passionate devotion she had resolved to secure against all comers, vogue la galère! Time might pulverise these mementoes but at least their elements would belong to her for ever. She was a most strange girl.

Walter wiped his boots on the Aubusson of Otto Olaf's Empire otto-man, beat on his glass of Golden Guinea with his fizz-whisk for silence to fall and paid out his discourse, in a pawl-and-ratchet monotone that could never be unsaid, as follows:

"It is on record that a lady member of the Lower House, and feme covert what is more, rose to her feet, those feet—for she was of Dublin stock—that Swift, rebuking the women of this country for their disregard of Shank's mare, described as being fit for nothing better than to be laid aside, and declared: 'I would rather commit adultery than suffer one drop of intoxicating liquor to pass my lips.' To which a gross baker, returned in the Labour interest, retorted: 'Wouldn't we all rather do that, Maam?' "

This opening passage was rather too densely packed to gain the general suffrage. On Otto Olaf it took effect some five minutes later, causing him to laugh in a helpless and hysterical manner. The sight of Walter, ranging to and fro on his fantastic upholstery as though he were caged or contesting an election, had capsized his whole nervous system and his heart was filling up rapidly with evil and madness.

" 'Il faut marcher avec son temps' said a Deputy of the extreme Right. 'Cela dépend' answered Briand in his sepulchral sneer 'dans quoi il marche.' So do not heckle me, Herrschaften, because that would about finish me."

He dropped his head, like a pelican after a long journey, pricked up the ears of his fearful moustache and shuffled and shifted his feet like one surprised in a dishonourable course of action. "He is out of his head" said the chief of the ill-intentioned ladies. Otto Olaf sidled up to the dumb-waiter. Una sat down with great ostentation on a pouf. "Let me know when he starts" she said. Thelma's eyes were darting this way and that in search of orange-blossom, Belacqua was watching Thelma and the Alba was watching him. James and Hermione, emboldened by the molasses, were trying themselves on before a Regence trumeau.

Mrs. bboggs was manoeuvring for a vantage-ground that would bring both husband and lover into her field of vision. The usual precautionary plain-clothes man, standing head and shoulders out of the ruck, was reading his paper. Two splendid mixers found themselves adjacent. "Drunk" said the first, "well lit" agreed the second, and they exchanged a long look of intelligence.

In fairness to Walter it must be said that he was far from being penetrate with this hangdog façade, behind which all was mercy-seat al fresco and Shekinah and himself, in the smartest mail, having his wounds dressed by the Alba-Morgen and looking through the orchards at the sun setting awkwardly in the blue shallows. Coming to with a start, shedding his cloak of dejection, he spoke the first words that he came across in his head:

> "Semper ibi juvenis cum virgine, nulla senectus
> Nullaque vis morbi, nullus dolor. . . ."

Mrs. bboggs, having already trembled to hear the belated chuckling of Otto Olaf and to observe his stealthy movements as he called in all the castle puddings on the dumb-waiter, was hardly surprised when he now opened rapid fire on his enemy with these. But Walter was able to block such trivial missiles, even caught one and ate it, while the old man's strength, and with it his rage, was soon spent. His arteries began to fray, with the fatal result as aforesaid, from this moment.

"I raise this glass" said Walter, extending it low down and a little to the left before him like a buckler, "this glorious bumper, on behalf of those present and the many prevented by age, sickness, infirmity or previous engagement from being with us, to you, dearest Thelma, whom we all love, and to you, Mr. Shuah, whom Thelma loving and being loved of her we all love too I feel sure, now on the threshold of your bliss, and to such and so many consummations, earthy and other, as you have in mind."

He plied the whisk, dealt himself a slow uppercut with the glass, and drank.

"I close these eyes" he proceeded, fixing them on Mrs. bboggs and returning the glass to its base, "and I see them in that memorable island,

Avalon, Atlantis, Hesperides, Ui Breasail, I don't insist, lapped in the Sia-
mese haecceity of puffect love, revelling in the most delightful natural
surroundings. Oh may that star, that radiant radical of their desire, not
of mine, my friends, nor yet of yours, for no two stars, as Saint Paul tells
us, are on a par in the matter of glory, delight them without ceasing with
legitimate inflexions!" He unleashed what was left of the glorious bum-
per. "To Hymen's gracious mussy and protection we commit them, now,
henceforth and for evermore. Slainte."

This was the end of Walter's speech, and a very good end for such
a bad speech every one felt it to be, but as he remained upright on the
ottoman in a rapt and suspended pose, drinking in the plaudits, Belac-
qua assumed that there was some yet to come and so was startled to hear
the voice of Una, whom the least semblance of procrastination invariably
threw into the most dreadful passion, calling on him petulantly to do
the needful: "Now Mr. Shuah, now then Mr. Shuah, we're waiting on yer
Mr. Shuah." This sordid hitch caused his acknowledgment to be rather
less cordial than he had intended. He made it from where he stood, in
the white voice of which he was a master:

"I have to thank: Miss bboggs, who henceforward may be so addressed
without the least ambiguity, for her as always timely reminder; Mr. Draf-
fin, for his kind torrents of meiosis; Mr. and Mrs. small double bee, for
their Bounty; the Maids, with special reference to Belle-Belle their leader,
for their finely calculated offices this day, something more than merely
buttress and less than *vis a tergo*; the Skyrm and Näutzsche, who I am
glad to see have not yet done rising to the occasion; my faithful friend
and best of men, Tiny Hairy Capper Quin, tipping the scale, day in day
out, for me and for many, whose spiritual body is by now I feel confident
a *fait accompli*; the entire Church staff; the Abbé Gabriel; as many, in fine,
as have found the time to witness and acclaim, in how small a way soever,
this instant of the whirligig. Eleleu. Jou Jou."

A student of Plutarch found himself rubbing shoulders with a physi-
cist of the modern school.

"There you have him" said the first "in a nutshell."

"This bivalve world" said the other.

Their eyes met and filled with tears.

Whatever small chance these words of Belacqua might have had of giving satisfaction was more than cancelled by his having been observed, in a dumbshow portmanteau of Selah and sigh of relief, to check off on his fingers each acknowledgment as it was made. Thelma marched to the door in an atmosphere of silence and shock, opened it and closed it behind her, which expression of independence rather cut the ground away from under Una, who had planned to sit down with a bang on the pouf, just at the moment when her services were obviously most needed, and thus put an open slight on the bride.

Hairy on the other hand, faithful to the last to his commission, reported smartly for duty.

"Slip out quick" said Belacqua "and run her behind into the lane off Denmark Street."

The guests were now adjourning stiffly to the drawing-room, Walter and Otto Olaf polarised in bitter tig about the person of the Alba, Otto Olaf being it, while Hermione and James, he propelling her in a tomb-deep armchair on casters, closed the recession. This grotesque equipage was brought to a standstill in the passage in consequence of the passenger's putting her feet to the ground, whether from coquetry or fatigue we leave it to the reader to determine.

"My crutches Jim" she said.

Jim went back for the crutches, Walter took sanctuary with Hermione, the Alba sent Otto Olaf flying, Jim came back with the sweeps, Hermione got them under her somehow, Walter rejoined the Alba. They remained all four quietly where they were, in the passage, discussing ways and means, severally first, then, when their interests were overheard to coincide, together. Four heads are better than two, eight than four, and so on.

After a fairly decent interval Belacqua excused himself just for a moment (as he did, it may be remembered, to the Poet in the Grosvenor), left the room, sprang up the stairs, caught up his bride like a Cossack and conveyed her by clandestine ways down to the garden that lay behind the house. He opened the wicket into the lane with the key that his love had fondly hoped would facilitate his suit in its early stages, and in another moment they had been clear of the abhorred premises when the sound of a broken-winded hue in the garden caused him to turn back. This proceeded from that irrepressible quartet, Hermione, the Alba, Walter and James, perspiring, suppliant, making their getaway.

Belacqua stood like a stock at gaze, with an overwhelming sense that all this would happen to him again, in a dream or subsequent existence. Then he stepped to the one side, Thelma to the other, of the wicket, Caudine exit, saying to himself, as he watched the fugitives storm the postern like women boarding a tram: "It is right that they who are loved should live." It was from this moment that he used to date in after years his crucial loss of interest in himself, as in a grape beyond his grasp.

But the alarm had been given, faces sprang up in the windows, Una began to scream havoc fit to burst, the mixers and the plain-clothes man came plunging up the garden in the van of pursuit. Belacqua threw them a tub in the form of Hairy, locked the wicket on the outside and committed himself and his wife to the Morgan, fast but noisy.

As for the other four, they did not feel safe until they reached the Cappella Lane, superb cenotheca, in Charlemont House. Nobody would ever think of looking for them there.

Lucy was *atra cura* in the dicky the best part of the way down to Galway.

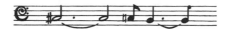

They all stopped for a drink. Thelma, as ever on his wrong side, began to insist that she was Mrs. Shuah, making his little heart go pit-a-pat. He turned a face that she had never seen upon her.

"Do you ever hear tell of a babylan?" he said.

Now Thelma was a brave girl.

"A what did you say?" she said.

Belacqua went to the trouble of spelling the strange word.

"Never" she said. "What is it? Something to eat?"

"Oh" he said "you're thinking of a baba."

"Well then" she said.

His eyes were parched, he closed them and saw, clearer than ever before, the mule, up to its knees in mire, and astride its back a beaver, flogging it with a wooden sword.

But she was not merely brave, she was discreet as well.

"Your veronica" she said "that I wanted so much, where is it gone?"

He clapped his hand to the place. Alas! the tassel had drooped, wormed its stem out of the slit, fallen to the ground and been trodden underfoot.

"Gone west" he said.

They went further.

The Smeraldina's Billet Doux

Bel Bel by own bloved, *allways* and for *ever* mine!!

Your letter is soked with tears death is the onely thing. I had been crying bitterly, tears! tears! tears! and nothing els, then your letter cam with more tears, after I had read it ofer and ofer again I found I had ink spots on my face. The tears are rolling down my face. It is very early in the morning, the sun is riseing behind the black trees and soon that will change, the sky will be blue and the trees a golden brown, but there is one thing that dosent change, this pain and thos tears. Oh! Bel I love you terrible, I want you terrible, I want your body your soft white body Nagelnackt! My body needs you so terrible, my hands and lips and breasts and everything els on me, sometimes I find it very hard to keep my promise but I have kept it up till now and will keep on doing so untill we meet again and I can at last have you, at last be the Geliebte. Whitch is the greater: the pain of being away from eachother, or the pain of being with eachother, crying at eachother beauty? I sopose the last is the greater, otherwise we would of given up all hope of ever being anything els but miserable.

I was at a grand Film last night, first of all there wasent *any* of the usual hugging and kissing, I think I have never enjoyed or felt so sad at a Film as at that one, *Sturm über Asien*, if it comes to Dublin you must go and see it, the same Regie as *Der Lebende Leichnam*, it was realey something quite different from all other Films, nothing to do with Love (as everybody understands the word) no silly girls makeing sweet faces, nearly all old people from Asien with marvellous faces, black lakes and grand Landschaften. Comeing home there was a new moon, it looked so grand ofer the black trees that it maid me cry. I opened my arms wide and tryed to imagine that you were lieing against my breasts and looking up at me like you did those moonlight nights when we walked together under the big chestnut trees with the stars shineing through the branches.

I met a new girl, very beautiful, pitch black hairs and very pale, she onely talks Egyptian. She told me about the man she loves, at present he is in Amerika far away in some lonely place and wont be back for the next three years and cant writ to her because there is no post office where he is staying and she onely gets a letter every 4 months, imagine if we only got a letter from each other every 4 months what sort of state we would be in by now, the poor girl I am very sorry for her. We went to a 5 o'clock tea dance, it was rather boreing but quite amuseing to see the people thinking of nothing but what they have on and the men settling their tyes every 5 minutes. On the way home I sudenly got in to a terrible state of sadness and woulden say a word, of course they were rageing with me, at the moment I dident care a dam, when I got in to the bus I got out a little Book and pencil and wrot down 100 times: Bloved Bloved Bloved Bel Bel Bel, I felt as if I never longed so much in my life for the man I love, to be with him, with him. I want you so much in every sence of the word, you and onely you. After I got out of the bus and was walking down the street I yelled out wahnsinnig wahnsinnig! wahnsinnig! Frau Schlank brought down your sock and that made me cry more than ever. I dont think I will send it to you, I will put it in to the drawer with your sweet letter. I had allso a letter from a man who asked me to go out with him to dance on Saturday evening, I sopose I will go. I know my bloved dosent mind and it makes the time go round quicker, the man is a bit of a fool but dances quite well and is the right hight for me. A flirt is very amuseing but shouldent go further than that.

Then I met the old man with the pipe and he told me I had a blue letter and then the fat man with the keys in the passage and he said Grüss Gott but I dident hear him.

Soon I will be counting the hours untill I can go to the station and find you amongst the crowded platform but I dont think I will be able to wear my grey costume if it is too cold and then I will have to wear Mammy furcoat. You will be by me on the 23th wont you Bel, my Bel with the beautiful lips and hands and eyes and face and everything that is on you, and now with your poor sore face it would make no diffrence. Two more weeks of agony pain and sadness! 14 more days oh! God and thos sleepless nights!!! How long? How long?

I had a very queer dream last night about you and me in a dark forest, we were lieing together on a path, when sudenly you changed in to a baby and dident know what love was and I was trying to tell you that I loved you more than anything on earth but you dident understand and wouldent have any thing to do with me but it was all a dream so it dosent count. There is no object in me trying to tell you how much I love you because I will never succeed, I know that for sirten. Is he the man I have allways been looking for? Yes! but then why cant he give that what I have been longing for for the last 6 months? I ofen wonder what is on you that makes me love you so greatly. I love you über alles in dieser Welt, mehr als alles auf Himmel, Erde und Hölle. One thing I thank God for that our love is so vast. I ofen wonder who I am to thank that you are born and that we met, I sopose I beter not start trying to find out whose fault it is that you are born. It comes back to the same thing, and that is, that I onely know ONE THING and that is that I LOVE YOU AND I AM ALL-WAYS YOUR SMERALDINA and that is the onely thing that matters most in our life YOU LOVE ME AND ARE ALLWAYS MY BEL.

Analiese is hacking round on the piano and there is no peace so I will stop. Now I am going to go on reading my Book called Die Grosse Liebe and then perhaps I will try and struggel through the Beethoven sonate, it is the onely thing that can take me away from my misery, I love playing quietly to myself in the evenings it gives me such a rest.

Bel! Bel! Bel! your letter has just come! Even if you cease to be all and allways mine!!! Oh! God how could you ever say such a thing, for lord sake dont!!! for god sake dont ever suggest such a thing again! I just berry my head in my hands and soke your letter with tears . . . Bel! Bel! how could you ever doubt me? Meine Ruh ist hin mein Herz ist schwer ich finde Sie nimmer und nimmer mehr. (Goethes Faust.) Lord Lord Lord for god sake tell me strate away what agsactly I have done. Is everything indiffrent to you? Evedintly you cant be bothered with a goat like me. If I dont stop writing you wont be able to read this letter because it will be all ofer tears. Bel! Bel! my love is so vast that when I am introduced to some young man and he starts doing the polite I get a quivver all ofer. I *know* what I am lifeing for, your last letter is allways on my breast when I wake up in the morning and see the sun rise. Ich seh' Dich nicht mehr Tränen hindernmich! My God! my true dog! my baby!

I must get a new nib, this old pen is gone to the dogs, I can't writ with it any more, it is the one I got from Wollworth so you can imagine how good it must bc.

Mammy wanted me to go out for a walk this afternoon, but I hate walking, I get so tired putting one foot delibertely in front of the other. Do you remember last summer (of course he dose) and how lovely it was lie-ing hearing the bees summing and the birds singing, and the big butter-fly that cam past, it looked grand, it was dark brown with yellow spots and looked so beautiful in the sun, and my body was quite brown *all* ofer and I dident feel the cold any more. Now the snow is all melted and the wood is as black as ever and the sky is allways grey except in the early morning and even then onc can onely see spots of red between the black clouds.

My hairs are freshily washed and I have a bit more energie than usual but still feel very passiv. For god sake dont overdo yourself and try and not get drunk again, I mean in that way that makes you sick.

We cam home in the bus this evening but we dident go that way through the fields with all the little paths because the big road was mended. Mammy allways asks after you. She says the time is *flying*, it will be *no* time untill Xmas and she says she hopes Frau Holle makes her bed ofen. I heard her saying to Daddy, I wonder how it is that Ivy and Bill get on my nerves when they go on together and Smerry and Bel never did. She ment when we are sitting on eachother knee and so on, I think it is because the love between Ivy and Bill is not real, there allways sems to be some sort of affection about it.

I curse the old body all day asswell because I have some dam thing on my leg so that I can barely walk, I don't know what it is or how it got there but it is there and full of matter to hell with it.

Today is one of the days when I see everything more clearer than ever and I am sure everything *will* go *right* in the end.

Der Tag wird kommen und die stille
NACHT!!!

I dont genau know when but if I dident think so I would cullaps with this agony, thes terrible long dark nights and onely your image to console me. I like the little white statue so much and am longing for the day when you and I will be standing like that and not haveing to think that there is somebody outside that can come in any minute.

Arschlochweh is married and gone to the Schweiz with his wife.

You ask me to give you a taske. I think I have gived you a big enough a taske. I am longing to see the "thing" you wrot about my "beauty" (as *you* call it) I must say (without wanting any complements) I cant see anything very much to writ about except the usual rot men writ about women.

Darling Bel I must stop. My bed is lonely without me and your photograph is waiting to be kissed so I better give them both peace. Soon it will all take an end, you will be by me and will feel that marvellous pain again that we did in the dark mountains and the big black lake blow and will walk in the fields covered with cowslips and Flieder and will hold once more in your arms

your own sad bloved
SMERALDINA

P.S. One day nearer to the silent Night!!!

Yellow

The night-nurse bounced in on the tick of five and turned
on the light. Belacqua waked feeling greatly refreshed and eager to wres-
tle with this new day. He had underlined, as quite a callow boy, a phrase
in Hardy's *Tess*, won by dint of cogging in the Synod: *When grief ceases to be
speculative, sleep sees her opportunity.* He had manipulated that sentence for
many years now, emending its terms, as joy for grief, to answer his occa-
sions, even calling upon it to bear the strain of certain applications for
which he feared it had not been intended, and still it held good through
it all. He waked with it now in his mind, as though it had been there all
the time he slept, holding that fragile place against dreams.

The nurse brought a pot of tea and a glass of strong salts on a tray.

"Pfui!" exclaimed Belacqua.

But the callous girl preferred to disregard this.

"When are they doing me?" he asked.

"You are down for twelve" she said.

Down . . . !

She took herself off.

He drank the salts and two cups of tea and be damned to the whole of
them. Then of course he was wide awake, poor fellow. But what cared he,
what cared saucy Belacqua? He switched off the lamp and lay back on his
back in this the darkest hour, smoking.

Carry it off as he might, he was in a dreadful situation. At twelve sharp he would be sliced open—zeep!—with a bistoury. This was the idea that his mind for the moment was in no fit state to entertain. If this Hunnish idea once got a foothold in his little psyche in its present unready condition, topsy-turvy after yesterday's debauch of anxiety and then the good night's sleep coming on top of that, it would be annihilated. The psyche, not the idea, which was precisely the reverse of what he wished. For himself, to do him justice, he did not care. His mind might cave in for all he cared, he was tired of the old bastardo. But the unfortunate part of it was that this would appear in his behaviour, he would scream and kick and bite and scratch when they came for him, beg for execution to be stayed and perhaps even wet the bed, and what a reflection on his late family that would be! The grand old family Huguenot guts, he could not do the dirty on them like that. (To say nothing of his natural anxiety to be put to rights with as little fuss as possible.)

My sufferings under the anaesthetic, he reflected, will be exquisite, but I shall not remember them.

He dashed out his cigarette and put on the lamp, this not so much for the company of the light as in order to postpone daybreak until he should feel a little more sure of himself. Daybreak, with its suggestion of a nasty birth, he could not bear. Downright and all as he was, he could not bear the sight of this punctilious and almost, he sometimes felt, superfluous delivery. This was mere folly and well he knew it. He tried hard to cure himself, to frighten or laugh himself out of this weakness, but to no avail. He would grow tired and say to himself: I am what I am. That was the end of all his meditations and endeavours: I am what I am. He had read the phrase somewhere and liked it and made it his own.

But God at least was good, as He usually is if we only know how to take Him, in this way, that six hours separated him (Belacqua) from the ordeal, six hours were allotted to him in which to make up his mind, as a pretty drab her face for an enemy. His getting the fleam in the neck, his suffering the tortures of the damned while seeming to slumber as peacefully as a little child, were of no consequence, as hope saved they were not, so long as his mind were master of the thought of them. What he had to do, and had with typical slackness put off doing till the last moment, was to arrange a hot reception in his mind for the thought of all the little acts of kindness that he was to endure before the day was out. Then he would be able to put a good face on it. Otherwise not. Otherwise he would bite, scratch, etc., when they came for him. Now the good face was all that concerned him, the bold devil-may-care expression. (Except of course that he was also anxious to be made well with the least possible ado.) He did not pause to consider himself in this matter, the light that the coming ordeal would shed on his irrevocable self, because he really was tired of that old bastardo. No, his whole concern was with other people, the lift-boy, nurses and sisters, the local doc coming to put him off, the eminent surgeon, the handy man at hand to clean up and put the bits into the incinerator, and all the friends of his late family, who would ferret out the whole truth. It did not matter about him, he was what he was. But these outsiders, the family guts and so on and so forth, all these things had to be considered.

An asthmatic in the room overhead was coughing his heart up. God bless you, thought Belacqua, you make things easier for me. But when did the unfortunate sleep? During the day, the livelong day, through the stress of the day. At twelve sharp he would be sound, or, better again, just dozing off. Meantime he coughed, as Crusoe laboured to bring his gear ashore, the snugger to be.

Belacqua made a long arm and switched off the lamp. It threw shadows. He would close his eyes, he would bilk the dawn in that way. What were the eyes anyway? The posterns of the mind. They were safer closed.

If only he were well-bred or, failing that, plucky. Blue blood or gamecock! Even if he lived in his mind as much as was his boast. Then he need not be at all this pains to make himself ready. Then it would only be a question of finding a comfortable position in the strange bed, trying to sleep or reading a book, waiting calmly for the angelus. But he was an indolent bourgeois poltroon, very talented up to a point, but not fitted for private life in the best and brightest sense, in the sense to which he referred when he bragged of how he furnished his mind and lived there, because it was the last ditch when all was said and done. But he preferred not to wait till then, he fancied it might be wiser to settle down there straight away and not wait till he was kicked into it by the world, just at the moment maybe when he was beginning to feel at home in the world. He could no more go back into his heart in that way than he could keep out of it altogether. So now there was nothing for it but to lie on his back in the dark and exercise his talent. Unless of course he chose to distress the friends of his late family (to say nothing of perhaps jeopardising the cure for which the friends of his late family were paying). But he had too much of the grocer's sense of honour for that. Rather than have that happen he would persist with his psyche, he would ginger up his little psyche for the occasion.

Poor Belacqua, he seems to be having a very dull, irksome morning, preparing for the fray in this manner. But he will make up for it later on, there is a good time coming for him later on, when the doctors have given him a new lease of apathy.

What were his tactics in this crisis?

In a less tight corner he might have been content to barricade his mind against the idea. But this was at the best a slipshod method, since the idea, how blatant an enemy soever and despite the strictest guard, was almost certain to sidle in sooner or later under the skirts of a friend, and then the game was up. Still, in the ordinary run of adversity, he would doubtless have bowed to his natural indolence and adopted such a course, he would have been content merely to think of other things and hope for the best. But this was no common or garden fix, he was properly up against it this time, there could be no question of half-measures on this melancholy occasion.

His plan therefore was not to refuse admission to the idea, but to keep it at bay until his mind was ready to receive it. Then let it in and pulverise it. Obliterate the bastard. He ground his teeth in the bed. Flitter the fucker, tear it into pieces like a priest. So far so good. But by what means. Belacqua ransacked his mind for a suitable engine of destruction.

At this crucial point the good God came to his assistance with a phrase from a paradox of Donne: *Now among our wise men, I doubt not but many would be found, who would laugh at Heraclitus weeping, none which would weep at Democritus laughing.* This was a godsend and no error. Not the phrase as a judgement, but its terms, the extremes of wisdom that it tendered to Belacqua. It is true that he did not care for these black and white alternatives as a rule. Indeed he even went so far as to hazard a little paradox on his own account, to the effect that between contraries no alternation was possible. But was it the moment for a man to be nice? Belacqua snatched eagerly at the issue. Was it to be laughter or tears? It came to the same thing in the end, but which was it to be *now*? It was too late to arrange for the luxury of both. Now in a moment he would fill his mind with one or other of these two orders of rays, shall we say ultra-red and ultra-violet, and prepare to perforate his adversary.

Really, thought Belacqua, I cannot remember having ever spent a more dreary morning; but needs must, that was a true saying, when the devil drives.

At this all-important juncture of his delirium Belacqua found himself blinking his eyes rapidly, a regular nictation, so that little flaws of dawn gushed into his mind. This had not been done with intent, but when he found that it seemed to be benefiting him in some curious way he kept it up, until gradually the inside of his skull began to feel sore. Then he desisted and went back to the dilemma.

Here, as indeed at every crux of the enterprise, he sacrificed sense of what was personal and proper to himself to the desirability of making a certain impression on other people, an impression almost of gallantry. He must efface himself altogether and do the little soldier. It was this paramount consideration that made him decide in favour of Bim and Bom, Grock, Democritus, whatever you are pleased to call it, and postpone its dark converse to a less public occasion. This was an abnegation if you like, for Belacqua could not resist a lachrymose philosopher and still less when, as was the case with Heraclitus, he was obscure at the same time. He was in his element in dingy tears and luxuriously so when these were furnished by a pre-Socratic man of acknowledged distinction. How often had he not exclaimed, skies being grey: "Another minute of this and I consecrate the remnant of my life to Heraclitus of Ephesus, I shall be that Delian diver who, after the third or fourth submersion, returns no more to the surface!"

But weeping in this charnel-house would be misconstrued. All the staff, from matron to lift-boy, would make the mistake of ascribing his tears, or, perhaps better, his tragic demeanor, not to the follies of humanity at large which of course covered themselves, but rather to the tumour the size of a brick that he had on the back of his neck. This would be a very natural mistake and Belacqua was not blaming them. No blame attached to any living person in this matter. But the news would get round that Belacqua, so far from grinning and bearing, had piped his eye, or had been on the point of doing so. Then he would be disgraced and, by extension, his late family also.

So now his course was clear. He would arm his mind with laughter, laughter is not quite the word but it will have to serve, at every point, then he would admit the idea and blow it to pieces. Smears, as after a gorge of blackberries, of hilarity, which is not quite the word either, would be adhering to his lips as he stepped smartly, *ohne Hast aber ohne Rast*, into the torture-chamber. His fortitude would be generally commended.

How did he proceed to put this plan into execution?

He has forgotten, he has no use for it any more.

The night-nurse broke in upon him at seven with another pot of tea and two cuts of toast.

"That's all you'll get now" she said.

The impertinent slut! Belacqua very nearly told her to work it up.

"Did the salts talk to you?" she said.

The sick man appraised her as she took his temperature and pulse. She was a tight trim little bit.

"They whispered to me" he said.

When she was gone he thought what an all but flawless brunette, so spick and span too after having been on the go all night, at the beck and call of the first lousy old squaw who let fall her book or could not sleep for the roar of the traffic in Merrion Row. What the hell did anything matter anyway!

Pale wales in the east beyond the Land Commission. The day was going along nicely.

The night-nurse came back for the tray. That made her third appearance, if he was not mistaken. She would very shortly be relieved, she would eat her supper and go to bed. But not to sleep. The place was too full of noise and light at that hour, her bed a refrigerator. She could not get used to this night-duty, she really could not. She lost weight and her face became cavernous. Also it was very difficult to arrange anything with her fiancé. What a life!

"See you later" she said.

There was no controverting this. Belacqua cast about wildly for a reply that would please her and do him justice at the same time. *Au plaisir* was of course the very thing, but the wrong language. Finally he settled on *I suppose so* and discharged it at her in a very half-hearted manner, when she was more than half out of the door. He would have been very much better advised to let it alone and say nothing.

While he was still wasting his valuable time cursing himself for a fool the door burst open and the day-nurse came in with a mighty rushing sound of starched apron. She was to have charge of him by day. She just missed being beautiful, this Presbyterian from Aberdeen. Aberdeen!

After a little conversation obiter Belacqua let fall casually, as though the idea had only just occurred to him, whereas in fact it had been tormenting him insidiously for some little time:

"Oh nurse the w.c. perhaps it might be as well to know."

Like that, all in a rush, without any punctuation.

When she had finished telling him he knew roughly where the place was. But he stupidly elected to linger on in the bed with his uneasy load, codding himself that it would be more decent not to act incontinent on intelligence of so intimate a kind. In his anxiety to give colour to this pause he asked Miranda when he was being done.

"Didn't the night-nurse tell you" she said sharply, "at twelve."

So the night-nurse had split. The treacherous darling!

He got up and set out, leaving Miranda at work on the bed. When he got back she was gone. He got back into the made bed.

Now the sun, that creature of habit, shone in through the window.

A little Aschenputtel, gummy and pert, skipped in with sticks and coal for the fire.

"Morning" she said.

"Yes" said Belacqua. But he retrieved himself at once. "What a lovely room" he exclaimed "all the morning sun."

No more was needed to give Aschenputtel his measure.

"Very lovely" she said bitterly "right on me fire." She tore down the blind. "Putting out me good fire" she said.

That was certainly one way of looking at it.

"I had one old one in here" she said "and he might be snoring but he wouldn't let the blind down."

Some old put had crossed her, that was patent.

"Not for God" she said "so what did I do?" She screwed round on her knees from building the fire. Belacqua obliged her.

"What was that?" he said.

She turned back with a chuckle to her task.

"I block it with a chair" she said "and his shirt over the back."

"Ha" exclaimed Belacqua.

"Again he'd be up" she exulted "don't you know." She laughed happily at the memory of this little deception. "I kep it off all right" she said.

She talked and talked and poor Belacqua, with his mind unfinished, had to keep his end up. Somehow he managed to create a very favourable impression.

"Well" she said at last, in an indescribable sing-song "g'bye now. See you later."

"That's right" said Belacqua.

Aschenputtel was engaged to be married to handy Andy, she had been for years. Meantime she gave him a dog's life.

Soon the fire was roaring up the chimney and Belacqua could not resist the temptation to get up and sit before it, clad only in his thin blue 100,000 Chemises pyjamas. The coughing aloft had greatly abated since he first heard it. The man was gradually settling down, it did not require a Sherlock Holmes to realize that. But on the grand old yaller wall, crowding in upon his left hand, a pillar of higher tone, representing the sun, was spinning out its placid deiseal. This dribble of time, thought Belacqua, like sanies into a bucket, the world wants a new washer. He would draw the blind, both blinds.

But he was foiled by the entry of the matron with the morning paper, this, save the mark, by way of taking his mind off it. It is impossible to describe the matron. She was all right. She made him nervous the way she flung herself about.

Belacqua turned on the flow:

"What a lovely morning" he gushed "a lovely room, all the morning sun."

The matron simply disappeared, there is no other word for it. The woman was there one moment and gone the next. It was extraordinary.

The theatre sister came in. What a number of women there seemed to be in this place! She was a great raw châteaubriant of a woman, like the one on the Wincarnis bottle. She took a quick look at his neck.

"Pah" she scoffed "that's nothing."

"Not at all" said Belacqua.

"Is that the lot?"

Belacqua did not altogether care for her tone.

"And a toe" he said "to come off, or rather portion of a toe."

"Top" she guffawed "and bottom."

There was no controverting this. But he had learnt his lesson. He let it pass.

This woman was found to improve on acquaintance. She had a coarse manner, but she was exceedingly gentle. She taught all her more likely patients to wind bandages. To do this well with the crazy little hand-windlass that she provided was no easy matter. The roll would become fusiform. But when one got to know the humours of the apparatus, then it could be coaxed into yielding the hard slender spools, perfect cylinders, that delighted her. All these willing slaves that passed through her hands, she blandished each one in turn. "I never had such tight straight bandages" she would say. Then, just as the friendship established on this basis seemed about to develop into something more—how shall I say?—substantial, the patient would all of a sudden be well enough to go home. Some malignant destiny pursued this splendid woman. Years later, when the rest of the staff was forgotten, she would drift into the mind. She marked down Belacqua for the bandages.

Miranda came back, this time with the dressing-tray. That voluptuous undershot cast of mouth, the clenched lips, almost bocca romana, how had he failed to notice it before? Was it the same woman?

"Now" she said.

She lashed into the part with picric and ether. It beat him to understand why she should be so severe on his little bump of amativeness. It was not septic to the best of his knowledge. Then why this severity? Merely on the off chance of its coming in for the fag-end of a dig? It was very strange. It had not even been shaved. It jutted out under the short hairs like a cuckoo's bill. He trusted it would come to no harm. Really he could not afford to have it curtailed. His little bump of amativeness.

When his entire nape was as a bride's adorned (bating the obscene stain of the picric) and so tightly bandaged that he felt his eyes bulging, she transferred her compassion to the toes. She scoured the whole phalanx, top and bottom. Suddenly she began to titter. Belacqua nearly kicked her in the eye, he got such a shock. How dared she trespass on his programme! He refusing to be tickled in this petty local way, trying with his teeth to reach his under-lip and gouging his palms, and she forgetting herself, there was no other word for it. There were limits, he felt, to Democritus.

"Such a lang tootsy" she giggled.

Heavenly father, the creature was bilingual. A lang tootsy! Belacqua swallowed his choler.

"Soon to be syne" he said in a loud voice. What his repartee lacked in wit it made up for in style. But it was lost on this granite Medusa.

"A long foot" he said agreeably "I know, or a long nose. But a long toe, what does that denote?"

No answer. Was the woman then altogether cretinous? Or did she not hear him? Belting away there with her urinous picric and cooling her porridge in advance. He would try her again.

"I say" he roared "that that toe you like so much will soon be only a memory." He could not put it plainer than that.

Her voice after his was scarcely audible. It went as follows:

"Yes"—the word died away and was repeated—"yes, his troubles are nearly over."

Belacqua broke down completely, he could not help it. This distant voice, like a cor anglais coming through the evening, and then the *his,* the *his* was the last straw. He buried his face in his hands, he did not care who saw him.

"I would like" he sobbed "the cat to have it, if I might."

She would never have done with her bandage, it cannot have measured less than a furlong. But of course it would never do to leave anything to chance, Belacqua could appreciate that. Still it seemed somehow disproportioned to the length of even his toe. At last she made all fast round his shin. Then she packed her tray and left. Some people go, others leave. Belacqua felt like the rejected of those two that night in a bed. He felt he had set Miranda somehow against him. Was this then the haporth of paint? Miranda on whom so much depended. Merde!

It was all Lister's fault. Those damned happy Victorians.

His heart gave a great leap in its box with a fulminating sense that he was all wrong, that anger would stand by him better than the other thing, the laugh seemed so feeble, so like a whinge in the end. But on second thoughts no, anger would turn aside when it came to the point, leaving him like a sheep. Anyhow it was too late to turn back. He tried cautiously what it felt like to have the idea in his mind. . . . Nothing happened, he felt no shock. So at least he had spiked the brute, that was something.

At this point he went downstairs and had a truly military evacuation, Army Service Corps. Coming back he did not doubt that all would yet be well. He whistled a snatch outside the duty-room. There was nothing left of his room when he got back but Miranda, Miranda more prognathous than ever, loading a syringe. Belacqua tried to make light of this.

"What now?" he said.

But she had the weapon into his bottom and discharged before he realized what was happening. Not a cry escaped him.

"Did you hear what I said?" he said. "I insist, it is my right, on knowing the meaning of this, the purpose of this injection, do you hear me?"

"It is what every patient gets" she said "before going down to the theatre."

Down to the theatre! Was there a conspiracy in this place to destroy him, body and soul? His tongue clave to his palate. They had desiccated his secretions. First blood to the profession!

The theatre-socks were the next little bit of excitement. Really the theatre seemed to take itself very seriously. To hell with your socks, he thought, it's your mind I want.

Now events began to move more rapidly. First of all an angel of the Lord came to his assistance with a funny story, really very funny indeed, it always made Belacqua laugh till he cried, about the parson who was invited to take a small part in an amateur production. All he had to do was to snatch at his heart when the revolver went off, cry "By God! I'm shot!" and drop dead. The parson said certainly, he would be most happy, if they would have no objection to his drawing the line at "By God!" on such a secular occasion. He would replace it, if they had no objection, by "Mercy!" or "Upon my word!" or something of that kind. "Oh my! I'm shot!" how would that be?

But the production was so amateur that the revolver went off indeed and the man of God was transfixed.

"Oh!" he cried "oh . . . ! . . . BY CHRIST! I *am* SHOT!"

It was a mercy that Belacqua was a dirty lowdown Low Church Protestant high-brow and able to laugh at this sottish jest. Laugh! How he did laugh, to be sure. Till he cried.

He got up and began to titivate himself. Now he could hear the asthmatic breathing if he listened hard. The day was out of danger, any fool could see that. A little sealed cardboard box lying on the mantelpiece caught his eye. He read the inscription: Fraisse's Ferruginous Ampoules for the Intensive Treatment of Anaemia by Intramuscular Squirtation. Registered Trademark—Mozart. The little Hexenmeister of Don Giovanni, now in his narrow cell for ever mislaid, dragged into bloodlessness! How very amusing. Really the world was in great form this morning.

Now two further women, there was no end to them, the one of a certain age, the other not, entered, ripping off their regulation cuffs as they advanced. They pounced on the bed. The precautionary oil-sheet, the cradle . . . Belacqua padded up and down before the fire, the ends of his pyjamas tucked like a cyclist's into the sinister socks. He would smoke one more cigarette, nor count the cost. It was astonishing, when he came to think of it, how the entire routine of this place, down to the meanest detail, was calculated to a cow's toe to promote a single end, the relief of suffering in the long run. Observe how he dots his i's now and crucifies his t's to the top of his bent. He was being put to his trumps.

Surreptitiously they searched his yellow face for signs of discomposure. In vain. It was a mask. But perhaps his voice would tremble. One, she whose life had changed, took it upon herself to say in a peevish tone:

"Sister Beamish won't bless you for soiling her good socks."

Sister Beamish would not bless him.

The voice of this person was in ruins, but she abused it further.

"Would you not stand on the mat?"

His mind was made up in a flash: he would stand on the mat. He would meet them in this matter. If he refused to stand on the mat he was lost in the eyes of these two women.

"Anything" he said "to oblige Sister Beamish."

Miranda was having a busy morning. Now she appeared for the fourth or fifth time, he had lost count, complete with shadowy assistants. The room seemed full of grey women. It was like a dream.

"If you have any false teeth" she said "you may remove them."

His hour was at hand, there was no blinking at the fact.

Going down in the lift with Miranda he felt his glasses under his hand. This was a blessed accident if you like, just when the silence was becoming awkward.

"Can I trust you with these?" he said.

She put them into her bosom. The divine creature! He would assault her in another minute.

"No smoking" she said "in the operating-theatre."

The surgeon was washing his invaluable hands as Belacqua swaggered through the antechamber. He that hath clean hands shall be stronger. Belacqua cut the surgeon. But he flashed a dazzling smile at the Wincarnis. She would not forget that in a hurry.

He bounced up on to the table like a bridegroom. The local doc was in great form, he had just come from standing best man, he was all togged up under his vestments. He recited his exhortation and clapped on the nozzle.

"Are you right?" said *Belacqua.*

The mixture was too rich, there could be no question about that. His heart was running away, terrible yellow yerks in his skull. "One of the best," he heard those words that did not refer to him. The expression reassured him. The best man clawed at his tap.

By Christ! he did die!

They had clean forgotten to auscultate him!

Draff

Shuah, Belacqua, in a Nursing Home.

Though this was stale news to Mrs. Shuah, for she had inserted it (by telephone) herself, yet she felt, on reading it in the morning after paper, a little shock of surprise, as on opening telegram confirming advance booking in crowded hotel. Then the thought of friends, their unassumed grief giving zest to their bacon and eggs, the first phrases of sympathy with her in this great loss modulating from porridge to marmalade, from whispers and gasps to the calm ejaculations of chat, in a dozen households that she could have mentioned, set in motion throughout her bodily economy, with results that plainly appeared at once on her face, the wheels of mourning. Whereupon she was without thought or feeling, just a slush, a teary coenaesthesis.

This particular Mrs. Shuah, as stated thus far at all events, does not sound very like Thelma née bboggs, nor is she. Thelma née bboggs perished of sunset and honeymoon that time in Connemara. Then shortly after that they suddenly seemed to be all dead, Lucy of course long since, Ruby duly, Winnie to decency, Alba Perdue in the natural course of being seen home. Belacqua looked round and the Smeraldina was the only sail in sight. In next to no time she had made up his mind by not merely loving but wanting him with such quasi-Gorgonesque impatience as her letter precited evinces. She and no other therefore is the Mrs. Shuah who now, after less than a year in the ultraviolet intimacy of the compound of ephebe and old woman that he was, reads in the paper that she had begun to survive him.

Bodies don't matter but hers went something like this: big enormous breasts, big breech, Botticelli thighs, knock-knees, square ankles, wobbly, poppata, mammose, slobbery-blubbery, bubbubbubbub, the real button-busting Weib, ripe. Then, perched away high out of sight on top of this porpoise prism, the sweetest little pale Pisanello of a birdface ever. She was like Lucrezia del Fede, pale and belle, a pale belle Braut, with a winter skin like an old sail in the wind. The root and the source of the athletic or aesthetic blob of a birdnose never palled, unless when he had a costive coryza himself, on Belacqua's forefinger pad and nail, with which he went probing and plumbing and boring the place just as for many years he polished his glasses (ecstasy of attrition!), or suffered the shakes and grace-note strangulations and enthrottlements of the Winkelmusik of Szopen or Pichon or Chopinek or Chopinetto or whoever it was embraced her heartily as sure as his name was Fred, dying all his life (thank you Mr. Auber) on a sickroom talent (thank you Mr. Field) and a Kleinmeister's Leidenschaftsucherei (thank you Mr. Beckett), or ascended across the Fulda or the Tolka or the Poddle or the Volga as the case might be, and he never dreaming that on each and all these occasions he was pandering to the most iniquitous excesses of a certain kind of sublimation. The wretched little wet rag of an upper lip, pugnozzling up and back in what you might nearly call a kind of a duck or a cobra sneer to the nostrils, was happily to some extent amended by the wanton pout of its fellow and the forward jaws to match—a brilliant recovery. The skull of this strapping girl was shaped like a wedge. The ears of course were shells, the eyes shafts of reseda (his favourite colour) into an oreless mind. The hair was as black as the pots and grew so thick and low athwart the temples that the brow was reduced to a fanlight (just the kind of shaped brow that he most admired). But what matter about bodies?

She got out of the narrow bed on the wrong side, but she was never clear in her mind as to which was the right side and which the wrong, and went into the room where he was laid out, the big bible wrapped in a napkin still under his chin. She stood at the end of the bed in her lotus chintz pyjamas, as glazed as those eyes that she could not see, and held her breath. His forehead, when she ventured to lay the back of her hand across it, was much less chilly than she had expected, but that no doubt was explained by her own peripheral circulation, which was wretched. She caught hold of his hands, folded, not on his breast as she would have wished, but lower down, and rearranged them. Scarcely had she gone down on her bended knees after having made this adjustment when a spasm of anxiety, lest there should be anything the matter with this corpse that rigor mortis had apparently passed over, straightened her up. She hoped it was all right. Baulked of her prayer, baulked of a last long look at the disaffected face, its contemptuous probity that would fall to pieces, she took herself off to prepare her weeds, for it would not do to be seen in lotus chintz. Black suited her, black and green had always been her colours. She found in her room what she had in mind, an Ethiope one-piece gashed and slashed with emerald insertions. She brought it to her work-table in the penannular bow-window, she sat down trembling and began to fix it. It was like being up in the sky in a bubble, the sun streaming in (through the curtains), the blue all round her. Soon the floor was strewn with the bright cuttings, it went to her heart to rip them they looked so lovely. Not a flower, not a flower sweet.

> One insertion in the Press
> Makes minus how many to make a black dress?

She was so sad and busy, the sobs were so quick to ripen and burst in her mind and the work was so nice, that she did not notice a fat drab demon approach the house nor hear his uproarious endeavours not to intrude on the gravel. Up came his card. Mr. Malacoda. Most respectfully desirous to measure. A sob, instead of bursting, withered. The Smeraldina whimpered that she was sorry but she could not admit this Mr. Malacoda, she could not have the Master measured. Mary Ann's leprous features were much abused with the usual. In a crisis like this, however, she was worth ten or fifteen of her mistress.

"He'd be about the Master's size" she said.

Just fancy her noticing that!

"Then why don't you tell him so" moaned the Smeraldina "and let do the best he can and not be coming up here to torment me."

What could an inch or so possibly matter this way or that? There was no question of having to skimp aragonite or peperino. The coffin was not going to eat him.

Mary Ann returned to the torment with the sad news that Mr. Malacoda was at that very moment springing up the stairs with a tape in his black claws. The Smeraldina started up, clutching the scissor, and began to plunge towards the door. But the thought of the thoral chintz brought her up short. Had again!

"You might at least bring me a cup of tea" she said.

Mary Ann left the room.

"And a lightly boiled egg" cried the Smeraldina.

A small wreath, of arum lilies needless to say, arrived in a box—anonymous. This the Smeraldina buried. She sought out the gardener, a slow shy slob of a man with a dripping moustache, and found him watering in a dazed and hopeless manner a bed of blighted sweet-william. Someone had stolen his rose, he mowed down the flowers with hard jets of water. She sent him flying up into the heart of the mountains with two sacks to gather bracken. Then he might go home. Herself she stripped a eucalyptus of its boughs.

The parson came churning up the avenue in bottom gear, confirmed his worst fears with a quick look at the windows, let fall his rustless allsteel in sorrow and anger on the gravel, and walked right in.

"I never knew anyone founder" he declared in a passionate way, "and I've seen a good many."

"No" said the Smeraldina.

"Automatic dispensation" he cried. "Strength from on high" snapping his thumb "like that. Meet in Paradize."

"Yes" said the Smeraldina.

"No sooner does he arrive" clasping his hands and looking up (why up?) "there where there is no time, than you burst in upon him."

"He's all right" said the Smeraldina. "I know that."

"Therefore be glad" cried the parson.

He pedalled away like a weaver's shuttle (but not before she had cove-nanted to be glad) to administer the Eucharist, of which he always carried an abundance in a satchel on the bracket of his bike, to a moneyed wether up the road whose tale was nearly told. Seven and six a time.

Capper Quin arrived on tiptire, in a car of his very own. He grappled with the widow, he simply could not help it. She was a sensible girl in some ways, she was not ashamed to let herself go in the arms of a man of her own weight at last. They broke away, carrot plucked from tin of grease, and Hairy stood humbly before her, hers to command. He was greatly improved, commerce with the things of time had greatly improved him. Now he could speak quite nicely, he did not simply have to abandon his periods in despair after a word or two.

She stood by while he freighted the car. The sacks distended with fern and bracken; the boughs of eucalyptus, piecemeal to meet the occasion, tied up in an old stable jacket; a superb shrub of verbena treated in the same way; a vat of moss; a bag of wire tholes. When all these things had been safely stowed and the car pointed in the right direction, Hairy fol-lowed her lead into the house and took up position, the crutch well split, the great feet splayed, swollen paws appaumée two dangling chunks of blood ballast, aborted mammae much in evidence, at gaze. Even Ireland has a few animals, now generally regarded as varieties, which have been ranked as species by some zoologists. He felt his face improving as grief modelled the features.

"Might I see him?" he whispered, like a priest asking for a book in the Trinity College Library.

She had herself supported up the stairs, she led the way into the death-chamber as though it belonged to her. They diverged, the body was between them on the bed like the keys between nations in Velásquez's *Lances*, like the water between Buda and Pest, and so on, hyphen of reality.

"Very beautiful" said Hairy.

"I think very" said the Smeraldina.

"They all are" said Hairy.

Shed a tear, damn you, she thought, I can't. But he went one better, he choked a whole bucketful back. His face improved rapidly.

They met again at the foot of the bed, like parallels made to for the sake of argument, and occupied this fresh viewpoint with heads together until the Smeraldina, feeling the absurdity of the position, detached herself, left the room and closed the door behind her, on the dying and the dead.

Hairy felt it was up to him now to feel something.

"You are quieter than humus" he said in his mind, "you will give the bowels of the earth a queer old lesson in quiet."

That was the best he could manage at the time. But bowels surely was hardly the right word. That was where Queen Anne had the gout.

The hands pious on the sternum were unseemly, defunct crusader, absolved from polite campaign. Hairy reached out with his endless arms and tugged at the marble members. Two nouns and two adjectives. Not a stir out of them. How stupid of him.

"This is final" he thought.

Belacqua had often looked forward to meeting the girls, Lucy especially, hallowed and transfigured beyond the veil. What a hope! Death had already cured him of that naïveté.

Hairy, anxious though he was to rejoin the Smeraldina while his face was at its best, before it relapsed into the workaday dumpling, steak and kidney pudding, had his work cut out to tear himself away. For he could not throw off the impression that he was letting slip a rare occasion to feel something really stupendous, something that nobody had ever felt before. But time pressed. The Smeraldina was pawing the ground, his own personal features were waning (or, perhaps better, waxing). In the end he took his leave without kneeling, without a prayer, but his brain quite prostrate and suppliant before this first fact of its experience. That was at least something. He would have welcomed a long Largo, on the black notes for preference.

In the cemetery the light was failing, the sea moonstone washing the countless toes turned up, the mountains swarthy Uccello behind the headstones. The loveliest little lap of earth you ever saw. Hairy shifted the roof of planks from off the brand-new pit and went down, down, down the narrow steps carefully not removed by the groundsman. His head came to rest below the surface of the earth. What a nerve the man had to be sure. The significance of this was lost on the Smeraldina, she merely crouched on the brink.

Well, to make a long story short, the pair of them between them, she feeding him from above, upholstered the grave: the floor with moss and fern, the walls with the verdure outstanding. Low down the clay was so hard that Hairy had to take his shoe to the tholes. However they made a great job of it, not a spot of clay showed when they had done, all was lush, green and most sweet smelling.

But soon it would be black and dark night, a chill wind arose, the pangs of light began on the foothills, the moonstone turned to ashes. The Smeraldina shivered, as well she might. Hairy, taking a last look round at his handiwork, was as snug as a bug in a rug. Belacqua lay dead on the bed with the timeless mock on the face. Hairy came up out of the hole, drew up the steps behind him, put back the planks and rubbed his hands with a sigh, labour ended, labour of love, painful duty.

All of a sudden the groundsman was there, a fine man in ruins, as drunk as he knew how, giving point to the consecrated ground. He was most moved by their attentions, without parallel in his experience of the forsaken. For his own part he could be relied on to work himself to the bone for the defunct, whom he had known well, not only as a man, but as a boy also. The Smeraldina had a quick vision of Belacqua as a boy, shinning up the larch trees, his breast expanding to the world.

Hairy feeling father, brother, husband, confessor, friend of the family (what family?) and the inevitable something more, did the heavy with the reeling groundsman. The Smeraldina played up. Belacqua, idealised something horrid, made the widow and her huge escort, who now stalked off, four lovely deaf ears, faces tilted slightly to the starry sky, one in this sordid matter.

"Home Hairy" she said.

Hairy quickened his step, enveloped her, helped her along.

"I don't see the moon" she said.

Like a jack-in-the-box the satellite obliged, let down her shining ladder to the shore. She had a long lonely climb before her.

The groundsman, cut to the quick, mindful of his lumbago, sat down on the planks and lowered his bottle of stout. Guinness for Thinness, stultifying stout. He had lost interest in all the shabby mysteries, he was beyond caring. He strained his ear for the future, and what did he hear? All the ancient punctured themes recurring, creeping up the treble out of sound. Very well. Let the essence of his being stay where it was, in liquor and liquor's harmonics, accepted gladly as the ultimate expression of his nonchalance. He rose and made his water agin a cypress.

That night Hairy lay in his bed, tossed and turned for various reasons, fell off at last into a troubled sleep, woke not at all refreshed to a day of wind and rain, the weather having broken in the small hours.

At midday to the Smeraldina, in bed indulging her most secret thoughts, salivating slightly for a lightly boiled egg, Mary Ann appeared. Mr. Malacoda. Keen to coffin. The Smeraldina observed in a bitter voice that if the man must coffin why coffin he must, surely there was no clear call on Mary Ann to make a point of pestering her with what could not be cured.

A thin wall, a good but thin wall, separated her from Mr. Malacoda and assistant ungulata, in a fever to have done. Cerements did not suit the defunct, with their riot of frills and lace they made him look like a pantomime baby.

When Hairy arrived it was the magic hour, Homer dusk, when the subliminal rats came abroad on their rounds. The little something extra that he felt he had come in for made great strides at the expense of its co-heirs. He agreed absolutely that cerements did not suit the defunct, somehow they made him look so put-upon and helpless, almost as though he had not done dying. He stayed to supper.

A point to bear in mind is that the Smeraldina was so naturally happy-go-lucky that she did not find it at all easy to feel deeply, or rather, perhaps better, be deeply sentimental. Her life had been springing leaks for as long as she cared to remember. A husband—and how!—was oakum in the end the same as everything else, prophylactic, a wire bandage of Jalade-Lafont. Belacqua had come unstuck like his own favour of veronica in *What a Misfortune*. Losers seekers. The position was not quite so simple as all that, there was some sentimental factor in play (or at work) complicating the position, but that was more or less it.

That night the weather so mended as to be more than merely clement for the ceremony. Malacoda and Co. turned up bright and early with their six cylinder hearse, black as Ulysses's cruiser. The demon, quite unable to control his impatience to cover, could only manage a quick flirt with Mary Ann. The Smeraldina was through with the death-chamber, not that she was callous, quite the reverse, but the livery of death, leaving aside its pale flag altogether, was too much for her. Hairy, more and more self-assured servitor, was of the same opinion. So let the good man cover by all means. That was what he was there for, that was what he was paid for. Let the whole nightmare brood walk up by all manner of means.

Now he was grinning up at the lid at last.

"No flowers" said Hairy.

God forbid!

"And no friends."

Need he ask!

The parson arrived in the nick of time. He had been casting out devils all morning, he was in a muck sweat.

Hairy scampered out into the sunlight and the balmy breeze, free of the house that was suddenly jerry-built mausoleum, with a message from his sweet ward to the driver whose name was Scarmiglione, a strongly worded message exhorting him to temper full speed with due caution. "Let her out" said Hairy in his pretentious jargon "to the irreducible coefficient of safety." Scarmiglione met this request with a look of petrified courtesy. On these trips he deferred to the speed-controlling washer of his own mind and conscience, and to none other. He was adamant in this matter. Hairy shrank away from the affable rictus.

All aboard. All souls at half-mast. Aye-aye.

Mary Ann found the gardener shut up in the toolshed, all of a heap on an upturned box, nervously tying knots in a piece of raffia. He was not neglecting his work, he was grieving.

"The only one" said Mary Ann, alluding to their late employer, "as ever I dreamed on," as though that could possibly interest the gardener. But what higher tribute could she pay? The gardener had secured his retreat, she could not come at him, she could only hold her livid farthing of a face at the broken window and commit copious nuisance with her opinions and impressions. She did not expect an answer, she did not pause for one, she received none. He heard the voice at a great distance, but could make no sense of it. For he was, temporarily at all events, just a clod of gloom, in which concern for his own state of health counted for more than he would have cared to admit. Was he overdoing things about the place? It was hard to say. He heard Mary Ann in the run, her voice raised in furious hallali, butchering a fowl for the table. He began to look about for his line. It was gone from its place. Someone had stolen his line. Some unauthorised person had taken his line, with the result that now he was helpless to put down his broccoli. He rose and let himself out, he slobbered out of darkness into light, he chose a place in the sun and settled, he was like a colossal fly trimming its load of typhus. Gradually he cheered up. Ten to one God was in his heaven.

Though the grave was deep the committal was neat, not a hitch; its words perhaps a trifle mis-directed on the vile, the sure and certain hope rather gobbled up in the fact of departure. The tone conveyed to "earth to earth" was a triumph of passionate and contemptuous reproach to all the living. How dared they continue full of misery! Pah!

"Now in Gaelic" said Hairy on the way home "they could not say that."

"What could they not say?" said the parson. He would not rest until he knew.

"O Death where is thy sting?" replied Hairy. "They have no words for these big ideas."

This was more than enough for the parson, a canon of the Church of Ireland, who hastily exclaimed, no doubt by way of a shining straw, to the Smeraldina:

"My wife would so much like to see you."

"O Anthrax" said Hairy "where is thy pustule?"

"She has been through the fire" said the parson, "she understands. My poor dear mother-in-law!"

"O G.P.I." said Hairy "where are thy rats?"

By the mercy of God the good canon was slow to wrath.

"And so on" said Hairy "and so forth. They can't say it once and for all. A spalpeen's babble."

Belacqua dead and buried, Hairy seemed to have taken on a new lease of life. He spoke well, with commendable assurance; he looked better, less obese cretin and spado than ever before; and he felt better, which was a great thing. Perhaps the explanation of this was that while Belacqua was alive Hairy could not be himself, or, if you prefer, could be nothing else. Whereas now the defunct, such of his parts at least as might be made to fit, could be pressed into service, incorporated in the daily ellipses of Capper Quin without his having to face the risk of exposure. Already Belacqua was not wholly dead, but merely mutilated. The Smeraldina appreciated this without thinking.

As for her, it was almost as though she had suffered the inverse change. She had died in part. She had definitely ceased to exist in that particular part which Belacqua had been at such pains to isolate, the public part so cruelly made private for his convenience, her last clandestine aspect[1] reduced to a radiograph and exploited to ginger his secret occasions. That was down the mine Daddy with the dead Sadomasochist. Her spiritual equivalent, to give it a name, had been measured, coffined and covered by Nick Malacoda. As material for anagogy (Greek g if you don't mind) the worms were welcome to her.

What was left was just a fine strapping lump of a girl or woman, theatre nurse in *Yellow* from the neck down, bursting with Lebensgeist at every suture, itching to be taken at her—very much so to speak—face value, and by force for preference.

Now it so happened that these two processes, a kind of marginal metabolism possibly you might call them, independent but of common origin, constructive in the case of the man, destructive and delightfully excrementitious in the case of the woman, culminated simultaneously on the drive back from the grave.

Hairy stopped the car.

---

1. What a competent poet once called the *bella menzogna*.

"Step down" he said to the parson, "I don't like you."

The parson appealed mutely to the Smeraldina. She had nothing whatever to say to him. Never again in this life would she occupy any position more partisan than that of a comfortably covered bone of contention, her mind was made up.

"Bill the executors" said Hairy "and out you hop."

The parson did as Hairy bid. He felt miserable. They did not even give him a chance to cock up the other cheek. He racked his brains for coals of fire. As the car began to move away he jumped up nimbly on the running-board, stooped forward in the lee of the windscreen and began, heedless of punctuation, in a lamentable voice:

". . . no more death neither sorrow nor crying neither shall there be any more—"

At which point, the car beginning to sway in a perilous manner, he was obliged to break off in order to save his life. He stood in the road, far from home, and hoped, without exactly making a prayer out of it, that they might be forgiven.

"Wouldn't he give you the sick" said Hairy "with his Noo Gefoozleum."

Little remains to be told. On their return they found the house in flames, the home to which Belacqua had brought three brides a raging furnace. It transpired that during their absence something had snapped in the brain of the gardener, who had ravished the servant girl and then set the premises on fire. He had neither given himself up nor tried to escape, he had shut himself up in the tool-shed and awaited arrest.

"Ravished Mary Ann" exclaimed the Smeraldina.

"So she deposes" said a high official of the Civic Guard. "It was she who raised the alarm."

Hairy looked this dignitary up and down.

"I don't see your fiddle" he said.

"Where is the girl?" asked the Smeraldina.

"She has gone home to her Mother" answered the high official.

She tried him again.

"Where is the gardener?"

But he had been expecting this question.

"He resisted arrest, he has been taken to hospital."

"Where are the heroes of the fire-brigade" said Hairy, entering into the spirit of the thing, "the boys of the old brigade, the Tara Street Cossacks? May we expect them today? They would act as a kind of antiphlogistic."

This Hairy was a revelation to the Smeraldina, he was indeed hairy.

"They are unavoidably detained" replied the Commissioner.

"Take me away" said the Smeraldina firmly, "the house is insured."

The Commissioner made a mental note of this suspicious circumstance.

Poor Smeraldina! She was more than ever at a loose end now.

"Why not come with me" said Hairy, "now that all this has happened, and be my love?"

"I don't understand" said the Smeraldina.

Hairy explained exactly what he meant. In the heart of the purple mountains the car conked out. Hairy had exhausted his petrol supply. But nothing daunted he continued to explain. He explained and explained, the same old thing over and over again. At last he too conked out.

"Perhaps after all" murmured the Smeraldina "this is what darling Bel would wish."

"What is?" cried Hairy aghast.

She handed him back his explanation in a nutshell.

"Darling Smerry!" cried Hairy. "What else?"

They fell silent. Hairy, gazing straight before him through the anti-dazzle windscreen, whose effect by the way on the mountains was to make them look not unlike the picture by Paul Henry, was inclined to think that it was about time they started to make a move. But this seemed out of the question. The Smeraldina, far far away with the corpse and her own spiritual equivalent in the bone-yard by the sea, was dwelling at length on how she would shortly gratify the former, even as it, while still unfinished, had that of Lucy,[1] and blot the latter for ever from her memory.

"We must think of an inscription" she said.

"He did mention one to me once" said Hairy, "now that I come to think of it, that he would have endorsed, but I can't recall it."

---

1. A most foully false analogy.

The groundsman stood deep in thought. What with the company of headstones sighing and gleaming like bones, the moon on the job, the sea tossing in her dreams and panting, and the hills observing their Attic vigil in the background, he was at a loss to determine off-hand whether the scene was of the kind that is termed romantic or whether it should not with more justice be deemed classical. Both elements were present, that was indisputable. Perhaps classico-romantic would be the fairest estimate. A classico-romantic scene.

Personally he felt calm and wistful. A classico-romantic working-man therefore. The words of the rose to the rose floated up in his mind: "No gardener has died, comma, within rosaceous memory." He sang a little song, he drank his bottle of stout, he dashed away a tear, he made himself comfortable.

So it goes in the world.

THE END

Stories, Texts, Novellas

First Love

I associate, rightly or wrongly, my marriage with the death of my father, in time. That other links exist, on other planes, between these two affairs, is not impossible. I have enough trouble as it is in trying to say what I think I know.

I visited, not so long ago, my father's grave, that I do know, and noted the date of his death, of his death alone, for that of his birth had no interest for me, on that particular day. I set out in the morning and was back by night, having lunched lightly in the graveyard. But some days later, wishing to know his age at death, I had to return to the grave, to note the date of his birth. These two limiting dates I then jotted down on a piece of paper, which I now carry about with me. I am thus in a position to affirm that I must have been about twenty-five at the time of my marriage. For the date of my own birth, I repeat, my own birth, I have never forgotten, I never had to note it down, it remains graven in my memory, the year at least, in figures that life will not easily erase. The day itself comes back to me, when I put my mind to it, and I often celebrate it, after my fashion, I don't say each time it comes back, for it comes back too often, but often.

Personally I have no bone to pick with graveyards, I take the air there willingly, perhaps more willingly than elsewhere, when take the air I must. The smell of corpses, distinctly perceptible under those of grass and humus mingled, I do not find unpleasant, a trifle on the sweet side perhaps, a trifle heady, but how infinitely preferable to what the living emit, their feet, teeth, armpits, arses, sticky foreskins and frustrated ovules. And when my father's remains join in, however modestly, I can almost shed a tear. The living wash in vain, in vain perfume themselves, they stink. Yes, as a place for an outing, when out I must, leave me my grave-yards and keep—you—to your public parks and beauty-spots. My sand-wich, my banana, taste sweeter when I'm sitting on a tomb, and when the time comes to piss again, as it so often does, I have my pick. Or I wander, hands clasped behind my back, among the slabs, the flat, the leaning and the upright, culling the inscriptions. Of these I never weary, there are always three or four of such drollery that I have to hold on to the cross, or the stele, or the angel, so as not to fall. Mine I composed long since and am still pleased with it, tolerably pleased. My other writings are no sooner dry than they revolt me, but my epitaph still meets with my approval. There is little chance unfortunately of its ever being reared above the skull that conceived it, unless the State takes up the matter. But to be unearthed I must first be found, and I greatly fear those gentlemen will have as much trouble finding me dead as alive. So I hasten to record it here and now, while there is yet time:

> Hereunder lies the above who up below
> So hourly died that he survived till now.

The second and last or rather latter line limps a little perhaps, but that is no great matter, I'll be forgiven more than that when I'm forgotten. Then with a little luck you hit on a genuine interment, with real live mourners and the odd relict rearing to throw herself into the pit. And nearly always that charming business with the dust, though in my expe-rience there is nothing less dusty than holes of this type, verging on muck for the most part, nor anything particularly powdery about the deceased, unless he happen to have died, or she, by fire. No matter, their little gimmick with the dust is charming. But my father's yard was not among my favourite. To begin with it was too remote, way out in the wilds of the country on the side of a hill, and too small, far too small, to go on with. Indeed it was almost full, a few more widows and they'd

be turning them away. I infinitely preferred Ohlsdorf, particularly the
Linne section, on Prussian soil, with its nine hundred acres of corpses
packed tight, though I knew no one there, except by reputation the wild
animal collector Hagenbeck. A lion, if I remember right, is carved on
his monument, death must have had for Hagenbeck the countenance of
a lion. Coaches ply to and fro, crammed with widows, widowers, orphans
and the like. Groves, rottoes, artificial lakes with swans, purvey consola-
tion to the inconsolable. It was December, I had never felt so cold, the
eel soup lay heavy on my stomach, I was afraid I'd die, I turned aside to
vomit, I envied them.

But to pass on to less melancholy matters, on my father's death I
had to leave the house. It was he who wanted me in the house. He was a
strange man. One day he said, Leave him alone, he's not disturbing any-
one. He didn't know I was listening. This was a view he must have often
voiced, but the other times I wasn't by. They would never let me see his
will, they simply said he had left me such a sum. I believed then, and still
believe, that he had stipulated in his will for me to be left the room I had
occupied in his lifetime and for food to be brought me there, as hith-
erto. He may even have given this the force of condition precedent. Pre-
sumably he liked to feel me under his roof, otherwise he would not have
opposed my eviction. Perhaps he merely pitied me. But somehow I think
not. He should have left me the entire house, then I'd have been all right,
the others too for that matter, I'd have summoned them and said, Stay,
stay by all means, your home is here. Yes, he was properly had, my poor
father, if his purpose was really to go on protecting me from beyond the
tomb. With regard to the money it is only fair to say they gave it to me
without delay, on the very day following the inhumation. Perhaps they
were legally bound to. I said to them, Keep this money and let me live on
here, in my room, as in Papa's lifetime. I added, God rest his soul, in the
hope of melting them. But they refused. I offered to place myself at their
disposal, a few hours every day, for the little odd maintenance jobs every
dwelling requires, if it is not to crumble away. Pottering is still just possi-
ble, I don't know why. I proposed in particular to look after the hothouse.
There I would have gladly whiled away the hours, in the heat, tending

the tomatoes, hyacinths, pinks and seedlings. My father and I alone, in that household, understood tomatoes. But they refused. One day, on my return from stool, I found my room locked and my belongings in a heap before the door. This will give you some idea how constipated I was, at this juncture. It was, I am now convinced, anxiety constipation. But was I genuinely constipated? Somehow I think not. Softly, softly. And yet I must have been, for how otherwise account for those long, those cruel sessions in the necessary house? At such times I never read, any more than at other times, never gave way to revery or meditation, just gazed dully at the almanac hanging from a nail before my eyes, with its chromo of a bearded stripling in the midst of sheep, Jesus no doubt, parted the cheeks with both hands and strained, heave! ho! heave! ho!, with the motions of one tugging at the oar, and only one thought in my mind, to be back in my room and flat on my back again. What can that have been but constipation? Or am I confusing it with the diarrhoea? It's all a muddle in my head, graves and nuptials and the different varieties of motion. Of my scanty belongings they had made a little heap, on the floor, against the door. I can still see that little heap, in the kind of recess full of shadow between the landing and my room. It was in this narrow space, guarded on three sides only, that I had to change, I mean exchange my dressing-gown and nightgown for my travelling costume, I mean shoes, socks, trousers, shirt, coat, greatcoat and hat, I can think of nothing else. I tried other doors, turning the knobs and pushing, or pulling, before I left the house, but none yielded. I think if I'd found one open I'd have barricaded myself in the room, they would have had to gas me out. I felt the house crammed as usual, the usual pack, but saw no one. I imagined them in their various rooms, all bolts drawn, every sense on the alert. Then the rush to the window, each holding back a little, hidden by the curtain, at the sound of the street door closing behind me, I should have left it open. Then the doors fly open and out they pour, men, women and children, and the voices, the sighs, the smiles, the hands, the keys in the hands, the blessed relief, the precautions rehearsed, if this then that, but if that then this, all clear and joy in every heart, come let's eat, the fumigation can wait. All imagination to be sure, I was already on my way, things may have passed quite differently, but who cares how things pass, provided they pass. All those lips that had kissed me, those hearts that had loved me (it is with the heart one loves, is it not, or am I confusing it with something else?), those hands that had played with mine and those minds that had almost made their own of me! Humans are truly strange. Poor Papa, a nice mug he must have felt that day if he could see me, see us, a nice mug on my account I mean. Unless in his great disembodied wisdom he saw further than his son whose corpse was not yet quite up to scratch.

But to pass on to less melancholy matters, the name of the woman with whom I was soon to be united was Lulu. So at least she assured me and I can't see what interest she could have had in lying to me, on this score. Of course one can never tell. She also disclosed her family name, but I've forgotten it. I should have made a note of it, on a piece of paper, I hate forgetting a proper name. I met her on a bench, on the bank of the canal, one of the canals, for our town boasts two, though I never knew which was which. It was a well situated bench, backed by a mound of solid earth and garbage, so that my rear was covered. My flanks too, partially, thanks to a pair of venerable trees, more than venerable, dead, at either end of the bench. It was no doubt these trees one fine day, aripple with all their foliage, that had sown the idea of a bench, in someone's fancy. To the fore, a few yards away, flowed the canal, if canals flow, don't ask me, so that from that quarter too the risk of surprise was small. And yet she surprised me. I lay stretched out, the night being warm, gazing up through the bare boughs interlocking high above me, where the trees clung together for support, and through the drifting cloud, at a patch of starry sky as it came and went. Shove up, she said. My first movement was to go, but my fatigue, and my having nowhere to go, dissuaded me from acting on it. So I drew back my feet a little way and she sat. Nothing more passed between us that evening and she soon took herself off, without another word. All she had done was sing, *sotto voce*, as to herself, and without the words fortunately, some old folk songs, and so disjointedly, skipping from one to another and finishing none, that even I found it strange. The voice, though out of tune, was not unpleasant. It breathed of a soul too soon wearied ever to conclude, that perhaps least arse-aching soul of all. The bench itself was soon more than she could bear and as for me, one look had been enough for her. Whereas in reality she was a most tenacious woman. She came back next day and the day after and all went off more or less as before. Perhaps a few words were exchanged. The next day it was raining and I felt in security. Wrong again. I asked her if she was resolved to disturb me every evening. I disturb you? she said. I felt her eyes on me. They can't have seen much, two eyelids at the most, with a hint of nose and brow, darkly, because of the dark. I thought we were easy, she said. You disturb me, I said, I can't stretch out with you there. The collar of my greatcoat was over my mouth and yet she heard me. Must you stretch out? she said. The mistake one makes is to speak to people. You have only to put your feet on my knees, she said. I didn't wait to be asked twice, under my miserable calves I felt her fat thighs. She began stroking my ankles. I considered kicking her in the cunt. You speak to people about stretching out and they immediately see a body at full length. What mattered to me in my dispeopled kingdom, that in regard to which the disposition of my carcass was the merest and most futile of accidents, was supineness in the mind, the dulling of the self and of that residue of execrable frippery known as the non-self and even the world, for short. But man is still today, at the age of twenty-five, at the mercy of an erection, physically too, from time to time, it's the common lot, even I was not immune, if that may be called an erection. It did not escape her naturally, women smell a rigid phallus ten miles away and wonder, How on earth did he spot me from there? One is no longer oneself, on such occasions, and it is painful to be no longer oneself, even more painful if possible than when one is. For when one is one knows what to do to be less so, whereas when one is not one is any old one irredeemably. What goes by the name of love is banishment, with now and then a postcard from the homeland, such is my considered opinion, this evening. When she had finished and my self been resumed, mine own, the mitigable, with the help of a brief torpor, it was alone. I sometimes wonder if that is not all invention, if in reality things did not take quite a different course, one I had no choice but to forget. And yet her image remains bound, for me, to that of the bench, not the bench by day, nor yet the bench by night, but the bench at evening, in such sort that to speak of the bench, as it appeared to me at evening, is to speak of her, for me. That proves nothing, but there is nothing I wish to prove. On the subject of the bench by day no words need be wasted, it never knew me, gone before morning and never back till dusk. Yes, in the daytime I foraged for food and marked down likely cover. Were you to enquire, as undoubtedly you itch, what I had done with the money my father had left me, the answer would be I had done nothing with it but leave it lie in my pocket. For I knew I would not be always young, and that summer does not last for ever either, nor even autumn, my mean soul told me so. In the end I told her I'd had enough. She disturbed me exceedingly, even absent. Indeed she still disturbs me, but no worse now than the rest. And it matters nothing to me now, to be disturbed, or so little, what does it mean, disturbed, and what would I do with myself if I wasn't? Yes, I've changed my system, it's the winning one at last, for the ninth or tenth time, not to mention not long now, not long till curtain down, on disturbers and disturbed, no more tattle about that, all that, her and the others, the shitball and heaven's high halls. So you don't want me to come any more, she said. It's incredible the way they repeat what you've just said to them, as if they risked faggot and fire in believing their ears. I told her to come just the odd time. I didn't understand women at that period. I still don't for that matter. Nor men either. Nor animals either. What I understand best, which is not saying much, are my pains. I think them through daily, it doesn't take long, thought moves so fast, but they are not only in my thought, not all. Yes, there are moments, particularly in the afternoon, when I go all syncretist, à la Reinhold. What equilibrium! But even them, my pains, I understand ill. That must come from my not being all pain and nothing else. There's the rub. Then they recede, or I, till they fill me with amaze and wonder, seen from a better planet. Not often, but I ask no more. Catch-cony life! To be nothing but pain, how that would simplify matters! Omnidolent! Impious dream. I'll tell them to you some day none the less, if I think of it, if I can, my strange pains, in detail, distinguishing between the different kinds, for the sake of clarity, those of the mind, those of the heart or emotional conative, those of the soul (none prettier than these) and finally those of the frame proper, first the inner or latent, then those affecting the surface, beginning with the hair and scalp and moving methodically down, without haste, all the way down to the feet beloved of the corn, the cramp, the kibe, the bunion, the hammer toe, the nail ingrown, the fallen arch, the common blain, the club foot, duck foot, goose foot, pigeon foot, flat foot, trench foot and other curiosities. And I'll tell by the same token, for those kind enough to listen, in accordance with a system whose inventor I forget, of those instants when, neither drugged, nor drunk, nor in ecstasy, one feels nothing. Next of course she desired to know what I meant by the odd time, that's what you get for opening your mouth. Once a week? Once in ten days? Once a fortnight? I replied less often, far less often, less often to the point of no more if she could, and if she could not the least often possible. And the next day (what is more) I abandoned the bench, less I must confess on her account than on its, for the site no longer answered my requirements, modest though they were, now that the air was beginning to strike chill, and for other reasons better not wasted on cunts like you, and took refuge in a deserted cowshed marked on one of my forays. It stood in the corner of a field richer on the surface in nettles than in grass and in mud than in nettles, but whose subsoil was perhaps possessed of exceptional qualities. It was in this byre, littered with dry and hollow cowclaps subsiding with a sigh at the poke of my finger, that for the first time in my life, and I would not hesitate to say the last if I had not to husband my cyanide, I had to contend with a feeling which gradually assumed, to my dismay, the dread name of love. What constitutes the charm of our country, apart of course from its scant population, and this without help of the meanest contraceptive, is that all is derelict, with the sole exception of history's ancient faeces. These are ardently sought after, stuffed and carried in procession. Wherever nauseated time has dropped a nice fat turd you will find our patriots, sniffing it up on all fours, their faces on fire. Elysium of the roofless. Hence my happiness at last. Lie down, all seems to say, lie down and stay down. I see no connexion between these remarks. But that one exists, and even more than one, I have little doubt, for my part. But what? Which? Yes, I loved her, it's the name I gave, still give alas, to what I was doing then. I had nothing to go by, having never loved before, but of course had heard of the thing, at home, in school, in brothel and at church, and read romances, in prose and verse, under the guidance of my tutor, in six or seven languages, both dead and living, in which it was handled at length. I was therefore in a position, in spite of all, to put a label on what I was about when I found myself inscribing the letters of Lulu in an old heifer pat or flat on my face in the mud under the moon trying to tear up the nettles by the roots. They were giant nettles, some full three foot high, to tear them up assuaged my pain, and yet it's not like me to do that to weeds, on the contrary, I'd smother them in manure if I had any. Flowers are a different matter. Love brings out the worst in man and no error. But what kind of love was this, exactly? Love-passion? Somehow I think not. That's the priapic one, is it not? Or is this a different variety? There are so many, are there not? All equally if not more delicious, are they not? Platonic love, for example, there's another just occurs to me. It's disinterested. Perhaps I loved her with a platonic love? But somehow I think not. Would I have been tracing her name in old cowshit if my love had been pure and disinterested? And with my devil's finger into the bargain, which I then sucked. Come now! My thoughts were all of Lulu, if that doesn't give you some idea nothing will. Anyhow I'm sick and tired of this name Lulu, I'll give her another, more like her, Anna for example, it's not more like her but no matter. I thought of Anna then, I who had learnt to think of nothing, nothing except my pains, a quick think through, and of what steps to take not to perish off-hand of hunger, or cold, or shame, but never on any account of living beings as such (I wonder what that means) whatever I may have said, or may still say, to the contrary or otherwise, on this subject. But I have always spoken, no doubt always shall, of things that never existed, or that existed if you insist, no doubt always will, but not with the existence I ascribe to them. Kepis, for example, exist beyond a doubt, indeed there is little hope of their ever disappearing, but personally I never wore a kepi. I wrote somewhere, They gave me . . . a hat. Now the truth is they never gave me a hat, I have always had my own hat, the one my father gave me, and I have never had any other hat than that hat. I may add it has followed me to the grave. I thought of

Anna then, long long sessions, twenty minutes, twenty-five minutes and even as long as half an hour daily. I obtain these figures by the addition of other, lesser figures. That must have been my way of loving. Are we to infer from this I loved her with that intellectual love which drew from me such drivel, in another place? Somehow I think not. For had my love been of this kind would I have stooped to inscribe the letters of Anna in time's forgotten cowplats? To divellicate urtica *plenis manibus*? And felt, under my tossing head, her thighs to bounce like so many demon bolsters? Come now! In order to put an end, to try and put an end, to this plight, I returned one evening to the bench, at the hour she had used to join me there. There was no sign of her and I waited in vain. It was December already, if not January, and the cold was seasonable, that is to say reasonable, like all that is seasonable. But one is the hour of the dial, and another that of changing air and sky, and another yet again the heart's. To this thought, once back in the straw, I owed an excellent night. The next day I was earlier to the bench, much earlier, night having barely fallen, winter night, and yet too late, for she was there already, on the bench, under the boughs tinkling with rime, her back to the frosted mound, facing the icy water. I told you she was a highly tenacious woman. I felt nothing. What interest could she have in pursuing me thus? I asked her, without sitting down, stumping to and fro. The cold had embossed the path. She replied she didn't know. What could she see in me, would she kindly tell me that at least, if she could. She replied she couldn't. She seemed warmly clad, her hands buried in a muff. As I looked at this muff, I remember, tears came to my eyes. And yet I forget what colour it was. The state I was in then! I have always wept freely, without the least benefit to myself, till recently. If I had to weep this minute I could squeeze till I was blue, I'm convinced not a drop would fall. The state I am in now! It was things made me weep. And yet I felt no sorrow. When I found myself in tears for no apparent reason it meant I had caught sight of something unbeknownst. So I wonder if it was really the muff that evening, if it was not rather the path, so iron hard and bossy as perhaps to feel like cobbles to my tread, or some other thing, some chance thing glimpsed below the threshold, that so unmanned me. As for her, I might as well never have laid eyes on her before. She sat all huddled and muffled up, her head sunk, the muff with her hands in her lap, her legs pressed tight together, her heels clear of the ground. Shapeless, ageless, almost lifeless, it might have been anything or anyone, an old woman or a little girl. And the way she kept on saying, I don't know, I can't. I alone did not know and could not. Is it on my account you came? I said. She managed yes to that. Well here I am, I said. And I? Had I not come on hers? Here we are, I said. I sat down beside her but sprang up again immediately as though scalded. I longed to be gone, to know if it was over. But before going, to be on the safe side, I asked her to sing me a song. I thought at first she was going to refuse, I mean simply not sing, but no, after a moment she began to sing and sang for some time, all the time the same song it seemed to me, without change of attitude. I did not know the song, I had never heard it before and shall never hear it again. It had something to do with lemon trees, or orange trees, I forget, that is all I remember, and for me that is no mean feat, to remember it had something to do with lemon trees, or orange trees, I forget, for of all the other songs I have ever heard in my life, and I have heard plenty, it being apparently impossible, physically impossible short of being deaf, to get through this world, even my way, without hearing singing, I have retained nothing, not a word, not a note, or so few words, so few notes, that, that what, that nothing, this sentence has gone on long enough. Then I started to go and as I went I heard her singing another song, or perhaps more verses of the same, fainter and fainter the further I went, then no more, either because she had come to an end or because I was gone too far to hear her. To have to harbour such a doubt was something I preferred to avoid, at that period. I lived of course in doubt, on doubt, but such trivial doubts as this, purely somatic as some say, were best cleared up without delay, they could nag at me like gnats for weeks on end. So I retraced my steps a little way and stopped. At first I heard nothing, then the voice again, but only just, so faintly did it carry. First I didn't hear it, then I did, I must therefore have begun hearing it, at a certain point, but no, there was no beginning, the sound emerged so softly from the silence and so resembled it. When the voice ceased at last I approached a little nearer, to make sure it had really ceased and not merely been lowered. Then in despair, saying, No knowing, no knowing, short of being beside her, bent over her, I turned on my heel and went, for good, full of doubt. But some weeks later, even more dead than alive than usual, I returned to the bench, for the fourth or fifth time since I had abandoned it, at roughly the same hour, I mean roughly the same sky, no, I don't mean that either, for it's always the same sky and never the same sky, what words are there for that, none I know, period. She wasn't there, then suddenly she was, I don't know how, I didn't see her come, nor hear her, all ears and eyes though I was. Let us say it was raining, nothing like a change, if only of weather. She had her umbrella up, naturally, what an outfit. I asked if she came every evening. No, she said, just the odd time. The bench was soaking wet, we paced up and down, not daring to sit. I took her arm, out of curiosity, to see if it would give me pleasure, it gave me none, I let it go. But why these particulars? To put off the evil hour. I saw her face a little clearer, it seemed normal to me, a face like millions of others. The eyes were crooked, but I didn't know that till later. It looked neither young nor old, the face, as though stranded between the vernal and the sere. Such ambiguity I found difficult to bear, at that period. As to whether it was beautiful, the face, or had once been beautiful, or could conceivably become beautiful, I confess I could form no opinion. I had seen faces in photographs I might have found beautiful had I known even vaguely in what beauty was supposed to consist. And my father's face, on his death-bolster, had seemed to hint at some form of aesthetics relevant to man. But the faces of the living, all grimace and flush, can they be described as objects? I admired in spite of the dark, in spite of my fluster, the way still or scarcely flowing water reaches up, as though athirst, to that falling from the sky. She asked if I would like her to sing something. I replied no, I would like her to say something. I thought she would say she had nothing to say, it would have been like her, and so was agreeably surprised when she said she had a room, most agreeably surprised, though I suspected as much. Who has not a room? Ah I hear the clamour. I have two rooms, she said. Just how many rooms do you have? I said. She said she had two rooms and a kitchen. The premises were expanding steadily, given time she would remember a bathroom.

Is it two rooms I heard you say? I said. Yes, she said. Adjacent? I said. At last conversation worthy of the name. Separated by the kitchen, she said. I asked her why she had not told me before. I must have been beside myself, at this period. I did not feel easy when I was with her, but at least free to think of something else than her, of the old trusty things, and so little by little, as down steps towards a deep, of nothing. And I knew that away from her I would forfeit this freedom.

There were in fact two rooms, separated by a kitchen, she had not lied to me. She said I should have fetched my things. I explained I had no things. It was at the top of an old house, with a view of the mountains for those who cared. She lit an oil-lamp. You have no current? I said. No, she said, but I have running water and gas. Ha, I said, you have gas. She began to undress. When at their wit's end they undress, no doubt the wisest course. She took off everything, with a slowness fit to enflame an elephant, except her stockings, calculated presumably to bring my concupiscence to the boil. It was then I noticed the squint. Fortunately she was not the first naked woman to have crossed my path, so I could stay, I knew she would not explode. I asked to see the other room which I had not yet seen. If I had seen it already I would have asked to see it again. Will you not undress? she said. Oh you know, I said, I seldom undress. It was the truth, I was never one to undress indiscriminately. I often took off my boots when I went to bed, I mean when I composed myself (composed!) to sleep, not to mention this or that outer garment according to the outer temperature. She was therefore obliged, out of common savoir faire, to throw on a wrap and light me the way. We went via the kitchen. We could just as well have gone via the corridor, as I realized later, but we went via the kitchen, I don't know why, perhaps it was the shortest way. I surveyed the room with horror. Such density of furniture defeats imagination. Not a doubt, I must have seen that room somewhere. What's this? I cried. The parlour, she said. The parlour! I began putting out the furniture through the door to the corridor. She watched, in sorrow I suppose, but not necessarily. She asked me what I was doing. She can't have expected an answer. I put it out piece by piece, and even two at a time, and stacked it all up in the corridor, against the outer wall. They were hundreds of pieces, large and small, in the end they blocked the door, making egress impossible, and *a fortiori* ingress, to and from the corridor. The door could be opened and closed, since it opened inwards, but had become impassable. To put it wildly. At least take off your hat, she said. I'll treat of my hat some other time perhaps. Finally the room was empty but for a sofa and some shelves fixed to the wall. The former I dragged to the back of the room, near the door, and next day took down the latter and put them out, in the corridor, with the rest. As I was taking them down, strange memory, I heard the word fibrome, or brone, I don't know which, never knew, never knew what it meant and never had the curiosity to find out. The things one recalls! And records! When all was in order at last I dropped on the sofa. She had not raised her little finger to help me. I'll get sheets and blankets, she said. But I wouldn't hear of sheets. You couldn't draw the curtain? I said. The window was frosted over. The effect was not white, because of the night, but faintly luminous none the less. This faint cold sheen, though I lay with my feet towards the door, was more than I could bear. I suddenly rose and changed the position of the sofa, that is to say turned it round so that the back, hitherto against the wall, was now on the outside and consequently the front, or way in, on the inside. Then I climbed back, like a dog into its basket. I'll leave you the lamp, she said, but I begged her to take it with her. And suppose you need something in the night, she said. She was going to start quibbling again, I could feel it. Do you know where the convenience is? she said. She was right, I was forgetting. To relieve oneself in bed is enjoyable at the time, but soon a source of discomfort. Give me a chamberpot, I said. But she did not possess one. I have a close-stool of sorts, she said. I saw the grandmother on it, sitting up very stiff and grand, having just purchased it, pardon, picked it up, at a charity sale, or perhaps won it in a raffle, a period piece, and now trying it out, doing her best rather, almost wishing someone could see her. That's the idea, procrastinate. Any old recipient, I said, I don't have the flux. She came back with a kind of saucepan, not a true saucepan for it had no handle, it was oval in shape with two lugs and a lid. My stewpan, she said. I don't need the lid, I said. You don't need the lid? she said. If I had said I needed the lid she would have said, You need the lid? I drew this utensil down under the blanket, I like something in my hand when sleeping, it reassures me, and my hat was still wringing. I turned to the wall. She caught up the lamp off the mantelpiece where she had set it down, that's the idea, every particular, it flung her waving shadow over me, I thought she was off, but no, she came stooping down towards me over the sofa back. All family possessions, she said. I in her shoes would have tiptoed away, but not she, not a stir. Already my love was waning, that was all that mattered. Yes, already I felt better, soon I'd be up to the slow descents again, the long submersions, so long denied me through her fault. And I had only just moved in! Try and put me out now, I said. I seemed not to grasp the meaning of these words, nor even hear the brief sound they made, till some seconds after having uttered them. I was so unused to speech that my mouth would sometimes open, of its own accord, and void some phrase or phrases, grammatically unexceptionable but entirely devoid if not of meaning, for on close inspection they would reveal one, and even several, at least of foundation. But I heard each word no sooner spoken. Never had my voice taken so long to reach me as on this occasion. I turned over on my back to see what was going on. She was smiling. A little later she went away, taking the lamp with her. I heard her steps in the kitchen and then the door of her room close behind her. Why behind her? I was alone at last, in the dark at last. Enough about that. I thought I was all set for a good night, in spite of the strange surroundings, but no, my night was most agitated. I woke next morning quite spent, my clothes in disorder, the blanket likewise, and Anna beside me, naked naturally. One shudders to think of her exertions. I still had the stewpan in my grasp. It had not served. I looked at my member. If only it could have spoken! Enough about that. It was my night of love.

Gradually I settled down, in this house. She brought my meals at the appointed hours, looked in now and then to see if all was well and make sure I needed nothing, emptied the stewpan once a day and did out the room once a month. She could not always resist the temptation to speak to me, but on the whole gave me no cause to complain. Sometimes I heard her singing in her room, the song traversed her door, then the kitchen, then my door, and in this way won to me, faint but indisputable. Unless it travelled by the corridor. This did not greatly incommode me, this occasional sound of singing. One day I asked her to bring me a hyacinth, live, in a pot. She brought it and put it on the mantelpiece, now the only place in my room to put things, unless you put them on the floor. Not a day passed without my looking at it. At first all went well, it even put forth a bloom or two, then it gave up and was soon no more than a limp stem hung with limp leaves. The bulb, half clear of the clay as though in search of oxygen, smelt foul. She wanted to remove it, but I told her to leave it. She wanted to get me another, but I told her I didn't want another. I was more seriously disturbed by other sounds, stifled giggles and groans, which filled the dwelling at certain hours of the night, and even of the day. I had given up thinking of her, quite given up, but still I needed silence, to live my life. In vain I tried to listen to such reasonings as that air is made to carry the clamours of the world, including inevitably much groan and giggle, I obtained no relief. I couldn't make out if it was always the same gent or more than one. Lovers' groans are so alike, and lovers' giggles. I had such horror then of these paltry perplexities that I always fell into the same error, that of seeking to clear them up. It took me a long time, my lifetime so to speak, to realize that the colour of an eye half seen, or the source of some distant sound, are closer to Giudecca in the hell of unknowing than the existence of God, or the origins of protoplasm, or the existence of self, and even less worthy than these to occupy the wise. It's a bit much, a lifetime, to achieve this consoling conclusion, it doesn't leave you much time to profit by it. So a fat lot of help it was when, having put the question to her, I was told they were clients she received in rotation. I could obviously have got up and gone to look through the keyhole. But what can you see, I ask you, through holes the likes of those? So you live by prostitution, I said. We live by prostitution, she said. You couldn't ask them to make less noise? I said, as if I believed her. I added, Or a different kind of noise. They can't help but yap and yelp, she said. I'll have to leave, I said. She found some old hangings in the family junk and hung them before our doors, hers and mine. I asked her if it would not be possible, now and then, to have a parsnip. A parsnip! she cried, as if I had asked for a dish of sucking Jew. I reminded her that the parsnip season was fast drawing to a close and that if, before it finally got there, she could feed me nothing but parsnips I'd be grateful. I like parsnips because they taste like violets and violets because they smell like parsnips. Were there no parsnips on earth violets would leave me cold and if violets did not exist I would care as little for parsnips as I do for turnips, or radishes. And even in the present state of their flora, I mean on this planet where parsnips and violets contrive to coexist, I could do without both with the utmost ease, the uttermost ease. One day she had the impudence to announce she was with child, and four or five months gone into the bargain, by me of all people! She offered me a side view of her belly. She even undressed, no doubt to prove she wasn't hiding a cushion under her skirt, and then of course for the pure plea-sure of undressing. Perhaps it's mere wind, I said, by way of consolation. She gazed at me with her big eyes whose colour I forget, with one big eye rather, for the other seemed riveted on the remains of the hyacinth. The more naked she was the more cross-eyed. Look, she said, stooping over her breasts, the haloes are darkening already. I summoned up my remaining strength and said, Abort, abort, and they'll blush like new. She had drawn back the curtain for a clear view of all her rotundities. I saw the mountain, impassible, cavernous, secret, where from morning to night I'd hear nothing but the wind, the curlews, the clink like distant silver of the stone-cutters' hammers. I'd come out in the daytime to the heather and gorse, all warmth and scent, and watch at night the distant city lights, if I chose, and the other lights, the lighthouses and lightships my father had named for me, when I was small, and whose names I could find again, in my memory, if I chose, that I knew. From that day forth things went from bad to worse, to worse and worse. Not that she neglected me, she could never have neglected me enough, but the way she kept plaguing me with *our* child, exhibiting her belly and breasts and saying it was due any moment, she could feel it lepping already. If it's lepping, I said, it's not mine. I might have been worse off than I was, in that house, that was cer-tain, it fell short of my ideal naturally, but I wasn't blind to its advantages. I hesitated to leave, the leaves were falling already, I dreaded the winter.

One should not dread the winter, it too has its bounties, the snow gives warmth and deadens the tumult and its pale days are soon over. But I did not yet know, at that time, how tender the earth can be for those who have only her and how many graves in her giving, for the living. What finished me was the birth. It woke me up. What that infant must have been going through! I fancy she had a woman with her, I seemed to hear steps in the kitchen, on and off. It went to my heart to leave a house without being put out. I crept out over the back of the sofa, put on my coat, greatcoat and hat, I can think of nothing else, laced up my boots and opened the door to the corridor. A mass of junk barred my way, but I scrabbled and barged my way through it in the end, regardless of the clatter. I used the word marriage, it was a kind of union in spite of all. Precautions would have been superfluous, there was no competing with those cries. It must have been her first. They pursued me down the stairs and out into the street. I stopped before the house door and listened. I could still hear them. If I had not known there was crying in the house I might not have heard them. But knowing it I did. I was not sure where I was. I looked among the stars and constellations for the Wains, but could not find them. And yet they must have been there. My father was the first to show them to me. He had shown me others, but alone, without him beside me, I could never find any but the Wains. I began playing with the cries, a little in the same way as I had played with the song, on, back, on, back, if that may be called playing. As long as I kept walking I didn't hear them, because of the footsteps. But as soon as I halted I heard them again, a little fainter each time, admittedly, but what does it matter, faint or loud, cry is cry, all that matters is that it should cease. For years I thought they would cease. Now I don't think so any more. I could have done with other loves perhaps. But there it is, either you love or you don't.

The Expelled

There were not many steps. I had counted them a thousand times, both going up and coming down, but the figure has gone from my mind. I have never known whether you should say one with your foot on the sidewalk, two with the following foot on the first step, and so on, or whether the sidewalk shouldn't count. At the top of the steps I fell foul of the same dilemma. In the other direction, I mean from top to bottom, it was the same, the word is not too strong. I did not know where to begin nor where to end, that's the truth of the matter. I arrived therefore at three totally different figures, without ever knowing which of them was right. And when I say that the figure has gone from my mind, I mean that none of the three figures is with me any more, in my mind. It is true that if I were to find, in my mind, where it is certainly to be found, one of these figures, I would find it and it alone, without being able to deduce from it the other two. And even were I to recover two, I would not know the third. No, I would have to find all three, in my mind, in order to know all three. Memories are killing. So you must not think of certain things, of those that are dear to you, or rather you must think of them, for if you don't there is the danger of finding them, in your mind, little by little. That is to say, you must think of them for a while, a good while, every day several times a day, until they sink forever in the mud. That's an order.

After all it is not the number of steps that matters. The important thing to remember is that there were not many, and that I have remembered.

Even for the child there were not many, compared to other steps he knew, from seeing them every day, from going up and coming down, and from playing on them at knuckle-bones and other games the very names of which he has forgotten. What must it have been like then for the man I had overgrown into?

The fall was therefore not serious. Even as I fell I heard the door slam, which brought me a little comfort, in the midst of my fall. For that meant they were not pursuing me down into the street, with a stick, to beat me in full view of the passers-by. For if that had been their intention they would not have shut the door, but left it open, so that the persons assembled in the vestibule might enjoy my chastisement and be edified. So, for once, they had confined themselves to throwing me out and no more about it. I had time, before coming to rest in the gutter, to conclude this piece of reasoning.

Under these circumstances nothing compelled me to get up immediately. I rested my elbow on the sidewalk, funny the things you remember, settled my ear in the cup of my hand and began to reflect on my situation, notwithstanding its familiarity. But the sound, fainter but unmistakable, of the door slammed again, roused me from my reverie, in which already a whole landscape was taking form, charming with hawthorn and wild roses, most dreamlike, and made me look up in alarm, my hands flat on the sidewalk and my legs braced for flight. But it was merely my hat sailing towards me through the air, rotating as it came. I caught it and put it on. They were most correct, according to their god. They could have kept this hat, but it was not theirs, it was mine, so they gave it back to me. But the spell was broken.

How describe this hat? And why? When my head had attained I shall not say its definitive but its maximum dimensions, my father said to me, Come, son, we are going to buy your hat, as though it had pre-existed from time immemorial in a pre-established place. He went straight to the hat. I personally had no say in the matter, nor had the hatter. I have often wondered if my father's purpose was not to humiliate me, if he was not jealous of me who was young and handsome, fresh at least, while he was already old and all bloated and purple. It was forbidden me, from that day forth, to go out bareheaded, my pretty brown hair blowing in the wind. Sometimes, in a secluded street, I took it off and held it in my hand, but trembling. I was required to brush it morning and evening. Boys my age with whom, in spite of everything, I was obliged to mix occasionally, mocked me. But I said to myself, It is not really the hat, they simply make merry at the hat because it is a little more glaring than the rest, for they have no finesse. I have always been amazed at my contemporaries' lack of finesse, I whose soul writhed from morning to night, in the mere quest of itself. But perhaps they were simply being kind, like those who make game of the hunchback's big nose. When my father died I could have got rid of this hat, there was nothing more to prevent me, but not I. But how describe it? Some other time, some other time.

I got up and set off. I forget how old I can have been. In what had just happened to me there was nothing in the least memorable. It was neither the cradle nor the grave of anything whatever. Or rather it resembled so many other cradles, so many other graves, that I'm lost. But I don't believe I exaggerate when I say that I was in the prime of life, what I believe is called the full possession of one's faculties. Ah yes, them I possessed all right. I crossed the street and turned back towards the house that had just ejected me, I who never turned back when leaving. How beautiful it was! There were geraniums in the windows. I have brooded over geraniums for years. Geraniums are artful customers, but in the end I was able to do what I liked with them. I have always greatly admired the door of this house, up on top of its little flight of steps. How describe it? It was a massive green door, encased in summer in a kind of green and white striped housing, with a hole for the thunderous wrought-iron knocker and a slit for letters, this latter closed to dust, flies and tits by a brass flap fitted with springs. So much for that description. The door was set between two pillars of the same colour, the bell being on that to the right. The curtains were in unexceptionable taste. Even the smoke rising from one of the chimney-pots seemed to spread and vanish in the air more sorrowful than the neighbours', and bluer. I looked up at the third and last floor and saw my window outrageously open. A thorough cleaning was in full swing. In a few hours they would close the window, draw the curtains and spray the whole place with disinfectant. I knew them. I would have gladly died in that house. In a sort of vision I saw the door open and my feet come out.

I wasn't afraid to look, for I knew they were not spying on me from behind the curtains, as they could have done if they had wished. But I knew them. They had all gone back into their dens and resumed their occupations.

And yet I had done them no harm.

I did not know the town very well, scene of my birth and of my first steps in this world, and then of all the others, so many that I thought all trace of me was lost, but I was wrong. I went out so little! Now and then I would go to the window, part the curtains and look out. But then I hastened back to the depths of the room, where the bed was. I felt ill at ease with all this air about me, lost before the confusion of innumerable prospects. But I still knew how to act at this period, when it was absolutely necessary. But first I raised my eyes to the sky, whence cometh our help, where there are no roads, where you wander freely, as in a desert, and where nothing obstructs your vision, wherever you turn your eyes, but the limits of vision itself. It gets monotonous in the end. When I was younger I thought life would be good in the middle of a plain, and I went to the Lüneburg heath. With the plain in my head I went to the heath. There were other heaths far less remote, but a voice kept saying to me, It's the Lüneburg heath you need. The element lüne must have had something to do with it. As it turned out the Lüneburg heath was most unsatisfactory, most unsatisfactory. I came home disappointed, and at the same time relieved. Yes, I don't know why, but I have never been disappointed, and I often was in the early days, without feeling at the same time, or a moment later, an undeniable relief.

I set off. What a gait. Stiffness of the lower limbs, as if nature had denied me knees, extraordinary splaying of the feet to right and left of the line of march. The trunk, on the contrary, as if by the effect of a compensatory mechanism, was as flabby as an old ragbag, tossing wildly to the unpredictable jolts of the pelvis. I have often tried to correct these defects, to stiffen my bust, flex my knees and walk with my feet in front of one another, for I had at least five or six, but it always ended in the same way, I mean with a loss of equilibrium, followed by a fall. A man must walk without paying attention to what he's doing, as he sighs, and when I walked without paying attention to what I was doing I walked in the way I have just described, and when I began to pay attention I managed a few steps of creditable execution and then fell. I decided therefore to be myself. This carriage is due, in my opinion, in part at least, to a certain leaning from which I have never been able to free myself completely and which left its stamp, as was only to be expected, on my impressionable years, those which govern the fabrication of character, I refer to the period which extends, as far as the eye can see, from the first totterings, behind a chair, to the third form, in which I concluded my studies. I had then the deplorable habit, having pissed in my trousers, or shat there, which I did fairly regularly early in the morning, about ten or half past ten, of persisting in going on and finishing my day as if nothing had happened. The very idea of changing my trousers, or of confiding in mother, who goodness knows asked nothing better than to help me, was unbearable, I don't know why, and till bedtime I dragged on with burning and stinking between my little thighs, or sticking to my bottom, the result of my incontinence. Whence this wary way of walking, with the legs stiff and wide apart, and this desperate rolling of the bust, no doubt intended to put people off the scent, to make them think I was full of gaiety and high spirits, without a care in the world, and to lend plausibility to my explanations concerning my nether rigidity, which I ascribed to hereditary rheumatism. My youthful ardour, in so far as I had any, spent itself in this effort, I became sour and mistrustful, a little before my time, in love with hiding and the prone position. Poor juvenile solutions, explaining nothing. No need then for caution, we may reason on to our heart's content, the fog won't lift.

The weather was fine. I advanced down the street, keeping as close as I could to the sidewalk. The widest sidewalk is never wide enough for me, once I set myself in motion, and I hate to inconvenience strangers. A policeman stopped me and said, The street for vehicles, the sidewalk for pedestrians. Like a bit of Old Testament. So I got back on the sidewalk, almost apologetically, and persevered there, in spite of an indescribable jostle, for a good twenty steps, till I had to fling myself to the ground to avoid crushing a child. He was wearing a little harness, I remember, with little bells, he must have taken himself for a pony, or a Clydesdale, why not. I would have crushed him gladly, I loathe children, and it would have been doing him a service, but I was afraid of reprisals. Everyone is a parent, that is what keeps you from hoping. One should reserve, on busy streets, special tracks for these nasty little creatures, their prams, hoops, sweets, scooters, skates, grandpas, grandmas, nannies, balloons and balls, all their foul little happiness in a word. I fell then, and brought down with me an old lady covered with spangles and lace, who must have weighed about sixteen stone. Her screams soon drew a crowd. I had high hopes she had broken her femur, old ladies break their femur easily, but not enough, not enough. I took advantage of the confusion to make off, muttering unintelligible oaths, as if I were the victim, and I was, but I couldn't have proved it. They never lynch children, babies, no matter what they do they are whitewashed in advance. I personally would lynch them with the utmost pleasure, I don't say I'd lend a hand, no, I am not a violent man, but I'd encourage the others and stand them drinks when it was done. But no sooner had I begun to reel on than I was stopped by a second policeman, similar in all respects to the first, so much so that I wondered whether it was not the same one. He pointed out to me that the sidewalk was for every one, as if it was quite obvious that I could not be assimilated to that category. Would you like me, I said, without think-ing for a single moment of Heraclitus, to get down in the gutter? Get down wherever you want, he said, but leave some room for others. If you can't bloody well get about like every one else, he said, you'd do better to stay at home. It was exactly my feeling. And that he should attribute to me a home was no small satisfaction. At that moment a funeral passed, as sometimes happens. There was a great flurry of hats and at the same time a flutter of countless fingers. Personally if I were reduced to making the sign of the cross I would set my heart on doing it right, nose, navel, left nipple, right nipple. But the way they did it, slovenly and wild, he seemed crucified all of a heap, no dignity, his knees under his chin and his hands anyhow. The more fervent stopped dead and muttered. As for the police-man, he stiffened to attention, closed his eyes and saluted. Through the windows of the cabs I caught a glimpse of the mourners conversing with animation, no doubt scenes from the life of their late dear brother in Christ, or sister. I seem to have heard that the hearse trappings are not the same in both cases, but I never could find out what the difference consists in. The horses were farting and shitting as if they were going to the fair. I saw no one kneeling.

But with us the last journey is soon done, it is in vain you quicken your pace, the last cab containing the domestics soon leaves you behind, the respite is over, the bystanders go their ways, you may look to your-self again. So I stopped a third time, of my own free will, and entered a cab. Those I had just seen pass, crammed with people hotly arguing, must have made a strong impression on me. It's a big black box, rock-ing and swaying on its springs, the windows are small, you curl up in a corner, it smells musty. I felt my hat grazing the roof. A little later I leant forward and closed the windows. Then I sat down again with my back to the horse. I was dozing off when a voice made me start, the cabman's. He had opened the door, no doubt despairing of making himself heard through the window. All I saw was his moustache. Where to? he said. He had climbed down from his seat on purpose to ask me that. And I who thought I was far away already. I reflected, searching in my memory for the name of a street, or a monument. Is your cab for sale? I said. I added, Without the horse. What would I do with a horse? But what would I do with a cab? Could I as much as stretch out in it? Who would bring me food? To the Zoo, I said. It is rare for a capital to be without a Zoo. I added, Don't go too fast. He laughed. The suggestion that he might go too fast to the Zoo must have amused him. Unless it was the prospect of being cabless. Unless it was simply myself, my own person, whose presence in the cab must have transformed it, so much so that the cabman, seeing me there with my head in the shadows of the roof and my knees against the window, had wondered perhaps if it was really his cab, really a cab. He hastens to look at his horse, and is reassured. But does one ever know oneself why one laughs? His laugh in any case was brief, which suggested

I was not the joke. He closed the door and climbed back to his seat. It was not long then before the horse got under way.

Yes, surprising though it may seem, I still had a little money at this time. The small sum my father had left me as a gift, with no restrictions, at his death, I still wonder if it wasn't stolen from me. Then I had none. And yet my life went on, and even in the way I wanted, up to a point. The great disadvantage of this condition, which might be defined as the absolute impossibility of all purchase, is that it compels you to bestir yourself. It is rare, for example, when you are completely penniless, that you can have food brought to you from time to time in your retreat. You are therefore obliged to go out and bestir yourself, at least one day a week. You can hardly have a home address under these circumstances, it's inevitable. It was therefore with a certain delay that I learnt they were looking for me, for an affair concerning me. I forget through what channel. I did not read the newspapers, nor do I remember having spoken with anyone during these years, except perhaps three or four times, on the subject of food. At any rate, I must have had wind of the affair one way or another, otherwise I would never have gone to see the lawyer, Mr. Nidder, strange how one fails to forget certain names, and he would never have received me. He verified my identity. That took some time. I showed him the metal initials in the lining of my hat, they proved nothing but they increased the probabilities. Sign, he said. He played with a cylindrical ruler, you could have felled an ox with it. Count, he said. A young woman, perhaps venal, was present at this interview, as a witness no doubt. I stuffed the wad in my pocket. You shouldn't do that, he said. It occurred to me that he should have asked me to count before I signed, it would have been more in order. Where can I reach you, he said, if necessary? At the foot of the stairs I thought of something. Soon after I went back to ask him where this money came from, adding that I had a right to know. He gave me a woman's name that I've forgotten. Perhaps she had dandled me on her knees while I was still in swaddling clothes and there had been some lovey-dovey. Sometimes that suffices. I repeat, in swaddling clothes, for any later it would have been too late, for lovey-dovey. It is thanks to this money then that I still had a little. Very little. Divided by my life to

come it was negligible, unless my conjectures were unduly pessimistic.
I knocked on the partition beside my hat, right in the cabman's back if
my calculations were correct. A cloud of dust rose from the upholstery. I
took a stone from my pocket and knocked with the stone, until the cab
stopped. I noticed that, unlike most vehicles, which slow down before
stopping, the cab stopped dead. I waited. The whole cab shook. The cab-
man, on his high seat, must have been listening. I saw the horse as with
my eyes of flesh. It had not lapsed into the drooping attitude of its brief-
est halts, it remained alert, its ears pricked up. I looked out of the win-
dow, we were again in motion. I banged again on the partition, until the
cab stopped again. The cabman got down cursing from his seat. I low-
ered the window to prevent his opening the door. Faster, faster. He was
redder than ever, purple in other words. Anger, or the rushing wind. I
told him I was hiring him for the day. He replied that he had a funeral
at three o'clock. Ah the dead. I told him I had changed my mind and no
longer wished to go to the Zoo. Let us not go to the Zoo, I said. He replied
that it made no difference to him where we went, provided it wasn't too
far, because of his beast. And they talk to us about the specificity of primi-
tive peoples' speech. I asked him if he knew of an eating-house. I added,
You'll eat with me. I prefer being with a regular customer in such places.
There was a long table with two benches of exactly the same length on
either side. Across the table he spoke to me of his life, of his wife, of
his beast, then again of his life, of the atrocious life that was his, chiefly
because of his character. He asked me if I realized what it meant to be out
of doors in all weathers. I learnt there were still some cabmen who spent
their day snug and warm inside their cabs on the rank, waiting for a cus-
tomer to come and rouse them. Such a thing was possible in the past, but
nowadays other methods were necessary, if a man was to have a little laid
up at the end of his days. I described my situation to him, what I had lost
and what I was looking for. We did our best, both of us, to understand, to
explain. He understood that I had lost my room and needed another, but
all the rest escaped him. He had taken it into his head, whence nothing
could ever dislodge it, that I was looking for a furnished room. He took
from his pocket an evening paper of the day before, or perhaps the day

before that again, and proceeded to run through the advertisements, five or six of which he underlined with a tiny pencil, the same that hovered over the likely outsiders. He underlined no doubt those he would have underlined if he had been in my shoes, or perhaps those concentrated in the same district, because of his beast. I would only have confused him by saying that I could tolerate no furniture in my room except the bed, and that all the other pieces, and even the very night table, had to be removed before I would consent to set foot in it. About three o'clock we roused the horse and set off again. The cabman suggested I climb up beside him on the seat, but for some time already I had been dreaming of the inside of the cab and I got back inside. We visited, methodically I hope, one after another, the addresses he had underlined. The short winter's day was drawing to a close. It seems to me sometimes that these are the only days I have ever known, and especially that most charming moment of all, just before night wipes them out. The addresses he had underlined, or rather marked with a cross, as common people do, proved fruitless one by one, and one by one he crossed them out with a diagonal stroke. Later he showed me the paper, advising me to keep it safe so as to be sure not to look again where I had already looked in vain. In spite of the closed windows, the creaking of the cab and the traffic noises, I heard him singing, all alone aloft on his high seat. He had preferred me to a funeral, this was a fact which would endure forever. He sang, *She is far from the land where her young hero*, those are the only words I remember. At each stop he got down from his seat and helped me get down from mine. I rang at the door he directed me to, and sometimes I disappeared inside the house. It was a strange feeling, I remember, a house all about me again, after so long. He waited for me on the sidewalk and helped me climb back into the cab. I was sick and tired of this cabman. He clambered back to his seat and we set off again. At a certain moment there occurred this. He stopped. I shook off my torpor and made ready to get down. But he did not come to open the door and offer me his arm, so that I was obliged to get down by myself. He was lighting the lamps. I love oil lamps, in spite of their having been, with candles, and if I except the stars, the first lights I ever knew. I asked him if I might light the second lamp, since he had already lit the first himself. He gave me his box of matches, I swung open on its hinges the little convex glass, lit and closed at once, so that the wick might burn steady and bright snug in its little house, sheltered from the wind. I had this joy. We saw nothing, by the light of these lamps, save the vague outlines of the horse, but the others saw them from afar, two yellow glows sailing slowly through the air. When the equipage turned an eye could be seen, red or green as the case might be, a bossy rhomb as clear and keen as stained glass.

After we had verified the last address the cabman suggested bringing me to a hotel he knew where I would be comfortable. That makes sense, cabman, hotel, it's plausible. With his recommendation I would want for nothing. Every convenience, he said, with a wink. I place this conversation on the sidewalk, in front of the house from which I had just emerged. I remember, beneath the lamp, the flank of the horse, hollow and damp, and on the handle of the door the cabman's hand in its woollen glove. The roof of the cab was on a level with my neck. I suggested we have a drink. The horse had neither eaten nor drunk all day. I mentioned this to the cabman, who replied that his beast would take no food till it was back in the stable. If it ate anything whatever, during work, were it but an apple or a lump of sugar, it would have stomach pains and colics that would root it to the spot and might even kill it. That was why he was compelled to tie its jaws together with a strap whenever for one reason or another he had to let it out of his sight, so that it would not have to suffer from the kind hearts of the passers-by. After a few drinks the cabman invited me to do his wife and him the honour of spending the night in their home. It was not far. Recollecting these emotions, with the celebrated advantage of tranquillity, it seems to me he did nothing else, all that day, but turn about his lodging. They lived above a stable, at the back of a yard. Ideal location, I could have done with it. Having presented me to his wife, extraordinarily full-bottomed, he left us. She was manifestly ill at ease, alone with me. I could understand her, I don't stand on ceremony on these occasions. No reason for this to end or go on. Then let it end. I said I would go down to the stable and sleep there. The cabman protested. I insisted. He drew his wife's attention to the pustule on top of my skull, for I had removed my hat out of civility. He should have that removed, she said. The cabman named a doctor he held in high esteem who had rid him of an induration of the seat. If he wants to sleep in the stable, said his wife, let him sleep in the stable. The cabman took the lamp from the table and preceded me down the stairs, or rather ladder, which descended to the stable, leaving his wife in the dark. He spread a horse blanket on the ground in a corner on the straw and left me a box of matches in case I needed to see clearly in the night. I don't remember what the horse was doing all this time. Stretched out in the dark I heard the noise it made as it drank, a noise like no other, the sudden gallop of the rats, and above me the muffled voices of the cabman and his wife as they criticized me. I held the box of matches in my hand, a big box of safety matches. I got up during the night and struck one. Its brief flame enabled me to locate the cab. I was seized, then abandoned, by the desire to set fire to the stable. I found the cab in the dark, opened the door, the rats poured out, I climbed in. As I settled down I noticed that the cab was no longer level, it was inevitable, with the shafts resting on the ground. It was better so, that allowed me to lie well back, with my feet higher than my head on the other seat. Several times during the night I felt the horse looking at me through the window and the breath of its nostrils. Now that it was unharnessed it must have been puzzled by my presence in the cab. I was cold, having forgotten to take the blanket, but not quite enough to go and get it. Through the window of the cab I saw the window of the stable, more and more clearly. I got out of the cab. It was not so dark now in the stable, I could make out the manger, the rack, the harness hanging, what else, buckets and brushes. I went to the door but couldn't open it. The horse didn't take its eyes off me. Don't horses ever sleep? It seemed to me the cabman should have tied it, to the manger for example. So I was obliged to leave by the window. It wasn't easy. But what is easy? I went out head first, my hands were flat on the ground of the yard while my legs were still thrashing to get clear of the frame. I remember the tufts of grass on which I pulled with both hands, in my efforts to extricate myself. I should have taken off my greatcoat and thrown it through the window, but that would have meant thinking of it. No sooner had I left the yard than I thought of something. Weakness. I slipped a banknote in the match box, went back to the yard and placed the box on the sill of the window through which I had just come. The horse was at the window. But after I had taken a few steps in the street I returned to the yard and took back my banknote. I left the matches, they were not mine. The horse was still at the window. I was sick and tired of this cabhorse. Dawn was just breaking. I did not know where I was. I made towards the rising sun, towards where I thought it should rise, the quicker to come into the light. I would have liked a sea horizon, or a desert one. When I am abroad in the morning, I go to meet the sun, and in the evening, when I am abroad, I follow it, till I am down among the dead. I don't know why I told this story. I could just as well have told another. Perhaps some other time I'll be able to tell another. Living souls, you will see how alike they are.

The Calmative

I don't know when I died. It always seemed to me I died old, about ninety years old, and what years, and that my body bore it out, from head to foot. But this evening, alone in my icy bed, I have the feeling I'll be older than the day, the night, when the sky with all its lights fell upon me, the same I had so often gazed on since my first stumblings on the distant earth. For I'm too frightened this evening to listen to myself rot, waiting for the great red lapses of the heart, the tearings at the caecal walls, and for the slow killings to finish in my skull, the assaults on unshakable pillars, the fornications with corpses. So I'll tell myself a story, I'll try and tell myself another story, to try and calm myself, and it's there I feel I'll be old, old, even older than the day I fell, calling for help, and it came. Or is it possible that in this story I have come back to life, after my death? No, it's not like me to come back to life, after my death.

What possessed me to stir when I wasn't with anybody? Was I being thrown out? No, I wasn't with anybody. I see a kind of den littered with empty tins. And yet we are not in the country. Perhaps it's just ruins, a ruined folly, on the skirts of the town, in a field, for the fields come right up to our walls, their walls, and the cows lie down at night in the lee of the ramparts. I have changed refuge so often, in the course of my rout, that now I can't tell between dens and ruins. But there was never any city but the one. It is true you often move along in a dream, houses and factories darken the air, trams go by, and under your feet wet from the grass there are suddenly cobbles. I only know the city of my childhood, I must have seen the other, but unbelieving. All I say cancels out, I'll have said nothing. Was I hungry itself? Did the weather tempt me? It was cloudy and cool, I insist, but not to the extent of luring me out. I couldn't get up at the first attempt, nor let us say at the second, and once up, propped against the wall, I wondered if I could go on, I mean up, propped against the wall. Impossible to go out and walk. I speak as though it all happened yesterday. Yesterday indeed is recent, but not enough. For what I tell this evening is passing this evening, at this passing hour. I'm no longer with these assassins, in this bed of terror, but in my distant refuge, my hands twined together, my head bowed, weak, breathless, calm, free, and older than I'll have ever been, if my calculations are correct. I'll tell my story in the past none the less, as though it were a myth, or an old fable, for this evening I need another age, that age to become another age in which I became what I was.

But little by little I got myself out and started walking with short steps among the trees, oh look, trees! The paths of other days were rank with tangled growth. I leaned against the trunks to get my breath and pulled myself forward with the help of boughs. Of my last passage no trace remained. They were the perishing oaks immortalized by d'Aubigné. It was only a grove. The fringe was near, a light less green and kind of tattered told me so, in a whisper. Yes, no matter where you stood, in this little wood, and were it in the furthest recess of its poor secrecies, you saw on every hand the gleam of this pale light, promise of God knows what fatuous eternity. Die without too much pain, a little, that's worth your while. Under the blind sky close with your own hands the eyes soon sockets, then quick into carrion not to mislead the crows. That's the advantage of death by drowning, one of the advantages, the crabs never get there too soon. But here a strange thing, I was no sooner free of the wood at last, having crossed unminding the ditch that girdles it, than thoughts came to me of cruelty, the kind that smiles. A lush pasture lay before me, nonsuch perhaps, who cares, drenched in evening dew or recent rain. Beyond this meadow to my certain knowledge a path, then a field and finally the ramparts, closing the prospect. Cyclopean and crenellated, standing out faintly

against a sky scarcely less sombre, they did not seem in ruins, viewed from
mine, but were, to my certain knowledge. Such was the scene offered to
me, in vain, for I knew it well and loathed it. What I saw was a bald man
in a brown suit, a comedian. He was telling a funny story about a fiasco.
Its point escaped me. He used the word snail, or slug, to the delight of all
present. The women seemed even more entertained than their escorts, if
that were possible. Their shrill laughter pierced the clapping and, when
this had subsided, broke out still here and there in sudden peals even
after the next story had begun, so that part of it was lost. Perhaps they had
in mind the reigning penis sitting who knows by their side and from that
sweet shore launched their cries of joy towards the comic vast, what a tal-
ent. But it's to me this evening something has to happen, to my body as
in myth and metamorphosis, this old body to which nothing ever hap-
pened, or so little, which never met with anything, loved anything, wished
for anything, in its tarnished universe, except for the mirrors to shatter,
the plane, the curved, the magnifying, the minifying, and to vanish in the
havoc of its images. Yes, this evening it has to be as in the story my father
used to read to me, evening after evening, when I was small, and he had
all his health, to calm me, evening after evening, year after year it seems
to me this evening, which I don't remember much about, except that it
was the adventures of one Joe Breem, or Breen, the son of a lighthouse-
keeper, a strong muscular lad of fifteen, those were the words, who swam
for miles in the night, a knife between his teeth, after a shark, I forget why,
out of sheer heroism. He might have simply told me the story, he knew it
by heart, so did I, but that wouldn't have calmed me, he had to read it to
me, evening after evening, or pretend to read it to me, turning the pages
and explaining the pictures that were of me already, evening after even-
ing the same pictures, till I dozed off on his shoulder. If he had skipped
a single word I would have hit him, with my little fist, in his big belly
bursting out of the old cardigan and unbuttoned trousers that rested
him from his office canonicals. For me now the setting forth, the strug-
gle and perhaps the return, for the old man I am this evening, older than
my father ever was, older than I shall ever be. I crossed the meadow with
little stiff steps at the same time limp, the best I could manage. Of my last

passage no trace remained, it was long ago. And the little bruised stems soon straighten up again, having need of air and light, and as for the broken their place is soon taken. I entered the town by what they call the Shepherds' Gate without having seen a soul, only the first bats like flying crucifixions, nor heard a sound except my steps, my heart in my breast and then, as I went under the arch, the hoot of an owl, that cry at once so soft and fierce which in the night, calling, answering, through my little wood and those nearby, sounded in my shelter like a tocsin. The further I went into the city the more I was struck by its deserted air. It was lit as usual, brighter than usual, although the shops were shut. But the lights were on in their windows with the object no doubt of attracting customers and prompting them to say, I say, I like that, not dear either, I'll come back tomorrow, if I'm still alive. I nearly said, Good God it's Sunday. The trams were running, the buses too, but few, slow, empty, noiseless, as if under water. I didn't see a single horse! I was wearing my long green greatcoat with the velvet collar, such as motorists wore about 1900, my father's, but that day it was sleeveless, a vast cloak. But on me it was still the same great dead weight, with no warmth to it, and the tails swept the ground, scraped it rather, they had grown so stiff, and I so shrunken. What would, what could happen to me in this empty place? But I felt the houses packed with people, lurking behind the curtains they looked out into the street or, crouched far back in the depths of the room, head in hands, were sunk in dream. Up aloft my hat, the same as always, I reached no further. I went right across the city and came to the sea, having followed the river to its mouth. I kept saying, I'll go back, unbelieving. The boats at anchor in the harbour, tied up to the jetty, seemed no less numerous than usual, as if I knew anything about what was usual. But the quays were deserted and there was no sign or stir of arrival or departure. But all might change from one moment to the next and be transformed like magic before my eyes. Then all the bustle of the people and things of the sea, the masts of the big craft gravely rocking and of the small more jauntily, I insist, and I'd hear the gulls' terrible cry and perhaps the sailors' cry. And I might slip unnoticed aboard a freighter outward bound and get far away and spend far away a few good months, perhaps even a year or two,

in the sun, in peace, before I died. And without going that far it would be
a sad state of affairs if in that unscandalizable throng I couldn't achieve a
little encounter that would calm me a little, or exchange a few words with
a navigator for example, words to carry away with me to my refuge, to add
to my collection. I waited sitting on a kind of topless capstan, saying, The
very capstans this evening are out of order. And I gazed out to sea, out
beyond the breakwaters, without sighting the least vessel. I could see
lights flush with the water. And the pretty beacons at the harbour mouth
I could see too, and others in the distance, flashing from the coast, the
islands, the headlands. But seeing still no sign or stir I made ready to go,
to turn away sadly from this dead haven, for there are scenes that call for
strange farewells. I had merely to bow my head and look down at my feet,
for it is in this attitude I always drew the strength to, how shall I say, I
don't know, and it was always from the earth, rather than from the sky,
notwithstanding its reputation, that my help came in time of trouble.
And there, on the flagstone, which I was not focussing, for why focus it, I
saw haven afar, where the black swell was most perilous, and all about me
storm and wreck. I'll never come back here, I said. But when with a thrust
of both hands against the rim of the capstan I heaved myself up I found
facing me a young boy holding a goat by a horn. I sat down again. He
stood there silent looking at me without visible fear or revulsion. Admit-
tedly the light was poor. His silence seemed natural to me, it befitted me
as the elder to speak first. He was barefoot and in rags. Haunter of the
waterfront he had stepped aside to see what the dark hulk could be aban-
doned on the quayside. Such was my train of thought. Close up to me
now with his little guttersnipe's eye there could be no doubt left in his
mind. And yet he stayed. Can this base thought be mine? Moved, for after
all that is what I must have come out for, in a way, and with little expecta-
tion of advantage from what might follow, I resolved to speak to him. So
I marshalled the words and opened my mouth, thinking I would hear
them. But all I heard was a kind of rattle, unintelligible even to me who
knew what was intended. But it was nothing, mere speechlessness due to
long silence, as in the wood that darkens the mouth of hell, do you
remember, I only just. Without letting go of his goat he moved right up

against me and offered me a sweet out of a twist of paper such as you could buy for a penny. I hadn't been offered a sweet for eighty years at least, but I took it eagerly and put it in my mouth, the old gesture came back to me, more and more moved since that is what I wanted. The sweets were stuck together and I had my work cut out to separate the top one, a green one, from the others, but he helped me and his hand brushed mine. And a moment later as he made to move away, hauling his goat after him, with a great gesticulation of my whole body I motioned him to stay and I said, in an impetuous murmur, Where are you off to, my little man, with your nanny? The words were hardly out of my mouth when for shame I covered my face. And yet they were the same I had tried to utter but a moment before. Where are you off to, my little man, with your nanny! If I could have blushed I would have, but there was not enough blood left in my extremities. If I had had a penny in my pocket I would have given it to him, for him to forgive me, but I did not have a penny in my pocket, nor anything resembling it. Nothing that could give pleasure to a little unfortunate at the mouth of life. I suspect I had nothing with me but my stone, that day, having gone out as it were without premeditation. Of his little person I was fated to see no more than the black curly hair and the pretty curve of the long bare legs all muscle and dirt. And the hand, so fresh and keen, I would not forget in a hurry either. I looked for better words to say to him, I found them too late, he was gone, oh not far, but far. Out of my life too he went without a care, not one of his thoughts would ever be for me again, unless perhaps when he was old and, delving in his boyhood, would come upon that gallows night and hold the goat by the horn again and linger again a moment by my side, with who knows perhaps a touch of tenderness, even of envy, but I have my doubts. Poor dear dumb beasts, how you will have helped me. What does your daddy do? that's what I would have said to him if he had given me the chance. Soon they were no more than a single blur which if I hadn't known I might have taken for a young centaur. I was nearly going to have the goat dung, then pick up a handful of the pellets so soon cold and hard, sniff and even taste them, no, that would not help me this evening. I say this evening as if it were always the same evening, but are there two evenings? I

went, intending to get back as fast as I could, but it would not be quite
empty-handed, repeating, I'll never come back here. My legs were pain-
ing me, every step would gladly have been the last, but the glances I darted
towards the windows, stealthily, showed me a great cylinder sweeping
past as though on rollers on the asphalt. I must indeed have been mov-
ing fast, for I overhauled more than one pedestrian, there are the first
men, without extending myself, I who in the normal way was left stand-
ing by cripples, and then I seemed to hear the footfalls die behind me.
And yet each little step would gladly have been the last. So much so that
when I emerged on a square I hadn't noticed on the way out, with a cathe-
dral looming on the far side, I decided to go in, if it was open, and hide,
as in the Middle Ages, for a space. I say cathedral, it may not have been, I
don't know, all I know is it would vex me in this story that aspires to be
the last, to have taken refuge in a common church. I remarked the Saxon
Stützenwechsel. Charming effect, but it didn't charm me. The brilliantly
lit nave appeared deserted. I walked round it several times without seeing
a soul. They were hiding perhaps, under the choir-stalls, or dodging
behind the pillars, like woodpeckers. Suddenly close to where I was, and
without my having heard the long preliminary rumblings, the organ
began to boom. I sprang up from the mat on which I lay before the altar
and hastened to the far end of the nave as if on my way out. But it was a
side aisle and the door I disappeared through was not the exit. For instead
of being restored to the night I found myself at the foot of a spiral stair-
case which I began to climb at top speed, mindless of my heart, like one
hotly pursued by a homicidal maniac. This staircase faintly lit by I know
not what means, slits perhaps, I mounted panting as far as the projecting
gallery in which it culminated and which, separated from the void by a
cynical parapet, encompassed a smooth round wall capped by a little
dome covered with lead or verdigrised copper, phew, if that's not clear.
People must have come here for the view, those who fall die on the way.
Flattening myself against the wall I started round, clockwise. But I had
hardly gone a few steps when I met a man revolving in the other direc-
tion, with the utmost circumspection. How I'd love to push him, or him
to push me, over the edge. He gazed at me wild-eyed for a moment and

then, not daring to pass me on the parapet side and surmising correctly that I would not relinquish the wall just to oblige him, abruptly turned his back on me, his head rather, for his back remained glued to the wall, and went back the way he had come so that soon there was nothing left of him but a left hand. It lingered a moment, then slid out of sight. All that remained to me was the vision of two burning eyes starting out of their sockets under a check cap. Into what nightmare thingness am I fallen? My hat flew off, but did not get far thanks to the string. I turned my head towards the staircase and lent an eye. Nothing. Then a little girl came into view followed by a man holding her by the hand, both pressed against the wall. He pushed her into the stairway, disappeared after her, turned and raised towards me a face that made me recoil. I could only see his bare head above the top step. When they were gone I called. I completed in haste the round of the gallery. No one. I saw on the horizon, where sky, sea, plain and mountain meet, a few low stars, not to be confused with the fires men light, at night, or that go alight alone. Enough. Back in the street I tried to find my way in the sky, where I knew the Bears so well. If I had seen someone I would have stopped him to ask, the most ferocious aspect would not have daunted me. I would have said, touching my hat, Pardon me your honour, the Shepherds' Gate for the love of God. I thought I could go no further, but no sooner had the impetus reached my legs than on I went, believe it or not, at a very fair pace. I wasn't returning empty-handed, not quite, I was taking back with me the virtual certainty that I was still of this world, of that world too, in a way. But I was paying the price. I would have done better to spend the night in the cathedral, on the mat before the altar, I would have continued on my way at first light, or they would have found me stretched out in the rigor of death, the genuine bodily article, under the blue eyes fount of so much hope, and put me in the evening papers. But suddenly I was descending a wide street, vaguely familiar, but in which I could never have set foot, in my lifetime. But soon realizing I was going downhill I turned about and set off in the other direction. For I was afraid if I went downhill of returning to the sea where I had sworn never to return. When I say I turned about I mean I wheeled round in a wide semi-circle without slowing down, for I was afraid if I stopped of not being able to start again, yes, I was afraid of that too. And this evening too I dare not stop. I was struck more and more by the contrast between the brightly lit streets and their deserted air. To say it distressed me, no, but I say it all the same, in the hope of calming myself. To say there was no one abroad, no, I would not go that far, for I remarked a number of shapes, male and female, strange shapes, but not more so than usual. As to what hour it might have been I had no idea, except that it must have been some hour of the night. But it might have been three or four in the morning just as it might have been ten or eleven in the evening, depending no doubt on whether one wondered at the scarcity of passers-by or at the extraordinary radiance shed by the street-lamps and traffic-lights. For at one or other of these no one could fail to wonder, unless he was out of his mind. Not a single private car, but admittedly from time to time a public vehicle, slow sweep of light silent and empty. It is not my wish to labour these antinomies, for we are needless to say in a skull, but I have no choice but to add the following few remarks. All the mortals I saw were alone and as if sunk in themselves. It must be a common sight, but mixed with something else I imagine. The only couple was two men grappling, their legs intertwined. I only saw one cyclist! He was going the same way as I was. All were going the same way as I was, vehicles too, I have only just realized it. He was pedalling slowly in the middle of the street, reading a newspaper which he held with both hands spread open before his eyes. Every now and then he rang his bell without interrupting his reading. I watched him recede till he was no more than a dot on the horizon. Suddenly a young woman perhaps of easy virtue, dishevelled and her dress in disarray, darted across the street like a rabbit. That is all I had to add. But here a strange thing, yet another, I had no pain whatever, not even in my legs. Weakness. A good night's nightmare and a tin of sardines would restore my sensitivity. My shadow, one of my shadows, flew before me, dwindled, slid under my feet, trailed behind me the way shadows will. This degree of opacity appeared to me conclusive. But suddenly ahead of me a man on the same side of the street and going the same way, to keep harping on the same thing lest I forget. The distance between us was considerable, seventy paces at least, and fearing he might escape me I quickened my step with the result I swept forward as if on rollers. This is not me, I said, let us make the most of it. Finding myself in an instant a bare ten paces in his rear I slowed down so as not to burst in on him and so heighten the aversion my person inspired even in its most abject and obsequious attitudes. And a moment later, keeping humbly in step with him, Excuse me your honour, the Shepherds' Gate for the love of God! At close quarters he appeared normal apart from that air already noted of ebbing inward. I drew a few steps ahead, turned, cringed, touched my hat and said, The right time for mercy's sake! I might as well not have existed. But what about the sweet? A light! I cried. Given my need of help I can't think why I did not bar his path. I couldn't have, that's all, I couldn't have touched him. Seeing a stone seat by the kerb I sat down and crossed my legs, like Walther. I must have dozed off, for the next thing was a man sitting beside me. I was still taking him in when he opened his eyes and set them on me, as if for the first time, for he shrank back unaffectedly. Where did you spring from? he said. To hear myself addressed again so soon impressed me greatly. What's the matter with you? he said. I tried to look like one with whom that only is the matter which is native to him. Forgive me your honour, I said, gingerly lifting my hat and rising a fraction from the seat, the right time for the love of God! He said a time, I don't remember which, a time that explained nothing, that's all I remember, and did not calm me. But what time could have done that? Oh I know, I know, one will come that will. But in the meantime? What's that you said? he said. Unfortunately I had said nothing. But I wriggled out of it by asking him if he could help me find my way which I had lost. No, he said, for I am not from these parts and if I am sitting on this slab it is because the hotels were full or would not let me in, I have no opinion. But tell me the story of your life, then we'll see. My life! I cried. Why yes, he said, you know, that kind of—what shall I say? He brooded for a time, no doubt trying to think of what life could well be said to be a kind. In the end he went on, testily, Come now, everyone knows that. He jogged me in the ribs. No details, he said, the main drift, the main drift. But as I remained silent he said, Shall I tell you mine, then you'll see what I mean. The account he then gave was brief and dense, facts, without comment. That's what I call a life, he said, do you follow me now? It wasn't bad, his story, positively fairy-like in places. But that Pauline, I said, are you still with her? I am, he said, but I'm going to leave her and set up with another, younger and plumper. You travel a lot, I said. Oh widely, widely, he said. Words were coming back to me, and the way to make them sound. All that's a thing of the past for you no doubt, he said. Do you think of spending some time among us? I said. This sentence struck me as particularly well turned. If it's not a rude question, he said, how old are you? I don't know, I said. You don't know! he cried. Not exactly, I said. Are thighs much in your thoughts, he said, arses, cunts and environs. I didn't follow. No more erections naturally, he said. Erections? I said. The penis, he said, you know what the penis is, there, between the legs. Ah that, I said. It thickens, lengthens, stiffens and rises, he said, does it not? I assented, though they were not the terms I would have used. That is what we call an erection, he said. He pondered, then exclaimed, Phenomenal! No? Strange right enough, I said. And there you have it all, he said. But what will become of her? I said. Who? he said. Pauline, I said. She will grow old, he said with tranquil assurance, slowly at first, then faster and faster, in pain and bitterness, pulling the devil by the tail. The face was not full, but I eyed it in vain, it remained clothed in its flesh instead of turning all chalky and channelled as with a gouge. The very vomer kept its cushion. It is true discussion was always bad for me. I longed for the tender nonsuch, I would have trodden it gently, with my boots in my hand, and for the shade of my wood, far from this terrible light. What are you grinning and bearing? he said. He held on his knees a big black bag, like a midwife's I imagine. It was full of glittering phials. I asked him if they were all alike. Oho no, he said, for every taste. He took one and held it out to me, saying, One and six. What did he want? To sell it to me? Proceeding on this hypothesis I told him I had no money. No money! he cried. All of a sudden his hand came down on the back of my neck, his sinewy fingers closed and with a jerk and a twist he had me up against him. But instead of dispatching me he began to murmur words so sweet that I went limp and my head fell forward in his lap. Between the caressing voice and the fingers rowelling my neck the contrast was striking. But gradually the two things merged in a devastating hope, if I dare say so, and I dare. For this evening I have nothing to lose that I can discern. And if I have reached this point (in my story) without anything having changed, for if anything had changed I think I'd know, the fact remains I have reached it, and that's something, and with nothing changed, and that's something too. It's no excuse for rushing matters. No, it must cease gently, as gently cease on the stairs the steps of the loved one, who could not love and will not come back, and whose steps say so, that she could not love and will not come back. He suddenly shoved me away and showed me the phial again. There you have it all, he said. It can't have been the same all as before. Want it? he said. No, but I said yes, so as not to vex him. He proposed an exchange. Give me your hat, he said. I refused. What vehemence! he said. I haven't a thing, I said. Try in your pockets, he said. I haven't a thing, I said, I came out without a thing. Give me a lace, he said. I refused. Long silence. And if you gave me a kiss, he said finally. I knew there were kisses in the air. Can you take off your hat? he said. I took it off. Put it back, he said, you look nicer with it on. I put it on. Come on, he said, give me a kiss and let there be an end to it. Did it not occur to him I might turn him down? No, a kiss is not a bootlace, he must have seen from my face that all passion was not quite spent. Come, he said. I wiped my mouth in its tod of hair and advanced it towards his. Just a moment, he said. My mouth stood still. You know what a kiss is? he said. Yes yes, I said. If it's not a rude question, he said, when was your last? Some time ago, I said, but I can still do them. He took off his hat, a bowler, and tapped the middle of his forehead. There, he said, and there only. He had a noble brow, white and high. He leaned forward, closing his eyes. Quick, he said. I pursed up my lips as mother had taught me and brought them down where he had said. Enough, he said. He raised his hand towards the spot, but left the gesture unfinished and put on his hat. I turned away and looked across the street. It was then I noticed we were sitting opposite a horse-butcher's. Here, he said, take it. I had forgotten. He rose. Standing he was quite short. One good turn, he said, with radiant smile. His teeth shone. I listened to his steps die away. How tell what remains. But it's the

end. Or have I been dreaming, am I dreaming? No no, none of that, for
dream is nothing, a joke, and significant what is worse. I said, Stay where
you are till day breaks, wait sleeping till the lamps go out and the streets
come to life. But I stood up and moved off. My pains were back, but with
something untoward which prevented my wrapping them round me. But
I said, Little by little you are coming to. From my gait alone, slow, stiff
and which seemed at every step to solve a statodynamic problem never
posed before, I would have been known again, if I had been known. I
crossed over and stopped before the butcher's. Behind the grille the cur-
tains were drawn, rough canvas curtains striped blue and white, colours
of the Virgin, and stained with great pink stains. They did not quite meet
in the middle, and through the chink I could make out the dim carcasses
of the gutted horses hanging from hooks head downwards. I hugged the
walls, famished for shadow. To think that in a moment all will be said, all
to do again. And the city clocks, what was wrong with them, whose great
chill clang even in my wood fell on me from the air? What else? Ah yes,
my spoils. I tried to think of Pauline, but she eluded me, gleamed an
instant and was gone, like the young woman in the street. So I went in the
atrocious brightness, buried in my old flesh, straining towards an issue
and passing them by to left and right, and my mind panting after this
and that and always flung back to where there was nothing. I succeeded
however in fastening briefly on the little girl, long enough to see her a
little more clearly than before, so that she wore a kind of bonnet and
clasped in her hand a book, of common prayer perhaps, and to try and
have her smile, but she did not smile, but vanished down the staircase
without having yielded me her little face. I had to stop. At first nothing,
then little by little, I mean rising up out of the silence till suddenly no
higher, a kind of massive murmur coming perhaps from the house that
was propping me up. That reminded me that the houses were full of peo-
ple, besieged, no, I don't know. When I stepped back to look at the win-
dows I could see, in spite of shutters, blinds and muslins, that many of
the rooms were lit. The light was so dimmed by the brilliancy flooding the
boulevard that short of knowing or suspecting it was not so one might
have supposed everyone sleeping. The sound was not continuous, but

broken by silences possibly of consternation. I thought of ringing at the door and asking for shelter and protection till morning. But suddenly I was on my way again. But little by little, in a slow swoon, darkness fell about me. I saw a mass of bright flowers fade in an exquisite cascade of paling colours. I found myself admiring, all along the house-fronts, the gradual blossoming of squares and rectangles, casement and sash, yellow, green, pink, according to the curtains and blinds, finding that pretty. Then at last, before I fell, first to my knees, as cattle do, then on my face, I was in a throng. I didn't lose consciousness, when I lose consciousness it will not be to recover it. They paid no heed to me, though careful not to walk on me, a courtesy that must have touched me, it was what I had come out for. It was well with me, sated with dark and calm, lying at the feet of mortals, fathom deep in the grey of dawn, if it was dawn. But reality, too tired to look for the right word, was soon restored, the throng fell away, the light came back and I had no need to raise my head from the ground to know I was back in the same blinding void as before. I said, Stay where you are, down on the friendly stone, or at least indifferent, don't open your eyes, wait for morning. But up with me again and back on the way that was not mine, on uphill along the boulevard. A blessing he was not waiting for me, poor old Breem, or Breen. I said, The sea is east, it's west I must go, to the left of north. But in vain I raised without hope my eyes to the sky to look for the Bears. For the light I steeped in put out the stars, assuming they were there, which I doubted, remembering the clouds.

The End

They clothed me and gave me money. I knew what the money was for, it was to get me started. When it was gone I would have to get more, if I wanted to go on. The same for the shoes, when they were worn out I would have to get them mended, or get myself another pair, or go on barefoot, if I wanted to go on. The same for the coat and trousers, needless to say, with this difference, that I could go on in my shirtsleeves, if I wanted. The clothes—shoes, socks, trousers, shirt, coat, hat—were not new, but the deceased must have been about my size. That is to say, he must have been a little shorter, a little thinner, for the clothes did not fit me so well in the beginning as they did at the end, the shirt especially, and it was many a long day before I could button it at the neck, or profit by the collar that went with it, or pin the skirts together between my legs in the way my mother had taught me. He must have put on his Sunday best to go to the consultation, perhaps for the first time, unable to bear it any longer. Be that as it may the hat was a bowler, in good shape. I said, Keep your hat and give me back mine. I added, Give me back my greatcoat. They replied that they had burnt them, together with my other clothes. I understood then that the end was near, at least fairly near. Later on I tried to exchange this hat for a cap, or a slouch which could be pulled down over my face, but without much success. And yet I could not go about bare-headed, with my skull in the state it was. At first this hat was too small, then it got used to me. They gave me a tie, after long discussion. It seemed a pretty tie to me, but I didn't like it. When it came at last I was too tired to send it back. But in the end it came in useful. It was blue, with kinds of little stars. I didn't feel well, but they told me I was well enough. They didn't say in so many words that I was as well as I would ever be, but that was the implication. I lay inert on the bed and it took three women to put on my trousers. They didn't seem to take much interest in my private parts which to tell the truth were nothing to write home about, I didn't take much interest in them myself. But they might have passed some remark. When they had finished I got up and finished dressing unaided. They told me to sit on the bed and wait. All the bedding had disappeared. It made me angry that they had not let me wait in the familiar bed, instead of leaving me standing in the cold, in these clothes that smelt of sulphur. I said, You might have left me in bed till the last moment. Men all in white came in with mallets in their hands. They dismantled the bed and took away the pieces. One of the women followed them out and came back with a chair which she set before me. I had done well to pretend I was angry. But to make it quite clear to them how angry I was that they had not left me in my bed, I gave the chair a kick that sent it flying. A man came in and made a sign to me to follow him. In the hall he gave me a paper to sign. What's this, I said, a safe-conduct? It's a receipt, he said, for the clothes and money you have received. What money? I said. It was then I received the money. To think I had almost departed without a penny in my pocket. The sum was not large, compared to other sums, but to me it seemed large. I saw the familiar objects, companions of so many bearable hours. The stool, for example, dearest of all. The long afternoons together, waiting for it to be time for bed. At times I felt its wooden life invade me, till I myself became a piece of old wood. There was even a hole for my cyst. Then the window-pane with the patch of frosting gone, where I used to press my eye in the hour of need, and rarely in vain. I am greatly obliged to you, I said, is there a law which prevents you from throwing me out naked and penniless? That would damage our reputation in the long run, he replied. Could they not possibly keep me a little longer, I said, I could make myself useful. Useful, he said, joking apart you would be willing to make yourself useful? A moment later he went on, If they believed you were really willing to make yourself useful they would keep you, I am sure. The number of times I had said I was going to make myself useful, I wasn't going to start that again. How weak I felt! Perhaps, I said, they would consent to take back the money and keep me a little longer. This is a charitable institution, he said, and the money is a gift you receive when you leave. When it is gone you will have to get more, if you wish to go on. Never come back here whatever you do, you would not be let in. Don't go to any of our branches either, they would turn you away. Exelmans! I cried. Come come, he said, and anyway no one understands a tenth of what you say. I'm so old, I said. You are not so old as all that, he said. May I stay here just a little longer, I said, till the rain is over. You may wait in the cloister, he said, the rain will go on all day. You may wait in the cloister till six o'clock, you will hear the bell. If anyone challenges you, you need only say you have permission to shelter in the cloister. Whose name will I give? I said. Weir, he said.

I had not been long in the cloister when the rain stopped and the sun came out. It was low and I reckoned it must be getting on for six, considering the season. I stayed there looking through the archway at the sun as it went down behind the cloister. A man appeared and asked me what I was doing. What do you want? were the words he used. Very friendly. I replied that I had Mr. Weir's permission to stay in the cloister till six o'clock. He went away, but came back immediately. He must have spoken to Mr. Weir in the interim, for he said, You must not loiter in the cloister now the rain is over.

Now I was making my way through the garden. There was that strange light which follows a day of persistent rain, when the sun comes out and the sky clears too late to be of any use. The earth makes a sound as of sighs and the last drops fall from the emptied, cloudless sky. A small boy, stretching out his hands and looking up at the blue sky, asked his mother how such a thing was possible. Fuck off, she said. I suddenly remembered I had not thought of asking Mr. Weir for a piece of bread. He would surely have given it to me. I had as a matter of fact thought of it during our conversation in the hall. I had said to myself, Let us first finish our conversation, then I'll ask. I knew well they would not keep me. I would gladly have turned back, but I was afraid one of the guards would stop me and tell me I would never see Mr. Weir again. That might have added to my sorrow. And anyway I never turned back on such occasions.

In the street I was lost. I had not set foot in this part of the city for a long time and it seemed greatly changed. Whole buildings had disappeared, the palings had changed position, and on all sides I saw, in great letters, the names of tradesmen I had never seen before and would have been at a loss to pronounce. There were streets where I remembered none, some I did remember had vanished and others had completely changed their names. The general impression was the same as before. It is true I did not know the city very well. Perhaps it was quite a different one. I did not know where I was supposed to be going. I had the great good fortune, more than once, not to be run over. My appearance still made people laugh, with that hearty jovial laugh so good for the health. By keeping the red part of the sky as much as possible on my right hand I came at last to the river. Here all seemed at first sight more or less as I had left it. But if I had looked more closely I would doubtless have discovered many changes. And indeed I subsequently did so. But the general appearance of the river, flowing between its quays and under its bridges, had not changed. Yes, the river still gave the impression it was flowing in the wrong direction. That's all a pack of lies I feel. My bench was still there. It was shaped to fit the curves of the seated body. It stood beside a watering trough, gift of a Mrs. Maxwell to the city horses, according to the inscription. During the short time I rested there several horses took advantage of this monument. The iron shoes approached and the jingle of the harness. Then silence. That was the horse looking at me. Then the noise of pebbles and mud that horses make when drinking. Then the silence again. That was the horse looking at me again. Then the pebbles again. Then the silence again. Till the horse had finished drinking or the driver deemed it had drunk its fill. The horses were uneasy. Once, when the noise stopped, I turned and saw the horse looking at me. The driver too was looking at me. Mrs. Maxwell would have been pleased if she could have seen her trough rendering such services to the city horses. When it was night, after a tedious twilight, I took off my hat which was paining me. I longed to be under cover again, in an empty place, close and warm, with artificial light, an oil-lamp for choice, with a pink shade for preference. From time to time someone would come to make sure I was all right and needed nothing. It was long since I had longed for anything and the effect on me was horrible.

In the days that followed I visited several lodgings, without much success. They usually slammed the door in my face, even when I showed my money and offered to pay a week in advance, or even two. It was in vain I put on my best manners, smiled and spoke distinctly, they slammed the door in my face before I could even finish my little speech. It was at this time I perfected a method of doffing my hat at once courteous and discreet, neither servile nor insolent. I slipped it smartly forward, held it a second poised in such a way that the person addressed could not see my skull, then slipped it back. To do that naturally, without creating an unfavourable impression, is no easy matter. When I deemed that to tip my hat would suffice, I naturally did no more than tip it. But to tip one's hat is no easy matter either. I subsequently solved this problem, always fundamental in time of adversity, by wearing a kepi and saluting in military fashion, no, that must be wrong, I don't know, I had my hat at the end. I never made the mistake of wearing medals. Some landladies were in such need of money that they let me in immediately and showed me the room. But I couldn't come to an agreement with any of them. Finally I found a basement. With this woman I came to an agreement at once. My oddities, that's the expression she used, did not alarm her. She nevertheless insisted on making the bed and cleaning the room once a week, instead of once a month as I requested. She told me that while she was cleaning, which would not take long, I could wait in the area. She added, with a great deal of feeling, that she would never put me out in bad weather. This woman was Greek, I think, or Turkish. She never spoke about herself. I somehow got the idea she was a widow or at least that her husband had left her. She had a strange accent. But so had I with my way of assimilating the vowels and omitting the consonants.

Now I didn't know where I was. I had a vague vision, not a real vision, I didn't see anything, of a big house five or six stories high, one of a block perhaps. It was dusk when I got there and I did not pay the same heed to my surroundings as I might have done if I had suspected they were to close about me. And by then I must have lost all hope. It is true that when I left this house it was a glorious day, but I never look back when leaving. I must have read somewhere, when I was small and still read, that it is better not to look back when leaving. And yet I sometimes did. But even without looking back it seems to me I should have seen something when leaving. But there it is. All I remember is my feet emerging from my shadow, one after the other. My shoes had stiffened and the sun brought out the cracks in the leather.

I was comfortable enough in this house, I must say. Apart from a few rats I was alone in the basement. The woman did her best to respect our agreement. About noon she brought me a big tray of food and took away the tray of the previous day. At the same time she brought me a clean chamber-pot. The chamber-pot had a large handle which she slipped over her arm, so that both her hands were free to carry the tray. The rest of the day I saw no more of her except sometimes when she peeped in to make sure nothing had happened to me. Fortunately I did not need affection. From my bed I saw the feet coming and going on the sidewalk. Certain evenings, when the weather was fine and I felt equal to it, I fetched my chair into the area and sat looking up into the skirts of the women passing by. Once I sent for a crocus bulb and planted it in the dark area, in an old pot. It must have been coming up to spring, it was probably not the right time for it. I left the pot outside, attached to a string I passed through the window. In the evening, when the weather was fine, a little light crept up the wall. Then I sat down beside the window and pulled on the string to keep the pot in the light and warmth. That can't have been easy, I don't see how I managed it. It was probably not the right thing for it. I manured it as best I could and pissed on it when the weather was dry. It may not have been the right thing for it. It sprouted, but never any flowers, just a wilting stem and a few chlorotic leaves. I would have liked to have a yellow crocus, or a hyacinth, but there, it was not to be. She wanted to take it away, but I told her to leave it. She wanted to buy me another, but I told her I didn't want another. What lacerated me most was the din of the newspaper boys. They went pounding by every day at the same hours, their heels thudding on the sidewalk, crying the names of their papers and even the headlines. The house noises disturbed me less. A little girl, unless it was a little boy, sang every evening at the same hour, somewhere above me. For a long time I could not catch the words. But hearing them day after day I finally managed to catch a few. Strange words for a little girl, or a little boy. Was it a song in my head or did it merely come from without? It was a sort of lullaby, I believe. It often sent me to sleep, even me. Sometimes it was a little girl who came. She had long red hair hanging down in two braids. I didn't know who she was. She lingered awhile in the room, then went away without a word. One day I had a visit from a policeman. He said I had to be watched, without explaining why. Suspicious, that was it, he told me I was suspicious. I let him talk. He didn't dare arrest me. Or perhaps he had a kind heart. A priest too, one day I had a visit from a priest. I informed him I belonged to a branch of the reformed church. He asked me what kind of clergyman I would like to see. Yes, there's that about the reformed church, you're lost, it's unavoidable. Perhaps he had a kind heart. He told me to let him know if I ever needed a helping hand. A helping hand! He gave me his name and explained where I could reach him. I should have made a note of it.

One day the woman made me an offer. She said she was in urgent need of cash and that if I could pay her six months in advance she would reduce my rent by one fourth during that period, something of that kind. This had the advantage of saving six weeks' (?) rent and the disadvantage of almost exhausting my small capital. But could you call that a disadvantage? Wouldn't I stay on in any case till my last penny was gone, and even longer, till she put me out? I gave her the money and she gave me a receipt.

One morning, not long after this transaction, I was awakened by a man shaking my shoulder. It could not have been much past eleven. He requested me to get up and leave his house immediately. He was most correct, I must say. His surprise, he said, was no less than mine. It was his house. His property. The Turkish woman had left the day before. But I saw her last night, I said. You must be mistaken, he said, for she brought the keys to my office no later than yesterday afternoon. But I just paid her six months' rent in advance, I said. Get a refund, he said. But I don't even know her name, I said, let alone her address. You don't know her name? he said. He must have thought I was lying. I'm sick, I said, I can't leave like this, without any notice. You're not so sick as all that, he said. He offered to send for a taxi, even an ambulance if I preferred. He said he needed the room immediately for his pig which even as he spoke was catching cold in a cart before the door and no one to look after him but a stray urchin whom he had never set eyes on before and who was probably busy tormenting him. I asked if he couldn't let me have another place, any old corner where I could lie down long enough to recover from the shock and decide what to do. He said he could not. Don't think I'm being unkind, he added. I could live here with the pig, I said, I'd look after him. The long months of peace, wiped out in an instant! Come now, come now, he said, get a grip on yourself, be a man, get up, that's enough. After all it was no concern of his. He had really been most patient. He must have visited the basement while I was sleeping.

I felt weak. Perhaps I was. I stumbled in the blinding light. A bus took me into the country. I sat down in a field in the sun. But it seems to me that was much later. I stuck leaves under my hat, all the way round, to make a shade. The night was cold. I wandered for hours in the fields. At last I found a heap of dung. The next day I started back to the city. They made me get off three buses. I sat down by the roadside and dried my clothes in the sun. I enjoyed doing that. I said to myself, There's nothing more to be done now, not a thing, till they are dry. When they were dry I brushed them with a brush, I think a kind of curry-comb, that I found in a stable. Stables have always been my salvation. Then I went to the house and begged a glass of milk and a slice of bread and butter. They gave me everything except the butter. May I rest in the stable? I said. No, they said. I still stank, but with a stink that pleased me. I much preferred it to my own which moreover it prevented me from smelling, except a waft now and then. In the days that followed I took the necessary steps to recover my money. I don't know exactly what happened, whether I couldn't find the address, or whether there was no such address, or whether the Greek woman was unknown there. I ransacked my pockets for the receipt, to try and decipher the name. It wasn't there. Perhaps she had taken it back while I was sleeping. I don't know how long I wandered thus, resting now in one place, now in another, in the city and in the country. The city had suffered many changes. Nor was the country as I remembered it. The general effect was the same. One day I caught sight of my son. He was striding along with a briefcase under his arm. He took off his hat and bowed and I saw he was as bald as a coot. I was almost certain it was he. I turned round to gaze after him. He went bustling along on his duck feet, bowing and scraping and flourishing his hat left and right. The insufferable son of a bitch.

One day I met a man I had known in former times. He lived in a cave by the sea. He had an ass that grazed winter and summer, over the cliffs, or along the little tracks leading down to the sea. When the weather was very bad this ass came down to the cave of his own accord and sheltered there till the storm was past. So they had spent many a night huddled together, while the wind howled and the sea pounded on the shore. With the help of this ass he could deliver sand, sea-wrack, and shells to the townsfolk, for their gardens. He couldn't carry much at a time, for the ass was old and small and the town was far. But in this way he earned a little money, enough to keep him in tobacco and matches and to buy a piece of bread from time to time. It was during one of these excursions that he met me, in the suburbs. He was delighted to see me, poor man. He begged me to go home with him and spend the night. Stay as long as you like, he said. What's wrong with your ass? I said. Don't mind him, he said, he doesn't know you. I reminded him that I wasn't in the habit of staying more than two or three minutes with anyone and that the sea did not agree with me. He seemed deeply grieved to hear it. So you won't come, he said. But to my amazement I got up on the ass and off we went, in the shade of the red chestnuts springing from the sidewalk. I held the ass by the mane, one hand in front of the other. The little boys jeered and threw stones, but their aim was poor, for they only hit me once, on the hat. A policeman stopped us and accused us of disturbing the peace. My friend replied that we were as nature had made us, the boys too were as nature had made them. It was inevitable, under these conditions, that the peace should be disturbed from time to time. Let us continue on our way, he said, and order will soon be restored throughout your beat. We followed the quiet, dustwhite inland roads with their hedges of hawthorn and fuchsia and their footpaths fringed with wild grass and daisies. Night fell. The ass carried me right to the mouth of the cave, for in the dark I could not have found my way down the path winding steeply to the sea. Then he climbed back to his pasture.

I don't know how long I stayed there. The cave was nicely arranged, I must say. I treated my crablice with salt water and seaweed, but a lot of nits must have survived. I put compresses of seaweed on my skull, which gave me great relief, but not for long. I lay in the cave and sometimes looked out at the horizon. I saw above me a vast trembling expanse without islands or promontories. At night a light shone into the cave at regular intervals. It was here I found the phial in my pocket. It was not broken, for the glass was not real glass. I thought Mr. Weir had confiscated all my belongings. My host was out most of the time. He fed me on fish. It is easy for a man, a proper man, to live in a cave, far from everybody. He invited me to stay as long as I liked. If I preferred to be alone he would gladly prepare another cave for me farther on. He would bring me food every day and drop in from time to time to make sure I was all right and needed nothing. He was kind. Unfortunately I did not need kindness. You wouldn't know of a lake dwelling? I said. I couldn't bear the sea, its splashing and heaving, its tides and general convulsiveness. The wind at least sometimes stops. My hands and feet felt as though they were full of ants. This kept me awake for hours on end. If I stayed here something awful would happen to me, I said, and a lot of good that would do me. You'd get drowned, he said. Yes, I said, or I'd jump off the cliff. And to think I couldn't live anywhere else, he said, in my cabin in the mountains I was very unhappy. Your cabin in the mountains? I said. He repeated the story of his cabin in the mountains, I had forgotten it, it was as though I were hearing it for the first time. I asked him if he still had it. He replied he had not seen it since the day he fled from it, but that he believed it was

still there, a little decayed no doubt. But when he urged me to take the
key I refused, saying I had other plans. You will always find me here, he
said, if you ever need me. Ah people. He gave me his knife.

What he called his cabin was a sort of wooden shed. The door had
been removed, for firewood, or for some other purpose. The glass had
disappeared from the window. The roof had fallen in at several places.
The interior was divided, by the remains of a partition, into two unequal
parts. If there had been any furniture it was gone. The vilest acts had been
committed on the ground and against the walls. The floor was strewn
with excrements, both human and animal, with condoms and vomit. In
a cowpad a heart had been traced, pierced by an arrow. And yet there was
nothing to attract tourists. I noticed the remains of abandoned nosegays.
They had been greedily gathered, carried for miles, then thrown away,
because they were cumbersome or already withered. This was the dwell-
ing to which I had been offered the key.

The scene was the familiar one of grandeur and desolation.

Nevertheless it was a roof over my head. I rested on a bed of ferns,
gathered at great labour with my own hands. One day I couldn't get up.
The cow saved me. Goaded by the icy mist she came in search of shelter.
It was probably not the first time. She can't have seen me. I tried to suck
her, without much success. Her udder was covered with dung. I took off
my hat and, summoning all my energy, began to milk her into it. The
milk fell to the ground and was lost, but I said to myself, No matter, it's
free. She dragged me across the floor, stopping from time to time only
to kick me. I didn't know our cows too could be so inhuman. She must
have recently been milked. Clutching the dug with one hand I kept my
hat under it with the other. But in the end she prevailed. For she dragged
me across the threshold and out into the giant streaming ferns, where I
was forced to let go.

As I drank the milk I reproached myself with what I had done. I could
no longer count on this cow and she would warn the others. More master
of myself I might have made a friend of her. She would have come every
day, perhaps accompanied by other cows. I might have learnt to make
butter, even cheese. But I said to myself, No, all is for the best.

Once on the road it was all downhill. Soon there were carts, but they all refused to take me up. In other clothes, with another face, they might have taken me up. I must have changed since my expulsion from the basement. The face notably seemed to have attained its climacteric. The humble, ingenuous smile would no longer come, nor the expression of candid misery, showing the stars and the distaff. I summoned them, but they would not come. A mask of dirty old hairy leather, with two holes and a slit, it was too far gone for the old trick of please your honour and God reward you and pity upon me. It was disastrous. What would I crawl with in future? I lay down on the side of the road and began to writhe each time I heard a cart approaching. That was so they would not think I was sleeping or resting. I tried to groan, Help! Help! But the tone that came out was that of polite conversation. My hour was not yet come and I could no longer groan. The last time I had cause to groan I had groaned as well as ever, and no heart within miles of me to melt. What was to become of me? I said to myself, I'll learn again. I lay down across the road at a narrow place, so that the carts could not pass without passing over my body, with one wheel at least, or two if there were four. But the day came when, looking round me, I was in the suburbs, and from there to the old haunts it was not far, beyond the stupid hope of rest or less pain.

So I covered the lower part of my face with a black rag and went and begged at a sunny corner. For it seemed to me my eyes were not completely spent, thanks perhaps to the dark glasses my tutor had given me. He had given me the *Ethics* of Geulincx. They were a man's glasses, I was a child. They found him dead, crumpled up in the water closet, his clothes in awful disorder, struck down by an infarctus. Ah what peace. The *Ethics* had his name (Ward) on the fly-leaf, the glasses had belonged to him. The bridge, at the time I am speaking of, was of brass wire, of the kind used to hang pictures and big mirrors, and two long black ribbons served as wings. I wound them round my ears and then down under my chin where I tied them together. The lenses had suffered, from rubbing in my pocket against each other and against the other objects there. I thought Mr. Weir had confiscated all my belongings. But I had no further need of these glasses and used them merely to soften the glare of the sun. I should never have mentioned them. The rag gave me a lot of trouble. I got it in the end from the lining of my greatcoat, no, I had no greatcoat now, of my coat then. The result was a grey rag rather than a black, perhaps even chequered, but I had to make do with it. Till afternoon I held my face raised towards the southern sky, then towards the western till night. The bowl gave me a lot of trouble. I couldn't use my hat because of my skull. As for holding out my hand, that was quite out of the question. So I got a tin and hung it from a button of my greatcoat, what's the matter with me, of my coat, at pubis level. It did not hang plumb, it leaned respectfully towards the passer-by, he had only to drop his mite. But that obliged him to come up close to me, he was in danger of touching me. In the end I got a bigger tin, a kind of big tin box, and I placed it on the sidewalk at my feet. But people who give alms don't much care to toss them, there's something contemptuous about this gesture which is repugnant to sensitive natures. To say nothing of their having to aim. They are prepared to give, but not for their gift to go rolling under the passing feet or under the passing wheels, to be picked up perhaps by some undeserving person. So they don't give. There are those, to be sure, who stoop, but generally speaking people who give alms don't much care to stoop. What they like above all is to sight the wretch from afar, get ready their penny, drop it in their stride and hear the God bless you dying away in the distance. Personally I never said that, nor anything like it, I wasn't much of a believer, but I did make a noise with my mouth. In the end I got a kind of board or tray and tied it to my neck and waist. It jutted out just at the right height, pocket height, and its edge was far enough from my person for the coin to be bestowed without danger. Some days I strewed it with flowers, petals, buds and that herb which men call fleabane, I believe, in a word whatever I could find. I didn't go out of my way to look for them, but all the pretty things of this description that came my way were for the board. They must have thought I loved nature. Most of the time I looked up at the sky, but without focussing it, for why focus it? Most of the time it was a mixture of white, blue and grey, and then at evening all the evening colours. I felt it weighing softly on my face, I rubbed my face against it, one cheek after the other, turning my head from side to side.

Now and then to rest my neck I dropped my head on my chest. Then I could see the board in the distance, a haze of many colours. I leaned against the wall, but without nonchalance, I shifted my weight from one foot to the other and my hands clutched the lapels of my coat. To beg with your hands in your pockets makes a bad impression, it irritates the workers, especially in winter. You should never wear gloves either. There were guttersnipes who swept away all I had earned, under cover of giving me a coin. It was to buy sweets. I unbuttoned my trousers discreetly to scratch myself. I scratched myself in an upward direction, with four nails. I pulled on the hairs, to get relief. It passed the time, time flew when I scratched myself. Real scratching is superior to masturbation, in my opinion. One can masturbate up to the age of seventy, and even beyond, but in the end it becomes a mere habit. Whereas to scratch myself properly I would have needed a dozen hands. I itched all over, on the privates, in the bush up to the navel, under the arms, in the arse, and then patches of eczema and psoriasis that I could set raging merely by thinking of them. It was in the arse I had the most pleasure. I stuck my forefinger up to the knuckle. Later, if I had to shit, the pain was atrocious. But I hardly shat any more. Now and then a flying machine flew by, sluggishly it seemed to me. Often at the end of the day I discovered the leg of my trousers all wet. That must have been the dogs. I personally pissed very little. If by chance the need came on me a little squirt in my fly was enough to relieve it. Once at my post I did not leave it till nightfall. I had no appetite, God tempered the wind to me. After work I bought a bottle of milk and drank it in the evening in the shed. Better still, I got a little boy to buy it for me, always the same, they wouldn't serve me, I don't know why. I gave him a penny for his pains. One day I witnessed a strange scene. Normally I didn't see a great deal. I didn't hear a great deal either. I didn't pay attention. Strictly speaking I wasn't there. Strictly speaking I believe I've never been anywhere. But that day I must have come back. For some time past a sound had been scarifying me. I did not investigate the cause, for I said to myself, It's going to stop. But as it did not stop I had no choice but to find out the cause. It was a man perched on the roof of a car and haranguing the passers-by. That at least was my interpretation. He was bellowing

so loud that snatches of his discourse reached my ears. Union . . . broth-
ers . . . Marx . . . capital . . . bread and butter . . . love. It was all Greek to
me. The car was drawn up against the kerb, just in front of me, I saw
the orator from behind. All of a sudden he turned and pointed at me, as
at an exhibit. Look at this down and out, he vociferated, this leftover. If
he doesn't go down on all fours, it's for fear of being impounded. Old,
lousy, rotten, ripe for the muckheap. And there are a thousand like him,
worse than him, ten thousand, twenty thousand—. A voice, Thirty thou-
sand. Every day you pass them by, resumed the orator, and when you have
backed a winner you fling them a farthing. Do you ever think? The voice,
God forbid. A penny, resumed the orator, tuppence—. The voice, Thrup-
pence. It never enters your head, resumed the orator, that your charity is
a crime, an incentive to slavery, stultification and organized murder. Take
a good look at this living corpse. You may say it's his own fault. Ask him
if it's his own fault. The voice, Ask him yourself. Then he bent forward
and took me to task. I had perfected my board. It now consisted of two
boards hinged together, which enabled me, when my work was done, to
fold it and carry it under my arm. I liked doing little odd jobs. So I took
off the rag, pocketed the few coins I had earned, untied the board, folded
it and put it under my arm. Do you hear me, you crucified bastard! cried
the orator. Then I went away, although it was still light. But generally
speaking it was a quiet corner, busy but not overcrowded, thriving and
well-frequented. He must have been a religious fanatic, I could find no
other explanation. Perhaps he was an escaped lunatic. He had a nice face,
a little on the red side.

I did not work every day. I had practically no expenses. I even man-
aged to put a little aside, for my very last days. The days I did not work I
spent lying in the shed. The shed was on a private estate, or what had
once been a private estate, on the riverside. This estate, the main entrance
to which opened on a narrow, dark and silent street, was enclosed with a
wall, except of course on the river front, which marked its northern
boundary for a distance of about thirty yards. From the last quays beyond
the water the eyes rose to a confusion of low houses, wasteland, hoard-
ings, chimneys, steeples and towers. A kind of parade ground was also to

be seen, where soldiers played football all the year round. Only the ground-floor windows—no, I can't. The estate seemed abandoned. The gates were locked and the paths were overgrown with grass. Only the ground-floor windows had shutters. The others were sometimes lit at night, faintly, now one, now another. At least that was my impression. Perhaps it was reflected light. In this shed, the day I adopted it, I found a boat, upside down. I righted it, chocked it up with stones and pieces of wood, took out the thwarts and made my bed inside. The rats had difficulty in getting at me, because of the bulge of the hull. And yet they longed to. Just think of it, living flesh, for in spite of everything I was still living flesh. I had lived too long among rats, in my chance dwellings, to share the dread they inspire in the vulgar. I even had a soft spot in my heart for them. They came with such confidence towards me, it seemed without the least repugnance. They made their toilet with catlike gestures. Toads at evening, motionless for hours, lap flies from the air. They like to squat where cover ends and open air begins, they favour thresholds. But I had to contend now with water rats, exceptionally lean and ferocious. So I made a kind of lid with stray boards. It's incredible the number of boards I've come across in my lifetime, I never needed a board but there it was, I had only to stoop and pick it up. I liked doing little odd jobs, no, not particularly, I didn't mind. It completely covered the boat, I'm referring again to the lid. I pushed it a little towards the stern, climbed into the boat by the bow, crawled to the stern, raised my feet and pushed the lid back to the bow till it covered me completely. But what did my feet push against? They pushed against a cross bar I nailed to the lid for that purpose, I liked these little odd jobs. But it was better to climb into the boat by the stern and pull back the lid with my hands till it completely covered me, then push it forward in the same way when I wanted to get out. As holds for my hands I planted two spikes just where I needed them. These little odds and ends of carpentry, if I may so describe it, carried out with whatever tools and material I chanced to find, gave me a certain pleasure. I knew it would soon be the end, so I played the part, you know, the part of—how shall I say, I don't know. I was comfortable enough in this boat, I must say. The lid fitted so well I had to pierce a hole. It's no good closing your eyes, you must leave them open in the dark, that is my opinion. I am not speaking of sleep, I am speaking of what I believe is called waking. In any case, I slept very little at this period, I wasn't sleepy, or I was too sleepy, I don't know, or I was afraid, I don't know. Flat then on my back I saw nothing except, dimly, just above my head, through the tiny chinks, the grey light of the shed. To see nothing at all, no, that's too much. I heard faintly the cries of the gulls ravening about the mouth of the sewer nearby. In a spew of yellow foam, if my memory serves me right, the filth gushed into the river and the slush of birds above screaming with hunger and fury. I heard the lapping of water against the slip and against the bank and the other sound, so different, of open wave, I heard it too. I too, when I moved, felt less boat than wave, or so it seemed to me, and my stillness was the stillness of eddies. That may seem impossible. The rain too, I often heard it, for it often rained. Sometimes a drop, falling through the roof of the shed, exploded on me. All that composed a rather liquid world. And then of course there was the voice of the wind or rather those, so various, of its playthings. But what does it amount to? Howling, soughing, moaning, sighing. What I would have liked was hammer strokes, bang bang bang, clanging in the desert. I let farts to be sure, but hardly ever a real crack, they oozed out with a sucking noise, melted in the mighty never. I don't know how long I stayed there. I was very snug in my box, I must say. It seemed to me I had grown more independent of recent years. That no one came any more, that no one could come any more, to ask me if I was all right and needed nothing, distressed me then but little. I was all right, yes, quite so, and the fear of getting worse was less with me. As for my needs, they had dwindled as it were to my dimensions and become, if I may say so, of so exquisite a quality as to exclude all thought of succour. To know I had a being, however faint and false, outside of me, had once had the power to stir my heart. You become unsociable, it's inevitable. It's enough to make you wonder sometimes if you are on the right planet. Even the words desert you, it's as bad as that. Perhaps it's the moment when the vessels stop communicating, you know, the vessels. There you are still between the two murmurs, it must be the same old song as ever, but Christ you wouldn't think so. There were times when

I wanted to push away the lid and get out of the boat and couldn't, I was so indolent and weak, so content deep down where I was. I felt them hard upon me, the icy, tumultuous streets, the terrifying faces, the noises that slash, pierce, claw, bruise. So I waited till the desire to shit, or even to piss, lent me wings. I did not want to dirty my nest! And yet it sometimes happened, and even more and more often. Arched and rigid I edged down my trousers and turned a little on my side, just enough to free the hole. To contrive a little kingdom, in the midst of the universal muck, then shit on it, ah that was me all over. The excrements were me too, I know, I know, but all the same. Enough, enough, the next thing I was having visions, I who never did, except sometimes in my sleep, who never had, real visions, I'd remember, except perhaps as a child, my myth will have it so. I knew they were visions because it was night and I was alone in my boat. What else could they have been? So I was in my boat and gliding on the waters. I didn't have to row, the ebb was carrying me out. Anyway I saw no oars, they must have taken them away. I had a board, the remains of a thwart perhaps, which I used when I came too close to the bank, or when a pier came bearing down on me or a barge at its moorings. There were stars in the sky, quite a few. I didn't know what the weather was doing, I was neither cold nor warm and all seemed calm. The banks receded more and more, it was inevitable, soon I saw them no more. The lights grew fainter and fewer as the river widened. There on the land men were sleeping, bodies were gathering strength for the toil and joys of the morrow. The boat was not gliding now, it was tossing, buffeted by the choppy waters of the bay. All seemed calm and yet foam was washing aboard. Now the sea air was all about me, I had no other shelter than the land, and what does it amount to, the shelter of the land, at such a time. I saw the beacons, four in all, including a lightship. I knew them well, even as a child I had known them well. It was evening, I was with my father on a height, he held my hand. I would have liked him to draw me close with a gesture of protective love, but his mind was on other things. He also taught me the names of the mountains. But to have done with these visions I also saw the lights of the buoys, the sea seemed full of them, red and green, and to my surprise even yellow. And on the slopes of the mountain, now rearing its unbroken bulk behind the town, the fires turned from gold to red, from red to gold. I knew what it was, it was the gorse burning. How often I had set a match to it myself, as a child. And hours later, back in my home, before I climbed into bed, I watched from my high window the fires I had lit. That night then, all aglow with distant fires, on sea, on land and in the sky, I drifted with the currents and the tides. I noticed that my hat was tied, with a string I suppose, to my button-hole. I got up from my seat in the stern and a great clanking was heard. That was the chain. One end was fastened to the bow and the other round my waist. I must have pierced a hole beforehand in the floor-boards, for there I was down on my knees prying out the plug with my knife. The hole was small and the water rose slowly. It would take a good half hour, everything included, barring accidents. Back now in the stern-sheets, my legs stretched out, my back well propped against the sack stuffed with grass I used as a cushion, I swallowed my calmative. The sea, the sky, the mountains and the islands closed in and crushed me in a mighty systole, then scattered to the uttermost confines of space. The memory came faint and cold of the story I might have told, a story in the likeness of my life, I mean without the courage to end or the strength to go on.

Texts for Nothing

1

Suddenly, no, at last, long last, I couldn't any more, I couldn't go on. Someone said, You can't stay here. I couldn't stay there and I couldn't go on. I'll describe the place, that's unimportant. The top, very flat, of a mountain, no, a hill, but so wild, so wild, enough. Quag, heath up to the knees, faint sheep-tracks, troughs scooped deep by the rains. It was far down in one of these I was lying, out of the wind. Glorious prospect, but for the mist that blotted out everything, valleys, loughs, plain and sea. How can I go on, I shouldn't have begun, no, I had to begin. Someone said, perhaps the same, What possessed you to come? I could have stayed in my den, snug and dry, I couldn't. My den, I'll describe it, no, I can't. It's simple, I can do nothing any more, that's what you think. I say to the body, Up with you now, and I can feel it struggling, like an old hack foundered in the street, struggling no more, struggling again, till it gives up. I say to the head, Leave it alone, stay quiet, it stops breathing, then pants on worse than ever. I am far from all that wrangle, I shouldn't bother with it, I need nothing, neither to go on nor to stay where I am, it's truly all one to me, I should turn away from it all, away from the body, away from the head, let them work it out between them, let them cease, I can't, it's I would have to cease. Ah yes, we seem to be more than one, all deaf, not even, gathered together for life. Another said, or the same, or the first, they all have the same voice, the same ideas, All you had to do was stay at home. Home. They wanted me to go home. My dwelling-place. But for the mist, with good eyes, with a telescope, I could see it from here. It's not just tiredness, I'm not just tired, in spite of the climb. It's not that I want to stay here either. I had heard tell, I must have heard tell of the view, the distant sea in hammered lead, the so-called golden vale so often sung, the double valleys, the glacial loughs, the city in its haze, it was all on every tongue. Who are these people anyway? Did they follow me up here, go before me, come with me? I am down in the hole the centuries have dug, centuries of filthy weather, flat on my face on the dark earth sodden with the creeping saffron waters it slowly drinks. They are up above, all round me, as in a graveyard. I can't raise my eyes to them, what a pity, I wouldn't see their faces, their legs perhaps, plunged in the heath. Do they see me, what can they see of me? Perhaps there is no one left, perhaps they are all gone, sickened. I listen and it's the same thoughts I hear, I mean the same as ever, strange. To think in the valley the sun is blazing all down the ravelled sky. How long have I been here, what a question, I've often wondered. And often I could answer, An hour, a month, a year, a century, depending on what I meant by here, and me, and being, and there I never went looking for extravagant meanings, there I never much varied, only the here would sometimes seem to vary. Or I said, I can't have been here long, I wouldn't have held out. I hear the curlews, that means close of day, fall of night, for that's the way with curlews, silent all day, then crying when the darkness gathers, that's the way with those wild creatures and so short-lived, compared with me. And that other question I know so well too, What possessed you to come?, unanswerable, so that I answered, To change, or, It's not me, or, Chance, or again, To see, or again, years of great sun, Fate, I feel that other coming, let it come, it won't catch me napping. All is noise, unending suck of black sopping peat, surge of giant ferns, heathery gulfs of quiet where the wind drowns, my life and its old jingles. To change, to see, no, there's no more to see, I've seen it all, till my eyes are blear, nor to get away from harm, the harm is done, one day the harm was done, the day my feet dragged me out that must go their ways, that I let go their ways and drag me here, that's what possessed me to come. And what I'm doing, all-important, breathing in and out and saying, with words like smoke, I can't go, I can't stay, let's see what happens next. And in the way of sensation? My God I can't complain, it's himself all right, only muffled, like buried in snow, less the warmth, less the drowse, I can follow them well, all the voices, all the parts, fairly well, the cold is eating me, the wet too, at least I presume so, I'm far. My rheumatism in any case is no more than a memory, it hurts me no more than my mother's did, when it hurt her. Eye ravening patient in the haggard vulture face, perhaps it's carrion time. I'm up there and I'm down here, under my gaze, foundered, eyes closed, ear cupped against the sucking peat, we're of one mind, all of one mind, always were, deep down, we're fond of one another, we're sorry for one another, but there it is, there's nothing we can do for one another. One thing at least is certain, in an hour it will be too late, in half-an-hour it will be night, and yet it's not, not certain, what is not certain, absolutely certain, that night prevents what day permits, for those who know how to go about it, who have the will to go about it, and the strength, the strength to try again. Yes, it will be night, the mist will clear, I know my mist, for all my distraction, the wind freshen and the whole night sky open over the mountain, with its lights, including the Bears, to guide me once again on my way, let's wait for night. All mingles, times and tenses, at first I only had been here, now I'm here still, soon I won't be here yet, toiling up the slope, or in the bracken by the wood, it's larch, I don't try to understand, I'll never try to understand any more, that's what you think, for the moment I'm here, always have been, always shall be, I won't be afraid of the big words any more, they are not big. I don't remember coming, I can't go, all my little company, my eyes are closed and I feel the wet humus harsh against my cheek, my hat is gone, it can't be gone far, or the wind has swept it away, I was attached to it. Sometimes it's the sea, other times the mountains, often it was the forest, the city, the plain too, I've flirted with the plain too, I've given myself up for dead all over the place, of hunger, of old age, murdered, drowned, and then for no reason, of tedium, nothing like breathing your last to put new life in you, and then the rooms, natural death, tucked up in bed, smothered in household gods, and always muttering, the same old mutterings, the same old stories, the same old questions and answers, no malice in me, hardly any, stultior stultissimo, never an imprecation, not such a fool, or else it's gone from mind. Yes, to the end, always muttering, to lull me and keep me company, and all ears always, all ears for the old stories, as when my father took me on his knee and read me the one about Joe Breem, or Breen, the son of a lighthouse-keeper, evening after evening, all the long winter through. A tale, it was a tale for children, it all happened on a rock, in the storm, the mother was dead and the gulls came beating against the light, Joe jumped into the sea, that's all I remember, a knife between his teeth, did what was to be done and came back, that's all I remember this evening, it ended happily, it began unhappily and it ended happily, every evening, a comedy, for children. Yes, I was my father and I was my son, I asked myself questions and answered as best I could, I had it told to me evening after evening, the same old story I knew by heart and couldn't believe, or we walked together, hand in hand, silent, sunk in our worlds, each in his worlds, the hands forgotten in each other. That's how I've held out till now. And this evening again it seems to be working, I'm in my arms, I'm holding myself in my arms, without much tenderness, but faithfully, faithfully. Sleep now, as under that ancient lamp, all twined together, tired out with so much talking, so much listening, so much toil and play.

2

Above is the light, the elements, a kind of light, sufficient to see by, the living find their ways, without too much trouble, avoid one another, unite, avoid the obstacles, without too much trouble, seek with their eyes, close their eyes, halting, without halting, among the elements, the living. Unless it has changed, unless it has ceased. The things too must still be there, a little more worn, a little even less, many still standing where they stood in the days of their indifference. Here you are under a different glass, not long habitable either, it's time to leave it. You are there, there it is, where you are will never long be habitable. Go then, no, better stay, for where would you go, now that you know? Back above? There are limits. Back in that kind of light. See the cliffs again, be again between the cliffs and the sea, reeling shrinking with your hands over your ears, headlong, innocent, suspect, noxious. Seek, by the excessive light of night, a demand commensurate with the offer, and go to ground empty-handed at the old crack of day. See Mother Calvet again, creaming off the garbage before the nightmen come. She must still be there. With her dog and her skeletal baby buggy. What could be more endurable? She wavered through the night, a kind of trident in her hand, muttering and ejaculating, Your highness! Your honour! The dog tottered on its hind-legs begging, hooked its paws over the rim of the can and snouted round with her in the muck. It got in her way, she cursed it for a lousy cur and let it have its way. There's a good memory. Mother Calvet. She knew what she liked, perhaps even what she would have liked. And beauty, strength, intelligence, the latest, daily, action, poetry, all one price for one and all. If only it could be wiped from knowledge. To have suffered under that miserable light, what a blunder. It let nothing show, it would have gone out, nothing terrible, nothing showed, of the true affair, it would have snuffed out. And now here, what now here, one enormous second, as in Paradise, and the mind slow, slow, nearly stopped. And yet it's changing, something is changing, it must be in the head, slowly in the head the ragdoll rotting, perhaps we're in a head, it's as dark as in a head before the worms get at it, ivory dungeon. The words too, slow, slow, the subject dies before it comes to the verb, words are stopping too. Better off then than when life was babble? That's it, that's it, the bright side. And the absence of others, does that count for so little? Pah others, that's nothing, others never inconvenienced anyone, and there must be a few here too, other others, invisible, mute, what does it matter. It's true you hid from them, hugged their walls, true, you miss that here, you miss the derivatives, here it's pure ache, pah you were saying that above and you a living mustard-plaster. So long as the words keep coming nothing will have changed, there are the old words out again. Utter, there's nothing else, utter, void yourself of them, here as always, nothing else. But they are failing, true, that's the change, they are failing, that's bad, bad. Or it's the dread of com-ing to the last, of having said all, your all, before the end, no, for that will be the end, the end of all, not certain. To need to groan and not be able, Jesus, better ration yourself, watch out for the genuine deathpangs, some are deceptive, you think you're home, start howling and revive, health-giving howls, better be silent, it's the only method, if you want to end, not a word but smiles, end rent with stifled imprecations, burst with speech-lessness, all is possible, what now. Perhaps above it's summer, a sum-mer Sunday, Mr. Joly is in the belfry, he has wound up the clock, now he's ringing the bells. Mr. Joly. He had only one leg and a half. Sunday. It was folly to be abroad. The roads were crawling with them, the same roads so often kind. Here at least none of that, no talk of a creator and nothing very definite in the way of a creation. Dry, it's possible, or wet, or slime, as before matter took ill. Is this stuff air that permits you to suffocate still, almost audibly at times, it's possible, a kind of air. What exactly is going on, exactly, ah old xanthic laugh, no, farewell mirth, good riddance, it was never droll. No, but one more memory, one last memory, it may help, to abort again. Piers pricking his oxen o'er the plain, no, for at the end of the furrow, before turning to the next, he raised his eyes to the sky and said, Bright again too early. And sure enough, soon after, the snow. In other words the night was black, when it fell at last, but no, strange, it wasn't, in spite of the buried sky. The way was long that led back to the den, over the fields, a winding way, it must still be there. When it comes to the top of the cliff it springs, some might think blindly, but no, wilily, like a goat, in hairpin zigzags towards the shore. Never had the sea so thundered from afar, the sea beneath the snow, though superlatives have lost most of their charm. The day had not been fruitful, as was only natural, considering the season, that of the very last leeks. It was none the less the return, to what no matter, the return, unscathed, always a matter for wonder. What happened? Is that the question? An encounter? Bang! No. Level with the farm of the Graves brothers a brief halt, opposite the lamplit window. A glow, red, afar, at night, in winter, that's worth having, that must have been worth having. There, it's done, it ends there, I end there. A far memory, far from the last, it's possible, the legs seem to be still working. A pity hope is dead. No. How one hoped above, on and off. With what diversity.

3

Leave, I was going to say leave all that. What matter who's speaking, someone said what matter who's speaking. There's going to be a departure, I'll be there, I won't miss it, it won't be me, I'll be here, I'll say I'm far from here, it won't be me, I won't say anything, there's going to be a story, someone's going to try and tell a story. Yes, no more denials, all is false, there is no one, it's understood, there is nothing, no more phrases, let us be dupes, dupes of every time and tense, until it's done, all past and done, and the voices cease, it's only voices, only lies. Here, depart from here and go elsewhere, or stay here, but coming and going. Start by stirring, there must be a body, as of old, I don't deny it, no more denials, I'll say I'm a body, stirring back and forth, up and down, as required. With a cluther of limbs and organs, all that is needed to live again, to hold out a little time, I'll call that living, I'll say it's me, I'll get standing, I'll stop thinking, I'll be too busy, getting standing, staying standing, stirring about, holding out, getting to tomorrow, tomorrow week, that will be ample, a week will be ample, a week in spring, that puts the jizz in you. It's enough to will it, I'll will it, will me a body, will me a head, a little strength, a little courage, I'm starting now, a week is soon served, then back here, this inextricable place, far from the days, the far days, it's not going to be easy. And why, come to think, no no, leave it, no more of that, don't listen to it all, don't say it all, it's all old, all one, once and for all. There you are now on your feet, I give you my word, I swear they're yours, I swear it's mine, get to work with your hands,

palp your skull, seat of the understanding, without which nix, then the
rest, the lower regions, you'll be needing them, and say what you're like,
have a guess, what kind of man, there has to be a man, or a woman, feel
between your legs, no need of beauty, nor of vigour, a week's a short
stretch, no one's going to love you, don't be alarmed. No, not like that, too
sudden, I gave myself a start. And to start with stop palpitating, no one's
going to kill you, no one's going to love you and no one's going to kill you,
perhaps you'll emerge in the high depression of Gobi, you'll feel at home
there. I'll wait for you here, no, I am alone, I alone am, this time it's I must
go. I know how I'll do it, I'll be a man, there's nothing else for it, a kind of
man, a kind of old tot, I'll have a nanny, I'll be her sweet pet, she'll give
me her hand, to cross over, she'll let me loose in the Green, I'll be good,
I'll sit quiet as a mouse in a corner and comb my beard, I'll tease it out, to
look more bonny, a little more bonny, if only it could be like that. She'll
say to me, Come, doty, it's time for bye-bye. I'll have no responsibility,
she'll have all the responsibility, her name will be Bibby, I'll call her Bibby,
if only it could be like that. Come, ducky, it's time for yum-yum. Who
taught me all I know, I alone, in the old wanderyears, I deduced it all from
nature, with the help of an all-in-one, I know it's not me, but it's too late
now, too late to deny it, the knowledge is there, the bits and scraps, flick-
ering on and off, turn about, winking on the storm, in league to fool me.
Leave it and go, it's time to go, to say so anyway, the moment has come, it's
not known why. What matter how you describe yourself, here or else-
where, fixed or mobile, without form or oblong like man, in the dark or
the light of the heavens, I don't know, it seems to matter, it's not going to
be easy. And if I went back to where all went out and on from there, no,
that would lead nowhere, never led anywhere, the memory of it has gone
out too, a great flame and then blackness, a great spasm and then no
more weight or traversable space. I tried throwing me off a cliff, collaps-
ing in the street in the midst of mortals, that led nowhere, I gave up. Take
the road again that cast me up here, then retrace it, or follow it on, wise
advice. That's so that I'll never stir again, dribble on here till time is done,
murmuring every ten centuries, It's not me, it's not true, it's not me, I'm
far. No no, I'll speak now of the future, I'll speak in the future, as when I

used to say, in the night, to myself, Tomorrow I'll put on my dark blue tie, with the yellow stars, and put it on, when night was past. Quick quick before I weep. I'll have a crony, my own vintage, my own bog, a fellow warrior, we'll relive our campaigns and compare our scratches. Quick quick. He'll have served in the navy, perhaps under Jellicoe, while I was potting at the invader from behind a barrel of Guinness, with my arquebuse. We have not long, that's the spirit, in the present, not long to live, it's our positively last winter, halleluiah. We wonder what will carry us off in the end. He's gone in the wind, I in the prostate rather. We envy each other, I envy him, he envies me, occasionally. I catheterize myself, unaided, with trembling hand, bent double in the public pisshouse, under cover of my cloak, people take me for a dirty old man. He waits for me to finish, sitting on a bench, coughing up his guts, spitting into a snuffbox which no sooner overflows than he empties it in the canal, out of civic-mindedness. We have well deserved of our motherland, she'll get us into the Incurables before we die. We spend our life, it's ours, trying to bring together in the same instant a ray of sunshine and a free bench, in some oasis of public verdure, we've been seized by a love of nature, in our sere and yellow, it belongs to one and all, in places. In a choking murmur he reads out to me from the paper of the day before, he had far far better been the blind one. The sport of kings is our passion, the dogs too, we have no political opinions, simply limply republican. But we also have a soft spot for the Windsors, the Hanoverians, I forget, the Hohenzollerns is it. Nothing human is foreign to us, once we have digested the racing news. No, alone, I'd be better off alone, it would be quicker. He'd nourish me, he had a friend a pork-butcher, he'd ram the ghost back down my gullet with black pudding. With his consolations, allusions to cancer, recollections of imperishable raptures, he'd prevent discouragement from sapping my foundations. And I, instead of concentrating on my own horizons, which might have enabled me to throw them under a lorry, would let my mind be taken off them by his. I'd say to him, Come on, gunner, leave all that, think no more about it, and it's I would think no more about it, besotted with brotherliness. And the obligations! I have in mind particularly the appointments at ten in the morning, hail rain or shine, in front of

Duggan's, thronged already with sporting men fevering to get their bets out of harm's way before the bars open. We were, there we are past and gone again, so much the better, so much the better, most punctual I must say. To see the remains of Vincent arriving in sheets of rain, with the brave involuntary swagger of the old tar, his head swathed in a bloody clout and a glitter in his eye, was for the acute observer an example of what man is capable of, in his pursuit of pleasure. With one hand he sustained his sternum, with the heel of the other his spinal column, as if tempted to break into a hornpipe, no, that's all memories, last shifts older than the flood. See what's happening here, where there's no one, where nothing happens, get something to happen here, someone to be here, then put an end to it, have silence, get into silence, or another sound, a sound of other voices than those of life and death, of lives and deaths everyone's but mine, get into my story in order to get out of it, no, that's all meaningless. Is it possible I'll sprout a head at last, all my very own, in which to brew poisons worthy of me, and legs to kick my heels with, I'd be there at last, I could go at last, it's all I ask, no, I can't ask anything. Just the head and the two legs, or one, in the middle, I'd go hopping. Or just the head, nice and round, nice and smooth, no need of lineaments, I'd go rolling, down-hill, almost a pure spirit, no, that wouldn't work, all is uphill from here, the leg is unavoidable, or the equivalent, perhaps a few annular joints, contractile, great ground to be covered with them. To set out from Duggan's door, on a spring morning of rain and shine, not knowing if you'll ever get to evening, what's wrong with that? It would be so easy. To be bedded in that flesh or in another, in that arm held by a friendly hand, and in that hand, without arms, without hands, and without soul in those trembling souls, through the crowd, the hoops, the toy balloons, what's wrong with that? I don't know, I'm here, that's all I know, and that it's still not me, it's of that the best has to be made. There is no flesh anywhere, nor any way to die. Leave all that, to want to leave all that, not knowing what that means, all that, it's soon said, soon done, in vain, nothing has stirred, no one has spoken. Here, nothing will happen here, no one will be here, for many a long day. Departures, stories, they are not for tomorrow. And the voices, wherever they come from, have no life in them.

4

Where would I go, if I could go, who would I be, if I could be, what would I say, if I had a voice, who says this, saying it's me? Answer simply, someone answer simply. It's the same old stranger as ever, for whom alone accusative I exist, in the pit of my inexistence, of his, of ours, there's a simple answer. It's not with thinking he'll find me, but what is he to do, living and bewildered, yes, living, say what he may. Forget me, know me not, yes, that would be the wisest, none better able than he. Why this sudden affability after such desertion, it's easy to understand, that's what he says, but he doesn't understand. I'm not in his head, nowhere in his old body, and yet I'm there, for him I'm there, with him, hence all the confusion. That should have been enough for him, to have found me absent, but it's not, he wants me there, with a form and a world, like him, in spite of him, me who am everything, like him who is nothing. And when he feels me void of existence it's of his he would have me void, and vice versa, mad, mad, he's mad. The truth is he's looking for me to kill me, to have me dead like him, dead like the living. He knows all that, but it's no help his knowing it, I don't know it, I know nothing. He protests he doesn't reason and does nothing but reason, crooked, as if that could improve matters. He thinks words fail him, he thinks because words fail him he's on his way to my speechlessness, to being speechless with my speechlessness, he would like it to be my fault that words fail him, of course words fail him. He tells his story every five minutes, saying it is not his, there's cleverness for you. He would like it to be my fault that he has no story, of course he has no story, that's no reason for trying to foist one on me. That's how he reasons, wide of the mark, but wide of what mark, answer us that. He has me say things saying it's not me, there's profundity for you, he has me who say nothing say it's not me. All that is truly crass. If at least he would dignify me with the third person, like his other figments, not he, he'll be satisfied with nothing less than me, for his me. When he had me, when he was me, he couldn't get rid of me quick enough, I didn't exist, he couldn't have that, that was no kind of life, of course I didn't exist, any more than he did, of course it was no kind of life, now he has it, his kind of life, let him lose it, if he wants to be in peace, with a bit of luck. His life, what a mine, what a life, he can't have that, you can't fool him, ergo it's not his, it's not him, what a thought, treat him like that, like a vulgar Molloy, a common Malone, those mere mortals, happy mortals, have a heart, land him in that shit, who never stirred, who is none but me, all things considered, and what things, and how considered, he had only to keep out of it. That's how he speaks, this evening, how he has me speak, how he speaks to himself, how I speak, there is only me, this evening, here, on earth, and a voice that makes no sound because it goes towards none, and a head strewn with arms laid down and corpses fighting fresh, and a body, I nearly forgot. This evening, I say this evening, perhaps it's morning. And all these things, what things, all about me, I won't deny them any more, there's no sense in that any more. If it's nature perhaps it's trees and birds, they go together, water and air, so that all may go on, I don't need to know the details, perhaps I'm sitting under a palm. Or it's a room, with furniture, all that's required to make life comfortable, dark, because of the wall outside the window. What am I doing, talking, having my figments talk, it can only be me. Spells of silence too, when I listen, and hear the local sounds, the world sounds, see what an effort I make, to be reasonable. There's my life, why not, it is one, if you like, if you must, I don't say no, this evening. There has to be one, it seems, once there is speech, no need of a story, a story is not compulsory, just a life, that's the mistake I made, one of the mistakes, to have wanted a story for myself, whereas life alone is enough. I'm making progress, it was time, I'll learn to keep my foul mouth shut before I'm done, if nothing foreseen crops up. But he who somehow comes and goes, unaided from place to place, even though nothing happens to him, true, what of him? I stay here, sitting, if I'm sitting, often I feel sitting, sometimes standing, it's one or the other, or lying down, there's another possibility, often I feel lying down, it's one of the three, or kneeling. What counts is to be in the world, the posture is immaterial, so long as one is on earth. To breathe is all that is required, there is no obligation to ramble, or receive company, you may even believe yourself dead on condition you make no bones about it, what more liberal regimen could be imagined, I don't know, I don't imagine. No point under such circumstances in saying I am somewhere else, someone else, such as I am I have all I need to hand, for to do what, I don't know, all I have to do, there I am on my own again at last, what a relief that must be. Yes, there are moments, like this moment, when I seem almost restored to the feasible. Then it goes, all goes, and I'm far again, with a far story again, I wait for me afar for my story to begin, to end, and again this voice cannot be mine. That's where I'd go, if I could go, that's who I'd be, if I could be.

5

I'm the clerk, I'm the scribe, at the hearings of what cause I know not. Why want it to be mine, I don't want it. There it goes again, that's the first question this evening. To be judge and party, witness and advocate, and he, attentive, indifferent, who sits and notes. It's an image, in my helpless head, where all sleeps, all is dead, not yet born, I don't know, or before my eyes, they see the scene, the lids flicker and it's in. An instant and then they close again, to look inside the head, to try and see inside, to look for me there, to look for someone there, in the silence of quite a different justice, in the toils of that obscure assize where to be is to be guilty. That is why nothing appears, all is silent, one is frightened to be born, no, one wishes one were, so as to begin to die. One, meaning me, it's not the same thing, in the dark where I will in vain to see there can't be any willing. I could get up, take a little turn, I long to, but I won't. I know where I'd go, I'd go into the forest, I'd try and reach the forest, unless that's where I am, I don't know where I am, in any case I stay. I see what it is, I seek to be like the one I seek, in my head, that my head seeks, that I bid my head seek, with its probes, within itself. No, don't pretend to seek, don't pretend to think, just be vigilant, the eyes staring behind the lids, the ears straining for a voice not from without, were it only to sound an instant, to tell another lie. I hear, that must be the voice of reason again, that the vigil is in vain, that I'd be better advised to take a little turn, the way you manoeuvre a tin soldier. And no doubt it's the same voice answers that I can't, I who but a moment ago seemed to think I could, unless it's old shuttlecock sentiment chiming in, full stop, got all that. Why did Pozzo leave home, he had a castle and retainers. Insidious question, to remind me I'm in the dock. Sometimes I hear things that seem for a moment judicious, for a moment I'm sorry they are not mine. Then what a relief, what a relief to know I'm mute for ever, if only it didn't distress me. And deaf, it seems to me sometimes that deaf I'd be less distressed, at being mute, listen to that, what a relief not to have that on my conscience. Ah yes, I hear I have a kind of conscience, and on top of that a kind of sensibility, I trust the orator is not forgetting anything, and without ceasing to listen or drive the old quill I'm afflicted by them, I heard, it's noted. This evening the session is calm, there are long silences when all fix their eyes on me, that's to make me fly off my hinges, I feel on the brink of shrieks, it's noted. Out of the corner of my eye I observe the writing hand, all dimmed and blurred by the—by the reverse of farness. Who are all these people, gentlemen of the long robe, according to the image, but according to it alone, there are others, there will be others, other images, other gentlemen. Shall I never see the sky again, never be free again to come and go, in sunshine and in rain, the answer is no, all answer no, it's well I didn't ask anything, that's the kind of extravagance I envy them, till the echoes die away. The sky, I've heard—the sky and earth, I've heard great accounts of them, now that's pure word for word, I invent nothing. I've noted, I must have noted many a story with them as setting, they create the atmosphere. Between them where the hero stands a great gulf is fixed, while all about they flow together more and more, till they meet, so that he finds himself as it were under glass, and yet with no limit to his movements in all directions, let him understand who can, that is no part of my attributions. The sea too, I am conversant with the sea too, it belongs to the same family, I have even gone to the bottom more than once, under various assumed names, don't make me laugh, if only I could laugh, all would vanish, all what, who knows, all, me, it's noted. Yes, I see the scene, I see the hand, it comes creeping out of shadow, the shadow of my head, then scurries back, no connexion with me. Like a little creepy crawly it ventures out an instant, then goes back in again, the things one has to listen to, I say it as I hear it. It's the clerk's hand, is he entitled to the wig, I don't know, formerly perhaps. What do I do when silence falls, with rhetorical intent, or denoting lassitude, perplexity, consternation, I rub to and fro against my lips, where they meet, the first knuckle of my forefinger, but it's the head that moves, the hand rests, it's to such details the liar pins his hopes. That's the way this evening, tomorrow will be different, perhaps I'll appear before the council, before the justice of him who is all love, unforgiving and justly so, but subject to strange indulgences, the accused will be my soul, I prefer that, perhaps someone will ask pity for my soul, I mustn't miss that, I won't be there, neither will God, it doesn't matter, we'll be represented. Yes, it can't be much longer now, I haven't been damned for what seems an eternity, yes, but sufficient unto the day, this evening I'm the scribe. This evening, it's always evening, always spoken of as evening, even when it's morning, it's to make me think night is at hand, bringer of rest. The first thing would be to believe I'm there, if I could do that I'd lap up the rest, there'd be none more credulous than me, if I were there. But I am, it's not possible otherwise, just so, it's not possible, it doesn't need to be possible. It's tiring, very tiring, in the same breath to win and lose, with concomitant emotions, one's heart is not of stone, to record the doom, don the black cap and collapse in the dock, very tiring, in the long run, I'm tired of it, I'd be tired of it, if I were me. It's a game, it's getting to be a game, I'm going to rise and go, if it's not me it will be someone, a phantom, long live all our phantoms, those of the dead, those of the living and those of those who are not born. I'll follow him, with my sealed eyes, he needs no door, needs no thought, to issue from this imaginary head, mingle with air and earth and dissolve, little by little, in exile. Now I'm haunted, let them go, one by one, let the last desert me and leave me empty, empty and silent. It's they murmur my name, speak to me of me, speak of a me, let them go and speak of it to others, who will not believe them either, or who will believe them too. Theirs all these voices, like a rattling of chains in my head, rattling to me that I have a head. That's where the court sits this evening, in the depths of that vaulty night, that's where I'm clerk and scribe, not understanding what I hear, not knowing what I write. That's where the council will be tomorrow, prayers will be offered for my soul, as for that of one dead, as for that of an infant dead in its dead mother, that it may not go to Limbo, sweet thing theology. It will be another evening, all happens at evening, but it will be the same night, it too has its evenings, its mornings and its evenings, there's a pretty conception, it's to make me think day is at hand, disperser of phantoms. And now birds, the first birds, what's this new trouble now, don't forget the question-mark. It must be the end of the session, it's been calm, on the whole. Yes, that's sometimes the way, there are suddenly birds and all goes silent, an instant. But the phantoms come back, it's in vain they go abroad, mingle with the dying, they come back and slip into the coffin, no bigger than a matchbox, it's they have taught me all I know, about things above, and all I'm said to know about me, they want to create me, they want to make me, like the bird the birdikin, with larvae she fetches from afar, at the peril—I nearly said at the peril of her life! But sufficient unto the day, those are other minutes. Yes, one begins to be very tired, very tired of one's toil, very tired of one's quill, it falls, it's noted.

6

How are the intervals filled between these apparitions? Do my keepers snatch a little rest and sleep before setting about me afresh, how would that be? That would be very natural, to enable them to get back their strength. Do they play cards, the odd rubber, bowls, to recruit their spirits, are they entitled to a little recreation? I would say no, if I had a say, no recreation, just a short break, with something cold, even though they should not feel inclined, in the interests of their health. They like their work, I feel it in my bones! No, I mean how filled for me, they don't come into this. Wretched acoustics this evening, the merest scraps, literally. The news, do you remember the news, the latest news, in slow letters of light, above Piccadilly Circus, in the fog? Where were you standing, in the doorway of the little tobacconist's closed for the night on the corner of Glasshouse Street was it, no, you don't remember, and for cause. Sometimes that's how it is, in a way, the eyes take over, and the silence, the sighs, like the sighs of sadness weary with crying, or old, that suddenly feels old and sighs for itself, for the happy days, the long days, when it cried it would never perish, but it's far from common, on the whole. My keepers, why keepers, I'm in no danger of stirring an inch, ah I see, it's to make me think I'm a prisoner, frantic with corporeality, rearing to get out and away. Other times it's male nurses, white from head to foot, even their shoes are white, and then it's another story, but the burden is the same. Other times it's like ghouls, naked and soft as worm, they grovel round me gloating on the corpse, but I have no more success dead than dying. Other times it's great clusters of bones, dangling and knocking with a clatter of castanets, it's clean and gay like coons, I'd join them with a will if it could be here and now, how is it nothing is ever here and now? It's varied, my life is varied, I'll never get anywhere. I know, there is no one here, neither me nor anyone else, but some things are better left unsaid, so I say nothing. Elsewhere perhaps, by all means, elsewhere, what elsewhere can there be to this infinite here? I know, if my head could think I'd find a way out, in my head, like so many others, and out of worse than this, the world would be there again, in my head, with me much as in the beginning. I would know that nothing had changed, that a little resolution is all that is needed to come and go under the changing sky, on the moving earth, as all along the long summer days too short for all the play, it was known as play, if my head could think. The air would be there again, the shadows of the sky drifting over the earth, and that ant, that ant, oh most excellent head that can't think. Leave it, leave it, nothing leads to anything, nothing of all that, my life is varied, you can't have everything, I'll never get anywhere, but when did I? When I laboured, all day long and let me add, before I forget, part of the night, when I thought that with perseverance I'd get at me in the end? Well look at me, a little dust in a little nook, stirred faintly this way and that by breath straying from the lost without. Yes, I'm here for ever, with the spinners and the dead flies, dancing to the tremor of their meshed wings, and it's well pleased I am, well pleased, that it's over and done with, the puffing and panting after me up and down their Tempe of tears. Sometimes a butterfly comes, all warm from the flowers, how weak it is, and quick dead, the wings crosswise, as when resting, in the sun, the scales grey. Blot, words can be blotted and the mad thoughts they invent, the nostalgia for that slime where the Eternal breathed and his son wrote, long after, with divine idiotic finger, at the feet of the adulteress, wipe it out, all you have to do is say you said nothing and so say nothing again. What can have become then of the tissues I was, I can see them no more, feel them no more, flaunting and fluttering all about and inside me, pah they must be still on their old prowl somewhere, passing themselves off as me. Did I ever believe in them, did I ever believe I was there, somewhere in that ragbag, that's more the line, of enquiry, perhaps I'm still there, as large as life, merely convinced I'm not. The eyes, yes, if these memories are mine, I must have believed in them an instant, believed it was me I saw there dimly in the depths of their glades. I can see me still, with those of now, sealed this long time, staring with those of then, I must have been twelve, because of the glass, a round shaving-glass, double-faced, faithful and magnifying, staring into one of the others, the true ones, true then, and seeing me there, imagining I saw me there, lurking behind the bluey veils, staring back sightlessly, at the age of twelve, because of the glass, on its pivot, because of my father, if it was my father, in the bathroom, with its view of the sea, the lightships at night, the red harbour light, if these memories concern me, at the age of twelve, or at the age of forty, for the mirror remained, my father went but the mirror remained, in which he had so greatly changed, my mother did her hair in it, with twitching hands, in another house, with no view of the sea, with a view of the mountains, if it was my mother, what a refreshing whiff of life on earth. I was, I was, they say in Purgatory, in Hell too, admirable singulars, admirable assurance. Plunged in ice up to the nostrils, the eyelids caked with frozen tears, to fight all your battles o'er again, what tranquillity, and know there are no more emotions in store, no, I can't have heard aright. How many hours to go, before the next silence, they are not hours, it will not be silence, how many hours still, before the next silence? Ah to know for sure, to know that this thing has no end, this thing, this thing, this farrago of silence and words, of silence that is not silence and barely murmured words. Or to know it's life still, a form of life, ordained to end, as others ended and will end, till life ends, in all its forms. Words, mine was never more than that, than this pell-mell babel of silence and words, my viewless form described as ended, or to come, or still in progress, depending on the words, the moments, long may it last in that singular way. Apparitions, keepers, what childishness, and ghouls, to think I said ghouls, do I as much as know what they are, of course I don't, and how the intervals are filled, as if I didn't know, as if there were two things, some other thing besides this thing, what is it, this unnamable thing that I name and name and never wear out, and I call that words. It's because I haven't hit on the right ones, the killers, haven't yet heaved them up from that heart-burning glut of words, with what words shall I name my unnamable words? And yet I have high hopes, I give you my word, high hopes, that one day I may tell a story, hear a story, yet another, with men, kinds of men as in the days when I played all regardless or nearly, worked and played. But first stop talking and get on with your weeping, with eyes wide open that the precious liquid may spill freely, without burning the lids, or the crystalline humour, I forget, whatever it is it burns. Tears, that could be the tone, if they weren't so easy, the true tone and tenor at last. Besides not a tear, not one, I'd be in greater danger of mirth, if it wasn't so easy. No, grave, I'll be grave, I'll close my ears, close my mouth and be grave. And when they open again it may be to hear a story, tell a story, in the true sense of the words, the word hear, the word tell, the word story, I have high hopes, a little story, with living creatures coming and going on a habitable earth crammed with the dead, a brief story, with night and day coming and going above, if they stretch that far, the words that remain, and I've high hopes, I give you my word.

7

Did I try everything, ferret in every hold, secretly, silently, patiently, listening? I'm in earnest, as so often, I'd like to be sure I left no stone unturned before reporting me missing and giving up. In every hold, I mean in all those places where there was a chance of my being, where once I used to lurk, waiting for the hour to come when I might venture forth, tried and trusty places, that's all I meant when I said in every hold. Once, I mean in the days when I still could move, and feel myself moving, painfully, barely, but unquestionably changing position on the whole, the trees were witness, the sands, the air of the heights, the cobblestones. This tone is promising, it is more like that of old, of the days and nights when in spite of all I was calm, treading back and forth the futile road, knowing it short and easy seen from Sirius, and deadly calm at the heart of my frenzies. My question, I had a question, ah yes, did I try everything, I can see it still, but it's passing, lighter than air, like a cloud, in moonlight, before the skylight, before the moon, like the moon, before the skylight. No, in its own way, I know it well, the way of an evening shadow you follow with your eyes, thinking of something else, yes, that's it, the mind elsewhere, and the eyes too, if the truth were known, the eyes elsewhere too. Ah if there must be speech at least none from the heart, no, I have only one desire, if I have it still. But another thing, before the ones that matter, I have just time, if I make haste, in the trough of all this time just time. Another thing, I call that another thing, the old thing

I keep on not saying till I'm sick and tired, revelling in the flying instants, I call that revelling, now's my chance and I talk of revelling, it won't come back in a hurry if I remember right, but come back it must with its riot of instants. It's not me in any case, I'm not talking of me, I've said it a million times, no point in apologizing again, for talking of me, when there's X, that paradigm of human kind, moving at will, complete with joys and sorrows, perhaps even a wife and brats, forebears most certainly, a carcass in God's image and a contemporary skull, but above all endowed with movement, that's what strikes you above all, with his likeness so easy to take and his so instructive soul, that really, no, to talk of oneself, when there's X, no, what a blessing I'm not talking of myself, enough vile parrot I'll kill you. And what if all this time I had not stirred hand or foot from the third-class waiting-room of the South-Eastern Railway Terminus, I never dared wait first on a third-class ticket, and were still there waiting to leave, for the south-east, the south rather, east lay the sea, all along the track, wondering where on earth to alight, or my mind absent, elsewhere. The last train went at twenty-three thirty, then they closed the station for the night. What thronging memories, that's to make me think I'm dead, I've said it a million times. But the same return, like the spokes of a turning wheel, always the same, and all alike, like spokes. And yet I wonder, whenever the hour returns when I have to wonder that, if the wheel in my head turns, I wonder, so given am I to thinking with my blood, or if it merely swings, like a balance-wheel in its case, a minute to and fro, seeing the immensity to measure and that heads are only wound up once, so given am I to thinking with my breath. But tut there I am far again from that terminus and its pretty neo-Doric colonnade, and far from that heap of flesh, rind, bones and bristles waiting to depart it knows not where, somewhere south, perhaps asleep, its ticket between finger and thumb for the sake of appearances, or let fall to the ground in the great limpness of sleep, perhaps dreaming it's in heaven, alit in heaven, or better still the dawn, waiting for the dawn and the joy of being able to say, I've the whole day before me, to go wrong, to go right, to calm down, to give up, I've nothing to fear, my ticket is valid for life. Is it there I came to a stop, is that me still waiting there, sitting up stiff and straight on the edge of the seat, knowing the dangers of laisser-aller, hands on thighs, ticket between finger and thumb, in that great room dim with the platform gloom as dispensed by the quarter-glass self-closing door, locked up in those shadows, it's there, it's me. In that case the night is long and singularly silent, for one who seems to remember the city sounds, confusedly, sunk now to a single sound, the impossible confused memory of a single confused sound, lasting all night, swelling, dying, but never for an instant broken by a silence the like of this deafening silence. Whence it should follow, but does not, that the third-class waiting-room of the South-Eastern Railway Terminus must be struck from the list of places to visit, see above, centuries above, that this lump is no longer me and that search should be made elsewhere, unless it be abandoned, which is my feeling. But not so fast, all cities are not eternal, that of this pensum is perhaps among the dead, and the station in ruins where I sit waiting, erect and rigid, hands on thighs, the tip of the ticket between finger and thumb, for a train that will never come, never go, natureward, or for day to break behind the locked door, through the glass black with the dust of ruin. That is why one must not hasten to conclude, the risk of error is too great. And to search for me elsewhere, where life persists, and me there, whence all life has withdrawn, except mine, if I'm alive, no, it would be a loss of time. And personally, I hear it said, personally I have no more time to lose, and that that will be all for this evening, that night is at hand and the time come for me too to begin.

8

Only the words break the silence, all other sounds have ceased. If I were silent I'd hear nothing. But if I were silent the other sounds would start again, those to which the words have made me deaf, or which have really ceased. But I am silent, it sometimes happens, no, never, not one second. I weep too without interruption. It's an unbroken flow of words and tears. With no pause for reflection. But I speak softer, every year a little softer. Perhaps. Slower too, every year a little slower. Perhaps. It is hard for me to judge. If so the pauses would be longer, between the words, the sentences, the syllables, the tears, I confuse them, words and tears, my words are my tears, my eyes my mouth. And I should hear, at every little pause, if it's the silence I say when I say that only the words break it. But nothing of the kind, that's not how it is, it's for ever the same murmur, flowing unbroken, like a single endless word and therefore meaningless, for it's the end gives the meaning to words. What right have you then, no, this time I see what I'm up to and put a stop to it, saying, None, none. But get on with the stupid old threne and ask, ask until you answer, a new question, the most ancient of all, the question were things always so. Well I'm going to tell myself something (if I'm able), pregnant I hope with promise for the future, namely that I begin to have no very clear recollection of how things were before (I was!), and by before I mean elsewhere, time has turned into space and there will be no more time, till I get out of here. Yes, my past has thrown me out, its gates have slammed behind me, or I burrowed my way out alone, to linger a moment free in a dream of days and nights, dreaming of me moving, season after season, towards the last, like the living, till suddenly I was here, all memory gone. Ever since nothing but fantasies and hope of a story for me somehow, of having come from somewhere and of being able to go back, or on, somehow, some day, or without hope. Without what hope, haven't I just said, of seeing me alive, not merely inside an imaginary head, but a pebble sand to be, under a restless sky, restless on its shore, faint stirs day and night, as if to grow less could help, ever less and less and never quite be gone. No truly, no matter what, I say no matter what, hoping to wear out a voice, to wear out a head, or without hope, without reason, no matter what, without reason. But it will end, a desinence will come, or the breath fail better still, I'll be silence, I'll know I'm silence, no, in the silence you can't know, I'll never know anything. But at least get out of here, at least that, no? I don't know. And time begin again, the steps on the earth, the night the fool implores at morning and the morning he begs at evening not to dawn. I don't know, I don't know what all that means, day and night, earth and sky, begging and imploring. And I can desire them? Who says I desire them, the voice, and that I can't desire anything, that looks like a contradiction, it may be for all I know. Me, here, if they could open, those little words, open and swallow me up, perhaps that is what has happened. If so let them open again and let me out, in the tumult of light that sealed my eyes, and of men, to try and be one again. Or if I'm guilty let me be forgiven and graciously authorized to expiate, coming and going in passing time, every day a little purer, a little deader. The mistake I make is to try and think, even the way I do, such as I am I shouldn't be able, even the way I do. But whom can I have offended so grievously, to be punished in this inexplicable way, all is inexplicable, space and time, false and inexplicable, suffering and tears, and even the old convulsive cry, It's not me, it can't be me. But am I in pain, whether it's me or not, frankly now, is there pain? Now is here and here there is no frankness, all I say will be false and to begin with not said by me, here I'm a mere ventriloquist's dummy, I feel nothing, say nothing, he holds me in his arms and moves my lips with a string, with a fish-hook, no, no need of lips, all is dark, there is no one, what's the matter with my head, I must have left it in Ireland, in a saloon, it must be there still, lying on the bar, it's all it deserved. But that other who is me, blind and deaf and mute, because of whom I'm here, in this black silence, helpless to move or accept this voice as mine, it's as him I must disguise myself till I die, for him in the meantime do my best not to live, in this pseudo-sepulture claiming to be his. Whereas to my certain knowledge I'm dead and kicking above, somewhere in Europe probably, with every plunge and suck of the sky a little more overripe, as yesterday in the pump of the womb. No, to have said so convinces me of the contrary, I never saw the light of day, any more than he, ah if no were content to cut yes's throat and never cut its own. Watch out for the right moment, then not another word, is that the only way to have being and habitat? But I'm here, that much at least is certain, it's in vain I keep on saying it, it remains true. Does it? It's hard for me to judge. Less true and less certain in any case than when I say I'm on earth, come into the world and assured of getting out, that's why I say it, patiently, variously, trying to vary, for you never know, it's perhaps all a question of hitting on the right aggregate. So as to be here no more at last, to have never been here, but all this time above, with a name like a dog to be called up with and distinctive marks to be had up with, the chest expanding and contracting unaided, panting towards the grand apnoea. The right aggregate, but there are four million possible, nay probable, according to Aristotle, who knew everything. But what is this I see, and how, a white stick and an ear-trumpet, where, Place de la République, at Pernod time, let me look closer at this, it's perhaps me at last. The trumpet, sailing at ear level, suddenly resembles a steam-whistle, of the kind thanks to which my steamers forge fearfully through the fog. That should fix the period, to the nearest half-century or so. The stick gains ground, tapping with its ferrule the noble bassamento of the United Stores, it must be winter, at least not summer. I can also just discern, with a final effort of will, a bowler hat which seems to my sorrow a sardonic synthesis of all those that never fitted me and, at the other extremity, similarly suspicious, a complete pair of brown boots lacerated and gaping. These insignia, if I may so describe them, advance in concert, as though connected by the traditional human excipient, halt, move on again, confirmed by the vast show windows. The level of the hat, and consequently of the trumpet, hold out some hope for me as a dying dwarf or at least hunchback. The vacancy is tempting, shall I enthrone my infirmities, give them this chance again, my dream infirmities, that they may take flesh and move, deteriorating, round and round this grandiose square which I hope I don't confuse with the Bastille, until they are deemed worthy of the adjacent Père Lachaise or, better still, prematurely relieved trying to cross over, at the hour of night's young thoughts. No, the answer is no. For even as I moved, or when the moment came, affecting beyond all others, to hold out my hand, or hat, without previous song, or any other form of concession to self-respect, at the terrace of a café, or in the mouth of the underground, I would know it was not me, I would know I was here, begging in another dark, another silence, for another alm, that of being or of ceasing, better still, before having been. And the hand old in vain would drop the mite and the old feet shuffle on, towards an even vainer death than no matter whose.

9

If I said, There's a way out there, there's a way out somewhere, the rest would come. What am I waiting for then, to say it? To believe it? And what does that mean, the rest? Shall I answer, try and answer, or go on as though I had asked nothing? I don't know, I can't know beforehand, nor after, nor during, the future will tell, some future instant, soon, or late, I won't hear, I won't understand, all dies so fast, no sooner born. And the yeses and noes mean nothing in this mouth, no more than sighs it sighs in its toil, or answers to a question not understood, a question unspoken, in the eyes of a mute, an idiot, who doesn't understand, never understood, who stares at himself in a glass, stares before him in the desert, sighing yes, sighing no, on and off. But there is reasoning somewhere, moments of reasoning, that is to say the same things recur, they drive one another out, they draw one another back, no need to know what things. It's mechanical, like the great colds, the great heats, the long days, the long nights, of the moon, such is my conviction, for I have convictions, when their turn comes round, then stop having them, that's how it goes, it must be supposed, at least it must be said, since I have just said it. The way out, this evening it's the turn of the way out, isn't it like a duo, or a trio, yes, there are moments when it's like that, then they pass and it's not like that any more, never was like that, is like nothing, no resemblance with anything, of no interest. What variety and at the same time what monotony, how varied it is and at the same time how, what's the word, how monotonous. What agitation and at the same time what calm, what vicissitudes within what changelessness. Moments of hesitation not so much rare as frequent, if one had to choose, and soon overcome in favour of the old crux, on which at first all depends, then much, then little, then nothing. That's right, wordshit, bury me, avalanche, and let there be no more talk of any creature, nor of a world to leave, nor of a world to reach, in order to have done, with worlds, with creatures, with words, with misery, misery. Which no sooner said, Ah, says I, punctually, if only I could say, There's a way out there, there's a way out somewhere, then all would be said, it would be the first step on the long travelable road, destination tomb, to be trod without a word, tramp tramp, little heavy irrevocable steps, down the long tunnels at first, then under the mortal skies, through the days and nights, faster and faster, no, slower and slower, for obvious reasons, and at the same time faster and faster, for other obvious reasons, or the same, obvious in a different way, or in the same way, but at a different moment of time, a moment earlier, a moment later, or at the same moment, there is no such thing, there would be no such thing, I recapitulate, impossible. Would I know where I came from, no, I'd have a mother, I'd have had a mother, and what I came out of, with what pain, no, I'd have forgotten, what is it makes me say that, what is it makes me say this, whatever it is makes me say all, and it's not certain, not certain the way the mother would be certain, the way the tomb would be certain, if there was a way out, if I said there was a way out, make me say it, demons, no, I'll ask for nothing. Yes, I'd have a mother, I'd have a tomb, I wouldn't have come out of here, one doesn't come out of here, here are my tomb and mother, it's all here this evening, I'm dead and getting born, without having ended, helpless to begin, that's my life. How reasonable it is and what am I complaining of? Is it because I'm no longer slinking to and fro before the graveyard, saying, God grant I'm buriable before the curtain drops, is that my grievance, it's possible. I was well inspired to be anxious, wondering on what score, and I asked myself, as I came and went, on what score I could possibly be anxious, and found the answer and answered, saying, It's not me, I haven't yet appeared, I haven't yet been noticed, and saying further, Oh yes it is, it's me all right, and ceasing to be what is more, then quickening my step, so as to arrive before the next onslaught, as though it were on time I trod, and saying further, and so forth. I can scarcely have gone unperceived, all this time, and yet you wouldn't have thought so, that I didn't go unperceived. I don't refer to the spoken salutation, I'd have been the first to be perturbed by that, almost as much as by the bow, kiss or handshake. But the other signs, irrepressible, with which the fellow-creature unwillingly betrays your presence, the shudders and wry faces, nothing of that nature either it would seem, except possibly on the part of certain hearse-horses, in spite of their blinkers and strict funereal training, but perhaps I flatter myself. Truly I can't recall a single face, proof positive that I was not there, no, proof of nothing. But the fact that I was not molested, can I have remained insensible to that? Alas I fear they could have subjected me to the most gratifying brutalities, I won't go so far as to say without my knowledge, but without my being encouraged, as a result, to feel myself there rather than elsewhere. And I may well have spent one half of my life in the prisons of their Arcady, purging the delinquencies of the other half, all unaware of any break or lull in my problematic patrolling, unconstrained, before the gates of the graveyard. But what if weary of seeing me relieve myself, of seeing me resume, after each forced vacation, my beat before the gates of the graveyard, what if finally they had plucked up heart and slightly stressed their blows, just enough to confer death, without any mutilation of the corpse, there, at the gates of the graveyard, where that very morning I had reappeared, no sooner set at large, and resumed by old offence, to and fro, with step now slow and now precipitate, like that of the conspirator Catilina plotting the ruin of the fatherland, saying, It's not me, yes, it's me, and further, There's a way out there, no no, I'm getting mixed, I must be getting mixed, confusing here and there, now and then, just as I confused them then, the here of then, the then of there, with other spaces, other times, dimly discerned, but not more dimly than now, now that I'm here, if I'm here, and no longer there, coming and going before the graveyard, perplexed. Or did I end up by simply sitting down, with my back to the wall, all the long night before me when the dead lie waiting, on the beds where they died, shrouded or coffined, for the sun to rise? What am I doing now, I'm trying to see where I am, so as to be able to go elsewhere, should occasion arise, or else simply to say, You have merely to wait till they come and fetch you, that's my impression at times. Then it goes and I see it's not that, but something else, difficult to grasp, and which I don't grasp, or which I do grasp, it depends, and it comes to the same, for it's not that either, but something else, some other thing, or the first back again, or still the same, always the same thing proposing itself to my perplexity, then disappearing, then proposing itself again, to my perplexity still unsated, or momentarily dead, of starvation. The graveyard, yes, it's there I'd return, this evening it's there, borne by my words, if I could get out of here, that is to say if I could say, There's a way out there, there's a way out somewhere, to know exactly where would be a mere matter of time, and patience, and sequency of thought, and felicity of expression. But the body, to get there with, where's the body? It's a minor point, a minor point. And I have no doubts, I'd get there somehow, to the way out, sooner or later, if I could say, There's a way out there, there's a way out somewhere, the rest would come, the other words, sooner or later, and the power to get there, and the way to get there, and pass out, and see the beauties of the skies, and see the stars again.

10

Give up, but it's all given up, it's nothing new, I'm nothing new. Ah so there was something once, I had something once. It may be thought there was, so long as it's known there was not, never anything, but giving up. But let us suppose there was not, that is to say let us suppose there was, something once, in a head, in a heart, in a hand, before all opened, emptied, shut again and froze. This is most reassuring, after such a fright, and emboldens me to go on, once again. But there is not silence. No, there is utterance, somewhere someone is uttering. Inanities, agreed, but is that enough, is that enough, to make sense? I see what it is, the head has fallen behind, all the rest has gone on, the head and its anus the mouth, or else it has gone on alone, all alone on its old prowls, slobbering its shit and lapping it back off the lips like in the days when it fancied itself. But the heart's not in it any more, nor is the appetite what it was. So home to roost it comes among my other assets, home yet again, and no trickery involved, that old past ever new, ever ended, ever ending, with all its hidden treasures of promise for tomorrow, and of consolation for today. And I'm in good hands again, they hold my head from behind, intriguing detail, as at the hairdresser's, the forefingers close my eyes, the middle fingers my nostrils, the thumbs stop up my ears, but imperfectly, to enable me to hear, but imperfectly, while the four remaining busy themselves with my jaws and tongue, to enable me to suffocate, but imperfectly, and to utter, for my good, what I must utter, for my future good, well-known ditty, and in particular to observe without delay, speaking of the passing moment, that worse have been known to pass, that it will pass in time, a mere moment of respite which but for this first aid might have proved fatal, and that one day I shall know again that I once was, and roughly who, and how to go on, and speak unaided, nicely, about number one and his pale imitations. And it is possible, just, for I must not be too affirmative at this stage, it would not be in my interest, that other fingers, quite a different gang, other tentacles, that's more like it, other charitable suckers, waste no more time trying to get it right, will take down my declarations, so that at the close of the interminable delirium, should it ever resume, I may not be reproached with having faltered. This is awful, awful, at least there's that to be thankful for. And perhaps beside me, and all around, other souls are being licked into shape, souls swooned away, or sick with over-use, or because no use could be found for them, but still fit for use, or fit only to be cast away, pale imitations of mine. Or has it knelled here at last for our committal to flesh, as the dead are committed to the ground, in the hour of their death at last, and at the place where they die, to keep the expenses down, or for our reassignment, souls of the stillborn, or dead before the body, or still young in the midst of the ruins, or never come to life through incapacity or for some other reason, or the immortal type, there must be a few of them too, whose bodies were always wrong, but patience there's a true one in pickle, among the unborn hordes, the true sepulchral body, for the living have no room for a second. No, no souls, or bodies, or birth, or life, or death, you've got to go on without any of that junk, that's all dead with words, with excess of words, they can say nothing else, they say there is nothing else, that here it's that and nothing else, but they won't say it eternally, they'll find some other nonsense, no matter what, and I'll be able to go on, no, I'll be able to stop, or start, another guzzle of lies but piping hot, it will last my time, it will be my time and place, my voice and silence, a voice of silence, the voice of my silence. It's with such prospects they exhort you to have patience, whereas you are patient, and calm, somehow somewhere calm, what calm here, ah that's an idea, say how calm it is here, and how fine I feel, and how silent I am, I'll start right away, I'll say what calm and silence, which nothing has ever broken, nothing will ever break, which saying I don't break, or saying I'll be saying, yes, I'll say all that tomorrow, yes, tomorrow evening, some other evening, not this evening, this evening it's too late, too late to get things right, I'll go to sleep, so that I may say, hear myself say, a little later, I've slept, he's slept, but he won't have slept, or else he's sleeping now, he'll have done nothing, nothing but go on, doing what, doing what he does, that is to say, I don't know, giving up, that's it, I'll have gone on giving up, having had nothing, not being there.

11

When I think, no, that won't work, when come those who knew me, perhaps even know me still, by sight of course, or by smell, it's as though, it's as if, come on, I don't know, I shouldn't have begun. If I began again, setting my mind to it, that sometimes gives good results, it's worth trying, I'll try it, one of these days, one of these evenings, or this evening, why not this evening, before I disappear, from up there, from down here, scattered by the everlasting words. What am I saying, scattered, isn't that just what I'm not, just what I'm not, I was wandering, my mind was wandering, just the very thing I'm not. And it's still the same old road I'm trudging, up yes and down no, towards one yet to be named, so that he may leave me in peace, be in peace, be no more, have never been. Name, no, nothing is namable, tell, no, nothing can be told, what then, I don't know, I shouldn't have begun. Add him to the repertory, there we have it, and execute him, as I execute me, one dead bar after another, evening after evening, and night after night, and all through the days, but it's always evening, why is that, why is it always evening, I'll say why, so as to have said it, have it behind me, an instant. It's time that can't go on at the hour of the serenade, unless it's dawn, no, I'm not in the open, I'm under the ground, or in my body somewhere, or in another body, and time devours on, but not me, there we have it, that's why it's always evening, to let me have the best to look forward to, the long black night to sleep in, there, I've answered, I've answered something. Or it's in the head, like a minute time switch, a second time switch, or it's like a patch of sea, under the passing lighthouse beam, a passing patch of sea under the passing beam. Vile words to make me believe I'm here, and that I have a head, and a voice, a head believing this, then that, then nothing more, neither in itself, nor in anything else, but a head with a voice belonging to it, or to others, other heads, as if there were two heads, as if there were one head, or headless, a headless voice, but a voice. But I'm not deceived, for the moment I'm not deceived, for the moment I'm not there, nor anywhere else what is more, neither as head, nor as voice, nor as testicle, what a shame, what a shame I'm not appearing anywhere as testicle, or as cunt, those areas, a female pubic hair, it sees great sights, peeping down, well, there it is, can't be helped, that's how it is. And I let them say their say, my words not said by me, me that word, that word they say, but say in vain. We're getting on, getting on, and when come those who knew me, quick quick, it's as though, no, premature. But peekaboo here I come again, just when most needed, like the square root of minus one, having terminated my humanities, this should be worth seeing, the livid face stained with ink and jam, caput mortuum of a studious youth, ears akimbo, eyes back to front, the odd stray hair, foaming at the mouth, and chewing, what is it chewing, a gob, a prayer, a lesson, a little of each, a prayer got by rote in case of emergency before the soul resigns and bubbling up all arsy-varsy in the old mouth bereft of words, in the old head done with listening, there I am old, it doesn't take long, a snotty old nipper, having terminated his humanities, in the two-stander urinal on the corner of the Rue d'Assas was it, with the leak making the same gurgle as sixty years ago, my favourite because of the encouragement like mother hissing to baby on pot, my brow glued to the partition among the graffiti, straining against the prostate, belching up Hail Marys, buttoned as to the fly, I invent nothing, through absent-mindedness, or exhaustion, or insouciance, or on purpose, to promote priming, I know what I mean, or one-armed better still, no arms, no hands, better by far, as old as the world and no less hideous, amputated on all sides, erect on my trusty stumps, bursting with old piss, old prayers, old lessons, soul, mind and carcass finishing neck and neck, not to mention the gobchucks, too painful to mention, sobs made mucus, hawked up from the heart, now I have a heart, now I'm complete, apart from a few extremities, having terminated their humanities, then their career, and with that not in the least pretentious, making no demands, rent with ejaculations, Jesus, Jesus. Evenings, evenings, what evenings they were then, made of what, and when was that, I don't know, made of friendly shadows, friendly skies, of time cloyed, resting from devouring, until its midnight meats, I don't know, any more than then, when I used to say, from within, or from without, from the coming night or from under the ground, Where am I, to mention only space, and in what semblance, and since when, to mention also time, and till when, and who is this clot who doesn't know where to go, who can't stop, who takes himself for me and for whom I take myself, anything at all, the old jangle. Those evenings then, but what is this evening made of, this evening now that never ends, in whose shadows I'm alone, that's where I am, where I was then, where I've always been, it's from them I spoke to myself, spoke to him, where has he vanished, the one I saw then, is he still in the street, it's probable, it's possible, with no voice speaking to him, I don't speak to him any more, I don't speak to me any more, I have no one left to speak to, and I speak, a voice speaks that can be none but mine, since there is none but me. Yes, I have lost him and he has lost me, lost from view, lost from hearing, that's what I wanted, is it possible, that I wanted that, wanted this, and he, what did he want, he wanted to stop, perhaps he has stopped, I have stopped, but I never stirred, perhaps he is dead, I am dead, but I never lived. But he moved, proof of animation, through those evenings, moving too, evenings with an end, evenings with a night, never saying a word, unable to say a word, not knowing where to go, unable to stop, listening to my cries, hearing a voice crying that it was no kind of life, as if he didn't know, as if the allusion was to his, which was a kind of one, there's the difference, those were the days, I didn't know where I was, nor in what semblance, nor since when, nor till when, whereas now, there's the difference, now I know, it's not true, but I say it just the same, there's the difference, I'm saying it now, I'll say it soon, I'll say it in the end, then end, I'll be free to end, I won't be any more, it won't be worth it any more, it won't be necessary any more, it won't be possible any more, but it's not worth it now, it's not necessary now, it's not possible now, that's how the reasoning runs. No, something better must be found, a better reason, for this to stop, another word, a better idea, to put in the negative, a new no, to cancel all the others, all the old noes that buried me down here, deep in this place which is not one, which is merely a moment for the time being eternal, which is called here, and in this being which is called me and is not one, and in this impossible voice, all the old noes dangling in the dark and swaying like a ladder of smoke, yes, a new no, that none says twice, whose drop will fall and let me down, shadow and babble, to an absence less vain than inexistence. Oh I know it won't happen like that, I know that nothing will happen, that nothing has happened and that I'm still, and particularly since the day I could no longer believe it, what is called flesh and blood somewhere above in their gonorrhoeal light, cursing myself heartily. And that is why, when comes the hour of those who knew me, this time it's going to work, when comes the hour of those who knew me, it's as though I were among them, that is what I had to say, among them watching me approach, then watching me recede, shaking my head and saying, Is it really he, can it possibly be he, then moving on in their company along a road that is not mine and with every step takes me further from that other not mine either, or remaining alone where I am, between two parting dreams, knowing none, known of none, that finally is what I had to say, that is all I can have had to say, this evening.

12

It's a winter night, where I was, where I'm going, remembered, imagined, no matter, believing in me, believing it's me, no, no need, so long as the others are there, where, in the world of the others, of the long mortal ways, under the sky, with a voice, no, no need, and the power to move, now and then, no need either, so long as the others move, the true others, but on earth, beyond all doubt on earth, for as long as it takes to die again, wake again, long enough for things to change here, for something to change, to make possible a deeper birth, a deeper death, or resurrection in and out of this murmur of memory and dream. A winter night, without moon or stars, but light, he sees his body, all the front, part of the front, what makes them light, this impossible night, this impossible body, it's me in him remembering, remembering the true night, dreaming of the night without morning, and how will he manage tomorrow, to endure tomorrow, the dawning, then the day, the same as he managed yesterday, to endure yesterday. Oh I know, it's not me, not yet, it's a veteran, inured to days and nights, but he forgets, he thinks of me, more than is wise, and it's a far cry to morning, perhaps it has time never to dawn at last. That's what he says, with his voice soon to leave him, perhaps tonight, and he says, How light it is, how shall I manage tomorrow, how did I manage yesterday, pah it's the end, it's a far cry to morning, and who's this speaking in me, and who's this disowning me, as though I had taken his place, usurped his life, that old shame that kept me from living, the shame of my living that kept me from living, and so on, muttering, the old inanities, his chin on his heart, his arms dangling, sagging at the knees, in the night. Will they succeed in slipping me into him, the memory and dream of me, into him still living, amn't I there already, wasn't I always there, like a stain of remorse, is that my night and contumacy, in the dungeons of this moribund, and from now till he dies my last chance to have been, and who is this raving now, pah there are voices everywhere, ears everywhere, one who speaks saying, without ceasing to speak, Who's speaking?, and one who hears, mute, uncomprehending, far from all, and bodies everywhere, bent, fixed, where my prospects must be just as good, just as poor, as in this firstcomer. And none will wait, he no more than the others, none ever waited to die for me to live in him, so as to die with him, but quick quick all die, saying, Quick quick let us die, without him, as we lived, before it's too late, lest we won't have lived. And this other now, obviously, what's to be said of this latest other, with his babble of homeless mes and untenanted hims, this other without number or person whose abandoned being we haunt, nothing. There's a pretty three in one, and what a one, what a no one. So, I'm supposed to say now, it's the moment, so that's the earth, these expiring vitals set aside for me which no sooner taken over would be set aside for another, many thanks, and here the laugh, the long silent guffaw of the knowing non-exister, at hearing ascribed to him such pregnant words, confess you're not the man you were, you'll end up riding a bicycle. That's the accountants' chorus, opining like a single man, and there are more to come, all the peoples of the earth would not suffice, at the end of the billions you'd need a god, unwitnessed witness of witnesses, what a blessing it's all down the drain, nothing ever as much as begun, nothing ever but nothing and never, nothing ever but lifeless words.

13

Weaker still the weak old voice that tried in vain to make me, dying away as much as to say it's going from here to try elsewhere, or dying down, there's no telling, as much as to say it's going to cease, give up trying. No voice ever but it in my life, it says, if speaking of me one can speak of life, and it can, it still can, or if not of life, there it dies, if this, if that, if speaking of me, there it dies, but who can the greater can the less, once you've spoken of me you can speak of anything, up to the point where, up to the time when, there it dies, it can't go on, it's been its death, speaking of me, here or elsewhere, it says, it murmurs. Whose voice, no one's, there is no one, there's a voice without a mouth, and somewhere a kind of hearing, something compelled to hear, and somewhere a hand, it calls that a hand, it wants to make a hand, or if not a hand something somewhere that can leave a trace, of what is made, of what is said, you can't do with less, no, that's romancing, more romancing, there is nothing but a voice murmuring a trace. A trace, it wants to leave a trace, yes, like air leaves among the leaves, among the grass, among the sand, it's with that it would make a life, but soon it will be the end, it won't be long now, there won't be any life, there won't have been any life, there will be silence, the air quite still that trembled once an instant, the tiny flurry of dust quite settled. Air, dust, there is no air here, nor anything to make dust, and to speak of instants, to speak of once, is to speak of nothing, but there it is, those are the expressions it employs. It has always spoken, it will always speak, of things that don't exist, or only exist elsewhere, if you like, if you must, if that may be called existing. Unfortunately it is not a question of elsewhere, but of here, ah there are the words out at last, out again, that was the only chance, get out of here and go elsewhere, go where time passes and atoms assemble an instant, where the voice belongs perhaps, where it sometimes says it must have belonged, to be able to speak of such figments. Yes, out of here, but how when here is empty, not a speck of dust, not a breath, the voice's breath alone, it breathes in vain, nothing is made. If I were here, if it could have made me, how I would pity it, for having spoken so long in vain, no, that won't do, it wouldn't have spoken in vain if I were here, and I wouldn't pity it if it had made me, I'd curse it, or bless it, it would be in my mouth, cursing, blessing, whom, what, it wouldn't be able to say, in my mouth it wouldn't have much to say, that had so much to say in vain. But this pity, all the same, it wonders, this pity that is in the air, though no air here for pity, but it's the expression, it wonders should it stop and wonder what pity is doing here and if it's not hope gleaming, another expression, evilly among the imaginary ashes, the faint hope of a faint being after all, human in kind, tears in its eyes before they've had time to open, no, no more stopping and wondering, about that or anything else, nothing will stop it any more, in its fall, or in its rise, perhaps it will end on a castrato scream. True there was never much talk of the heart, literal or figurative, but that's no reason for hoping, what, that one day there will be one, to send up above to break in the galanty show, pity. But what more is it waiting for now, when there's no doubt left, no choice left, to stick a sock in its death-rattle, yet another locution. To have rounded off its cock-and-bullshit in a coda worthy of the rest? Last everlasting questions, infant languors in the end sheets, last images, end of dream, of being past, passing and to be, end of lie. Is it possible, is that the possible thing at last, the extinction of this black nothing and its impossible shades, the end of the farce of making and the silencing of silence, it wonders, that voice which is silence, or it's me, there's no telling, it's all the same dream, the same silence, it and me, it and him, him and me, and all our train, and all theirs, and all theirs, but whose, whose dream, whose silence, old questions, last questions, ours who are dream and silence, but it's ended, we're ended who never were, soon there will be nothing where there was never anything, last images. And whose the shame, at every mute micromillisyllable, and unslakable infinity of remorse delving ever deeper in its bite, at having to hear, having to say, fainter than the faintest murmur, so many lies, so many times the same lie lyingly denied, whose the screaming silence of no's knife in yes's wound, it wonders. And wonders what has become of the wish to know, it is gone, the heart is gone, the head is gone, no one feels anything, asks anything, seeks anything, says anything, hears anything, there is only silence. It's not true, yes, it's true, it's true and it's not true, there is silence and there is not silence, there is no one and there is someone, nothing prevents anything. And were the voice to cease quite at last, the old ceasing voice, it would not be true, as it is not true that it speaks, it can't speak, it can't cease. And were there one day to be here, where there are no days, which is no place, born of the impossible voice the unmakable being, and a gleam of light, still all would be silent and empty and dark, as now, as soon now, when all will be ended, all said, it says, it murmurs.

From an Abandoned Work

Up bright and early that day, I was young then, feeling awful, and out, mother hanging out of the window in her nightdress weeping and waving. Nice fresh morning, bright too early as so often. Feeling really awful, very violent. The sky would soon darken and rain fall and go on falling, all day, till evening. Then blue and sun again a second, then night. Feeling all this, how violent and the kind of day, I stopped and turned. So back with bowed head on the look out for a snail, slug or worm. Great love in my heart too for all things still and rooted, bushes, boulders and the like, too numerous to mention, even the flowers of the field, not for the world when in my right senses would I ever touch one, to pluck it. Whereas a bird now, or a butterfly, fluttering about and getting in my way, all moving things, getting in my path, a slug now, getting under my feet, no, no mercy. Not that I'd go out of my way to get at them, no, at a distance often they seemed still, then a moment later they were upon me. Birds with my piercing sight I have seen flying so high, so far, that they seemed at rest, then the next minute they were all about me, crows have done this. Ducks are perhaps the worst, to be suddenly stamping and stumbling in the midst of ducks, or hens, any class of poultry, few things are worse. Nor will I go out of my way to avoid such things, when avoidable, no, I simply will not go out of my way, though I have never in my life been on my way anywhere, but simply on my way. And in this way I have gone through great thickets, bleeding, and deep into bogs, water too, even the sea in some moods and been carried out of my course, or driven back, so as not to drown. And that is perhaps how I shall die at last if they don't catch me, I mean drowned, or in fire, yes, perhaps that is how I shall do it at last, walking furious headlong into fire and dying burnt to bits. Then I raised my eyes and saw my mother still in the window waving, waving me back or on I don't know, or just waving, in sad helpless love, and I heard faintly her cries. The window-frame was green, pale, the house-wall grey and my mother white and so thin I could see past her (piercing sight I had then) into the dark of the room, and on all that full the not long risen sun, and all small because of the distance, very pretty really the whole thing, I remember it, the old grey and then the thin green surround and the thin white against the dark, if only she could have been still and let me look at it all. No, for once I wanted to stand and look at something I couldn't with her there waving and fluttering and swaying in and out of the window as though she were doing exercises, and for all I know she may have been, not bothering about me at all. No tenacity of purpose, that was another thing I didn't like in her. One week it would be exercises, and the next prayers and Bible reading, and the next gardening, and the next playing the piano and singing, that was awful, and then just lying about and resting, always changing. Not that it mattered to me, I was always out. But let me get on now with the day I have hit on to begin with, any other would have done as well, yes, on with it and out of my way and on to another, enough of my mother for the moment. Well then for a time all well, no trouble, no birds at me, nothing across my path except at a great distance a white horse followed by a boy, or it might have been a small man or woman. This is the only completely white horse I remember, what I believe the Germans call a Schimmel, oh I was very quick as a boy and picked up a lot of hard knowledge, Schimmel, nice word, for an English speaker. The sun was full upon it, as shortly before on my mother, and it seemed to have a red band or stripe running down its side, I thought perhaps a bellyband, perhaps the horse was going somewhere to be harnessed, to a trap or suchlike. It crossed my path a long way off, then vanished, behind greenery I suppose, all I noticed was the sudden appearance of the horse, then disappearance. It was bright white, with the sun on it, I had never seen such a horse, though often heard of them, and never saw another. White I must say has always affected me strongly, all white things, sheets, walls and so on, even flowers, and then just white, the thought of white, without more. But let me get on with this day and get it over. All well then for a time, just the violence and then this white horse, when suddenly I flew into a most savage rage, really blinding. Now why this sudden rage I really don't know, these sudden rages, they made my life a misery. Many other things too did this, my sore throat for example, I have never known what it is to be without a sore throat, but the rages were the worst, like a great wind suddenly rising in me, no, I can't describe. It wasn't the violence getting worse in any case, nothing to do with that, some days I would be feeling violent all day and never have a rage, other days quite quiet for me and have four or five. No, there's no accounting for it, there's no accounting for anything, with a mind like the one I always had, always on the alert against itself, I'll come back on this perhaps when I feel less weak. There was a time I tried to get relief by beating my head against something, but I gave it up. The best thing I found was to start running. Perhaps I should mention here I was a very slow walker. I didn't dally or loiter in any way, just walked very slowly, little short steps and the feet very slow through the air. On the other hand I must have been quite one of the fastest runners the world has ever seen, over a short distance, five or ten yards, in a second I was there. But I could not go on at that speed, not for breathlessness, it was mental, all is mental, figments. Now the jog trot on the other hand, I could no more do that than I could fly. No, with me all was slow, and then these flashes, or gushes, vent the pent, that was one of those things I used to say, over and over, as I went along, vent the pent, vent the pent. Fortunately my father died when I was a boy, otherwise I might have been a professor, he had set his heart on it. A very fair scholar I was too, no thought, but a great memory. One day I told him about Milton's cosmology, away up in the mountains we were, resting against a huge rock looking out to sea, that impressed him greatly. Love too, often in my thoughts, when a boy, but not a great deal compared to other boys, it kept me awake I found. Never loved anyone I think, I'd remember. Except in my dreams, and there it was animals, dream animals, nothing like what you see walking about the country, I couldn't describe them, lovely creatures they were, white mostly. In a way perhaps it's a pity, a good woman might have been the making of me, I might be sprawling in the sun now sucking my pipe and patting the bottoms of the third generation, looked up to and respected, wondering what there was for dinner, instead of stravaging the same old roads in all weathers, I was never much of a one for new ground. No, I regret nothing, all I regret is having been born, dying is such a long tiresome business I always found. But let me get on now from where I left off, the white horse and then the rage, no connexion I suppose. But why go on with all this, I don't know, some day I must end, why not now. But these are thoughts, not mine, no matter, shame upon me. Now I am old and weak, in pain and weakness murmur why and pause, and the old thoughts well up in me and over into my voice, the old thoughts born with me and grown with me and kept under, there's another. No, back to that far day, any far day, and from the dim granted ground to its things and sky the eyes raised and back again, raised again and back again again, and the feet going nowhere only somehow home, in the morning out from home and in the evening back home again, and the sound of my voice all day long muttering the same old things I don't listen to, not even mine it was at the end of the day, like a marmoset sitting on my shoulder with its bushy tail, keeping me company. All this talking, very low and hoarse, no wonder I had a sore throat. Perhaps I should mention here that I never talked to anyone, I think my father was the last one I talked to. My mother was the same, never talked, never answered, since my father died. I asked her for the money, I can't go back on that now, those must have been my last words to her. Sometimes she cried out on me, or implored, but never long, just a few cries, then if I looked up the poor old thin lips pressed tight together and the body turned away and just the corners of the eyes on me, but it was rare. Sometimes in the night I heard her, talking to herself I suppose, or praying out loud, or reading out loud, or reciting her hymns, poor woman. Well after the horse and rage I don't know, just on, then I suppose the slow turn, wheeling more and more to the one or other hand, till facing home, then home. Ah my father and mother, to think they are probably in paradise, they were so good. Let me go to hell, that's all I ask, and go on cursing them there, and them look down and hear me, that might take some of the shine off their bliss. Yes, I believe all their blather about the life to come, it cheers me up, and unhappiness like mine, there's no annihilating that. I was mad of course and still am, but harmless, I passed for harmless, that's a good one. Not of course that I was really mad, just strange, a little strange, and with every passing year a little stranger, there can be few stranger creatures going about than me at the present day. My father, did I kill him too as well as my mother, perhaps in a way I did, but I can't go into that now, much too old and weak. The questions float up as I go along and leave me very confused, breaking up I am. Suddenly they are there, no, they float up, out of an old depth, and hover and linger before they die away, questions that when I was in my right mind would not have survived one second, no, but atomized they would have been, before as much as formed, atomized. In twos often they came, one hard on the other, thus, How shall I go on another day? and then, How did I ever go on another day? Or, Did I kill my father? and then, Did I ever kill anyone? That kind of way, to the general from the particular I suppose you might say, question and answer too in a way, very addling. I strive with them as best I can, quickening my step when they come on, tossing my head from side to side and up and down, staring agonizedly at this and that, increasing my murmur to a scream, these are helps. But they should not be necessary, something is wrong here, if it was the end I would not so much mind, but how often I have said, in my life, before some new awful thing, It is the end, and it was not the end, and yet the end cannot be far off now, I shall fall as I go along and stay down or curl up for the night as usual among the rocks and before morning be gone. Oh I know I too shall cease and be as when I was not yet, only all over instead of in store, that makes me happy, often now my murmur falters and dies and I weep for happiness as I go along and for love of this old earth that has carried me so long and whose uncomplainingness will soon be mine. Just under the surface I shall be, all together at first, then separate and drift, through all the earth and perhaps in the end through a cliff into the sea, something of me. A ton of worms in an acre, that is a wonderful thought, a ton of worms, I believe it. Where did I get it, from a dream, or a book read in a nook when a boy, or a word overheard as I went along, or in me all along and kept under till it could give me joy, these are the kind of horrid thoughts I have to contend with in the way I have said. Now is there nothing to add to this day with the white horse and white mother in the window, please read again my descriptions of these, before I get on to some other day at a later time, nothing to add before I move on in time skipping hundreds and even thousands of days in a way I could not at the time, but had to get through somehow until I came to the one I am coming to now, no, nothing, all has gone but mother in the window, the violence, rage and rain. So on to this second day and get it over and out of the way and on to the next. What happens now is I was set on and pursued by a family or tribe, I do not know, of stoats, a most extraordinary thing, I think they were stoats. Indeed if I may say so I think I was fortunate to get off with my life, strange expression, it does not sound right somehow. Anyone else would have been bitten and bled to death, perhaps sucked white, like a rabbit, there is that word white again. I know I could never think, but if I could have, and then had, I would just have lain down and let myself be destroyed, as the rabbit does. But let me start as always with the morning and the getting out. When a day comes back, whatever the reason, then its morning and its evening too are there, though in themselves quite unremarkable, the going out and coming home, there is a remarkable thing I find. So up then in the grey of dawn, very weak and shaky after an atrocious night little dreaming what lay in store, out and off. What time of year, I really do not know, does it matter. Not wet really, but dripping, everything dripping, the day might rise, did it, no, drip drip all day long, no sun, no change of light, dim all day, and still, not a breath, till night, then black, and a little wind, I saw some stars, as I neared home. My stick of course, by a merciful providence, I shall not say this again, when not mentioned my stick is in my hand, as I go along. But not my long coat, just my jacket, I could never bear the long coat, flapping about my legs, or rather one day suddenly I turned against it, a sudden violent dislike. Often when dressed to go I would take it out and put it on, then stand in the middle of the room unable to move, until at last I could take it off and put it back on its hanger, in the cupboard. But I was hardly down the stairs and out into the air when the stick fell from my hand and I just sank to my knees to the ground and then forward on my face, a most extraordinary thing, and then after a little over on my back, I could never lie on my face for any length of time, much as I loved it, it made me feel sick, and lay there, half an hour perhaps, with my arms along my sides and the palms of my hands against the pebbles and my eyes wide open straying over the sky. Now was this my first experience of this kind, that is the question that immediately assails one. Falls I had had in plenty, of the kind after which unless a limb broken you pick yourself up and go on, cursing God and man, very different from this. With so much life gone from knowledge how to know when all began, all the variants of the one that one by one their venom staling follow upon one another, all life long, till you succumb. So in some way even olden things each time are first things, no two breaths the same, all a going over and over and all once and never more. But let me get up now and on and get this awful day over and on to the next. But what is the sense of going on with all this, there is none. Day after unremembered day until my mother's death, then in a new place soon old until my own. And when I come to this night here among the rocks with my two books and the strong starlight it will have passed from me and the day that went before, my two books, the little and the big, all past and gone, or perhaps just moments here and there still, this little sound perhaps now that I don't understand so that I gather up my things and go back into my hole, so bygone they can be told. Over, over, there is a soft place in my heart for all that is over, no, for the being over, I love the word, words have been my only loves, not many. Often all day long as I went along I have said it, and sometimes I would be saying vero, oh vero. Oh but for those awful fidgets I have always had I would have lived my life in a big empty echoing room with a big old pendulum clock, just listening and dozing, the case open so that I could watch the swinging, moving my eyes to and fro, and the lead weights dangling lower and lower till I got up out of my chair and wound them up again, once a week. The third day was the look I got from the roadman, suddenly I see that now, the ragged old brute bent double down in the ditch leaning on his spade or whatever it was and leering around and up at me from under the brim of his slouch, the red mouth, how is it I wonder I saw him at all, that is more like it, the day I saw the look I got from Balfe, I went in terror of him as a child. Now he is dead and I resemble him. But let us get on and leave these old scenes and come to these, and my reward. Then it will not be as now, day after day, out, on, round, back, in, like leaves turning, or torn out and thrown crumpled away, but a long unbroken time without before or after, light or dark, from or towards or at, the old half knowledge of when and where gone, and of what, but kinds of things still, all at once, all going, until nothing, there was never anything, never can be, life and death all nothing, that kind of thing, only a voice dreaming and droning on all around, that is something, the voice that once was in your mouth. Well once out on the road and free of the property what then, I really do not know, the next thing I was up in the bracken lashing about with my stick making the drops fly and cursing, filthy language, the same words over and over, I hope nobody heard me. Throat very bad, to swallow was torment, and something wrong with an ear, I kept poking at it without relief, old wax perhaps pressing on the drum. Extraordinary still over the land, and in me too all quite still, a coincidence, why the curses were pouring out of me I do not know, no, that is a foolish thing to say, and the lashing about with the stick, what possessed me mild and weak to be doing that, as I struggled along. Is it the stoats now, no, first I just sink down again and disappear in the ferns, up to my waist they were as I went along. Harsh things these great ferns, like starched, very woody, terrible stalks, take the skin off your legs through your trousers, and then the holes they hide, break your leg if you're not careful, awful English this, fall and vanish from view, you could lie there for weeks and no one hear you, I often thought of that up in the mountains, no, that is a foolish thing to say, just went on, my body doing its best without me.

All Strange Away

Imagination dead imagine. A place, that again. Never another question. A place, then someone in it, that again. Crawl out of the frowsy deathbed and drag it to a place to die in. Out of the door and down the road in the old hat and coat like after the war, no, not that again. Five foot square, six high, no way in, none out, try for him there. Stool, bare walls when the light comes on, women's faces on the walls when the light comes on. In a corner when the light comes on tattered syntaxes of Jolly and Draeger Praeger Draeger, all right. Light off and let him be, on the stool, talking to himself in the last person, murmuring, no sound, Now where is he, no, Now he is here. Sitting, standing, walking, kneeling, crawling, lying, creeping, in the dark and in the light, try all. Imagine light. Imagine light. No visible source, glare at full, spread all over, no shadow, all six planes shining the same, slow on, ten seconds on earth to full, same off, try that. Still his crown touches the ceiling, moving not, say a lifetime of walking bowed and full height when brought to a stand. It goes out, no matter, start again, another place, someone in it, keep glaring, never see, never find, no end, no matter. He says, no sound, The longer he lives and so the further goes the smaller they grow, the reasoning being the fuller he fills the space and so on, and the emptier, same reasoning. Hell this light from nothing no reason any moment, take off his coat, no, naked, all right, leave it for the moment. Sheets of black paper, stick them to the wall with cobweb and spittle, no good, shine like the rest. Imagine what needed, no more, any given moment, needed no more, gone, never was. Light flows, eyes close, stay closed till it ebbs, no, can't do that, eyes stay open, all right, look at that later. Black bag over his head, no good, all the rest still in light, front, sides, back, between the legs. Black shroud, start search for pins. Light on, down on knees, sights pin, makes for it, light out, gets pin in dark, light on, sights another, light out, so on, years of time on earth. Back on the stool in the shroud saying, That's better, now he's better, and so sits and never stirs, clutching it to him where it gapes, till it all perishes and rots off of him and hangs off of him in black flitters. Light out, long dark, candle and matches, imagine them, strike one to light, light on, blow out, light out, strike another, light on, so on. Light out, strike one to light, light on, light all the same, candlelight in light, blow out, light out, so on. No candle, no matches, no need, never were. As he was, in the dark any length, then the light when it flows till it ebbs any length, then again, so on, sitting, standing, walking, kneeling, crawling, lying, creeping, all any length, no paper, no pins, no candle, no matches, never were, talking to himself no sound in the last person any length, five foot square, six high, all white when light at full, no way in, none out. Falling on his knees in the dark to murmur, no sound, Fancy is his only hope. Surprised by light in this posture, hope and fancy on his lips, crawling lifelong habit to a corner here shadowless and similarly sinking head to ground here shining back into his eyes. Imagine eyes burnt ashen blue and lashes gone, lifetime of unseeing glaring, jammed open, one lightning wince per minute on earth, try that. Have him say, no sound, No way in, none out, he's not here. Tighten it round him, three foot square, five high, no stool, no sitting, no kneeling, no lying, just room to stand and revolve, light as before, faces as before, syntaxes upended in opposite corners. The back of his head touches the ceiling, say a lifetime of standing bowed. Call floor angles deasil a, b, c and d and ceiling likewise e, f, g and h, say Jolly at b and Draeger at d, lean him for rest with feet at a and head at g, in dark and light, eyes glaring, murmuring, He's not here, no sound, Fancy is his only hope. Physique, flesh and fell, nail him to that while still tender, nothing clear, place again. Light as before, all white still when at full, flaking plaster or the like, floor like bleached dirt, aha. Faces now naked bodies, eye level, two per wall, eight in all, all right, details later. All six planes hot when shining, aha. So dark and cold any length, shivering more or less, feeble slaps want of room at all flesh within reach, little stamps of hampered feet, so on. Same system light and heat with sweat more or less, cringing away from walls, burning soles, now one, now the other. Murmur unaffected, He's not here, no sound, Fancy dead, gaping eyes unaffected. See how light stops at five soft and mild for bodies, eight no more, one per wall, four in all, say all of Emma. First face alone, lovely beyond words, leave it at that, then deasil breasts alone, then thighs and cunt alone, then arse and hole alone, all lovely beyond words. See how he crouches down and back to see, back of head against face when eyes on cunt, against breasts when on hole, and vice versa, all most clear. So in this soft and mild, crouched down and back with hands on knees to hold himself together, say deasil first from face through hole then back through face, murmuring, Imagine him kissing, caressing, licking, sucking, fucking and buggering all this stuff, no sound. Then halt and up to position of rest, back of head touching the ceiling, gaze on ground, lifetime of unbloody bowed unseeing glaring. Imagine lifetime, gems, evenings with Emma and the flights by night, no, not that again. Physique, too soon, perhaps never, vague bowed body bonewhite when light at full, nothing clear but ashen glare as imagined, no, attitudes too with play of joints most clear more various now. For nine and nine eighteen that is four feet and more across in which to kneel, arse on heels, hands on thighs, trunk best bowed and crown on ground. And even sit, knees drawn up, trunk best bowed, head between knees, arms round knees to hold all together. And even lie, arse to knees say diagonal ac, feet say at d, head on left cheek at b. Price to pay and highest lying more flesh touching glowing ground. But say not glowing enough to burn and turning over, see how that works. Arse to knees, say bd, feet say at c, head on right cheek at a. Then arse to knees say again ac, but feet at b and head on left cheek at d. Then arse to knees say again bd, but feet at a and head on right cheek at c. So on other four possibilities when begin again. All that most clear. Imaginable too flat on back, knees drawn up, hands holding shins to hold all together, glare on ceiling, whereas flat on face by no stretch. Place then most clear

so far but of him nothing and perhaps never save jointed segments vari-
ously disposed white when light at full. And always there among them
somewhere the glaring eyes now clearer still in that flashes of vision few
and far now rive their unseeingness. So for example as chance may have
it on the ceiling a flyspeck or the insect itself or a strand of Emma's motte.
Then lost and all the remaining field for hours of time on earth. Imagi-
nation dead imagine to lodge a second in that glare a dying common
house or dying window fly, then fall the five feet to the dust and die and
fall. No, no image, no fly here, no life or dying here but his, a speck of dirt.
Or hers since sex not seen so far, say Emma standing, turning, sitting,
kneeling, lying, in dark and light, saying to herself, She's not here, no
sound, Fancy is her only hope, and Emmo on the walls, first the face, hand-
some beyond words, then deasil details later. And how crouching down
and back she turns murmuring, Fancy her being all kissed, licked, sucked,
fucked and so on by all that, no sound, hands on knees to hold herself
together. Till halt and up, no, no image, down, for her down, to sit or kneel,
kneel, arse on heels, hands on thighs, trunk bowed, breasts hanging, crown
on ground, eyes glaring, no, no image, eyes closed, long lashes black when
light, no more glare, never was, long black hair strewn when light, mur-
muring, no sound, Fancy dead. Any length, in dark and light, then topple
left, arse to knees say db, feet say at c, head on left cheek at a, left breast
puckered in the dust, hands, imagine hands. Imagine hands. Let her lie so
from now on, have always lain so, head on left cheek in black hair at a and
the rest the only way, never sat, never knelt, never stood, no Emmo, no
need, never was. Imagine hands. Left on ball of right shoulder holding
enough not to slip, right lightly clenched on ground, something in this
hand, imagine later, something soft, clench tight, then lax and still any
length, then tight again, so on, imagine later. Highest point from ground
top to swell of right haunch, say twenty inches, slim woman. Ceiling
wrong now, down two foot, perfect cube now, three foot every way, always
was, light as before, all bonewhite when at full as before, floor like bleached
dirt, something there, leave it for the moment. Waste height, sixteen
inches, strange, say some reason unimaginable now, imagine later, imagi-
nation dead imagine all strange away. Jolly and Draeger gone, never were.

So far then hollow cube three foot overall, no way in imagined yet, none out. Black cold any length, then light slow up to full glare say ten seconds still and hot glare any length all ivory white all six planes no shadow, then down through deepening greys and gone, so on. Walls and ceiling flaking plaster or suchlike, floor like bleached dirt, aha, something there, leave it for the moment. Call floor angles deasil a, b, c and d and in here Emma lying on her left side, arse to knees along diagonal db with arse towards d and knees towards b though neither at either because too short and waste space here too some reason yet to be imagined. On left side then arse to knees db and consequently arse to crown along wall da though not flush because arse out with head on left cheek at a and remaining segment knees to feet along bc not flush because knees out with feet at c. In dark and light. Slow fade of ivory flesh when ebb ten seconds and gone. Long black hair when light strewn over face and adjacent floor. Uncover right eye and cheekbone vivid white for long black lashes when light. Say again though no real image puckered tip of left breast, leave right a mere name. Left hand clinging to right shoulder ball, right more faint loose fist on ground till fingers tighten as though to squeeze, imagine later, then loose again and still any length, so on. Murmuring, no sound, though say lips move with faint stir of hair, whether none emitted or air too rare, Fancy is her only hope, or, She's not here, or, Fancy dead, suggesting moments of discouragement, imagine other murmurs. In dark and light, no, dark alone, say murmurs now in dark alone as though in light all ears all six planes all ears when shining whereas in dark unheard, this a well-known thing. And yet no sound, well say a sound too faint for mortal ear. Imagine other murmurs. So great need of words not daring till at last slow ebb ten seconds, too fast, thirty now, great need not daring till at last slow ebb thirty seconds on earth through a thousand darkening greys till out and incontinent, Fancy dead, for instance if spirits low, no sound. But see how the light dies down and from half down or more slow up again to full and the words down again that were trembling up, all right, say mere delay, dark must be in the end, say dark and light here equal in the end that is when all done with dead imagining and measures taken dark and light seen equal in the end. And indeed how stay of flow or ebb at any grey any length and even on the very sill of black any length till at last in and black and at long last the murmur too faint for mortal ear. But murmurs in long dark so long that longing no but need for light as in long light for dark murmurs sometimes as great a space apart as from on earth a winter to a summer day and coming on that great silence, She's not here, for instance if in better spirits or, Fancy is her only hope, too faint for mortal ear. And other times to imagine other extreme so hard on one another any order and sometimes when all spent if not assuaged a second time in some quite different so run together that a mere torrent of hope and unhope mingled and submission amounting to nothing, get all this clearer later. Imagine other murmurs, Mother mother, Mother in heaven, Mother of God, God in heaven, combinations with Christ and Jesus, other proper names in great numbers say of loved ones for the most part and cherished haunts, imagine as needed, unsupported interjections, ancient Greek philosophers ejaculated with place of origin when possible suggesting pursuit of knowledge at some period, completed propositions such as, She is not here, the exception, imagine others, This is not possible, there is one, and here another of exceptional length, In a hammock in the sun in here the name of some bewitching site she lies sleeping. But sudden gleam that whatever words given to let fall soundless in the dark that if no sound better none, all right, try sound and if no better say quite speechless, imagine sound and not till then all that black hair toss back into the corner baring face as about to when this happened. Quite audible then now for her and if other ears there with her in the dark for them and if ears low down in the wall at a for them a voice without meaning, hear that. Then further quite expressionless, ohs and ahs copulate cold and no more feeling apparently in hammock than in Jesus Christ Almighty. And finally for the moment and then that face the tailaway so common in untrained speakers leaving sometimes in some doubt such things as which Diogenes and what fancy her only. Such then the sound roughly and if no clearer so then all the storm unspoken and the silence unbroken unless sound of light and dark or at the moments of change a sound of flow thirty seconds till full then silence any length till sound of ebb thirty seconds till black then silence any length, that might repay hearing and she hearing open then her eyes to lightening or darkening greys and not close them then to keep them closed till next sound of change till full light or dark, that might well be imagined. But at the same time say here all sound most doubtful though still too soon to deny and that in the end that is when all gone from mind and all mind gone that then none ever been but only silent flesh unless with the faint rise and fall of breast the breath to whip up to a pant if too faint alone and all others denied but still too soon. Hollow cube then three foot overall, full glare, head on left cheek in angle a and the rest the only way and say though no clear image now the long black hair now scattered clear of face on floor so clear when strewn on face now gone some reason, come back to that later, and on the face now bare all the glare for the moment. Gone the remembered long black lashes vivid white so clear before through gap in hair before all tossed back and lost some reason and face quite bare suggesting perhaps confusion then with errant threads of hair itself confused then with long lashes and so gone with hair or some other reason now quite gone. Cease here from face a space to note how place no longer cube but rotunda three foot diameter eighteen inches high supporting a dome semicircular in section as in the Pantheon at Rome or certain beehive tombs and consequently three foot from ground to vertex that is at its highest point no lower than before with loss of floor space in the neighbourhood of two square feet or six square inches per lost angle and consequences for recumbent readily imaginable and of cubic an even higher figure, all right, resume face. But a, b, c and d now where any pair of right-angled diameters meet circumference meaning tighter fit for Emma with loss if folded as before of nearly one foot from crown to arse and of more than one from arse to knees and of nearly one from knees to feet though she still might be mathematically speaking more than seven foot long and merely a question of refolding in such a way that if head on left cheek at new a and feet at new c then arse no longer at new d but somewhere between it and new c and knees no longer at new b but somewhere between it and new a with segments angled more acutely that is head almost touching knees and feet almost touching arse, all that most clear. Rotunda then three foot diameter and three from ground to vertex, full glare, head on left cheek at a no longer new, when suddenly clear these dimensions faulty and small woman scarce five foot fully extended making rotunda two foot diameter and two from ground to verge, full glare, face on left cheek at a and long segment that is from crown to arse now necessarily along diagonal too hastily assigned to middle with result face on left cheek with crown against wall at a and no longer feet but *arse* against wall at c there being no alternative and knees against wall ab a few inches from face and feet against wall bc a few inches from arse there being no alternatives and in this way the body tripled or trebled up and wedged in the only possible way in one half of the available room leaving the other empty, aha.

DIAGRAM

Arms and hands as before for the moment. Rotunda then two foot across and at its highest two foot high, full glare, face on left cheek at a, long black hair gone, long black lashes on white cheekbone gone, glare from above for features on this bonewhite undoubted face right profile still hungering for missing lashes burning down for commissure of lids at least when like say without hesitation hell gaping they part and the black eye appears, leave now this face for the moment. Glare now on hands most womanly clear and womanly especially right still loosely clenched as before but no longer on ground since corrected pose but now on outer of right knee just where it swells to thigh while left still loosely hitched to right shoulder ball as before. All that most clear. That black eye still yawning before going down to former to see what all this squeezing note how the other slips a little way down slope of upper arm then back up to ball, imagine squeeze again. Loose clench any length then crush down most womanly straining knuckles five seconds then back lax any length, all right, now down while fingers loose and in between tips and palm that tiny chink, full glare all this time. No real image but say like red no grey say like something grey and when again squeeze firm down five seconds say faint hiss then silence then back loose two seconds and say faint pop and so arrive though no true image at small grey punctured rubber ball or small grey ordinary rubber bulb such as on earth attached to bottle of

scent or suchlike that when squeezed a jet of scent but here alone. So lit-
tle by little all strange away. Avalanche white lava mud seethe lid over eye
permitting return to face of which finally only that it could be nothing
else, all right. Thence on to neck in health by nature blank chunk nearer
to healthy natural neck with even hint of jugular and cords suggesting
perhaps past her best and thence on down to other meat when suddenly
when least expected all this prying pointless and enough for the moment
and perhaps for ever this place so clear now when light at full and this
body hinged and crooked as only the human man or woman living or not
when light at full without all this poking and prying about for cracks
holes and appendages. Rotunda then as before no change for the moment
in dark and light no visible source spread even no shadow slow on thirty
seconds to full same off to black two foot high at highest six and a half
round good measure, wall peeling plaster or the like supporting dome
semi-circular in section same surface, floor bleached dirt or similar, head
wedged against wall at a with blank face on left cheek and the rest the
only way that is arse wedged against wall at c and knees wedged against
wall ab a few inches from face and feet wedged against wall bc a few inches
from arse, puckered tip of left breast no real image but maintain for the
moment, left hand most clear and womanly lightly clasping right shoul-
der ball so lightly that slip from time to time down slope of right upper
arm then back up to clasp, right no less on upper outer right knee lightly
clasping any length small grey rubber sprayer bulb or grey punctured
rubber ball then squeeze five seconds on earth faint hiss relax two sec-
onds and pop or not, black right eye like maintain hell gaping any length
then seethe of lid to cover imagine frequency later and motive, left also
at same time or not or never imagine later, all contained in one hemi-
cycle leaving other vacant, aha. All that if not yet quite complete quite
clear and little change likely unless perhaps to complete unless perhaps
somehow light sudden gleam perhaps better fixed and all this flowing
and ebbing to full and empty more harm than good and better unchang-
ing black or glare one or the other or between the two soft white unchang-
ing but leave for the moment as seen from outset and never doubted
slow on and off thirty seconds to glare and black any length through slow

lightening and darkening greys from nothing for no reason yet imagined. Sleep stirring now some time add now with nightmares unimaginable making waking sweet and lying waking till longing for sleep again with dread of demons, perhaps some glimpse of demons later. Dread then in rotunda now with longing and sweet relief but so faint and weak no more than weak tremors of a hothouse leaf. Memories of past felicity no save one faint with faint ripple of sorrow of a lying side by side, look at this closer later. Imagine turning over with help of hinge of neck to bow head towards breast and so temporarily shorten long segment unwedging crown and arse with play enough to writhe till finally head wedged against wall at a as before but on right cheek and arse against wall at c as before but on right cheek and knees against wall a few inches from face as before but wall ad and feet against wall a few inches from arse as before but wall cd and so all tripled up and wedged as before but on the other side to rest the other and within the other hemicycle leaving the other vacant, aha, all that most clear. Clear further how at some earlier more callow stage this writhe again and again in vain through weakness or natural awkwardness or want of pliancy or want of resolution and how halfway through on back with legs just clear how after some time in the balance thus the fall back to where she lay head wedged against wall at a with blank face on left cheek and arse against wall at c and knees against wall ab and feet against wall bc with left hand clutching lightly right shoulder ball and right on upper outer knee small grey sprayer bulb or grey punctured rubber ball with disappointment naturally tinged perhaps with relief and this again and again till final renouncement with faint sweet relief, faint disappointment will have been here too. Sleep if maintained with cacodemons making waking in light and dark if this maintained faint sweet relief and the longing for it again and to be gone again a folly to be resisted again in vain. No memories of felicity save with faint ruffle of sorrow of a lying side by side and of misfortune none, look closer later. So in rotunda up to now with disppointment and relief with dread and longing sorrow all so weak and faint no more than faint tremors of a leaf indoors on earth in winter to survive till spring. Glare back now where all no light immeasurable turmoil no sound black soundless storm of

which on earth all being well say one millionth stilled to mean and of that
as much again by the more fortunate all being well vented as only humans
can. All gone now and never been never stilled never voiced all back
whence never sundered unstillable turmoil no sound, She's not here,
Fancy is her only, Mother mother, Mother in heaven and of God, God in
heaven, Christ and Jesus all combinations, loved ones and places, philos-
ophers and all mere cries, In a hammock etc. and all such, leaving only
for the moment, Fancy dead, try that again with spirant barely parting
lips in murmur and faint stir of white dust or not in light and dark if this
maintained or dark alone as though ears when shining and dead uncer-
tain in dying fall of amateur soliloquy when not known for certain. Last
look oh not farewell but last for now on right side tripled up and wedged
in half the room head against wall at a and arse against wall at c and
knees against wall ab an inch or so from head and feet against wall bc an
inch or so from arse. Then look away then back for left hand clasping
lightly right shoulder ball any length till slip and back to clasp and right
on upper outer knee any length grey sprayer bulb or small grey punctured
rubber ball till squeeze with hiss and loose again with pop or not. Long
black hair and lashes gone and puckered breast no details to add to these
for the moment save normal neck with hint of cords and jugular and
black bottomless eye. Within apart from fancy dead and with faint sorrow
faint memory of a lying side by side and in sleep demons not yet imag-
ined all dark unappeasable turmoil no sound and so exhaled only for the
moment with faint sound, Fancy dead, to which now add for old mind's
sake sorrow vented in simple sighing sound black vowel a and further so
that henceforth here no other sounds than these say gone now and never
were sprayer bulb or punctured rubber ball and nothing ever in that hand
lightly closed on nothing any length till for no reason yet imagined fin-
gers tighten then relax no sound and to the same end slip of left hand
down slope of right upper arm no sound and same purpose none of
breath to the end that here henceforth no other sounds than these and
never were that is than sop to mind faint sighing sound for tremor of sor-
row at faint memory of a lying side by side and fancy murmured dead.

Imagination Dead Imagine

No trace anywhere of life, you say, pah, no difficulty there, imagination not dead yet, yes, dead, good, imagination dead imagine. Islands, waters, azure, verdure, one glimpse and vanished, endlessly, omit. Till all white in the whiteness the rotunda. No way in, go in, measure. Diameter three feet, three feet from ground to summit of the vault. Two diameters at right angles AB CD divide the white ground into two semi-circles ACB BDA. Lying on the ground two white bodies, each in its semi-circle. White too the vault and the round wall eighteen inches high from which it springs. Go back out, a plain rotunda, all white in the whiteness, go back in, rap, solid throughout, a ring as in the imagination the ring of bone. The light that makes all so white no visible source, all shines with the same white shine, ground, wall, vault, bodies, no shadow. Strong heat, surfaces hot but not burning to the touch, bodies sweating. Go back out, move back, the little fabric vanishes, ascend, it vanishes, all white in the whiteness, descend, go back in. Emptiness, silence, heat, whiteness, wait, the light goes down, all grows dark together, ground, wall, vault, bodies, say twenty seconds, all the greys, the light goes out, all vanishes. At the same time the temperature goes down, to reach its minimum, say freezing-point, at the same instant that the black is reached, which may seem strange. Wait, more or less long, light and heat come back, all grows white and hot together, ground, wall, vault, bodies, say twenty seconds, all the greys, till the initial level is reached whence the fall began. More or less long, for there may intervene, experience shows, between end of fall and beginning of rise, pauses of varying length, from the fraction of the second to what would have seemed, in other times, other places, an eternity. Same remark for the other pause, between end of rise and beginning of fall. The extremes, as long as they last, are perfectly stable, which in the case of the temperature may seem strange, in the beginning. It is possible too, experience shows, for rise and fall to stop short at any point and mark a pause, more or less long, before resuming, or revers-ing, the rise now fall, the fall rise, these in their turn to be completed, or to stop short and mark a pause, more or less long, before resuming, or again reversing, and so on, till finally one or the other extreme is reached. Such variations of rise and fall, combining in countless rhythms, com-monly attend the passage from white and heat to black and cold, and vice versa. The extremes alone are stable as is stressed by the vibration to be observed when a pause occurs at some intermediate stage, no matter what its level and duration. Then all vibrates, ground, wall, vault, bodies, ashen or leaden or between the two, as may be. But on the whole, expe-rience shows, such uncertain passage is not common. And most often, when the light begins to fail, and along with it the heat, the movement continues unbroken until, in the space of some twenty seconds, pitch black is reached and at the same instant say freezing-point. Same remark for the reverse movement, towards heat and whiteness. Next most fre-quent is the fall or rise with pauses of varying length in these feverish greys, without at any moment reversal of the movement. But whatever its uncertainties the return sooner or later to a temporary calm seems assured, for the moment, in the black dark or the great whiteness, with attendant temperature, world still proof against enduring tumult. Redis-covered miraculously after what absence in perfect voids it is no longer quite the same, from this point of view, but there is no other. Externally all is as before and the sighting of the little fabric quite as much a matter of chance, its whiteness merging in the surrounding whiteness. But go in and now briefer lulls and never twice the same storm. Light and heat remain linked as though supplied by the same source of which still no trace. Still on the ground, bent in three, the head against the wall at B, the arse against the wall at A, the knees against the wall between B and C, the feet against the wall between C and A, that is to say inscribed in the semicircle ACB, merging in the white ground were it not for the long hair of strangely imperfect whiteness, the white body of a woman finally. Similarly inscribed in the other semicircle, against the wall his head at A, his arse at B, his knees between A and D, his feet between D and B, the partner. On their right sides therefore both and back to back head to arse. Hold a mirror to their lips, it mists. With their left hands they hold their left legs a little below the knee, with their right hands their left arms a little above the elbow. In this agitated light, its great white calm now so rare and brief, inspection is not easy. Sweat and mirror notwithstanding they might well pass for inanimate but for the left eyes which at incalculable intervals suddenly open wide and gaze in unblinking exposure long beyond what is humanly possible. Piercing pale blue the effect is striking, in the beginning. Never the two gazes together except once, when the beginning of one overlapped the end of the other, for about ten seconds. Neither fat nor thin, big nor small, the bodies seem whole and in fairly good condition, to judge by the surfaces exposed to view. The faces too, assuming the two sides of a piece, seem to want nothing essential. Between their absolute stillness and the convulsive light the contrast is striking, in the beginning, for one who still remembers having been struck by the contrary. It is clear however, from a thousand little signs too long to imagine, that they are not sleeping. Only murmur ah, no more, in this silence, and at the same instant for the eye of prey the infinitesimal shudder instantaneously suppressed. Leave them there, sweating and icy, there is better elsewhere. No, life ends and no, there is nothing elsewhere, and no question now of ever finding again that white speck lost in whiteness, to see if they still lie still in the stress of that storm, or of a worse storm, or in the black dark for good, or the great whiteness unchanging, and if not what they are doing.

Enough

All that goes before forget. Too much at a time is too much. That gives the pen time to note. I don't see it but I hear it there behind me. Such is the silence. When the pen stops I go on. Sometimes it refuses. When it refuses I go on. Too much silence is too much. Or it's my voice too weak at times. The one that comes out of me. So much for the art and craft.

I did all he desired. I desired it too. For him. Whenever he desired something so did I. He only had to say what thing. When he didn't desire anything neither did I. In this way I didn't live without desires. If he had desired something for me I would have desired it too. Happiness for example or fame. I only had the desires he manifested. But he must have manifested them all. All his desires and needs. When he was silent he must have been like me. When he told me to lick his penis I hastened to do so. I drew satisfaction from it. We must have had the same satisfactions. The same needs and the same satisfactions.

One day he told me to leave him. It's the verb he used. He must have been on his last legs. I don't know if by that he meant me to leave him for good or only to step aside a moment. I never asked myself the question. I never asked myself any questions but his. Whatever it was he meant I made off without looking back. Gone from reach of his voice I was gone from his life. Perhaps it was that he desired. There are questions you see and don't ask yourself. He must have been on his last legs. I on the contrary was far from on my last legs. I belonged to an entirely different generation. It didn't last. Now that I'm entering night I have kinds of gleams in my skull. Stony ground but not entirely. Given three or four lives I might have accomplished something.

I cannot have been more than six when he took me by the hand. Barely emerging from childhood. But it didn't take me long to emerge altogether. It was the left hand. To be on the right was more than he could bear. We advanced side by side hand in hand. One pair of gloves was enough. The free or outer hands hung bare. He did not like to feel against his skin the skin of another. Mucous membrane is a different matter. Yet he sometimes took off his glove. Then I had to take off mine. We would cover in this way a hundred yards or so linked by our bare extremities. Seldom more. That was enough for him. If the question were put to me I would say that odd hands are ill-fitted for intimacy. Mine never felt at home in his. Sometimes they let each other go. The clasp loosened and they fell apart. Whole minutes often passed before they clasped again. Before his clasped mine again.

They were cotton gloves rather tight. Far from blunting the shapes they sharpened them by simplifying. Mine was naturally too loose for years. But it didn't take me long to fill it. He said I had Aquarius hands. It's a mansion above.

All I know comes from him. I won't repeat this apropos of all my bits of knowledge. The art of combining is not my fault. It's a curse from above. For the rest I would suggest not guilty.

Our meeting. Though very bowed already he looked a giant to me. In the end his trunk ran parallel with the ground. To counterbalance this anomaly he held his legs apart and sagged at the knees. His feet grew more and more flat and splay. His horizon was the ground they trod. Tiny moving carpet of turf and trampled flowers. He gave me his hand like a tired old ape with the elbow lifted as high as it would go. I had only to straighten up to be head and shoulders above him. One day he halted and fumbling for his words explained to me that anatomy is a whole.

In the beginning he always spoke walking. So it seems to me now. Then sometimes walking and sometimes still. In the end still only. And the voice getting fainter all the time. To save him having to say the same thing twice running I bowed right down. He halted and waited for me to get into position. As soon as out of the corner of his eye he glimpsed my head alongside his the murmurs came. Nine times out of ten they did not concern me. But he wished everything to be heard including the ejaculations and broken paternosters that he poured out to the flowers at his feet.

He halted then and waited for my head to arrive before telling me to leave him. I snatched away my hand and made off without looking back. Two steps and I was lost to him for ever. We were severed if that is what he desired.

His talk was seldom of geodesy. But we must have covered several times the equivalent of the terrestrial equator. At an average speed of roughly three miles per day and night. We took flight in arithmetic. What mental calculations bent double hand in hand! Whole ternary numbers we raised in this way to the third power sometimes in downpours of rain. Graving themselves in his memory as best they could the ensuing cubes accumulated. In view of the converse operation at a later stage. When time would have done its work.

If the question were put to me suitably framed I would say yes indeed the end of this long outing was my life. Say about the last seven thousand miles. Counting from the day when alluding for the first time to his infirmity he said he thought it had reached its peak. The future proved him right. That part of it at least we were to make past of together.

I see the flowers at my feet and it's the others I see. Those we trod down with equal step. It is true they are the same.

Contrary to what I had long been pleased to imagine he was not blind. Merely indolent. One day he halted and fumbling for his words described his vision. He concluded by saying he thought it would get no worse. How far this was not a delusion I cannot say. I never asked myself the question. When I bowed down to receive his communications I felt on my eye a glint of blue bloodshot apparently affected.

He sometimes halted without saying anything. Either he had finally nothing to say or while having something to say he finally decided not to say it. I bowed down as usual to save him having to repeat himself and we remained in this position. Bent double heads touching silent hand in hand. While all about us fast on one another the minutes flew. Sooner or later his foot broke away from the flowers and we moved on. Perhaps only to bait again after a few steps. So that he might say at last what was in his heart or decide not to say it again.

Other main examples suggest themselves to the mind. Immediate continuous communication with immediate redeparture. Same thing with delayed redeparture. Delayed continuous communication with immediate redeparture. Same thing with delayed redeparture. Immediate discontinuous communication with immediate redeparture. Same thing with delayed redeparture. Delayed discontinuous communication with immediate redeparture. Same thing with delayed redeparture.

It is then I shall have lived then or never. Ten years at the very least. From the day he drew the back of his left hand lingeringly over his sacral ruins and launched his prognostic. To the day of my supposed disgrace. I can see the place a step short of the crest. Two steps forward and I was descending the other slope. If I had looked back I would not have seen him.

He loved to climb and therefore I too. He clamoured for the steepest slopes. His human frame broke down into two equal segments. This thanks to the shortening of the lower by the sagging knees. On a gradient of one in one his head swept the ground. To what this taste was due I cannot say. To love of the earth and the flowers' thousand scents and hues. Or to cruder imperatives of an anatomical order. He never raised the question. The crest once reached alas the going down again.

In order from time to time to enjoy the sky he resorted to a little round mirror. Having misted it with his breath and polished it on his calf he looked in it for the constellations. I have it! he exclaimed referring to the Lyre or the Swan. And often he added that the sky seemed much the same.

We were not in the mountains however. There were times I discerned on the horizon a sea whose level seemed higher than ours. Could it be the bed of some vast evaporated lake or drained of its waters from below? I never asked myself the question.

The fact remains we often came upon this sort of mound some three hundred feet in height. Reluctantly I raised my eyes and discerned the nearest often on the horizon. Or instead of moving on from the one we had just descended we ascended it again.

I am speaking of our last decade comprised between the two events described. It veils those that went before and must have resembled it like blades of grass. To those engulfed years it is reasonable to impute my education. For I don't remember having learnt anything in those I remember. It is with this reasoning I calm myself when brought up short by all I know.

I set the scene of my disgrace just short of a crest. On the contrary it was on the flat in a great calm. If I had looked back I would have seen him in the place where I had left him. Some trifle would have shown me my mistake if mistake there had been. In the years that followed I did not exclude the possibility of finding him again. In the place where I had left him if not elsewhere. Or of hearing him call me. At the same time telling myself he was on his last legs. But I did not count on it unduly. For I hardly raised my eyes from the flowers. And his voice was spent. And as if that were not enough I kept telling myself he was on his last legs. So it did not take me long to stop counting on it altogether.

I don't know what the weather is now. But in my life it was eternally mild. As if the earth had come to rest in spring. I am thinking of our hemisphere. Sudden pelting downpours overtook us. Without noticeable darkening of the sky. I would not have noticed the windlessness if he had not spoken of it. Of the wind that was no more. Of the storms he had ridden out. It is only fair to say there was nothing to sweep away. The very flowers were stemless and flush with the ground like water-lilies. No brightening our buttonholes with these.

We did not keep tally of the days. If I arrive at ten years it is thanks to our podometer. Total milage divided by average daily milage. So many days. Divide. Such a figure the night before the sacrum. Such another the eve of my disgrace. Daily average always up to date. Subtract. Divide.

Night. As long as day in this endless equinox. It falls and we go on. Before dawn we are gone.

Attitude at rest. Wedged together bent in three. Second right angle at the knees. I on the inside. We turn over as one man when he manifests the desire. I can feel him at night pressed against me with all his twisted length. It was less a matter of sleeping than of lying down. For we walked in a half sleep. With his upper hand he held and touched me where he wished. Up to a certain point. The other was twined in my hair. He murmured of things that for him were no more and for me could not have been. The wind in the overground stems. The shade and shelter of the forests.

He was not given to talk. An average of a hundred words per day and night. Spaced out. A bare million in all. Numerous repeats. Ejaculations. Too few for even a cursory survey. What do I know of man's destiny? I could tell you more about radishes. For them he had a fondness. If I saw one I would name it without hesitation.

We lived on flowers. So much for sustenance. He halted and without having to stoop caught up a handful of petals. Then moved munching on. They had on the whole a calming action. We were on the whole calm. More and more. All was. This notion of calm comes from him. Without him I would not have had it. Now I'll wipe out everything but the flowers. No more rain. No more mounds. Nothing but the two of us dragging through the flowers. Enough my old breasts feel his old hand.

Ping

All known all white bare white body fixed one yard legs joined like sewn. Light heat white floor one square yard never seen. White walls one yard by two white ceiling one square yard never seen. Bare white body fixed only the eyes only just. Traces blurs light grey almost white on white. Hands hanging palms front white feet heels together right angle. Light heat white planes shining white bare white body fixed ping fixed elsewhere. Traces blurs signs no meaning light grey almost white. Bare white body fixed white on white invisible. Only the eyes only just light blue almost white. Head haught eyes light blue almost white silence within. Brief murmurs only just almost never all known. Traces blurs signs no meaning light grey almost white. Legs joined like sewn heels together right angle. Traces alone unover given black light grey almost white on white. Light heat white walls shining white one yard by two. Bare white body fixed one yard ping fixed elsewhere. Traces blurs signs no meaning light grey almost white. White feet toes joined like sewn heels together right angle invisible. Eyes alone unover given blue light blue almost white. Murmur only just almost never one second perhaps not alone. Given rose only just bare white body fixed one yard white on white invisible. All white all known murmurs only just almost never always the same all known. Light heat hands hanging palms front white on white invisible. Bare white body fixed ping fixed elsewhere. Only the eyes only just light blue almost white fixed front. Ping murmur only just almost never one second perhaps a way out. Head haught eyes light blue almost white fixed front ping murmur ping silence. Eyes holes light blue almost white mouth white seam like sewn invisible. Ping murmur perhaps a nature one second almost never that much memory almost never. White walls each its trace grey blur signs no meaning light grey almost white. Light heat all known all white planes meeting invisible. Ping murmur only just almost never one second perhaps a meaning that much memory almost never. White feet toes joined like sewn heels together right angle ping elsewhere no sound. Hands hanging palms front legs joined like sewn. Head haught eyes holes light blue almost white fixed front silence within. Ping elsewhere always there but that known not. Eyes holes light blue alone unover given blue light blue almost white only colour fixed front. All white all known white planes shining white ping murmur only just almost never one second light time that much memory almost never. Bare white body fixed one yard ping fixed elsewhere white on white invisible heart breath no sound. Only the eyes given blue light blue almost white fixed front only colour alone unover. Planes meeting invisible one only shining white infinite but that known not. Nose ears white holes mouth white seam like sewn invisible. Ping murmurs only just almost never one second always the same all known. Given rose only just bare white body fixed one yard invisible all known without within. Ping perhaps a nature one second with image same time a little less blue and white in the wind. White ceiling shining white one square yard never seen ping perhaps way out there one second ping silence. Traces alone unover given black grey blurs signs no meaning light grey almost white always the same. Ping perhaps not alone one second with image always the same same time a little less that much memory almost never ping silence. Given rose only just nails fallen white over. Long hair fallen white invisible over. White scars invisible same white as flesh torn of old given rose only just. Ping image only just almost never one second light time blue and white in the wind. Head haught nose ears white holes mouth white seam like sewn invisible over. Only the eyes given blue fixed front light blue almost white only colour alone unover. Light heat white planes shining white one only shining white infinite but that known not. Ping a nature only just almost never one second with image same time a little less blue and white in the wind. Traces blurs light grey eyes holes light blue almost white fixed front ping a meaning only just almost never ping silence. Bare white one yard fixed ping fixed elsewhere no sound legs joined like sewn heels together right angle hands hanging palms front. Head haught eyes holes light blue almost white fixed front silence within. Ping elsewhere always there but that known not. Ping perhaps not alone one second with image same time a little less dim eye black and white half closed long lashes imploring that much memory almost never. Afar flash of time all white all over all of old ping flash white walls shining white no trace eyes holes light blue almost white last colour ping white over. Ping fixed last elsewhere legs joined like sewn heels together right angle hands hanging palms front head haught eyes white invisible fixed front over. Given rose only just one yard invisible bare white all known without within over. White ceiling never seen ping of old only just almost never one second light time white floor never seen ping of old perhaps there. Ping of old only just perhaps a meaning a nature one second almost never blue and white in the wind that much memory henceforth never. White planes no trace shining white one only shining white infinite but that known not. Light heat all known all white heart breath no sound. Head haught eyes white fixed front old ping last murmur one second perhaps not alone eye unlustrous black and white half closed long lashes imploring ping silence ping over.

Lessness

Ruins true refuge long last towards which so many false time out of mind. All sides endlessness earth sky as one no sound no stir. Grey face two pale blue little body heart beating only upright. Blacked out fallen open four walls over backwards true refuge issueless.

Scattered ruins same grey as the sand ash grey true refuge. Four square all light sheer white blank planes all gone from mind. Never was but grey air timeless no sound figment the passing light. No sound no stir ash grey sky mirrored earth mirrored sky. Never but this changelessness dream the passing hour.

He will curse God again as in the blessed days face to the open sky the passing deluge. Little body grey face features crack and little holes two pale blue. Blank planes sheer white eye calm long last all gone from mind.

Figment light never was but grey air timeless no sound. Blank planes touch close sheer white all gone from mind. Little body ash grey locked rigid heart beating face to endlessness. On him will rain again as in the blessed days of blue the passing cloud. Four square true refuge long last four walls over backwards no sound.

Grey sky no cloud no sound no stir earth ash grey sand. Little body same grey as the earth sky ruins only upright. Ash grey all sides earth sky as one all sides endlessness.

He will stir in the sand there will be stir in the sky the air the sand. Never but in dream the happy dream only one time to serve. Little body little block heart beating ash grey only upright. Earth sky as one all sides endlessness little body only upright. In the sand no hold one step more in the endlessness he will make it. No sound not a breath same grey all sides earth sky body ruins.

Slow black with ruin true refuge four walls over backwards no sound. Legs a single block arms fast to sides little body face to endlessness. Never but in vanished dream the passing hour long short. Only upright little body grey smooth no relief a few holes. One step in the ruins in the sand on his back in the endlessness he will make it. Never but dream the days and nights made of dreams of other nights better days. He will live again the space of a step it will be day and night again over him the endlessness.

In four split asunder over backwards true refuge issueless scattered ruins. Little body little block genitals overrun arse a single block grey crack overrun. True refuge long last issueless scattered down four walls over backwards no sound. All sides endlessness earth sky as one no stir not a breath. Blank planes sheer white calm eye light of reason all gone from mind. Scattered ruins ash grey all sides true refuge long last issueless.

Ash grey little body only upright heart beating face to endlessness. Old love new love as in the blessed days unhappiness will reign again. Earth sand same grey as the air sky ruins body fine ash grey sand. Light refuge sheer white blank planes all gone from mind. Flatness endless little body only upright same grey all sides earth sky body ruins. Face to white calm touch close eye calm long last all gone from mind. One step more one alone all alone in the sand no hold he will make it.

Blacked out fallen open true refuge issueless towards which so many false time out of mind. Never but silence such that in imagination this wild laughter these cries. Head through calm eye all light white calm all gone from mind. Figment dawn dispeller of figments and the other called dusk.

He will go on his back face to the sky open again over him the ruins the sand the endlessness. Grey air timeless earth sky as one same grey as the ruins flatness endless. It will be day and night again over him the endlessness the air heart will beat again. True refuge long last scattered ruins same grey as the sand.

Face to calm eye touch close all calm all white all gone from mind. Never but imagined the blue in a wild imagining the blue celeste of poesy. Little void mighty light four square all white blank planes all gone from mind. Never was but grey air timeless no stir not a breath. Heart beating little body only upright grey face features overrun two pale blue. Light white touch close head through calm eye light of reason all gone from mind.

Little body same grey as the earth sky ruins only upright. No sound not a breath same grey all sides earth sky body ruins. Blacked out fallen open four walls over backwards true refuge issueless.

No sound no stir ash grey sky mirrored earth mirrored sky. Grey air timeless earth sky as one same grey as the ruins flatness endless. In the sand no hold one step more in the endlessness he will make it. It will be day and night again over him the endlessness the air heart will beat again.

Figment light never was but grey air timeless no sound. All sides endlessness earth sky as one no stir not a breath. On him will rain again as in the blessed days of blue the passing cloud. Grey sky no cloud no sound no stir earth ash grey sand.

Little void mighty light four square all white blank planes all gone from mind. Flatness endless little body only upright same grey all sides earth sky body ruins. Scattered ruins same grey as the sand ash grey true refuge. Four square true refuge long last four walls over backwards no sound. Never but this changelessness dream the passing hour. Never was but grey air timeless no sound figment the passing light.

In four split asunder over backwards true refuge issueless scattered ruins. He will live again the space of a step it will be day and night again over him the endlessness. Face to white calm touch close eye calm long last all gone from mind. Grey face two pale blue little body heart beating only upright. He will go on his back face to the sky open again over him the ruins the sand the endlessness. Earth sand same grey as the air sky ruins body fine ash grey sand. Blank planes touch close sheer white all gone from mind.

Heart beating little body only upright grey face features overrun two pale blue. Only upright little body grey smooth no relief a few holes. Never but dream the days and nights made of dreams of other nights better days. He will stir in the sand there will be stir in the sky the air the sand. One step in the ruins in the sand on his back in the endlessness he will make it. Never but silence such that in imagination this wild laughter these cries.

True refuge long last scattered ruins same grey as the sand. Never was but grey air timeless no stir not a breath. Blank planes sheer white calm eye light of reason all gone from mind. Never but in vanished dream the passing hour long short. Four square all light sheer white blank planes all gone from mind.

Blacked out fallen open true refuge issueless towards which so many false time out of mind. Head through calm eye all light white calm all gone from mind. Old love new love as in the blessed days unhappiness will reign again. Ash grey all sides earth sky as one all sides endlessness. Scattered ruins ash grey all sides true refuge long last issueless. Never but in dream the happy dream only one time to serve. Little body grey face features crack and little holes two pale blue.

Ruins true refuge long last towards which so many false time out of mind. Never but imagined the blue in a wild imagining the blue celeste of poesy. Light white touch close head through calm eye light of reason all gone from mind.

Slow black with ruin true refuge four walls over backwards no sound. Earth sky as one all sides endlessness little body only upright. One step more one alone all alone in the sand no hold he will make it. Ash grey little body only upright heart beating face to endlessness. Light refuge sheer white blank planes all gone from mind. All sides endlessness earth sky as one no sound no stir.

Legs a single block arms fast to sides little body face to endlessness. True refuge long last issueless scattered down four walls over backwards no sound. Blank planes sheer white eye calm long last all gone from mind. He will curse God again as in the blessed days face to the open sky the passing deluge. Face to calm eye touch close all calm all white all gone from mind.

Little body little block heart beating ash grey only upright. Little body ash grey locked rigid heart beating face to endlessness. Little body little block genitals overrun arse a single block grey crack overrun. Figment dawn dispeller of figments and the other called dusk.

The Lost Ones

Abode where lost bodies roam each searching for its lost one. Vast enough for search to be in vain. Narrow enough for flight to be in vain. Inside a flattened cylinder fifty metres round and sixteen high for the sake of harmony. The light. Its dimness. Its yellowness. Its omnipresence as though every separate square centimetre were agleam of the some twelve million of total surface. Its restlessness at long intervals suddenly stilled like panting at the last. Then all go dead still. It is perhaps the end of their abode. A few seconds and all begins again. Consequences of this light for the searching eye. Consequences for the eye which having ceased to search is fastened to the ground or raised to the distant ceiling where none can be. The temperature. It oscillates with more measured beat between hot and cold. It passes from one extreme to the other in about four seconds. It too has its moments of stillness more or less hot or cold. They coincide with those of the light. Then all go dead still. It is perhaps the end of all. A few seconds and all begins again. Consequences of this climate for the skin. It shrivels. The bodies brush together with a rustle of dry leaves. The mucous membrane itself is affected. A kiss makes an indescribable sound. Those with stomach still to copulate strive in vain. But they will not give in. Floor and wall are of solid rubber or such-like. Dash against them foot or fist or head and the sound is scarcely heard. Imagine then the silence of the steps. The only sounds worthy of the name result from the manipulation of the ladders or the thud of bodies striking against one another or of one against itself as when in sudden fury it beats its breast. Thus flesh and bone subsist. The ladders. These are the only objects. They are single without exception and vary greatly in size. The shortest measure not less than six metres. Some are fitted with a sliding extension. They are propped against the wall without regard to harmony. Bolt upright on the top rung of the tallest the tallest climbers can touch the ceiling with their fingertips. Its composition is no less familiar therefore than that of floor and wall. Dash a rung against it and the sound is scarcely heard. These ladders are in great demand. At the foot of each at all times or nearly a little queue of climbers. And yet it takes courage to climb. For half the rungs are missing and this without regard to harmony. If only every second one were missing no great harm would be done. But the want of three in a row calls for acrobatics. These ladders are nevertheless in great demand and in no danger of being reduced to mere uprights runged at their extremities alone. For the need to climb is too widespread. To feel it no longer is a rare deliverance. The missing rungs are in the hands of a happy few who use them mainly for attack and self-defence. Their solitary attempts to brain themselves culminate at the best in brief losses of consciousness. The purpose of the ladders is to convey the searchers to the niches. Those whom these entice no longer climb simply to get clear of the ground. It is the custom not to climb two or more at a time. To the fugitive fortunate enough to find a ladder free it offers certain refuge until the clamours subside. The niches or alcoves. These are cavities sunk in that part of the wall which lies above an imaginary line running midway between floor and ceiling and features therefore of its upper half alone. A more or less wide mouth gives rapid access to a chamber of varying capacity but always sufficient for a body in reasonable command of its joints to enter in and similarly once in to crouch down after a fashion. They are disposed in irregular quincunxes roughly ten metres in diameter and cunningly out of line. Such harmony only he can relish whose long experience and detailed knowledge of the niches are such as to permit a perfect mental image of the entire system. But it is doubtful that such a one exists. For each climber has a fondness for certain niches and refrains as far as possible from the others. A certain number are connected by tunnels opened in the thickness of the wall and attaining in some cases no fewer than fifty metres in length. But most have no other way out than the way in. It is as though at a certain stage discouragement had prevailed. To be noted in support of this wild surmise the existence of a long tunnel abandoned blind. Woe the body that rashly enters here to be compelled finally after long efforts to crawl back backwards as best it can the way it came. Not that this drama is peculiar to the unfinished tunnel. One has only to consider what inevitably must ensue when two bodies enter a normal tunnel at the same time by opposite ends. Niches and tunnels are subject to the same light and climate as the rest of the abode. So much for a first aperçu of the abode.

One body per square metre or two hundred bodies in all round numbers. Whether relatives near and far or friends in varying degree many in theory are acquainted. The gloom and press make recognition difficult. Seen from a certain angle these bodies are of four kinds. Firstly those perpetually in motion. Secondly those who sometimes pause. Thirdly those who short of being driven off never stir from the coign they have won and when driven off pounce on the first free one that offers and freeze again. That is not quite accurate. For if among these sedentary the need to climb is dead it is none the less subject to strange resurrections. The quidam then quits his post in search of a free ladder or to join the nearest or shortest queue. The truth is that no searcher can readily forego the ladder. Paradoxically the sedentary are those whose acts of violence most disrupt the cylinder's quiet. Fourthly those who do not search or non-searchers sitting for the most part against the wall in the attitude which wrung from Dante one of his rare wan smiles. By non-searchers and despite the abyss to which this leads it is finally impossible to understand other than ex-searchers. To rid this notion of some of its virulence one has only to suppose the need to search no less resurrectable than that of the ladder and those eyes to all appearances for ever cast down or closed possessed of the strange power suddenly to kindle again before passing face and body. But enough will always subsist to spell for this little people the extinction soon or late of its last remaining fires. A languishing happily unperceived because of its slowness and the resurgences that make up for it in part and the inattention of those concerned dazed by the passion preying on them still or by the state of languor into which imperceptibly they are already fallen. And far from being able to imagine their last state when every body will be still and every eye vacant they will come to it unwitting and be so unawares. Then light and climate will be changed in a way impossible to foretell. But the former may be imagined extinguished as purposeless and the latter fixed not far from freezing point. In cold darkness motionless flesh. So much roughly speaking for these bodies seen from a certain angle and for this notion and its consequences if it is maintained.

Inside a cylinder fifty metres round and sixteen high for the sake of harmony or a total surface of roughly twelve hundred square metres of which eight hundred mural. Not counting the niches and tunnels. Omnipresence of a dim yellow light shaken by a vertiginous tremolo between contiguous extremes. Temperature agitated by a like oscillation but thirty or forty times slower in virtue of which it falls rapidly from a maximum of twenty-five degrees approximately to a minimum of approximately five whence a regular variation of five degrees per second. That is not quite accurate. For it is clear that at both extremes of the shuttle the difference can fall to as little as one degree only. But this remission never lasts more than a little less than a second. At great intervals suspension of the two vibrations fed no doubt from a single source and resumption together after a lull of varying duration but never exceeding ten seconds or thereabouts. Corresponding abeyance of all motion among the bodies in motion and heightened fixity of the motionless. Only objects fifteen single ladders propped against the wall at irregular intervals. In the upper half of the wall disposed quincuncially for the sake of harmony a score of niches some connected by tunnels.

From time immemorial rumour has it or better still the notion is abroad that there exists a way out. Those who no longer believe so are not immune from believing so again in accordance with the notion requiring as long as it holds that here all should die but with so gradual and to put it plainly so fluctuant a death as to escape the notice even of a visitor. Regarding the nature of this way out and its location two opinions divide without opposing all those still loyal to that old belief. One school swears by a secret passage branching from one of the tunnels and leading in the words of the poet to nature's sanctuaries. The other dreams of a trapdoor hidden in the hub of the ceiling giving access to a flue at the end of which the sun and other stars would still be shining. Conversion is frequent either way and such a one who at a given moment would hear of nothing but the tunnel may well a moment later hear of nothing but the trapdoor and a moment later still give himself the lie again. The fact remains none the less that of these two persuasions the former is declining in favour of the latter but in a manner so desultory and slow and of course with so little effect on the comportment of either sect that to perceive it one must be in the secret of the gods. This shift has logic on its side. For those who believe in a way out possible of access as via a tunnel it would be and even without any thought of putting it to account may be tempted by its quest. Whereas the partisans of the trapdoor are spared this demon by the fact that the hub of the ceiling is out of reach. Thus by insensible degrees the way out transfers from the tunnel to the ceiling prior to never having been. So much for a first aperçu of this credence so singular in itself and by reason of the loyalty it inspires in the hearts of so many possessed. Its fatuous little light will be assuredly the last to leave them always assuming they are darkward bound.

Bolt upright on the top rung of the great ladder fully extended and reared against the wall the tallest climbers can touch the edge of the ceiling with their fingertips. On the same ladder planted perpendicular at the centre of the floor the same bodies would gain half a metre and so be enabled to explore at leisure the fabulous zone decreed out of reach and which therefore in theory is in no wise so. For such recourse to the ladder is conceivable. All that is needed is a score of determined volunteers joining forces to keep it upright with the help if necessary of other ladders acting as stays or struts. An instant of fraternity. But outside their explosions of violence this sentiment is as foreign to them as to butterflies. And this owing not so much to want of heart or intelligence as to the ideal preying on one and all. So much for this inviolable zenith where for amateurs of myth lies hidden a way out to earth and sky.

The use of the ladders is regulated by conventions of obscure origin which in their precision and the submission they exact from the climbers resemble laws. Certain infractions unleash against the culprit a collective fury surprising in creatures so peaceable on the whole and apart from the grand affair so careless of one another. Others on the contrary scarcely ruffle the general indifference. This at first sight is strange. All rests on the rule against mounting the ladder more than one at a time. It remains taboo therefore to the climber waiting at its foot until such time as his predecessor has regained the ground. Idle to imagine the confusion that would result from the absence of such a rule or from its non-observance. But devised for the convenience of all there is no question of its applying without restriction or as a licence for the unprincipled climber to engross the ladder beyond what is reasonable. For without some form of curb he might take the fancy to settle down permanently in one of the niches or tunnels leaving behind him a ladder out of service for good and all. And were others to follow his example as inevitably they must the spectacle would finally be offered of one hundred and eighty-five searchers less the vanquished committed for all time to the ground. Not to mention the intolerable presence of properties serving no purpose. It is therefore understood that after a certain interval difficult to assess but unerringly timed by all the ladder is again available meaning at the disposal in the same conditions of him due next to climb easily recognizable by his position at the head of the queue and so much the worst for the abuser. The situation of this latter having lost his ladder is delicate indeed and seems to exclude a priori his ever returning to the ground. Happily sooner or later he succeeds in doing so thanks to a further provision giving priority at all times to descent over ascent. He has therefore merely to watch at the mouth of his niche for a ladder to present itself and immediately start down quite easy in his mind knowing full well that whoever below is on the point of mounting if not already on his way up will give way in his favour. The worst that can befall him is a long vigil because of the ladders' mobility. It is indeed rare for a climber when it

comes to his turn to content himself with the same niche as his prede-
cessor and this for obvious reasons that will appear in due course. But
rather he makes off with his ladder followed by the queue and plants
it under one or other of the five niches available by reason of the dif-
ference in number between these and the ladders. But to return to the
unfortunate having outstayed his time it is clear that his chances of
rapid redescent will be increased though far from doubled if thanks to
a tunnel he disposes of two niches from which to watch. Though even
in this event he usually prefers and invariably if the tunnel is a long one
to plump for one only lest a ladder should present itself at one or the
other and he still crawling between the two. But the ladders do not serve
only as vehicles to the niches and tunnels and those whom these have
ceased if only temporarily to entice use them simply to get clear of the
ground. They mount to the level of their choice and there stay and set-
tle standing as a rule with their faces to the wall. This family of climbers
too is liable to exceed the allotted time. It is in order then for him due
next for the ladder to climb in the wake of the offender and by means
of one or more thumps on the back bring him back to a sense of his
surroundings. Upon which he unfailingly hastens to descend preceded
by his successor who has then merely to take over the ladder subject to
the usual conditions. This docility in the abuser shows clearly that the
abuse is not deliberate but due to a temporary derangement of his inner
timepiece easy to understand and therefore to forgive. Here is the rea-
son why this in reality infrequent infringement whether on the part of
those who push on up to the niches and tunnels or of those who halt
on the way never gives rise to the fury vented on the wretch with no bet-
ter sense than to climb before his time and yet whose precipitancy one
would have thought quite as understandable and consequently forgiv-
able as the converse excess. This is indeed strange. But what is at stake
is the fundamental principle forbidding ascent more than one at a time
the repeated violation of which would soon transform the abode into a
pandemonium. Whereas the belated return to the ground hurts finally
none but the laggard himself. So much for a first aperçu of the climb-
ers' code.

Similarly the transport of the ladders is not left to the good pleasure of the carriers who are required to hug the wall at all times eddywise. This is a rule no less strict than the prohibition to climb more than one at a time and not lightly to be broken. Nothing more natural. For if for the sake of the shortcut it were permitted to carry the ladder slap through the press or skirting the wall at will in either direction life in the cylinder would soon become untenable. All along the wall therefore a belt about one metre wide is reserved for the carriers. To this zone those also are confined who wait their turn to climb and must close their ranks and flatten themselves as best they can with their backs to the wall so as not to encroach on the arena proper.

It is curious to note the presence within this belt of a certain number of sedentary searchers sitting or standing against the wall. Dead to the ladders to all intents and purposes and a source of annoyance for both climbers and carriers they are nevertheless tolerated. The fact is that these sort of semi-sages among whom all ages are to be admired from old age to infancy inspire in those still fitfully fevering if not a cult at least a certain deference. They cling to this as to a homage due to them and are morbidly susceptible to the least want of consideration. A sedentary searcher stepped on instead of over is capable of such an outburst of fury as to throw the entire cylinder into a ferment. Cleave also to the wall both sitting and standing four vanquished out of five. They may be walked on without their reacting.

To be noted finally the care taken by the searchers in the arena not to overflow on the climbers' territory. When weary of searching among the throng they turn towards this zone it is only to skirt with measured tread its imaginary edge devouring with their eyes its occupants. Their slow round counter-carrier-wise creates a second even narrower belt respected in its turn by the main body of searchers. Which suitably lit from above would give the impression at times of two narrow rings turning in opposite directions about the teeming precinct.

One body per square metre of available surface or two hundred bodies in all round numbers. Bodies of either sex and all ages from old age to infancy. Sucklings who having no longer to suck huddle at gaze in

the lap or sprawled on the ground in precocious postures. Others a lit-
tle more advanced crawl searching among the legs. Picturesque detail a
woman with white hair still young to judge by her thighs leaning against
the wall with eyes closed in abandonment and mechanically clasping to
her breast a mite who strains away in an effort to turn its head and look
behind. But such tiny ones are comparatively few. None looks within
himself where none can be. Eyes cast down or closed signify abandon-
ment and are confined to the vanquished. These precisely to be counted
on the fingers of one hand are not necessarily still. They may stray unsee-
ing through the throng indistinguishable to the eye of flesh from the still
unrelenting. These recognize them and make way. They may wait their
turn at the foot of the ladders and when it comes ascend to the niches or
simply leave the ground. They may crawl blindly in the tunnels in search
of nothing. But normally abandonment freezes them both in space and
in their pose whether standing or sitting as a rule profoundly bowed. It
is this makes it possible to tell them from the sedentary devouring with
their eyes in heads dead still each body as it passes by. Standing or sitting
they cleave to the wall all but one in the arena stricken rigid in the midst
of the fevering. These recognize him and keep their distance. The spent
eyes may have fits of the old craving just as those who having renounced
the ladder suddenly take to it again. So true it is that when in the cylinder
what little is possible is not so it is merely no longer so and in the least
less the all of nothing if this notion is maintained. Then the eyes sud-
denly start to search afresh as famished as the unthinkable first day until
for no clear reason they as suddenly close again or the head falls. Even
so a great heap of sand sheltered from the wind lessened by three grains
every second year and every following increased by two if this notion is
maintained. If then the vanquished have still some way to go what can
be said of the others and what better name be given them than the fair
name of searchers? Some and indeed by far the greater number never
pause except when they line up for a ladder or watch out at the mouth of
a niche. Some come to rest from time to time all but the unceasing eyes.
As for the sedentary if they never stir from the coign they have won it is
because they have calculated their best chance is there and if they seldom

or never ascend to the niches and tunnels it is because they have done so too often in vain or come there too often to grief. An intelligence would be tempted to see in these the next vanquished and continuing in its stride to require of those still perpetually in motion that they all soon or late one after another be as those who sometimes pause and of these that they finally be as the sedentary and of the sedentary that they be in the end as the vanquished and of the two hundred vanquished thus obtained that all in due course each in his turn be well and truly vanquished for good and all each frozen in his place and attitude. But let these families be numbered in order of maturity and experience shows that it is possible to graduate from one to three skipping two and from one to four skipping two or three or both and from two to four skipping three. In the other direction the ill-vanquished may at long intervals and with each relapse more briefly revert to the state of the sedentary who in their turn count a few chronic waverers prone to succumb to the ladder again while remaining dead to the arena. But never again will they ceaselessly come and go who now at long intervals come to rest without ceasing to search with their eyes. In the beginning then unthinkable as the end all roamed without respite including the nurselings in so far as they were borne except of course those already at the foot of the ladders or frozen in the tunnels the better to listen or crouching all eyes in the niches and so roamed a vast space of time impossible to measure until a first came to a standstill followed by a second and so on. But as to at this moment of time and there will be no other numbering the faithful who endlessly come and go impatient of the least repose and those who every now and then stand still and the sedentary and the so-called vanquished may it suffice to state that at this moment of time to the nearest body in spite of the press and gloom the first are twice as many as the second who are three times as many as the third who are four times as many as the fourth namely five vanquished in all. Relatives and friends are well represented not to speak of mere acquaintances. Press and gloom make recognition difficult. Man and wife are strangers two paces apart to mention only this most intimate of all bonds. Let them move on till they are close enough to touch and then without pausing on their way exchange a look. If they recognize each other it does not appear. Whatever it is they are searching for it is not that.

What first impresses in this gloom is the sensation of yellow it imparts not to say of sulphur in view of the associations. Then how it throbs with constant unchanging beat and fast but not so fast that the pulse is no longer felt. And finally much later that ever and anon there comes a momentary lull. The effect of those brief and rare respites is unspeakably dramatic to put it mildly. Those who never know a moment's rest stand rooted to the spot often in extravagant postures and the stillness heightened tenfold of the sedentary and vanquished makes that which is normally theirs seem risible in comparison. The fists on their way to smite in anger or discouragement freeze in their arcs until the scare is past and the blow can be completed or volley of blows. Similarly without entering into tedious details those surprised in the act of climbing or carrying a ladder or making unmakable love or crouched in the niches or crawling in the tunnels as the case may be. But a brief ten seconds at most and the throbbing is resumed and all is as before. Those interrupted in their coming and going start coming and going again and the motionless relax. The lovers buckle to anew and the fists carry on where they left off. The murmur cut off as though by a switch fills the cylinder again. Among all the components the sum of which it is the ear finally distinguishes a faint stridulence as of insects which is that of the light itself and the one invariable. Between the extremes that delimit the vibration the difference is of two or three candles at the most. So that the sensation of yellow is faintly tinged with one of red. Light in a word that not only dims but blurs into the bargain. It might safely be maintained that the eye grows used to these conditions and in the end adapts to them were it not that just the contrary is to be observed in the slow deterioration of vision ruined by this fiery flickering murk and by the incessant straining for ever vain with concomitant moral distress and its repercussion on the organ. And were it possible to follow over a long enough period of time eyes blue for preference as being the most perishable they would be seen to redden more and more in an ever widening glare and their pupils little by little to dilate till the whole orb was devoured. And all by such slow and insensible degrees to be sure as to pass unperceived even by those most concerned if this notion is maintained. And the thinking being coldly intent on all these data and evidences could scarcely escape at the close of his analysis the mistaken conclusion that instead of speaking of the vanquished with the slight taint of pathos attaching to the term it would be more correct to speak of the blind and leave it at that. Once the first shocks of surprise are finally past this light is further unusual in that far from evincing one or more visible or hidden sources it appears to emanate from all sides and to permeate the entire space as though this were uniformly luminous down to its least particle of ambient air. To the point that the ladders themselves seem rather to shed than to receive light with this slight reserve that light is not the word. No other shadows then than those cast by the bodies pressing on one another wilfully or from necessity as when for example on a breast to prevent its being lit or on some private part the hand descends with vanished palm. Whereas the skin of a climber alone on his ladder or in the depths of a tunnel glistens all over with the same red-yellow glister and even some of its folds and recesses in so far as the air enters in. With regard to the temperature its oscillation is between much wider extremes and at a much lower frequency since it takes not less than four seconds to pass from its minimum of five degrees to its maximum of twenty-five and inversely namely an average of only five degrees per second. Does this mean that with every passing second there is a rise or fall of five degrees exactly neither more nor less? Not quite. For it is clear there are two periods in the scale namely from twenty-one degrees on on the way up and from nine on on the way down when this difference will not be reached. Out of the eight seconds therefore required for a single rise and fall it is only during a bare six and a half that the bodies suffer the maximum increment of heat or cold which with the help of a little addition or better still division works out nevertheless at some twenty years respite per century in this domain. There is something disturbing at first sight in the relative slowness of this vibration compared to that of the light. But this is a disturbance analysis makes short work of. For on due reflection the difference to be considered is not one of speed but of space travelled. And if that required of the temperature were reduced to the equivalent of a few candles there would be nothing to choose mutatis mutandis between the two effects. But that would not answer the needs of the cylinder. So all is for the best. The more so as the two storms have this in common that when one is cut off as though by magic then in the same breath the other also as though again the two were connected somewhere to a single commutator. For in the cylinder alone are certitudes to be found and without nothing but mystery. At vast intervals then the bodies enjoy ten seconds at most of unbroken warmth or cold or between the two. But this cannot be truly accounted for respite so great is the other tension then.

The bed of the cylinder comprises three distinct zones separated by clear-cut mental or imaginary frontiers invisible to the eye of flesh. First an outer belt roughly one metre wide reserved for the climbers and strange to say favoured by most of the sedentary and vanquished. Next a slightly narrower inner belt where those weary of searching in mid-cylinder slowly revolve in Indian file intent on the periphery. Finally the arena proper representing an area of one hundred and fifty square metres round numbers and chosen hunting ground of the majority. Let numbers be assigned to these three zones and it appears clearly that from the third to the second and inversely the searcher moves at will whereas on entering and leaving the first he is held to a certain discipline. One example among a thousand of the harmony that reigns in the cylinder between order and licence. Thus access to the climbers' reserve is authorized only when one of them leaves it to rejoin the searchers of the arena or exceptionally those of the intermediate zone. While infringement of this rule is rare it does none the less occur as when for example a particularly nervous searcher can no longer resist the lure of the niches and tries to steal in among the climbers without the warrant of a departure. Whereupon he is unfailingly ejected by the queue nearest to the point of trespass and the matter goes no further. No choice then for the searcher wishing to join the climbers but to watch for his opportunity among the searchers of the intermediate zone or searcher-watchers or simply watchers. So much for access to the ladders. In the other direction the passage is not free either and once among the climbers the watcher is

there for some time and more precisely the highly variable time it takes
to advance from the tail to the head of the queue adopted. For no less
than the freedom for each body to climb is the obligation once in the
queue of its choice to queue on to the end. Any attempt to leave prema-
turely is sharply countered by the other members and the offender put
back in his place. But once at the very foot of the ladder with between him
and it only one more return to the ground the aspirant is free to rejoin
the searchers of the arena or exceptionally the watchers of the intermedi-
ate zone without opposition. It is therefore on those at the head of their
lines as being the most likely to create the vacancy so ardently desired
that the eyes of the second-zone watchers are fixed as they burn to enter
the first. The objects of this scrutiny continue so up to the moment they
exercise their right to the ladder and take it over. For the climber may
reach the head of the queue with the firm resolve to ascend and then feel
this melt little by little and gather in its stead the urge to depart but still
without the power to decide him till the very last moment when his pre-
decessor is actually on the way down and the ladder virtually his at last.
To be noted also the possibility for the climber to leave the queue once
he has reached the head and yet not leave the zone. This merely requires
his joining one of the other fourteen queues at his disposal or more sim-
ply still his returning to the tail of his own. But it is exceptional for a
body in the first place to leave its queue and in the second having excep-
tionally done so not to leave the zone. No alternative then once among
the climbers but to stay there at least the time it takes to advance from
the last place to the first of the chosen queue. This time varies according
to the length of the latter and the more or less prolonged occupation of
the ladder. Some users keep it till the last moment. For others one half
or any other fraction of this time is enough. The short queue is not nec-
essarily the most rapid and such a one starting tenth may well find him-
self first before such another starting fifth assuming of course they start
together. This being so no wonder that the choice of the queue is deter-
mined by considerations having nothing to do with its length. Not that
all choose nor even the greater number. The tendency would be rather
to join straightway the queue nearest to the point of penetration on

condition however that this does not involve motion against the stream. For one entering this zone head-on the nearest queue is on the right and if it does not please it is only by going right that a more pleasing can be found. Some could thus revolve through thousands of degrees before settling down to wait were it not for the rule forbidding them to exceed a single circuit. Any attempt to elude it is quelled by the queue nearest to the point of full circle and the culprit compelled to join its ranks since obviously the right to turn back is denied him too. That a full round should be authorized is eloquent of the tolerant spirit which in the cylinder tempers discipline. But whether chosen or first to hand the queue must be suffered to the end before the climber may leave the zone. First chance of departure therefore at any moment between arrival at head of queue and predecessor's return to ground. There remains to clarify in this same context the situation of the body which having accomplished its queue and let pass the first chance of departure and exercised its right to the ladder returns to the ground. It is now free again to depart without further ado but with no compulsion to do so. And to remain among the climbers it has merely to join again in the same conditions as before the queue so lately left with departure again possible from the moment the head is reached. And should it for some reason or another feel like a little change of queue and ladder it is entitled for the purpose of fixing its choice to a further full circuit in the same way as on first arrival and in the same conditions with this slight difference that having already suffered one queue to the end it is free at any moment of the new revolution to leave the zone. And so on infinitely. Whence theoretically the possibility for those already among the climbers never to leave and never to arrive for those not yet. That there exists no regulation tending to forestall such injustice shows clearly it can never be more than temporary. As indeed it cannot. For the passion to search is such that no place may be left unsearched. To the watcher nevertheless on the qui vive for a departure the wait may seem interminable. Sometimes unable to endure it any longer and fortified by the long vacation he renounces the ladder and resumes his search in the arena. So much roughly speaking for the main ground divisions and the duties and prerogatives of the bodies in

their passage from one to another. All has not been told and never shall
be. What principle of priority obtains among the watchers always in force
and eager to profit by the first departure from among the climbers and
whose order of arrival on the scene cannot be established by the queue
impracticable in their case or by any other means? Is there not reason to
fear a saturation of the intermediate zone and what would be its conse-
quences for the bodies as a whole and particularly for those of the arena
thus cut off from the ladders? Is not the cylinder doomed in a more or
less distant future to a state of anarchy given over to fury and violence?
To these questions and many more the answers are clear and easy to give.
It only remains to dare. The sedentary call for no special remark since
only the ladders can wean them from their fixity. The vanquished are
obviously in no way concerned.

The effect of this climate on the soul is not to be underestimated. But
it suffers certainly less than the skin whose entire defensive system from
sweat to goose bumps is under constant stress. It continues none the
less feebly to resist and indeed honourably compared to the eye which
with the best will in the world it is difficult not to consign at the close
of all its efforts to nothing short of blindness. For skin in its own way
as it is not to mention its humours and lids it has not merely one adver-
sary to contend with. This desiccation of the envelope robs nudity of
much of its charm as pink turns grey and transforms into a rustling of
nettles the natural succulence of flesh against flesh. The mucous mem-
brane itself is affected which would not greatly matter were it not for its
hampering effect on the work of love. But even from this point of view
no great harm is done so rare is erection in the cylinder. It does occur
none the less followed by more or less happy penetration in the near-
est tube. Even man and wife may sometimes be seen in virtue of the law
of probabilities to come together again in this way without their knowl-
edge. The spectacle then is one to be remembered of frenzies prolonged
in pain and hopelessness long beyond what even the most gifted lovers
can achieve in camera. For male or female all are acutely aware how rare
the occasion is and how unlikely to recur. But here too the desisting and
deathly still in attitudes verging at times on the obscene whenever the

vibrations cease and for as long as this crisis lasts. Stranger still at such times all the questing eyes that suddenly go still and fix their stare on the void or on some old abomination as for instance other eyes and then the long looks exchanged by those fain to look away. Irregular intervals of such length separate these lulls that for forgetters the likes of these each is the first. Whence invariably the same vivacity of reaction as to the end of a world and the same brief amaze when the twofold storm resumes and they start to search again neither glad nor even sorry.

Seen from below the wall presents an unbroken surface all the way round and up to the ceiling. And yet its upper half is riddled with niches. This paradox is explained by the levelling effect of the dim omnipresent light. None has ever been known to seek out a niche from below. The eyes are seldom raised and when they are it is to the ceiling. Floor and ceiling bear no sign or mark apt to serve as a guide. The feet of the ladders pitched always at the same points leave no trace. The same is true of the skulls and fists dashed against the wall. Even did such marks exist the light would prevent their being seen. The climber making off with his ladder to plant it elsewhere relies largely on feel. He is seldom out by more than a few centimetres and never by more than a metre at most because of the way the niches are disposed. On the spur of his passion his agility is such that even this deviation does not prevent him from gaining the nearest if not the desired niche and thence though with greater labour from regaining the ladder for the descent. There does none the less exist a north in the guise of one of the vanquished or better one of the women vanquished or better still the woman vanquished. She squats against the wall with her head between her knees and her legs in her arms. The left hand clasps the right shinbone and the right the left forearm. The red hair tarnished by the light hangs to the ground. It hides the face and whole front of the body down to the crutch. The left foot is crossed on the right. She is the north. She rather than some other among the vanquished because of her greater fixity. To one bent for once on taking his bearings she may be of help. For the climber averse to avoidable acrobatics a given niche may lie so many paces or meters to east or west of the woman vanquished without of course his naming her thus or

otherwise even in his thoughts. It goes without saying that only the van-
quished hide their faces though not all without exception. Standing or
sitting with head erect some content themselves with opening their eyes
no more. It is of course forbidden to withhold the face or other part from
the searcher who demands it and may without fear of resistance remove
the hand from the flesh it hides or raise the lid to examine the eye. Some
searchers there are who join the climbers with no thought of climbing
and simply in order to inspect at close hand one or more among the
vanquished or sedentary. The hair of the woman vanquished has thus
many a time been gathered up and drawn back and the head raised and
the face laid bare and whole front of the body down to the crutch. The
inspection once completed it is usual to put everything carefully back
in place as far as possible. It is enjoined by a certain ethics not to do
unto others what coming from them might give offence. This precept
is largely observed in the cylinder in so far as it does not jeopardize the
quest which would clearly be a mockery if in case of doubt it were not
possible to check certain details. Direct action with a view to their elu-
cidation is generally reserved for the persons of the sedentary and van-
quished. Face or back to the wall these normally offer but a single aspect
and so may have to be turned the other way. But wherever there is motion
as in the arena or among the watchers and the possibility of encompass-
ing the object there is no call for such manipulations. There are times of
course when a body has to be brought to a stand and disposed in a cer-
tain position to permit the inspection at close hand of a particular part
or the search for a scar or birthblot for example. To be noted finally the
immunity in this respect of those queueing for a ladder. Obliged for want
of space to huddle together over long periods they appear to the observer
a mere jumble of mingled flesh. Woe the rash searcher who carried away
by his passion dare lay a finger on the least among them. Like a single
body the whole queue falls on the offender. Of all the scenes of violence
the cylinder has to offer none approaches this.

So on infinitely until towards the unthinkable end if this notion is
maintained a last body of all by feeble fits and starts is searching still.
There is nothing at first sight to distinguish him from the others dead

still where they stand or sit in abandonment beyond recall. Lying down is unheard of in the cylinder and this pose solace of the vanquished is for ever denied them here. Such privation is partly to be explained by the dearth of floor space namely a little under one square metre at the disposal of each body and not to be eked out by that of the niches and tunnels reserved for the search alone. Thus the prostration of those withered ones filled with the horror of contact and compelled to brush together without ceasing is denied its natural end. But the persistence of the twofold vibration suggests that in this old abode all is not yet quite for the best. And sure enough there he stirs this last of all if a man and slowly draws himself up and some time later opens his burnt eyes. At the foot of the ladders propped against the wall with scant regard to harmony no climber waits his turn. The aged vanquished of the third zone has none about him now but others in his image motionless and bowed. The mite still in the white-haired woman's clasp is no more than a shadow in her lap. Seen from the front the red head sunk to the uttermost exposes part of the nape. There he opens then his eyes this last of all if a man and some time later threads his way to that first among the vanquished so often taken for a guide. On his knees he parts the heavy hair and raises the unresisting head. Once devoured the face thus laid bare the eyes at a touch of the thumbs open without demur. In those calm wastes he lets his wander till they are the first to close and the head relinquished falls back into its place. He himself after a pause impossible to time finds at last his place and pose whereupon dark descends and at the same instant the temperature comes to rest not far from freezing point. Hushed in the same breath the faint stridulence mentioned above whence suddenly such silence as to drown all the faint breathings put together. So much roughly speaking for the last state of the cylinder and of this little people of searchers one first of whom if a man in some unthinkable past for the first time bowed his head if this notion is maintained.

Fizzles

1

He is barehead, barefoot, clothed in a singlet and tight trousers too short for him, his hands have told him so, again and again, and his feet, feeling each other and rubbing against the legs, up and down calves and shins. To this vaguely prison garb none of his memories answer, so far, but all are of heaviness, in this connexion, of fullness and of thickness. The great head where he toils is all mockery, he is forth again, he'll be back again. Some day he'll see himself, his whole front, from the chest down, and the arms, and finally the hands, first rigid at arm's length, then close up, trembling, to his eyes. He halts, for the first time since he knows he's under way, one foot before the other, the higher flat, the lower on its toes, and waits for a decision. Then he moves on. Spite of the dark he does not grope his way, arms outstretched, hands agape and the feet held back just before the ground. With the result he must often, namely at every turn, strike against the walls that hem his path, against the right-hand when he turns left, the left-hand when he turns right, now with his foot, now with the crown of his head, for he holds himself bowed, because of the rise, and because he always holds himself bowed, his back humped, his head thrust forward, his eyes cast down. He loses his blood, but in no great quantity, the little wounds have time to close before being opened again, his pace is so slow. There are places where the walls almost meet, then it is the shoulders take the shock. But instead of stopping short, and even turning back, saying to himself, This is the end of the road, nothing now but to return to the other terminus and start again, instead he attacks the narrow sideways and so finally squeezes through, to the great hurt of his chest and back. Do his eyes, after such long exposure to the gloom, begin to pierce it? No, and this is one of the reasons he shuts them more and more, more and more often and for ever longer spells. For his concern is increasingly to spare himself needless fatigue, such as that come of staring before him, and even all about him, hour after hour, day after day, and never seeing a thing. This is not the time to go into his wrongs, but perhaps he was wrong not to persist, in his efforts to pierce the gloom. For he might well have succeeded, in the end, up to a point, which would have brightened things up for him, nothing like a ray of light, from time to time, to brighten things up for one. And all may yet grow light, at any moment, first dimly and then—how can one say?—then more and more, till all is flooded with light, the way, the ground, the walls, the vault, without his being one whit the wiser. The moon may appear, framed at the end of the vista, and he in no state to rejoice and quicken his step, or on the contrary wheel and run, while there is yet time. For the moment however no complaints, which is the main. The legs notably seem in good shape, that is a blessing, Murphy had first-rate legs. The head is still a little weak, it needs time to get going again, that part does. No sign of insanity in any case, that is a blessing. Meagre equipment, but well balanced. The heart? No complaints. It's going again, enough to see him through. But see how now, having turned right for example, instead of turning left a little further on he turns right again. And see how now again, yet a little further on, instead of turning left at last he turns right yet again. And so on until, instead of turning right yet again, as he expected, he turns left at last. Then for a time his zigzags resume their tenor, deflecting him alternately to right and left, that is to say bearing him onward in a straight line more or less, but no longer the same straight line as when he set forth, or rather as when he suddenly realized he was forth, or perhaps after all the same. For if there are long periods when the right predominates, there are others when the left prevails. It matters little in any case, so long as he keeps on climbing. But see how now a little further on the ground falls away so sheer that he has to rear violently backwards in order not to fall. Where is it then that life awaits him, in relation to his starting-point, to the point rather at which he suddenly realized he was started, above or below? Or will they cancel out in the end, the long gentle climbs and headlong steeps? It matters little in any case, so long as he is on the right road, and that he is, for there are no others, unless he has let them slip by unnoticed, one after another. Walls and ground, if not of stone, are no less hard, to the touch, and wet. The former, certain days, he stops to lick. The fauna, if any, is silent. The only sounds, apart from those of the body on its way, are of fall, a great drop dropping at last from a great height and bursting, a solid mass that leaves its place and crashes down, lighter particles collapsing slowly. Then the echo is heard, as loud at first as the sound that woke it and repeated sometimes a good score of times, each time a little weaker, no, sometimes louder than the time before, till finally it dies away. Then silence again, broken only by the sound, intricate and faint, of the body on its way. But such sounds of fall are not common and mostly silence reigns, broken only by the sounds of the body on its way, of the bare feet on the wet ground, of the laboured breathing, of the body striking against the walls or squeezing through the narrows, of the clothes, singlet and trousers, espousing and resisting the movements of the body, coming unstuck from the damp flesh and sticking to it again, tattering and fluttered where in tatters already by sudden flurries as suddenly stilled, and finally of the hands as now and then they pass, back and forth, over all those parts of the body they can reach without fatigue. He himself has yet to drop. The air is foul. Sometimes he halts and leans against a wall, his feet wedged against the other. He has already a number of memories, from the memory of the day he suddenly knew he was there, on this same path still bearing him along, to that now of having halted to lean against the wall, he has a little past already, even a smatter of settled

ways. But it is all still fragile. And often he surprises himself, both mov-
ing and at rest, but more often moving, for he seldom comes to rest, as
destitute of history as on that first day, on this same path, which is his
beginning, on days of great recall. But usually now, the surprise once past,
memory returns and takes him back, if he will, far back to that first instant
beyond which nothing, when he was already old, that is to say near to
death, and knew, though unable to recall having lived, what age and death
are, with other momentous matters. But it is all still fragile. And often he
suddenly begins, in these black windings, and makes his first steps for
quite a while before realizing they are merely the last, or latest. The air is
so foul that only he seems fitted to survive it who never breathed the
other, the true life-giving, or so long ago as to amount to never. And such
true air, coming hard on that of here, would very likely prove fatal, after a
few lungfuls. But the change from one to the other will no doubt be gen-
tle, when the time comes, and gradual, as the man draws closer and closer
to the open. And perhaps even now the air is less foul than when he
started, than when he suddenly realized he was started. In any case little
by little his history takes shape, with if not yet exactly its good days and
bad, at least studded with occasions passing rightly or wrongly for out-
standing, such as the straitest narrow, the loudest fall, the most lingering
collapse, the steepest descent, the greatest number of successive turns
the same way, the greatest fatigue, the longest rest, the longest—aside
from the sound of the body on its way—silence. Ah yes, and the most
rewarding passage of the hands, on the one hand, the feet, on the other,
over all those parts of the body within their reach. And the sweetest wall
lick. In a word all the summits. Then other summits, hardly less elevated,
such as a shock so rude that it rivalled the rudest of all. Then others still,
scarcely less eminent, a wall lick so sweet as to vie with the second sweet-
est. Then little or nothing of note till the minima, these too unforgetta-
ble, on days of great recall, a sound of fall so muted by the distance, or for
want of weight, or for lack of space between departure and arrival, that it
was perhaps his fancy. Or again, second example, no, not a good example.
Other landmarks still are provided by first times, and even second. Thus
the first narrow, for example, no doubt because he was not expecting it,

impressed him quite as strongly as the straitest, just as the second col-
lapse, no doubt because he was expecting it, was no less than the briefest
never to be forgotten. So with one thing and another little by little his
history takes shape, and even changes shape, as new maxima and minima
tend to cast into the shade, and toward oblivion, those momentarily glo-
rified, and as fresh elements and motifs, such as these bones of which
more very shortly, and at length, in view of their importance, contribute
to enrich it.

2

Horn came always at night. I received him in the dark. I had come to bear everything bar being seen. In the beginning I would send him away after five or six minutes. Till he learnt to go of his own accord, once his time was up. He consulted his notes by the light of an electric torch. Then he switched it off and spoke in the dark. Light silence, dark speech. It was five or six years since anyone had seen me, to begin with myself. I mean the face I had pored over so, all down the years. Now I would resume that inspection, that it may be a lesson to me, in my mirrors and looking-glasses so long put away. I'll let myself be seen before I'm done. I'll call out, if there is a knock, Come in! But I speak now of five or six years ago. These allusions to now, to before and after, and all such yet to come, that we may feel ourselves in time. I had more trouble with the body proper. I masked it as best I could, but when I got out of bed it was sure to show. For I was now beginning, then if you prefer, to get out of bed again. Then there is the matter of its injuries. But the body was of less consequence. Whereas the face, no, not at any price. Hence Horn at night. When he forgot his torch he made shift with matches. Were I to ask, for example, And her gown that day?, then he switched on, thumbed through his notes, found the particular, switched off and answered, for example, The yellow. He did not like one to interrupt him and I must confess I seldom had call to. Interrupting him one night I asked him to light his face. He did so, briefly, switched off and resumed the thread.

Interrupting again I asked him to be silent for a moment. That night things went no further. But the next, or more likely the next but one, I desired him at the outset to light his face and keep it lit till further notice. The light, bright at first, gradually died down to no more than a yellow glimmer which then, to my surprise, persisted undiminished some little while. Then suddenly it was dark again and Horn went away, the five or six minutes having presumably expired. But here one of two things, either the final extinction had coincided, by some prank of chance, with the close of the session, or else Horn, knowing his time to be up, had cut off the last dribs of current. I still see, sometimes, that waning face disclosing, more and more clearly the more it entered shadow, the one I remembered. In the end I said to myself, as unaccountably it lingered on, No doubt about it, it is he. It is in outer space, not to be confused with the other, that such images develop. I need only interpose my hand, or close my eyes, to banish them, or take off my eyeglasses for them to fade. This is a help, but not a real protection, as we shall see. I try to keep before me therefore, as far as possible, when I get up, some such unbroken plane as that which I command from my bed, I mean the ceiling. For I have taken to getting up again. I thought I had made my last journey, the one I must now try once more to elucidate, that it may be a lesson to me, the one from which it were better I had never returned. But the feeling gains on me that I must undertake another. So I have taken to getting up again and making a few steps in the room, holding on to the bars of the bed. What ruined me at bottom was athletics. With all that jumping and running when I was young, and even long after in the case of certain events, I wore out the machine before its time. My fortieth year had come and gone and I still throwing the javelin.

3: Afar a bird

Ruinstrewn land, he has trodden it all night long, I gave up, hugging the hedges, between road and ditch, on the scant grass, little slow steps, no sound, stopping ever and again, every ten steps say, little wary steps, to catch his breath, then listen, ruinstrewn land, I gave up before birth, it is not possible otherwise, but birth there had to be, it was he, I was inside, now he stops again, for the hundredth time that night say, that gives the distance gone, it's the last, hunched over his stick, I'm inside, it was he who wailed, he who saw the light, I didn't wail, I didn't see the light, one on top of the other the hands weigh on the stick, the head weighs on the hands, he has caught his breath, he can listen now, the trunk horizontal, the legs asprawl, sagging at the knees, same old coat, the stiffened tails stick up behind, day dawns, he has only to raise his eyes, open his eyes, raise his eyes, he merges in the hedge, afar a bird, a moment past he grasps and is fled, it was he had a life, I didn't have a life, a life not worth having, because of me, it's impossible I should have a mind and I have one, someone divines me, divines us, that's what he's come to, come to in the end, I see him in my mind, there divining us, hands and head a little heap, the hours pass, he is still, he seeks a voice for me, it's impossible I should have a voice and I have none, he'll find one for me, ill beseeming me, it will meet the need, his need, but no more of him, that image, the little heap of hands and head, the trunk horizontal, the jutting elbows, the eyes closed and the face rigid listening, the eyes hidden and the whole face hidden, that image and no more, never changing, ruinstrewn land, night recedes, he is fled, I'm inside, he'll do himself to death, because of me, I'll live it with him, I'll live his death, the end of his life and then his death, step by step, in the present, how he'll go about it, it's impossible I should know, I'll know, step by step, it's he will die, I won't die, there will be nothing of him left but bones, I'll be inside, nothing but a little grit, I'll be inside, it is not possible otherwise, ruinstrewn land, he is fled through the hedge, no more stopping now, he will never say I, because of me, he won't speak to anyone, no one will speak to him, he won't speak to himself, there is nothing left in his head, I'll feed it all it needs, all it needs to end, to say I no more, to open its mouth no more, confusion of memory and lament, of loved ones and impossible youth, clutching the stick in the middle he stumbles bowed over the fields, a life of my own I tried, in vain, never any but his, worth nothing, because of me, he said it wasn't one, it was, still is, the same, I'm still inside, the same, I'll put faces in his head, names, places, churn them all up together, all he needs to end, phantoms to flee, last phantoms to flee and to pursue, he'll confuse his mother with whores, his father with a roadman named Balfe, I'll feed him an old curdog, a mangy old curdog, that he may love again, lose again, ruinstrewn land, little panic steps

4

I gave up before birth, it is not possible otherwise, but birth there had to be, it was he, I was inside, that's how I see it, it was he who wailed, he who saw the light, I didn't wail, I didn't see the light, it's impossible I should have a voice, impossible I should have thoughts, and I speak and think, I do the impossible, it is not possible otherwise, it was he who had a life, I didn't have a life, a life not worth having, because of me, he'll do himself to death, because of me, I'll tell the tale, the tale of his death, the end of his life and his death, his death alone would not be enough, not enough for me, if he rattles it's he who will rattle, I won't rattle, he who will die, I won't die, perhaps they will bury him, if they find him, I'll be inside, he'll rot, I won't rot, there will be nothing of him left but bones, I'll be inside, nothing left but dust, I'll be inside, it is not possible otherwise, that's how I see it, the end of his life and his death, how he will go about it, go about coming to an end, it's impossible I should know, I'll know, step by step, impossible I should tell, I'll tell, in the present, there will be no more talk of me, only of him, of the end of his life and his death, of his burial if they find him, that will be the end, I won't go on about worms, about bones and dust, no one cares about them, unless I'm bored in his dust, that would surprise me, as stiff as I was in his flesh, here long silence, perhaps he'll drown, he always wanted to drown, he didn't want them to find him, he can't want now any more, but he used to want to drown, he usen't to want them to find him, deep water and a millstone, urge spent like all the others, but why one day to the left, to the left and not elsewhither, here long silence, there will be no more I, he'll never say I any more, he'll never say anything any more, he won't talk to anyone, no one will talk to him, he won't talk to himself, he won't think any more, he'll go on, I'll be inside, he'll come to a place and drop, why there and not elsewhere, drop and sleep, badly because of me, he'll get up and go on, badly because of me, he can't stay still any more, because of me, he can't go on any more, because of me, there's nothing left in his head, I'll feed it all it needs.

5

Closed place. All needed to be known for say is known. There is nothing but what is said. Beyond what is said there is nothing. What goes on in the arena is not said. Did it need to be known it would be. No interest. Not for imagining. Place consisting of an arena and a ditch. Between the two skirting the latter a track. Closed place. Beyond the ditch there is nothing. This is known because it needs to be said. Arena black vast. Room for millions. Wandering and still. Never seeing never hearing one another. Never touching. No more is known. Depth of ditch. See from the edge all the bodies on its bed. The millions still there. They appear six times smaller than life. Bed divided into lots. Dark and bright. They take up all its width. The lots still bright are square. Appear square. Just room for the average sized body. Stretched out diagonally. Bigger it has to curl up. Thus the width of the ditch is known. It would have been in any case. Sum the bright lots. The dark. Outnumbered the former by far. The place is already old. The ditch is old. In the beginning it was all bright. All bright lots. Almost touching. Faintly edged with shadow. The ditch seems straight. Then reappears a body seen before. A closed curve therefore. Brilliance of the bright lots. It does not encroach on the dark. Adamantine blackness of these. As dense at the edge as at the centre. But vertically it diffuses unimpeded. High above the level of the arena. As high above as the ditch is deep. In the black air towers of pale light. So many bright lots so many towers. So many bodies visible on the bed. The track follows the ditch all the way along. All the way round. It is on a higher level than the arena. A step higher. It is made of dead leaves. A reminder of beldam nature. They are dry. The heat and the dry air. Dead but not rotting. Crumbling into dust rather. Just wide enough for one. On it no two ever meet.

6

Old earth, no more lies, I've seen you, it was me, with my other's ravening eyes, too late. You'll be on me, it will be you, it will be me, it will be us, it was never us. It won't be long now, perhaps not tomorrow, nor the day after, but too late. Not long now, how I gaze on you, and what refusal, how you refuse me, you so refused. It's a cockchafer year, next year there won't be any, nor the year after, gaze your fill. I come home at nightfall, they take to wing, rise from my little oaktree and whirr away, glutted, into the shadows. I reach up, grasp the bough, pull myself up and go in. Three years in the earth, those the moles don't get, then guzzle guzzle, ten days long, a fortnight, and always the flight at nightfall. To the river perhaps, they head for the river. I turn on the light, then off, ashamed, stand at gaze before the window, the windows, going from one to another, leaning on the furniture. For an instant I see the sky, the different skies, then they turn to faces, agonies, loves, the different loves, happiness too, yes, there was that too, unhappily. Moments of life, of mine too, among others, no denying, all said and done. Happiness, what happiness, but what deaths, what loves, I knew at the time, it was too late then. Ah to love at your last and see them at theirs, the last minute loved ones, and be happy, why ah, uncalled for. No but now, now, simply stay still, standing before a window, one hand on the wall, the other clutching your shirt, and see the sky, a long gaze, but no, gasps and spasms, a childhood sea, other skies, another body.

7: Still

Bright at last close of a dark day the sun shines out at last
and goes down. Sitting quite still at valley window normally turn head
now and see it the sun low in the southwest sinking. Even get up cer-
tain moods and go stand by western window quite still watching it sink
and then the afterglow. Always quite still some reason some time past
this hour at open window facing south in small upright wicker chair
with armrests. Eyes stare out unseeing till first movement some time
past close though unseeing still while still light. Quite still again then all
quite quiet apparently till eyes open again while still light though less.
Normally turn head now ninety degrees to watch sun which if already
gone then fading afterglow. Even get up certain moods and go stand by
western window till quite dark and even some evenings some reason
long after. Eyes then open again while still light and close again in what
if not quite a single movement almost. Quite still again then at open
window facing south over the valley in this wicker chair though actu-
ally close inspection not still at all but trembling all over. Close inspec-
tion namely detail by detail all over to add up finally to this whole not
still at all but trembling all over. But casually in this failing light impres-
sion dead still even the hands clearly trembling and the breast faint rise
and fall. Legs side by side broken right angles at the knees as in that old
statue some old god twanged at sunrise and again at sunset. Trunk like-
wise dead plumb right up to top of skull seen from behind including

nape clear of chairback. Arms likewise broken right angles at the elbows forearms along armrests just right length forearms and rests for hands clenched lightly to rest on ends. So quite still again then all quite quiet apparently eyes closed which to anticipate when they open again if they do in time then dark or some degree of starlight or moonlight or both. Normally watch night fall however long from this narrow chair or standing by western window quite still either case. Quite still namely staring at some one thing alone such as tree or bush a detail alone if near if far the whole if far enough till it goes. Or by eastern window certain moods staring at some point on the hillside such as that beech in whose shade once quite still till it goes. Chair some reason always same place same position facing south as though clamped down whereas in reality no lighter no more movable imaginable. Or anywhere any ope staring out at nothing just failing light quite still till quite dark though of course no such thing just less light still when less did not seem possible. Quite still then all this time eyes open when discovered then closed then opened and closed again no other movement any kind though of course not still at all when suddenly or so it looks this movement impossible to follow let alone describe. The right hand slowly opening leaves the armrest taking with it the whole forearm complete with elbow and slowly rises opening further as it goes and turning a little deasil till midway to the head it hesitates and hangs half open trembling in mid air. Hangs there as if half inclined to return that is sink back slowly closing as it goes and turning the other way till as and where it began clenched lightly on end of rest. Here because of what comes now not midway to the head but almost there before it hesitates and hangs there trembling as if half inclined etc. Half no but on the verge when in its turn the head moves from its place forward and down among the ready fingers where no sooner received and held it weighs on down till elbow meeting armrest brings this last movement to an end and all still once more. Here back a little way to that suspense before head to rescue as if hand's need the greater and on down in what if not quite a single movement almost till elbow against rest. All quite still again then head in hand namely thumb on outer edge of right socket index ditto left and middle on left cheekbone plus as the hours pass lesser contacts each more or less now more now less with the faint stirrings of the various parts as night wears on. As if even in the dark eyes closed not enough and perhaps even more than ever necessary against that no such thing the further shelter of the hand. Leave it so all quite still or try listening to the sounds all quite still head in hand listening for a sound.

8: For to end yet again

For to end yet again skull alone in a dark place pent bowed
on a board to begin. Long thus to begin till the place fades followed by the
board long after. For to end yet again skull alone in the dark the void no
neck no face just the box last place of all in the dark the void. Place of
remains where once used to gleam in the dark on and off used to glimmer
a remain. Remains of the days of the light of day never light so faint as
theirs so pale. Thus then the skull makes to glimmer again in lieu of going
out. There in the end all at once or by degrees there dawns and magic lin-
gers a leaden dawn. By degrees less dark till final grey or all at once as if
switched on grey sand as far as eye can see beneath grey cloudless sky same
grey. Skull last place of all black void within without till all at once or by
degrees this leaden dawn at last checked no sooner dawned. Grey cloud-
less sky grey sand as far as eye can see long desert to begin. Sand pale as dust
ah but dust indeed deep to engulf the haughtiest monuments which too
it once was here and there. There in the end same grey invisible to any other
eye stark erect amidst his ruins the expelled. Same grey all that little body
from head to feet sunk ankle deep were it not for the eyes last bright of all.
The arms still cleave to the trunk and to each other the legs made for flight.
Grey cloudless sky ocean of dust not a ripple mock confines verge upon
verge hell air not a breath. Mingling with the dust slowly sinking some
almost fully sunk the ruins of the refuge. First change of all in the end a
fragment comes away and falls. With slow fall for so dense a body it lights

like cork on water and scarce breaks the surface. Thus then the skull last place of all makes to glimmer again in lieu of going out. Grey cloudless sky verge upon verge grey timeless air of those nor for God nor for his enemies. There again in the end way amidst the verges a light in the grey two white dwarfs. Long at first mere whiteness from afar they toil step by step through the grey dust linked by a litter same white seen from above in the grey air. Slowly it sweeps the dust so bowed the backs and long the arms compared with the legs and deep sunk the feet. Bleached as one same wilderness they are so alike the eye cannot tell them apart. They carry face to face and relay each other often so that turn about they backwards lead the way. His who follows who knows to shape the course much as the coxswain with light touch the skiff. Let him veer to the north or other cardinal point and promptly the other by as much to the antipode. Let one stop short and the other about this pivot slew the litter through a semi-circle and thereon the roles are reversed. Bone white of the sheet seen from above and the shafts fore and aft and the dwarfs to the crowns of their massy skulls. From time to time impelled as one they let fall the litter then again as one take it up again without having to stoop. It is the dung litter of laughable memory with shafts twice as long as the couch. Swelling the sheet now fore now aft as permutations list a pillow marks the place of the head. At the end of the arms the four hands open as one and the litter so close to the dust already settles without a sound. Monstrous extremities including skulls stunted legs and trunks monstrous arms stunted faces. In the end the feet as one lift clear the left forward backward the right and the amble resumes. Grey dust as far as eye can see beneath grey cloudless sky and there all at once or by degrees this whiteness to decipher. Yet to imagine if he can see it the last expelled amidst his ruins if he can ever see it and seeing believe his eyes. Between him and it bird's-eye view the space grows no less but has only even now appeared last desert to be crossed. Little body last stage of all stark erect still amidst his ruins all silent and marble still. First change of all a fragment comes away from mother ruin and with slow fall scarce stirs the dust. Dust having engulfed so much it can engulf no more and woe the little on the surface still. Or mere digestive torpor as once the boas which past with one last gulp clean sweep at last. Dwarfs distant whiteness sprung from nowhere motionless afar in the grey air where dust alone possible. Wilderness and carriage immemorial as one they advance as one retreat hither thither halt move on again. He facing forward will sometimes halt and hoist as best he can his head as if to scan the void and who knows alter course. Then on so soft the eye does not see them go driftless with heads sunk and lidded eyes. Long lifted to the horizontal faces closer and closer strain as it will the eye achieves no more than two tiny oval blanks. Atop the cyclopean dome rising sheer from jut of brow yearns white to the grey sky the bump of habitativity or love of home. Last change of all in the end the expelled falls headlong down and lies back to sky full little stretch amidst his ruins. Feet centre body radius falls unbending as a statue falls faster and faster the space of a quadrant. Eagle the eye that shall discern him now mingled with the ruins mingling with the dust beneath a sky forsaken of its scavengers. Breath has not left him though soundless still and exhaling scarce ruffles the dust. Eyes in their orbits blue still unlike the doll's the fall has not shut nor yet the dust stopped up. No fear henceforth of his ever having not to believe them before that whiteness afar where sky and dust merge. Whiteness neither on earth nor above of the dwarfs as if at the end of their trials the litter left lying between them the white bodies marble still. Ruins all silent marble still little body prostrate at attention wash blue deep in gaping sockets. As in the days erect the arms still cleave to the trunk and to each other the legs made for flight. Fallen unbending all his little length as though pushed from behind by some helping hand or by the wind but not a breath. Or murmur from some dreg of life after the lifelong stand fall fall never fear no fear of your rising again. Sepulchral skull is this then its last state all set for always litter and dwarfs ruins and little body grey cloudless sky glutted dust verge upon verge hell air not a breath? And dream of a way in a space with neither here nor there where all the footsteps ever fell can never fare nearer to anywhere nor from anywhere further away? No for in the end for to end yet again by degrees or as though switched on dark falls there again that certain dark that alone certain ashes can. Through it who knows yet another end beneath a cloudless sky same dark it earth and sky of a last end if ever there had to be another absolutely had to be.

One Evening

He was found lying on the ground. No one had missed him. No one was looking for him. An old woman found him. To put it vaguely. It happened so long ago. She was straying in search of wild flowers. Yellow only. With no eyes but for these she stumbled on him lying there. He lay face downward and arms outspread. He wore a greatcoat in spite of the time of year. Hidden by the body a long row of buttons fastened it all the way down. Buttons of all shapes and sizes. Worn upright the skirts swept the ground. That seems to hang together. Near the head a hat lay askew on the ground. At once on its brim and crown. He lay inconspicuous in the greenish coat. To catch an eye searching from afar there was only the white head. May she have seen him somewhere before? Somewhere on his feet before? Not too fast. She was all in black. The hem of her long black skirt trailed in the grass. It was close of day. Should she now move away into the east her shadow would go before. A long black shadow. It was lambing time. But there were no lambs. She could see none. Were a third party to chance that way theirs were the only bodies he would see. First that of the old woman standing. Then on drawing near it lying on the ground. That seems to hang together. The deserted fields. The old woman all in black stock still. The body stock still on the ground. Yellow at the end of the black arm. The white hair in the grass. The east foundering in night. Not too fast. The weather. Sky overcast all day till evening. In the west-north-west near the verge already the sun came out at last. Rain? A few drops if you will. A few drops in the morning if you will. In the present to conclude. It happened so long ago. Cooped indoors all day she comes out with the sun. She makes haste to gain the fields. Surprised to have seen no one on the way she strays feverishly in search of the wild flowers. Feverishly seeing the imminence of night. She remarks with surprise the absence of lambs in great numbers here at this time of year. She is wearing the black she took on when widowed young. It is to reflower the grave she strays in search of the flowers he had loved. But for the need of yellow at the end of the black arm there would be none. There are therefore only as few as possible. This is for her the third surprise since she came out. For they grow in plenty here at this time of year. Her old friend her shadow irks her. So much so that she turns to face the sun. Any flower wide of her course she reaches sidelong. She craves for sundown to end and to stray freely again in the long afterglow. Further to her distress the familiar rustle of her long black skirt in the grass. She moves with half-closed eyes as if drawn on into the glare. She may say to herself it is too much strangeness for a single March or April evening. No one abroad. Not a single lamb. Scarcely a flower. Shadow and rustle irksome. And to crown all the shock of her foot against a body. Chance. No one had missed him. No one was looking for him. Black and green of the garments touching now. Near the white head the yellow of the few plucked flowers. The old sunlit face. Tableau vivant if you will. In its way. All is silent from now on. For as long as she cannot move. The sun disappears at last and with it all shadow. All shadow here. Slow fade of afterglow. Night without moon or stars. All that seems to hang together. But no more about it.

As the story was told

As the story was told me I never went near the place during sessions. I asked what place and a tent was described at length, a small tent the colour of its surroundings. Wearying of this description I asked what sessions and these in their turn were described, their object, duration, frequency and harrowing nature. I hope I was not more sensitive than the next man, but finally I had to raise my hand. I lay there quite still for a time, then asked where I was while all this was going forward. In a hut, was the answer, a small hut in a grove some two hundred yards away, a distance even the loudest cry could not carry, but must die on the way. This was not so strange as at first sight it sounded when one considered the stoutness of the canvas and the sheltered situation of the hut among the trees. Indeed the tent might have been struck where it stood and moved forward fifty yards or so without inconvenience. Lying there with closed eyes in the silence which followed this information I began to see the hut, though unlike the tent it had not been described to me, but only its situation. It reminded me strongly of a summer-house in which as a child I used to sit quite still for hours on end, on the window-seat, the whole year round. It had the same five log walls, the same coloured glass, the same diminutiveness, being not more than ten feet across and so low of ceiling that the average man could not have held himself erect in it, though of course there was no such difficulty for the child. At the centre, facing the coloured panes, stood a small upright wicker chair with armrests, as against the summer-house's window-seat. I sat there very straight and still, with my arms along the rests, looking out at the orange light. It must have been shortly after six, the sessions closing punctually at that hour, for as I watched a hand appeared in the doorway and held out to me a sheet of writing. I took and read it, then tore it in four and put the pieces in the waiting hand to take away. A little later the whole scene disappeared. As the story was told me the man succumbed in the end to his ill-treatment, though quite old enough at the time to die naturally of old age. I lay there a long time quite still—even as a child I was unusually still and more and more so with the passing years—till it must have seemed the story was over. But finally I asked if I knew exactly what the man—I would like to give his name but cannot—what exactly was required of the man, what it was he would not or could not say. No, was the answer, after some little hesitation no, I did not know what the poor man was required to say, in order to be pardoned, but would have recognized it at once, yes, at a glance, if I had seen it.

neither

To and fro in shadow from inner to outershadow

from impenetrable self to impenetrable unself by way of neither

as between two lit refuges whose doors once neared gently close, once turned away from gently part again

beckoned back and forth and turned away

heedless of the way, intent on the one gleam or the other

unheard footfalls only sound

till at last halt for good, absent for good from self and other

then no sound

then gently light unfading on that unheeded neither

unspeakable home

Company

A voice comes to one in the dark. Imagine.

To one on his back in the dark. This he can tell by the pressure on his hind parts and by how the dark changes when he shuts his eyes and again when he opens them again. Only a small part of what is said can be verified. As for example when he hears, You are on your back in the dark. Then he must acknowledge the truth of what is said. But by far the greater part of what is said cannot be verified. As for example when he hears, You first saw the light on such and such a day. Sometimes the two are combined as for example, You first saw the light on such and such a day and now you are on your back in the dark. A device perhaps from the incontrovertibility of the one to win credence for the other. That then is the proposition. To one on his back in the dark a voice tells of a past. With occasional allusion to a present and more rarely to a future as for example, You will end as you now are. And in another dark or in the same another devising it all for company. Quick leave him.

Use of the second person marks the voice. That of the third that cankerous other. Could he speak to and of whom the voice speaks there would be a first. But he cannot. He shall not. You cannot. You shall not.

Apart from the voice and the faint sound of his breath there is no sound. None at least that he can hear. This he can tell by the faint sound of his breath.

Though now even less than ever given to wonder he cannot but sometimes wonder if it is indeed to and of him the voice is speaking. May not there be another with him in the dark to and of whom the voice is speaking? Is he not perhaps overhearing a communication not intended for him? If he is alone on his back in the dark why does the voice not say so? Why does it never say for example, You saw the light on such and such a day and now you are alone on your back in the dark? Why? Perhaps for no other reason than to kindle in his mind this faint uncertainty and embarrassment.

Your mind never active at any time is now even less than ever so. This is the type of assertion he does not question. You saw the light on such and such a day and your mind never active at any time is now even less than ever so. Yet a certain activity of mind however slight is a necessary adjunct of company. That is why the voice does not say, You are on your back in the dark and have no mental activity of any kind. The voice alone is company but not enough. Its effect on the hearer is a necessary complement. Were it only to kindle in his mind the state of faint uncertainty and embarrassment mentioned above. But company apart this effect is clearly necessary. For were he merely to hear the voice and it to have no more effect on him than speech in Bantu or in Erse then might it not as well cease? Unless its object be by mere sound to plague one in need of silence. Or of course unless as above surmised directed at another.

A small boy you come out of Connolly's Stores holding your mother by the hand. You turn right and advance in silence southward along the highway. After some hundred paces you head inland and broach the long steep homeward. You make ground in silence hand in hand through the warm still summer air. It is late afternoon and after some hundred paces the sun appears above the crest of the rise. Looking up at the blue sky and then at your mother's face you break the silence asking her if it is not in reality much more distant than it appears. The sky that is. The blue sky. Receiving no answer you mentally reframe your question and some hundred paces later look up at her face again and ask her if it does not appear much less distant than in reality it is. For some reason you could never fathom this question must have angered her exceedingly. For she shook off your little hand and made you a cutting retort you have never forgotten.

If the voice is not speaking to him it must be speaking to another. So with what reason remains he reasons. To another of that other. Or of him. Or of another still. To another of that other or of him or of another still. To one on his back in the dark in any case. Of one on his back in the dark whether the same or another. So with what reason remains he reasons and reasons ill. For were the voice speaking not to him but to another then it must be of that other it is speaking and not of him or of another still. Since it speaks in the second person. Were it not of him to whom it is speaking speaking but of another it would not speak in the second person but in the third. For example, He first saw the light on such and such a day and now he is on his back in the dark. It is clear therefore that if it is not to him the voice is speaking but to another it is not of him either but of that other and none other to that other. So with what reason remains he reasons ill. In order to be company he must display a certain mental activity. But it need not be of a high order. Indeed it might be argued the lower the better. Up to a point. The lower the order of mental activity the better the company. Up to a point.

You first saw the light in the room you most likely were conceived in. The big bow window looked west to the mountain. Mainly west. For being bow it looked also a little south and a little north. Necessarily. A little south to more mountain and a little north to foothill and plain. The midwife was none other than a Dr. Hadden or Haddon. Straggling grey moustache and hunted look. It being a public holiday your father left the house soon after his breakfast with a flask and a package of his

favourite egg sandwiches for a tramp in the mountains. There was noth-
ing unusual in this. But on that particular morning his love of walking
and wild scenery was not the only mover. But he was moved also to take
himself off and out of the way by his aversion to the pains and general
unpleasantness of labour and delivery. Hence the sandwiches which he
relished at noon looking out to sea from the lee of a great rock on the
first summit scaled. You may imagine his thoughts before and after as
he strode through the gorse and heather. When he returned at nightfall
he learned to his dismay from the maid at the back door that labour was
still in swing. Despite its having begun before he left the house full ten
hours earlier. He at once hastened to the coachhouse some twenty yards
distant where he housed his De Dion Bouton. He shut the doors behind
him and climbed into the driver's seat. You may imagine his thoughts
as he sat there in the dark not knowing what to think. Though footsore
and weary he was on the point of setting out anew across the fields in
the young moonlight when the maid came running to tell him it was
over at last. Over!

You are an old man plodding along a narrow country road. You have been
out since break of day and now it is evening. Sole sound in the silence
your footfalls. Rather sole sounds for they vary from one to the next. You
listen to each one and add it in your mind to the growing sum of those
that went before. You halt with bowed head on the verge of the ditch and
convert into yards. On the basis now of two steps per yard. So many since
dawn to add to yesterday's. To yesteryear's. To yesteryears'. Days other
than today and so akin. The giant tot in miles. In leagues. How often
round the earth already. Halted too at your elbow during these computa-
tions your father's shade. In his old tramping rags. Finally on side by side
from nought anew.

The voice comes to him now from one quarter and now from another.
Now faint from afar and now a murmur in his ear. In the course of a sin-
gle sentence it may change place and tone. Thus for example clear from
above his upturned face, You first saw the light at Easter and now. Then

a murmur in his ear, You are on your back in the dark. Or of course vice versa. Another trait its long silences when he dare almost hope it is at an end. Thus to take the same example clear from above his upturned face, You first saw the light of day the day Christ died and now. Then long after on his nascent hope the murmur, You are on your back in the dark. Or of course vice versa.

Another trait its repetitiousness. Repeatedly with only minor variants the same bygone. As if willing him by this dint to make it his. To confess, Yes I remember. Perhaps even to have a voice. To murmur, Yes I remember. What an addition to company that would be! A voice in the first person singular. Murmuring now and then, Yes I remember.

An old beggar woman is fumbling at a big garden gate. Half blind. You know the place well. Stone deaf and not in her right mind the woman of the house is a crony of your mother. She was sure she could fly once in the air. So one day she launched herself from a first-floor window. On the way home from kindergarten on your tiny cycle you see the poor old beggar woman trying to get in. You dismount and open the gate for her. She blesses you. What were her words? God reward you little master. Some such words. God save you little master.

A faint voice at loudest. It slowly ebbs till almost out of hearing. Then slowly back to faint full. At each slow ebb hope slowly dawns that it is dying. He must know it will flow again. And yet at each slow ebb hope slowly dawns that it is dying.

Slowly he entered dark and silence and lay there for so long that with what judgement remained he judged them to be final. Till one day the voice. One day! Till in the end the voice saying, You are on your back in the dark. Those its first words. Long pause for him to believe his ears and then from another quarter the same. Next the vow not to cease till hearing cease. You are on your back in the dark and not till hearing cease will this voice cease. Or another way. As in shadow he lay and only the odd sound slowly silence fell and darkness gathered. That were perhaps better company. For what odd sound? Whence the shadowy light?

You stand at the tip of the high board. High above the sea. In it your father's upturned face. Upturned to you. You look down to the loved trusted face. He calls to you to jump. He calls, Be a brave boy. The red round face. The thick moustache. The greying hair. The swell sways it under and sways it up again. The far call again, Be a brave boy. Many eyes upon you. From the water and from the bathing place.

The odd sound. What a mercy to have that to turn to. Now and then. In dark and silence to close as if to light the eyes and hear a sound. Some object moving from its place to its last place. Some soft thing softly stirring soon to stir no more. To darkness visible to close the eyes and hear if only that. Some soft thing softly stirring soon to stir no more.

By the voice a faint light is shed. Dark lightens while it sounds. Deepens when it ebbs. Lightens with flow back to faint full. Is whole again when it ceases. You are on your back in the dark. Had the eyes been open then they would have marked a change.

Whence the shadowy light? What company in the dark! To close the eyes and try to imagine that. Whence once the shadowy light. No source. As if faintly luminous all his little void. What can he have seen then above his upturned face. To close the eyes in the dark and try to imagine that.

Another trait the flat tone. No life. Same flat tone at all times. For its affirmations. For its negations. For its interrogations. For its exclamations. For its imperations. Same flat tone. You were once. You were never. Were you ever? Oh never to have been! Be again. Same flat tone.

Can he move? Does he move? Should he move? What a help that would be. When the voice fails. Some movement however small. Were it but of a hand closing. Or opening if closed to begin. What a help that would be in the dark! To close the eyes and see that hand. Palm upward filling the whole field. The lines. The fingers slowly down. Or up if down to begin. The lines of that old palm.

There is of course the eye. Filling the whole field. The hood slowly down. Or up if down to begin. The globe. All pupil. Staring up. Hooded. Bared. Hooded again. Bared again.

If he were to utter after all? However feebly. What an addition to company that would be! You are on your back in the dark and one day you will utter again. One day! In the end. In the end you will utter again. Yes I remember. That was I. That was I then.

You are alone in the garden. Your mother is in the kitchen making ready for afternoon tea with Mrs. Coote. Making the wafer-thin bread and butter. From behind a bush you watch Mrs. Coote arrive. A small thin sour woman. Your mother answers her saying, He is playing in the garden. You climb to near the top of a great fir. You sit a little listening to all the sounds. Then throw yourself off. The great boughs break your fall. The needles. You lie a little with your face to the ground. Then climb the tree again. Your mother answers Mrs. Coote again saying, He has been a very naughty boy.

What with what feeling remains does he feel about now as compared to then? When with what judgement remained he judged his condition final. As well enquire what he felt then about then as compared to before. When he still moved or tarried in remains of light. As then there was no then so there is none now.

In another dark or in the same another devising it all for company. This at first sight seems clear. But as the eye dwells it grows obscure. Indeed the longer the eye dwells the obscurer it grows. Till the eye closes and freed from pore the mind enquires, What does this mean? What finally does this mean that at first sight seemed clear? Till it the mind too closes as it were. As the window might close of a dark empty room. The single window giving on outer dark. Then nothing more. No. Unhappily no. Pangs of faint light and stirrings still. Unformulable gropings of the mind. Unstillable.

Nowhere in particular on the way from A to Z. Or say for verisimilitude the Ballyogan Road. That dear old back road. Somewhere on the Ballyogan Road in lieu of nowhere in particular. Where no truck any more. Somewhere on the Ballyogan Road on the way from A to Z. Head sunk totting up the tally on the verge of the ditch. Foothills to left. Croker's Acres ahead. Father's shade to right and a little to the rear. So many times already round the earth. Topcoat once green stiff with age and grime from chin to insteps. Battered once buff block hat and quarter boots still a match. No other garments if any to be seen. Out since break of day and night now falling. Reckoning ended on together from nought anew. As if bound for Stepaside. When suddenly you cut through the hedge and vanish hobbling east across the gallops.

For why or? Why in another dark or in the same? And whose voice asking this? Who asks, Whose voice asking this? And answers, His soever who devises it all. In the same dark as his creature or in another. For company. Who asks in the end, Who asks? And in the end answers as above? And adds long after to himself, Unless another still. Nowhere to be found. Nowhere to be sought. The unthinkable last of all. Unnamable. Last person. I. Quick leave him.

The light there was then. On your back in the dark the light there was then. Sunless cloudless brightness. You slip away at break of day and climb to your hiding place on the hillside. A nook in the gorse. East beyond the sea the faint shape of high mountain. Seventy miles away according to your Longman. For the third or fourth time in your life. The first time you told them and were derided. All you had seen was cloud. So now you hoard it in your heart with the rest. Back home at nightfall supperless to bed. You lie in the dark and are back in that light. Straining out from your nest in the gorse with your eyes across the water till they ache. You close them while you count a hundred. Then open and strain again. Again and again. Till in the end it is there. Palest blue against the pale sky. You lie in the dark and are back in that light. Fall asleep in that sunless cloudless light. Sleep till morning light.

Deviser of the voice and of its hearer and of himself. Deviser of himself for company. Leave it at that. He speaks of himself as of another. He says speaking of himself, He speaks of himself as of another. Himself he devises too for company. Leave it at that. Confusion too is company up to a point. Better hope deferred than none. Up to a point. Till the heart starts to sicken. Company too up to a point. Better a sick heart than none. Till it starts to break. So speaking of himself he concludes for the time being, For the time being leave it at that.

In the same dark as his creature or in another not yet imagined. Nor in what position. Whether standing or sitting or lying or in some other position in the dark. There are among the matters yet to be imagined. Matters of which as yet no inkling. The test is company. Which of the two darks is the better company. Which of all imaginable positions has the most to offer in the way of company. And similarly for the other matters yet to be imagined. Such as if such decisions irreversible. Let him for example after due imagination decide in favour of the supine position or prone and this in practice prove less companionable than anticipated. May he then or may he not replace it by another? Such as huddled with his legs drawn up within the semicircle of his arms and his head on his knees. Or in motion. Crawling on all fours. Another in another dark or in the same crawling on all fours devising it all for company. Or some other form of motion. The possible encounters. A dead rat. What an addition to company that would be! A rat long dead.

Might not the hearer be improved? Made more companionable if not downright human. Mentally perhaps there is room for enlivenment. An attempt at reflexion at least. At recall. At speech even. Conation of some

kind however feeble. A trace of emotion. Signs of distress. A sense of fail-
ure. Without loss of character. Delicate ground. But physically? Must he
lie inert to the end? Only the eyelids stirring on and off since technically
they must. To let in and shut out the dark. Might he not cross his feet? On
and off. Now left on right and now a little later the reverse. No. Quite out
of keeping. He lie with crossed feet? One glance dispels. Some movement
of the hands? A hand. A clenching and unclenching. Difficult to justify.
Or raised to brush away a fly. But there are no flies. Then why not let there
be? The temptation is great. Let there be a fly. For him to brush away. A
live fly mistaking him for dead. Made aware of its error and renewing it
incontinent. What an addition to company that would be! A live fly mis-
taking him for dead. But no. He would not brush away a fly.

You take pity on a hedgehog out in the cold and put it in an old hatbox
with some worms. This box with the hog inside you then place in a dis-
used hutch wedging the door open for the poor creature to come and go
at will. To go in search of food and having eaten to regain the warmth
and security of its box in the hutch. There then is the hedgehog in its
box in the hutch with enough worms to tide it over. A last look to make
sure all is as it should be before taking yourself off to look for something
else to pass the time heavy already on your hands at that tender age. The
glow at your good deed is slower than usual to cool and fade. You glowed
readily in those days but seldom for long. Hardly had the glow been kin-
dled by some good deed on your part or by some little triumph over your
rivals or by a word of praise from your parents or mentors when it would
begin to cool and fade leaving you in a very short time as chill and dim
as before. Even in those days. But not this day. It was on an autumn after-
noon you found the hedgehog and took pity on it in the way described
and you were still the better for it when your bedtime came. Kneeling at
your bedside you included it the hedgehog in your detailed prayer to God
to bless all you loved. And tossing in your warm bed waiting for sleep to
come you were still faintly glowing at the thought of what a fortunate
hedgehog it was to have crossed your path as it did. A narrow clay path
edged with sere box edging. As you stood there wondering how best to

pass the time till bedtime it parted the edging on the one side and was making straight for the edging on the other when you entered its life. Now the next morning not only was the glow spent but a great uneasiness had taken its place. A suspicion that all was perhaps not as it should be. That rather than do as you did you had perhaps better let good alone and the hedgehog pursue its way. Days if not weeks passed before you could bring yourself to return to the hutch. You have never forgotten what you found then. You are on your back in the dark and have never forgotten what you found then. The mush. The stench.

Impending for some time the following. Need for company not continuous. Moments when his own unrelieved a relief. Intrusion of voice at such. Similarly image of hearer. Similarly his own. Regret then at having brought them about and problem how dispel them. Finally what meant by his own unrelieved? What possible relief? Leave it at that for the moment.

Let the hearer be named H. Aspirate. Haitch. You Haitch are on your back in the dark. And let him know his name. No longer any question of his overhearing. Of his not being meant. Though logically none in any case. Of words murmured in his ear to wonder if to him! So he is. So that faint uneasiness lost. That faint hope. To one with so few occasions to feel. So inapt to feel. Asking nothing better in so far as he can ask anything than to feel nothing. Is it desirable? No. Would he gain thereby in companionability? No. Then let him not be named H. Let him be again as he was. The hearer. Unnamable. You.

Imagine closer the place where he lies. Within reason. To its form and dimensions a clue is given by the voice afar. Receding afar or there with abrupt saltation or resuming there after pause. From above and from all sides and levels with equal remoteness at its most remote. At no time from below. So far. Suggesting one lying on the floor of a hemispherical chamber of generous diameter with ear dead centre. How generous? Given faintness of voice at its least faint some sixty feet should suffice or thirty from ear to any given point of encompassing surface. So much for form and dimensions. And composition? What and where clue to that if any anywhere. Reserve for the moment. Basalt is tempting. Black basalt. But reserve for the moment. So he imagines to himself as voice and hearer pall. But further imagination shows him to have imagined ill. For with what right affirm of a faint sound that it is a less faint made fainter by farness and not a true faint near at hand? Or of a faint fading to fainter that it recedes and not in situ decreases. If with none then no light from the voice on the place where our old hearer lies. In immeasurable dark. Contourless. Leave it at that for the moment. Adding only, What kind of imagination is this so reason-ridden? A kind of its own.

Another devising it all for company. In the same dark as his creature or in another. Quick imagine. The same.

Might not the voice be improved? Made more companionable. Say changing now for some time past though no tense in the dark in that dim mind. All at once over and in train and to come. But for the other say for some time past some improvement. Same flat tone as initially imagined and same repetitiousness. No improving those. But less mobility. Less variety of faintness. As if seeking optimum position. From which to discharge with greatest effect. The ideal amplitude for effortless audition. Neither offending the ear with loudness nor through converse excess constraining it to strain. How far more companionable such an organ than it initially in haste imagined. How far more likely to achieve its object. To have the hearer have a past and acknowledge it. You were born on an Easter Friday after long labour. Yes I remember. The sun had not long sunk behind the larches. Yes I remember. As best to erode the drop must strike unwavering. Upon the place beneath.

The last time you went out the snow lay on the ground. You now on your back in the dark stand that morning on the sill having pulled the door gently to behind you. You lean back against the door with bowed head making ready to set out. By the time you open your eyes your feet have disappeared and the skirts of your greatcoat come to rest on the surface of the snow. The dark scene seems lit from below. You see yourself at that last outset leaning against the door with closed eyes waiting for the word from you to go. To be gone. Then the snowlit scene. You lie in the dark with closed eyes and see yourself there as described making ready to strike out and away across the expanse of light. You hear again the click of the door pulled gently to and the silence before the steps can start. Next thing you are on your way across the white pasture afrolic with lambs in spring and strewn with red placentae. You take the course you always take which is a beeline for the gap or ragged point in the quickset that forms the western fringe. Thither from your entering the pasture you need normally from eighteen hundred to two thousand paces depending on your humour and the state of the ground. But on this last morning many more will be required. Many many more. The beeline is so familiar to your feet that if necessary they could keep to it and you sightless with error on arrival of not more than a few feet north or south. And indeed without any such necessity unless from within this is what they normally do and not only here. For you advance if not with closed eyes though this as often as not at least with them fixed on the momentary ground before your feet. That is all of nature you have seen. Since finally you bowed your head. The fleeting ground before your feet. From time to time. You do not count your steps any more. For the simple reason they number each day the same. Average day in day out the same. The way being always the same. You keep count of the days and every tenth day multiply. And add. Your father's shade is not with you any more. It fell out long ago. You do not hear your footfalls any more. Unhearing unseeing you go your way. Day after day. The same way. As if there were no other any more. For you there is no other any more. You used never to halt except to make your reckoning. So as to plod on from nought anew. This need removed as we have seen there is none in theory to halt any more. Save perhaps a moment at the outermost point. To gather yourself together for the return. And yet you do. As never before. Not for tiredness. You are no more tired now than you always were. Not because of age. You are no older now than you always were. And yet you halt as never before. So that the same hundred yards you used to cover in a matter of three to four minutes may now take you anything from fifteen to twenty. The foot falls unbidden in midstep or next for lift cleaves to the ground bringing the body to a stand. Then a speechlessness whereof the gist, Can they go on? Or better, Shall they go on? The barest gist. Stilled when finally as always hitherto they do. You lie in the dark with closed eyes and see the scene. As you could not at the time. The dark cope of sky. The dazzling land. You at a standstill in the midst. The quarter boots sunk to the tops. The skirts of the greatcoat resting on the snow. In the old bowed head in the old block hat speechless misgiving. Halfway across the pasture on your beeline to the gap. The unerring feet fast. You look behind you as you could not then and see their trail. A great swerve. Withershins. Almost as if all at once the heart too heavy. In the end too heavy.

Bloom of adulthood. Imagine a whiff of that. On your back in the dark you remember. Ah you you remember. Cloudless May day. She joins you in the little summerhouse. A rustic hexahedron. Entirely of logs. Both larch and fir. Six feet across. Eight from floor to vertex. Area twenty-four square feet to furthest decimal. Two small multicoloured lights vis-à-vis. Small stained diamond panes. Under each a ledge. There on summer Sundays after his midday meal your father loved to retreat with *Punch* and a cushion. The waist of his trousers unbuttoned he sat on the one ledge turning the pages. You on the other with your feet dangling. When he chuckled you tried to chuckle too. When his chuckle died yours too. That you should try to imitate his chuckle pleased and tickled him greatly and sometimes he would chuckle for no other reason than to hear you try to chuckle too. Sometimes you turn your head and look out through a rose-red pane. You press your little nose against the pane and all without is rosy. The years have flown and there at the same place as then you sit in the bloom of adulthood bathed in rainbow light gazing before you. She is late. You close your eyes and try to calculate the volume. Simple sums you find a help in times of trouble. A haven. You arrive in the end at seven cubic yards approximately. Even still in the timeless dark you find figures a comfort. You assume a certain heart rate and reckon how many thumps a day. A week. A month. A year. And assuming a certain lifetime a lifetime. Till the last thump. But for the moment with hardly more than seventy American billion behind you you sit in the little summerhouse working out the volume. Seven cubic yards approximately. This strikes you for some reason as improbable and you set about your sun anew. But you have not made much headway when her light step is heard. Light for a woman of her size. You open with quickening pulse your eyes and a moment later that seems an eternity her face appears at the window. Mainly blue in this position the natural pallor you so admire as indeed from it no doubt wholly blue your own. For natural pallor is a property you have in common. The violet lips do not return your smile. Now this window being flush with your eyes from where you sit and the floor as near as no matter with the outer ground you cannot but wonder if she has not sunk to her knees. Knowing from experience that the height or length you have in common is the sum of equal segments. For when bolt upright or lying at full stretch you cleave face to face then your knees meet and your pubes and the hairs of your heads mingle. Does it follow from this that the loss of height for the body that sits is the same as for it that kneels? At this point assuming height of seat adjustable as in the case of certain piano stools you close your eyes the better with mental measure to measure and compare the first and second segments namely from sole to knee-pad and thence to pelvic girdle. How given you were both moving and at rest to the closed eye in your waking hours! By day and by night. To that perfect dark. That shadowless light. Simply to be gone. Or for affair as now. A single leg appears. Seen from above. You separate the segments and lay them side by side. It is as you half surmised. The upper is the longer and the sitter's loss the greater when seat at knee level. You leave the pieces lying there and open your eyes to find her sitting before you. All dead still. The ruby lips do not return your smile. Your gaze descends to the breasts. You do not remember them so big. To the abdomen. Same impression. Dissolve to your father's straining against the unbuttoned waistband. Can it be she is with child without your having asked for as much as her hand? You go back into your mind. She too did you but know it has closed her eyes. So you sit face to face in the little summerhouse. With eyes closed and your hands on your pubes. In that rainbow light. That dead still.

Wearied by such stretch of imagining he ceases and all ceases. Till feeling the need for company again he tells himself to call the hearer M at least. For readier reference. Himself some other character. W. Devising it all himself included for company. In the same dark as M when last heard of. In what posture and whether fixed or mobile left open. He says further to himself referring to himself, When last he referred to himself it was to say he was in the same dark as his creature. Not in another as once seemed possible. The same. As more companionable. And that his posture there remained to be devised. And to be decided whether fast or mobile. Which of all imaginable postures least liable to pall? Which of motion or of rest the more entertaining in the long run? And in the same breath too soon to say and why after all not say without further ado what can later be unsaid and what if it could not? What then? Could he now if he chose move out of the dark he chose when last heard of and away from his creature into another? Should he now decide to lie and come later to regret it could he then rise to his feet for example and lean against a wall or pace to and fro? Could M be reimagined in an easy chair? With hands free to go to his assistance? There in the same dark as his creature he leaves himself to these perplexities while wondering as every now and then he wonders in the back of his mind if the woes of the world are all they used to be. In his day.

M so far as follows. On his back in a dark place form and dimensions yet to be devised. Hearing on and off a voice of which uncertain whether addressed to him or to another sharing his situation. There being nothing to show when it describes correctly his situation that the description is not for the benefit of another in the same situation. Vague distress at the vague thought of his perhaps overhearing a confidence when he hears for example, You are on your back in the dark. Doubts gradually dashed as voice from questing far and wide closes in upon him. When it ceases no other sound than his breath. When it ceases long enough vague hope it may have said its last. Mental activity of a low order. Rare flickers of reasoning of no avail. Hope and despair and suchlike barely felt. How current situation arrived at unclear. No that then to compare to this now. Only eyelids move. When for relief from outer and inner dark they close and open respectively. Other small local movements eventually within moderation not to be despaired of. But no improvement by means of such achieved so far. Or on a higher plane by such addition to company as a movement of sustained sorrow or desire or remorse or curiosity or anger and so on. Or by some successful act of intellection as were he to think to himself referring to himself, Since he cannot think he will give up trying. Is there anything to add to this esquisse? His unnamability. Even M must go. So W reminds himself of his creature as so far created. W? But W too is creature. Figment.

Yet another then. Of whom nothing. Devising figments to temper his nothingness. Quick leave him. Pause and again in panic to himself, Quick leave him.

Devised deviser devising it all for company. In the same figment dark as his figments. In what posture and if or not as hearer in his for good not yet devised. Is not one immovable enough? Why duplicate this particular solace? Then let him move. Within reason. On all fours. A moderate crawl torso well clear of the ground eyes front alert. If this no better than nothing cancel. If possible. And in the void regained another motion. Or none. Leaving only the most helpful posture to be devised. But to be going on with let him crawl. Crawl and fall. Crawl again and fall again. In the same figment dark as his other figments.

From ranging far and wide as if in quest the voice comes to rest and constant faintness. To rest where? Imagine warily.

Above the upturned face. Falling tangent to the crown. So that in the faint light it sheds were there a mouth to be seen he would not see it. Roll as he might his eyes. Height from the ground?

Arm's length. Force? Low. A mother's stooping over cradle from behind. She moves aside to let the father look. In his turn he murmurs to the newborn. Flat tone unchanged. No trace of love.

You are on your back at the foot of an aspen. In its trembling shade. She at right angles propped on her elbows head between her hands. Your eyes opened and closed have looked in hers looking in yours. In your dark you look in them again. Still. You feel on your face the fringe of her long black hair stirring in the still air. Within the tent of hair your faces are hidden from view. She murmurs, Listen to the leaves. Eyes in each other's eyes you listen to the leaves. In their trembling shade.

Crawling and falling then. Crawling again and falling again. If this finally no improvement on nothing he can always fall for good. Or have never risen to his knees. Contrive how such crawl unlike the voice may serve to chart the area. However roughly. First what is the unit of crawl? Corresponding to the footstep of erect locomotion. He rises to all fours and makes ready to set out. Hands and knees angles of an oblong two foot long width irrelevant. Finally say left knee moves forward six inches thus half halving distance between it and homologous hand. Which then in due course in its turn moves forward by as much. Oblong now rhomboid. But for no longer than it takes right knee and hand to follow suit. Oblong restored. So on till he drops. Of all modes of crawl this the repent amble is possibly the least common. And so possibly of all the most diverting.

So as he crawls the mute count. Grain by grain in the mind. One two three four one. Knee hand knee hand two. One foot. Till say after five he falls. Then sooner or later on from nought anew. One two three four one. Knee hand knee hand two. Six. So on. In what he wills a beeline. Till having encountered no obstacle discouraged he heads back the way he came. From nought anew. Or in some quite different direction. In what he hopes a beeline. Till again with no dead end for his pains he renounces and embarks on yet another course. From nought anew. Well aware or little doubting how darkness may deflect. Withershins on account of the heart. Or conversely to shortest path convert deliberate veer. Be that as it may and crawl as he will no bourne as yet. As yet imaginable. Hand knee hand knee as he will. Bourneless dark.

Would it be reasonable to imagine the hearer as mentally quite inert? Except when he hears. That is when the voice sounds. For what if not it and his breath is there for him to hear? Aha! The crawl. Does he hear the crawl? The fall? What an addition to company were he but to hear the crawl. The fall. The rising to all fours again. The crawl resumed. And wonder to himself what in the world such sounds might signify. Reserve for a duller moment. What if not sound could set his mind in motion? Sight? The temptation is strong to decree there is nothing to see. But too late for the moment. For he sees a change of dark when he opens or shuts his eyes. And he may see the faint light the voice imagined to shed. Rashly imagined. Light infinitely faint it is true since now no more than a mere murmur. Here suddenly seen how his eyes close as soon as the voice sounds. Should they happen to be open at the time. So light as let be faintest light no longer perceived than the time it takes the lid to fall. Taste? The taste in his mouth? Long since dulled. Touch? The thrust of the ground against his bones. All the way from calcaneum to bump of philoprogenitiveness. Might not a notion to stir ruffle his apathy? To turn on his side. On his face. For a change. Let that much of want be conceded. With attendant relief that the days are no more when he could writhe in vain. Smell? His own? Long since dulled. And a barrier to others if any. Such as might have once emitted a rat long dead. Or some other carrion. Yet to be imagined. Unless the crawler smell. Aha! The crawling creator. Might the crawling creator be reasonably imagined to smell? Even fouler than his creature. Stirring now and then to wonder that mind so lost to wonder. To wonder what in the world can be making that alien smell. Whence in the world those wafts of villainous smell. How much more companionable could his creator but smell. Could he but smell his creator. Some sixth sense? Inexplicable premonition of impending ill? Yes or no? No. Pure reason? Beyond experience. God is love. Yes or no? No.

Can the crawling creator crawling in the same create dark as his crea-ture create while crawling? One of the questions he put to himself as between two crawls he lay. And if the obvious answer were not far to seek the most helpful was another matter. And many crawls were necessary and the like number of prostrations before he could finally make up his imagination on this score. Adding to himself without conviction in the same breath as always that no answer of his was sacred. Come what might the answer he hazarded in the end was no he could not. Crawl-ing in the dark in the way described was too serious a matter and too all-engrossing to permit of any other business were it only the conjur-ing of something out of nothing. For he had not only as perhaps too hast-ily imagined to cover the ground in this special way but rectigrade into the bargain to the best of his ability. And furthermore to count as he went adding half foot to half foot and retain in his memory the ever-changing sum of those gone before. And finally to maintain eyes and ears at a high level of alertness for any clue however small to the nature of the place to which imagination perhaps unadvisedly had consigned him. So while in the same breath deploring a fancy so reason-ridden and observing how revocable its flights he could not but answer finally no he could not. Could not conceivably create while crawling in the same create dark as his creature.

A strand. Evening. Light dying. Soon none left to die. No. No such thing then as no light. Died on to dawn and never died. You stand with your back to the wash. No sound but its. Ever fainter as it slowly ebbs. Till it slowly flows again. You lean on a long staff. Your hands rest on the knob and on them your head. Were your eyes to open they would first see far below in the last rays the skirt of your greatcoat and the uppers of your boots emerging from the sand. Then and it alone till it vanishes the shadow of the staff on the sand. Vanishes from your sight. Moonless star-less night. Were your eyes to open dark would lighten.

Crawls and falls. Lies. Lies in the dark with closed eyes resting from his crawl. Recovering. Physically and from his disappointment at having crawled again in vain. Perhaps saying to himself, Why crawl at all? Why not just lie in the dark with closed eyes and give up? Give up all. Have done with all. With bootless crawl and figments comfortless. But if on occasion so disheartened it is seldom for long. For little by little as he lies the craving for company revives. In which to escape from his own. The need to hear that voice again. If only saying again, You are on your back in the dark. Or if only, You first saw the light and cried at the close of the day when in darkness Christ at the ninth hour cried and died. The need eyes closed the better to hear to see that glimmer shed. Or with addition of some human weakness to improve the hearer. For example an itch beyond reach of the hand or better still within while the hand immovable. An unscratchable itch. What an addition to company that would be! Or last if not least resort to ask himself what precisely he means when he speaks of himself loosely as lying. Which in other words of all the innumerable ways of lying is likely to prove in the long run the most endearing. If having crawled in the way described he falls it would normally be on his face. Indeed given the degree of his fatigue and discouragement at this point it is hard to see how he could do otherwise. But once fallen and lying on his face there is no reason why he should not turn over on one or other of his sides or on his only back and so lie should any of these three postures offer better company than any of the other three. The supine though most tempting he must finally disallow as being already supplied by the hearer. With regard to the sidelong one glance is enough to dispel them both. Leaving him with no other choice than the prone. But how prone? Prone how? How disposed the legs? The arms? The head? Prone in the dark he strains to see how best he may lie prone. How most companionably.

See hearer clearer. Which of all the ways of lying supine the least likely in the long run to pall? After long straining eyes closed prone in the dark the following. But first naked or covered? If only with a sheet. Naked. Ghostly in the voice's glimmer that bonewhite flesh for company. Head resting mainly on occipital bump aforesaid. Legs joined at attention. Feet splayed ninety degrees. Hands invisibly manacled crossed on pubis. Other details as need felt. Leave him at that for the moment.

Numb with the woes of your kind you raise none the less your head from off your hands and open your eyes. You turn on without moving from your place the light above you. Your eyes light on the watch lying beneath it. But instead of reading the hour of night they follow round and round the second hand now followed and now preceded by its shadow. Hours later it seems to you as follows. At 60 seconds and 30 seconds shadow hidden by hand. From 60 to 30 shadow precedes hand at a distance increasing from zero at 60 to maximum at 15 and thence decreasing to new zero at 30. From 30 to 60 shadow follows hand at a distance increasing from zero at 30 to maximum at 45 and thence decreasing to new zero at 60. Slant light now to dial by moving either to either side and hand hides shadow at two quite different points as for example 50 and 20. Indeed at any two quite different points whatever depending on degree of slant. But however great or small the slant and more or less remote from initial 60 and 30 the new points of zero shadow the space between the two remains one of 30 seconds. The shadow emerges from under hand at any point whatever of its circuit to follow or precede it for the space of 30 seconds. Then disappears infinitely briefly before emerging again to precede or follow it for the space of 30 seconds again. And so on and on. This would seem to be the one constant. For the very distance itself between hand and shadow varies as the degree of slant. But however great or small this distance it invariably waxes and wanes from nothing to a maximum 15 seconds later and to nothing again 15 seconds later again respectively. And so on and on. This would seem to be a second constant. More might have been observed on the subject of this second hand and its shadow in their seemingly endless parallel rotation round and round the dial and other variables and constants brought to light and errors if any corrected in what had seemed so far. But unable to continue you bow your head back to where it was and with closed eyes return to the woes of your kind. Dawn finds you still in this position. The low sun shines on you through the eastern window and flings all along the floor your shadow and that of the lamp left lit above you. And those of other objects also.

What visions in the dark of light! Who exclaims thus? Who asks who exclaims, What visions in the shadeless dark of light and shade! Yet another still? Devising it all for company. What a further addition to company that would be! Yet another still devising it all for company. Quick leave him.

Somehow at any price to make an end when you could go out no more you sat huddled in the dark. Having covered in your day some twenty-five thousand leagues or roughly thrice the girdle. And never once over-stepped a radius of one from home. Home! So sat waiting to be purged the old lutist cause of Dante's first quarter-smile and now perhaps singing praises with some section of the blest at last. To whom here in any case farewell. The place is windowless. When as you sometimes do to void the fluid you open your eyes dark lessens. Thus you now on your back in the dark once sat huddled there your body having shown you it could go out no more. Out no more to walk the little winding back roads and interjacent pastures now alive with flocks and now deserted. With at your elbow for long years your father's shade in his old tramping rags and then for long years alone. Adding step after step to the ever mounting sum of those already accomplished. Halting now and then with bowed head to fix the score. Then on from nought anew. Huddled thus you find yourself imagining you are not alone while knowing full well that nothing has occurred to make this possible. The process continues none the less lapped as it were in its meaninglessness. You do not murmur in so many words, I know this doomed to fail and yet persist. No. For the first personal singular and a fortiori plural pronoun had never any place in your vocabulary. But without a word you view yourself to this effect as you would a stranger suffering say from Hodgkin's disease or if you prefer Percival Pott's surprised at prayer. From time to time with unexpected grace you lie. Simultaneously the various parts set out. The arms unclasp the knees. The head lifts. The legs start to straighten. The trunk tilts backwards. And together these and countless others continue on their respective ways till they can go no further and together come to rest. Supine now you resume your fable where the act of lying cut it short.

And persist till the converse operation cuts it short again. So in the dark now huddled and now supine you toil in vain. And just as from the former position to the latter the shift grows easier in time and more alacrious so from the latter to the former the reverse is true. Till from the occasional relief it was supineness becomes habitual and finally the rule. You now on your back in the dark shall not rise to your arse again to clasp your legs in your arms and bow down your head till it can bow down no further. But with face upturned for good labour in vain at your fable. Till finally you hear how words are coming to an end. With every inane word a little nearer to the last. And how the fable too. The fable of one with you in the dark. The fable of one fabling of one with you in the dark. And how better in the end labour lost and silence. And you as you always were.

Alone.

Ill Seen Ill Said

From where she lies she sees Venus rise. On. From where she lies when the skies are clear she sees Venus rise followed by the sun. Then she rails at the source of all life. On. At evening when the skies are clear she savours its star's revenge. At the other window. Rigid upright on her old chair she watches for the radiant one. Her old deal spindlebacked kitchen chair. It emerges from out the last rays and sinking ever brighter is engulfed in its turn. On. She sits on erect and rigid in the deepening gloom. Such helplessness to move she cannot help. Heading on foot for a particular point often she freezes on the way. Unable till long after to move on not knowing whither or for what purpose. Down on her knees especially she finds it hard not to remain so forever. Hand resting on hand on some convenient support. Such as the foot of her bed. And on them her head. There then she sits as though turned to stone face to the night. Save for the white of her hair and faintly bluish white of face and hands all is black. For an eye having no need of light to see. All this in the present as had she the misfortune to be still of this world.

The cabin. Its situation. Careful. On. At the inexistent centre of a formless place. Rather more circular than otherwise finally. Flat to be sure. To cross it in a straight line takes her from five to ten minutes. Depending on her speed and radius taken. Here she who loves to—here she who now can only stray never strays. Stones increasingly abound. Ever scanter even the rankest weed. Meagre pastures hem it round on which it slowly gains. With none to gainsay. To have gainsaid. As if doomed to spread. How come a cabin in such a place? How came? Careful. Before replying that in the far past at the time of its building there was clover growing to its very walls. Implying furthermore that it the culprit. And from it as from an evil core that the what is the wrong word the evil spread. And none to urge—none to have urged its demolition. As if doomed to endure. Question answered. Chalkstones of striking effect in the light of the moon. Let it be in opposition when the skies are clear. Quick then still under the spell of Venus quick to the other window to see the other marvel rise. How whiter and whiter as it climbs it whitens more and more the stones. Rigid with face and hands against the pane she stands and marvels long.

The two zones form a roughly circular whole. As though outlined by a trembling hand. Diameter. Careful. Say one furlong. On an average. Beyond the unknown. Mercifully. The feeling at times of being below sea level. Especially at night when the skies are clear. Invisible nearby sea. Inaudible. The entire surface under grass. Once clear of the zone of stones. Save where it has receded from the chalky soil. Innumerable white scabs all shapes and sizes. Of striking effect in the light of the moon. In the way of animals ovines only. After long hesitation. They are white and make do with little. Whence suddenly come no knowing nor whither as suddenly gone. Unshepherded they stray as they list. Flowers? Careful. Alone the odd crocus still at lambing time. And man? Shut of at last? Alas no. For will she not be surprised one day to find him gone? Surprised no she is beyond surprise. How many? A figure come what may. Twelve. Wherewith to furnish the horizon's narrow round. She raises her eyes and sees one. Turns away and sees another. So on. Always afar. Still or receding. She never once saw one come towards her. Or she forgets. She forgets. Are they always the same? Do they see her? Enough.

A moor would have better met the case. Were there a case better to meet. There had to be lambs. Rightly or wrongly. A moor would have allowed of them. Lambs for their whiteness. And for other reasons as yet obscure. Another reason. And so that there may be none. At lambing time. That from one moment to the next she may raise her eyes to find them gone. A moor would have allowed of them. In any case too late. And what lambs. No trace of frolic. White splotches in the grass. Aloof from the unheeding ewes. Still. Then a moment straying. Then still again. To think there is still life in this age. Gently gently.

She is drawn to a certain spot. At times. There stands a stone. It it is draws her. Rounded rectangular block three times as high as wide. Four. Her stature now. Her lowly stature. When it draws she must to it. She cannot see it from her door. Blindfold she could find her way. With herself she has no more converse. Never had much. Now none. As had she the misfortune to be still of this world. But when the stone draws then to her feet the prayer, Take her. Especially at night when the skies are clear. With moon or without. They take her and hall her before it. There she too as if of stone. But black. Sometimes in the light of the moon. Mostly of the stars alone. Does she envy it?

To the imaginary stranger the dwelling appears deserted. Under constant watch it betrays no sign of life. The eye glued to one or the other window has nothing but black drapes for its pains. Motionless against the door he listens long. No sound. Knocks. No answer. Watches all night in vain for the least glimmer. Returns at last to his own and avows, No one. She shows herself only to her own. But she has no own. Yes yes she has one. And who has her.

There was a time when she did not appear in the zone of stones. A long time. Was not therefore to be seen going out or coming in. When she appeared only in the pastures. Was not therefore to be seen leaving them. Save as though by enchantment. But little by little she began to appear. In the zone of stones. First darkly. Then more and more plain. Till in detail she could be seen crossing the threshold both ways and closing the door behind her. Then a time when within her walls she did not appear. A long time. But little by little she began to appear. Within her walls. Darkly. Time truth to tell still current. Though she within them no more. This long time.

Yes within her walls so far at the window only. At one or the other window. Rapt before the sky. And only half seen so far a pallet and a ghostly chair. Ill half seen. And how in her faint comings and goings she suddenly stops dead. And how hard set to rise up from off her knees. But there too little by little she begins to appear more plain. Within her walls. As well as other objects. Such as under her pillow—such as deep in some recess this still shadowy album. Perhaps in time be by her when she takes it on her knees. See the old fingers fumble through the pages. And what scenes they can possibly be that draw the head down lower still and hold it in thrall. In the meantime who knows no more than withered flowers. No more!

But quick seize her where she is best to be seized. In the pastures far from shelter. She crosses the zone of stones and is there. Clearer and clearer as she goes. Quick seeing she goes out less and less. And so to say only in winter. Winter in her winter haunts she wanders. Far from shelter. Head bowed she makes her slow wavering way across the snow. It is evening. Yet again. On the snow her long shadow keeps her company. The others are there. All about. The twelve. Afar. Still or receding. She raises her eyes and sees one. Turns away and sees another. Again she stops dead. Now the moment or never. But something forbids. Just time to begin to glimpse a fringe of black veil. The face must wait. Just time before the eye cast down. Where nothing to be seen in the grazing rays but snow. And how all about little by little her footprints are effaced.

What is it defends her? Even from her own. Averts the intent gaze. Incriminates the dearly won. Forbids divining her. What but life ending. Hers. The other's. But so otherwise. She needs nothing. Nothing utterable. Whereas the other. How need in the end? But how? How need in the end?

Times when she is gone. Long lapses of time. At crocus time it would be making for the distant tomb. To have that on the imagination! On top of the rest. Bearing by the stem or round her arm the cross or wreath. But she can be gone at any time. From one moment of the year to the next suddenly no longer there. No longer anywhere to be seen. Nor by the eye of flesh nor by the other. Then as suddenly there again. Long after. So on. Any other would renounce. Avow, No one. No one more. Any other than this other. In wait for her to reappear. In order to resume. Resume the— what is the word? What the wrong word?

Riveted to some detail of the desert the eye fills with tears. Imagination at wit's end spreads its sad wings. Gone she hears one night the sea as if afar. Plucks up her long skirt to make better haste and discovers her boots and stockings to the calf. Tears. Last example the flagstone before her door that by dint by dint her little weight has grooved. Tears.

Before left for the stockings the boots have time to be ill buttoned. Weeping over as weeping will see now the buttonhook larger than life. Of tarnished silver pisciform it hangs by its hook from a nail. It trembles faintly without cease. As if here without cease the earth faintly quaked. The oval handle is wrought to a semblance of scales. The shank a little bent leads up to the hook the eye so far still dry. A lifetime of hooking has lessened its curvature. To the point at certain moments of its seeming unfit for service. Child's play with a pliers to restore it. Was there once a time she did? Careful. Once once in a way. Till she could no more. No more bring the jaws together. Oh not for weakness. Since when it hangs useless from the nail. Trembling imperceptibly without cease. Silver shimmers some evenings when the skies are clear. Close-up then. In which in defiance of reason the nail prevails. Long this image till suddenly it blurs.

She is there. Again. Let the eye from its vigil be distracted a moment. At break or close of day. Distracted by the sky. By something in the sky. So that when it resumes the curtain may be no longer closed. Opened by her to let her see the sky. But even without that she is there. Without the curtain's being opened. Suddenly open. A flash. The suddenness of all! She still without stopping. On her way without starting. Gone without going. Back without returning. Suddenly it is evening. Or dawn. The eye rivets the bare window. Nothing in the sky will distract it from it more. While she from within looks her fill. Pfft occulted. Nothing having stirred.

Already all confusion. Things and imaginings. As of always. Confusion amounting to nothing. Despite precautions. If only she could be pure figment. Unalloyed. This old so dying woman. So dead. In the madhouse of the skull and nowhere else. Where no more precautions to be taken. No precautions possible. Cooped up there with the rest. Hovel and stones. The lot. And the eye. How simple all then. If only all could be pure figment. Neither be nor been nor by any shift to be. Gently gently. On. Careful.

Here to the rescue two lights. Two small skylights. Set in the high-pitched roof on either side. Each shedding dim light. No ceiling therefore. Necessarily. Otherwise with the curtains closed she would be in the dark. Day and night in the dark. And what of it? She is done with raising her eyes. Nearly done. But when she lies with them open she can just make out the rafters. In the dim light the skylights shed. An even dimmer light. As the panes slowly dimmen. All in black she comes and goes. The hem of her long black skirt brushes the floor. But most often she is still. Standing or sitting. Lying or on her knees. In the dim light the skylights shed. Otherwise with the curtains closed for preference she would be in the dark. In the dark day and night.

Next to emerge from the shadows an inner wall. Only slowly to dissolve in favour of a single space. East the bed. West the chair. A place divided by her use of it alone. How more desirable in every way an interior of a piece. The eye breathes again but not for long. For slowly it emerges again. Rises from the floor and slowly up to lose itself in the gloom. The semigloom. It is evening. The buttonhook glimmers in the last rays. The pallet scarce to be seen.

Weary of the inanimate the eye in her absence falls back on the twelve. Out of her sight as she of theirs. Alone turn where she may she keeps her eyes fixed on the ground. On the way at her feet where it has come to a stop. Winter evening. Not to be precise. All so bygone. To the twelve then for want of better the widowed eye. No matter which. In the distance stiff he stands facing front and the setting sun. Dark greatcoat reaching to the ground. Antiquated block hat. Finally the face caught full in the last rays. Quick enlarge and devour before night falls.

Having no need of light to see the eye makes haste. Before night falls. So it is. So itself belies. Then glutted—then torpid under its lid makes way for unreason. What if not her do they ring around? Careful. She who looks up no more looks up and sees them. Some among them. Still or receding. Receding. Those too closely seen who move to preserve their distance. While at the same time others advance. Those in the wake of her wandering. She never once saw one come towards her. Or she forgets. She forgets. Now some do. Towards but never nearer. Thus they keep her in the centre. More or less. What then if not her do they ring around? In their ring whence she disappears unhindered. Whence they let her disappear. Instead of disappearing in her company. So the unreasoning goes. While the eye digests its pittance. In its private dark. In the general dark.

As hope expires of her ever reappearing she reappears. At first sight little changed. It is evening. It will always be evening. When not night. She emerges at the fringe of the pastures and sets forward across them. Slowly with fluttering step as if wanting mass. Suddenly still and as suddenly on her way again. At this rate it will be black night before she reaches home. Home! But time slows all this while. Suits its speed to hers. Whence from beginning to end of her course no loss or but little of twilight. A matter at most of a candle or two. Bearing south as best she can she casts towards the moon to come her long black shadow. They come at last to the door holding a great key. At the same instant night. When not evening night.

Head bowed she stands exposed facing east. All dead still. All save hanging from a finger the old key polished by use. Trembling it faintly shimmers in the light of the moon.

Wooed from below the face consents at last. In the dim light reflected by the flag. Calm slab worn and polished by agelong comings and goings. Livid pallor. Not a wrinkle. How serene it seems this ancient mask. Worthy those worn by certain newly dead. True the light leaves to be desired. The lids occult the longed-for eyes. Time will tell them washen blue. Where tears perhaps not for nothing. Unimaginable tears of old. Lashes jet black remains of the brunette she was. Perhaps once was. When yet a lass. Yet brunette. Skipping the nose at the call of the lips these no sooner broached are withdrawn. The slab having darkened with the darkening sky. Black night henceforward. And at dawn an empty place. With no means of knowing whether she has gone in or under cover of darkness her ways again.

White stones more plentiful every year. As well say every instant. In a fair way if they persist to bury all. First zone rather more extensive than at first sight ill seen and every year rather more. Of striking effect in the light of the moon these millions of little sepulchres. But in her absence but cold comfort. From it then in the end to the second miscalled pastures. Leprous with white scars where the grass has receded from the chalky soil. In contemplation of this erosion the eye finds solace. Everywhere stone is gaining. Whiteness. More and more every year. As well say every instant. Everywhere every instant whiteness is gaining.

The eye will return to the scene of its betrayals. On centennial leave from where tears freeze. Free again an instant to shed them scalding. On the blest tears once shed. While exulting at the white heap of stone. Ever heaping for want of better on itself. Which if it persist will gain the skies. The moon. Venus.

From the stones she steps down into the pastures. As from one tier of a circus to the next. A gap time will fill. For faster than the stones invade it the other ground upheaves its own. So far in silence. A silence time will break. This great silence evening and night. Then all along the verge the muffled thud of stone on stone. Of those spilling their excess on those emergent. Only now and then at first. Then at ever briefer intervals. Till one continuous din. With none to hear. Decreasing as the levels draw together to silence once again. Evening and night. In the meantime she is suddenly sitting with her feet in the pastures. Were it not for the empty hands on the way who knows to the tomb. Back from it then more likely. On the way back from the tomb. Frozen true to her wont she seems turned to stone. Face to the further confines the eye closes in vain to see. At last they appear an instant. North where she passes them always. Shroud of radiant haze. Where to melt into paradise.

The long white hair stares in a fan. Above and about the impassive face. Stares as if shocked still by some ancient horror. Or by its continuance. Or by another. That leaves the face stonecold. Silence at the eye of the scream. Which say? Ill say. Both. All three. Question answered.

Seated on the stones she is seen from behind. From the waist up. Trunk black rectangle. Nape under frill of black lace. White half halo of hair. Face to the north. The tomb. Eyes on the horizon perhaps. Or closed to see the headstone. The withered crocuses. Endless evening. She lit aslant by the last rays. They make no difference. None to the black of the cloth. None to the white hair. It too dead still. In the still air. Voidlike calm as always. Evening and night. Suffice to watch the grass. How motionless it droops. Till under the relentless eye it shivers. With faintest shiver from its innermost. Equally the hair. Rigidly horrent it shivers at last for the eye about to abandon. And the old body itself. When it seems of stone. Is it not in fact ashiver from head to foot? Let her but go and stand still by the other stone. It white from afar in the pastures. And the eye go from one to the other. Back and forth. What calm then. And what storm. Beneath the weeds' mock calm.

Not possible any longer except as figment. Not endurable. Nothing for it but to close the eye for good and see her. Her and the rest. Close it for good and all and see her to death. Unremittent. In the shack. Over the stones. In the pastures. The haze. At the tomb. And back. And the rest. For good and all. To death. Be shut of it all. On to the next. Next figment. Close it for good this filthy eye of flesh. What forbids? Careful.

Such—such fiasco that folly takes a hand. Such bits and scraps. Seen no matter how and said as seen. Dread of black. Of white. Of void. Let her vanish. And the rest. For good. And the sun. Last rays. And the moon. And Venus. Nothing left but black sky. White earth. Or inversely. No more sky or earth. Finished high and low. Nothing but black and white. Everywhere no matter where. But black. Void. Nothing else. Contemplate that. Not another word. Home at last. Gently gently.

Panic past pass on. The hands. Seen from above. They rest on the pubis intertwined. Strident white. Their faintly leaden tinge killed by the black ground. Suspicion of lace at the wrists. To go with the frill. They tighten then loosen their clasp. Slow systole diastole. And the body that scandal. While its sole hands in view. On its sole pubis. Dead still to be sure. On the chair. After the spectacle. Slowly its spell unbinding. On and on they keep. Tightening and loosening their clasp. Rhythm of a labouring heart. Till when almost despaired of gently part. Suddenly gently. Spreading rise and in midair palms uppermost come to rest. Behold our hollows. Then after a moment as if to hide the lines fall back pronating as they go and light flat on head of thighs. Within an ace of the crotch. It is now the left hand lacks its third finger. A swelling no doubt—a swelling no doubt of the knuckle between first and second phalanges preventing one panic day withdrawal of the ring. The kind called keeper. Still as stones they defy as stones do the eye. Do they as much as feel the clad flesh? Does the clad flesh feel them? Will they then never quiver? This night assuredly not. For before they have—before the eye has time they mist. Who is to blame? Or what? They? The eye? The missing finger? The keeper? The cry? What cry? All five. All six. And the rest. All. All to blame. All.

Winter evening in the pastures. The snow has ceased. Her steps so light they barely leave a trace. Have barely left having ceased. Just enough to be still visible. Adrift the snow. Whither in her head while her feet stray thus? Hither and thither too? Or unswerving to the mirage? And where when she halts? The eye discerns afar a kind of stain. Finally the steep roof whence part of the fresh fall has slid. Under the low lowering sky the north is lost. Obliterated by the snow the twelve are there. Invisible were she to raise her eyes. She on the contrary immaculately black. Not having received a single flake. Nothing needed now but for them to start falling again which therefore they do. First one by one here and there. Then thicker and thicker plumb through the still air. Slowly she disappears. Together with the trace of her steps and that of the distant roof. How find her way home? Home! Even as the homing bird. Safe as the saying is and sound.

All dark in the cabin while she whitens afar. Silence but for the imaginary murmur of flakes beating on the roof. And every now and then a real creak. Her company. Here without having to close the eye sees her afar. Motionless in the snow under the snow. The buttonhook trembles from its nail as if a night like any other. Facing the black curtain the chair exudes its solitude. For want of a fellow-table. Far from it in a corner see suddenly an antique coffer. In its therefore no lesser solitude. It perhaps that creaks. And in its depths who knows the key. The key to close. But this night the chair. Its immovable air. Less than the—more than the empty seat the barred back is piteous. Here if she eats here she sits to eat. The eye closes in the dark and sees her in the end. With her right hand as large as life she holds the edge of the bowl resting on her knees. With her left the spoon dipped in the slop. She waits. For it to cool perhaps. But no. Merely frozen again just as about to begin. At last in a twin movement full of grace she slowly raises the bowl towards her lips while at the same time with equal slowness bowing her head to join it. Having set out at the same instant they meet halfway and there come to rest. Fresh rigor before the first spoonful slobbered largely back into the slop. Others no happier till time to part lips and bowl and slowly back with never a slip to their starting points. As smooth and even fro as to. Now again the rigid Memnon pose. With her right hand she holds the edge of the bowl. With her left the spoon dipped in the slop. So far so good. But before she can proceed she fades and disappears. Nothing now for the staring eye but the chair in its solitude.

One evening she was followed by a lamb. Reared for slaughter like the others it left them to follow her. In the present to conclude. All so bygone. Slaughter apart it is not like the others. Hanging to the ground in matted coils its fleece hides the little shanks. Rather than walk it seems to glide like a toy in tow. It halts at the same instant as she. At the same instant as she strays on. Stock still as she it waits with head like hers extravagantly bowed. Clash of black and white that far from muting the last rays amplify. It is now her puniness leaps to the eye. Thanks it would seem to the lowly creature next her. Brief paradox. For suddenly together they move on. Hither and thither towards the stones. There she turns and sits. Does she see the white body at her feet? Head haught now she gazes into emptiness. That profusion. Or with closed eyes sees the tomb. The lamb goes no further. Alone night fallen she makes for home. Home! As straight as were it to be seen.

Was it ever over and done with questions? Dead the whole brood no sooner hatched. Long before. In the egg. Long before. Over and done with answering. With not being able. With not being able not to want to know. With not being able. No. Never. A dream. Question answered.

What remains for the eye exposed to such conditions? To such vicissitude of hardly there and wholly gone. Why none but to open no more. Till all done. She done. Or left undone. Tenement and unreason. No more unless to rest. In the outward and so-called visible. That daub. Quick again to the brim the old nausea and shut again. On her. Till she be whole. Or abort. Question answered.

The coffer. Empty after long nocturnal search. Nothing. Save in the end in a cranny of dust a scrap of paper. Jagged along one edge as if torn from a diary. On its yellowed face in barely legible ink two letters followed by a number. Tu 17. Or Th. Tu or Th 17. Otherwise blank. Otherwise empty.

She reemerges on her back. Dead still. Evening and night. Dead still on her back evening and night. The bed. Careful. A pallet? Hardly if head as ill seen when on her knees. Praying if she prays. Pah she has only to grovel deeper. Or grovel elsewhere. Before the chair. Or the coffer. Or at the edge of the pastures with her head on the stones. A pallet then flat on the floor. No pillow. Hidden from chin to foot under a black covering she offers her face alone. Alone! Face defenceless evening and night. Quick the eyes. The moment they open. Suddenly they are there. Nothing having stirred. One is enough. One staring eye. Gaping pupil thinly nimbed with washen blue. No trace of humour. None any more. Unseeing. As if dazed by what seen behind the lids. The other plumbs its dark. Then opens in its turn. Dazed in its turn.

Incontinent the void. The zenith. Evening again. When not night it will be evening. Death again of deathless day. On the one hand embers. On the other ashes. Day without end won and lost. Unseen.

On resumption the head is covered. No matter. No matter now. Such the confusion now between real and—how say its contrary? No matter. That old tandem. Such now the confusion between them once so twain. And such the farrago from eye to mind. For it to make what sad sense of it may. No matter now. Such equal liars both. Real and—how ill say its contrary? The counter-poison.

Still fresh the coffer fiasco what now of all things but a trapdoor. So cunningly contrived that even to the lidded eye it scarcely shows. Careful. Raise it at once and risk another rebuff? No question. Simply savour in advance with in mind the grisly cupboard its conceivable contents. For the first time then wooden floor. Its boards in line with the trap's designed to conceal it. Promising this flagrant concern with camouflage. But beware. Question by the way what wood of all woods? Ebony why not? Ebony boards. Black on black the brushing skirt. Stark the skeleton chair death-paler than life.

While head included she lies hidden time for a turn in the pastures. No shock were she already dead. As of course she is. But in the meantime more convenient not. Still living then she lies hidden. Having for some reason covered her head. Or for no reason. Night. When not evening night. Winter night. No snow. For the sake of variety. To vary the monotony. The limp grass strangely rigid under the weight of the rime. Clawed by the long black skirt how if but heard it must murmur. Moonless star-studded sky reflected in the erosions filmed with ice. The silence merges into music infinitely far and as unbroken as silence. Ceaseless celestial winds in unison. For all all matters now. The stones gleam faintly afar and the cabin walls seen white at last. Said white. The guardians—the twelve are there but not at full muster. Well! Above all not understand. Simply note now those still faithful have moved apart. Such ill seen that night in the pastures. While head included she lies hidden. Under on closer inspection a long greatcoat. A man's by the buttons. The button-holes. Eyes closed does she see him?

White walls. High time. White as new. No wind. Not a breath. Unbeaten on by all that comes beating down. And mystery the sun has spared them. The sun that once beat down. So east and west sides the required clash. South gable no problem. But the other. That door. Careful. Black too? Black too. And the roof. Slates. More. Small slates black too brought from a ruined mansion. What tales had they tongues to tell. Their long tale told. Such the dwelling ill seen ill said. Outwardly. High time.

Changed the stone that draws her when revisited alone. Or she who changes it when side by side. Now alone it leans. Backward or forward as the case may be. Is it to nature alone it owes its rough-hewn air? Or to some too human hand forced to desist? As Michelangelo's from the regicide's bust. If there may not be no more questions let there at least be no more answers. Granite of no common variety assuredly. Black as jade the jasper that flecks its whiteness. On its what is the wrong word its uptilted face obscure graffiti. Scrawled by the ages for the eye to solicit in vain. Winter evenings on her doorstep she imagines she can see it glitter afar. When from their source in the west-south-west the last rays rake its averse face. Such ill seen the stone alone where it stands at the far fringe of the pastures. On her way out with the flowers as unerring as best she can she lingers by it. As on her way back with empty hands. Lingers by it a while on her way on. Towards the one or other abode. As unerring as best she can.

See them again side by side. Not quite touching. Lit aslant by the latest last rays they cast to the east-north-east their long parallel shadows. Evening therefore. Winter evening. It will always be evening. Always winter. When not night. Winter night. No more lambs. No more flowers. Empty-handed she shall go to the tomb. Until she go no more. Or no more return. So much for that. Undistinguishable the twin shadows. Till one at length more dense as if of a body better opaque. At length more still. As faintly at length the other trembles under the staring gaze. Throughout this confrontation the sun stands still. That is to say the earth. Not to recoil on until the parting. Then on its face over the pastures and then the stones the still living shadow slowly glides. Lengthening and fading more and more. But never quite away. Under the hovering eye.

Close-up of a dial. Nothing else. White disc divided in minutes. Unless it be in seconds. Sixty black dots. No figure. One hand only. Finest of fine black darts. It advances by fits and starts. No tick. Leaps from dot to dot with so lightning a leap that but for its new position it had not stirred. Whole nights may pass as may but a fraction of a second or any intermediate lapse of time soever before it flings itself from one degree to the next. None at any moment overleaping in all fairness be it said. Let it when discovered be pointing east. Having thus covered after its fashion assuming the instrument plumb the first quarter of its latest hour. Unless it be its latest minute. Then doubt certain—then despair certain nights of its ever attaining the last. Ever regaining north.

She reappears at evening at her window. When not night evening. If she will see Venus again she must open it. Well! First draw aside the curtain and then open. Head bowed she waits to be able. Mindful perhaps of evenings when she was able too late. Black night fallen. But no. In her head too pure wait. The curtain. Seen closer thanks to this hiatus it reveals itself at last for what it is. A black greatcoat. Hooked by its tails from the rod it hangs sprawling inside out like a carcass in a butcher's stall. Or better inside in for the pathos of the dangling arms. Same infinitesimal quaver as the buttonhook and passim. Another novelty the chair drawn up to the window. This to raise the line of sight on the fair prey loftier when first sighted than at first sight ill seen. What empty space henceforward. For long pacing to and fro in the gloom. Suddenly in a single gesture she snatches aside the coat and to again on a sky as black as it. And then? Careful. Have her sit? Lie? Kneel? Go? She too vacillates. Till in the end the back and forth prevails. Sends her wavering north and south from wall to wall. In the kindly dark.

She is vanishing. With the rest. The already ill seen bedimmed and ill seen again annulled. The mind betrays the treacherous eyes and the treacherous word their treacheries. Haze sole certitude. The same that reigns beyond the pastures. It gains them already. It will gain the zone of stones. Then the dwelling through all its chinks. The eye will close in vain. To see but haze. Not even. Be itself but haze. How can it ever be said? Quick how ever ill said before it submerges all. Light. In one treacherous word. Dazzling haze. Light in its might at last. Where no more to be seen. To be said. Gently gently.

The face yet again in the light of the last rays. No loss of pallor. None of cold. Suspended on the verge for this sight the westering sun. That is the eastering earth. The thin lips seem as if never again to part. Peeping from their join a suspicion of pulp. Unlikely site of olden kisses given and received. Or given only. Or received only. Impressive above all the corners imperceptibly upcurved. A smile? Is it possible? Ghost of an ancient smile smiled finally once and for all. Such ill half seen the mouth in the light of the last rays. Suddenly they leave it. Rather it leaves them. Off again to the dark. There to smile on. If smile is what it is.

Reexamined rid of light the mouth changes. Unexplainably. Lips as before. Same closure. Same hint of extruding pulp. At the corners same imperceptible laxness. In a word the smile still there if smile is what it is. Neither more nor less. Less! And yet no longer the same. True that light distorts. Particularly sunset. That mockery. True too that the eyes then agaze for the viewless planet are now closed. On other viewlessness. Of which more if ever anon. There the explanation at last. This same smile established with eyes open is with them closed no longer the same. Though between the two inspections the mouth unchanged. Utterly. Good. But in what way no longer the same? What there now that was not there? What there no more that was? Enough. Away.

Back after many winters. Long after in this endless winter. This endless heart of winter. Too soon. She as when fled. Where as when fled. Still or again. Eyes closed in the dark. To the dark. In their own dark. On the lips same minute smile. If smile is what it is. In short alive as she alone knows how neither more nor less. Less! Compared to true stone. Within as sadly as before all as at first sight ill seen. With the happy exception of the lights' enhanced opacity. Dim the light of day from them were day again to dawn. Without on the other hand some progress. Towards unbroken night. Universal stone. Day no sooner risen fallen. Scrapped all the ill seen ill said. The eye has changed. And its drivelling scribe. Absence has changed them. Not enough. Time to go again. Where still more to change. Whence back too soon. Changed but not enough. Strangers but not enough. To all the ill seen ill said. Then back again. Disarmed for to finish with it all at last. With her and her rags of sky and earth. And if again too soon go again. Change still more again. Then back again. Barring impediment. Ah. So on. Till fit to finish with it all at last. All the trash. In unbroken night. Universal stone. So first go. But first see her again. As when fled. And the abode. That under the changed eye it too may change. Begin. Just one parting look. Before all meet again. Then go. Barring impediment. Ah.

But see she suddenly no longer there. Where suddenly fled. Quick then the chair before she reappears. At length. Every angle. With what one word convey its change? Careful. Less. Ah the sweet one word. Less. It is less. The same but less. Whencesoever the glare. True that the light. See now how words too. A few drops mishaphazard. Then strangury. To say the least. Less. It will end by being no more. By never having been. Divine prospect. True that the light.

Suddenly enough and way for remembrance. Closed again to that end the vile jelly or opened again or left as it was however that was. Till all recalled. First finally by far hanging from their skirts two black greatcoats. Followed by the first hazy outlines of what possibly a hutch when suddenly enough. Remembrance! When all worse there than when first ill seen. The pallet. The chair. The coffer. The trap. Alone the eye has changed. Alone can cause to change. In the meantime nothing wanting. Wrong. The buttonhook. The nail. Wrong. There they are again. Still. Worse there than ever. Unchanged for the worse. Ope eye and at them to begin. But first the partition. It rid they too would be. It less they by as much.

It of all the properties doubtless the least obdurate. See the instant see it again when unaided it dissolved. So to say of itself. With no help from the eye. Not till long after to reappear. As if reluctantly. For what reason? For one not far to seek. For others then said obscure. One other above all. One other still far to seek. Analogy of the heart? The skull? Hear from here the howls of laughter of the damned.

Enough. Quicker. Quick see how all in keeping with the chair. Minimally less. No more. Well on the way to inexistence. As to zero the infinite. Quick say. And of her? As much. Quick find her again. In that black heart. That mock brain.

The sheet. Between tips of trembling fingers. In two. Four. Eight. Old frantic fingers. Not paper any more. Each eighth apart. In two. Four. Finish with the knife. Hack into shreds. Down the plughole. On to the next. White. Quick blacken.

Alone the face remains. Of the rest beneath its covering no trace. During the inspection a sudden sound. Startling without consequence for the gaze the mind awake. How explain it? And without going so far how say it? Far behind the eye the quest begins. What time the event recedes. When suddenly to the rescue it comes again. Forthwith the uncommon common noun collapsion. Reinforced a little later if not enfeebled by the infrequent slumberous. A slumberous collapsion. Two. Then far from the still agonizing eye a gleam of hope. By the grace of these modest beginnings. With in second sight the shack in ruins. To scrute together with the inscrutable face. All curiosity spent.

Later while the face still unyielding another sound of fall but this time sharp. Heightening the fond illusion of general havoc in train. Here a great leap into what brief future remains and summary puncture of that puny balloon. Far ahead to the instant when the coats will have gone from their rods and the buttonhook from its nail. And been hove the sigh no more than that. Sigh upon sigh till all sighed quite away. All the fond trash. Destined before being to be no more than that. Last sighs. Of relief.

Quick beforehand again two mysteries. Not even. Mild shocks. Not even. In such abeyance the mind then. And from then on. First the curtains gone without loss of dark. Sweet foretaste of the joy at journey's end. Second after long hesitation no trace of the fallen where they fell. No trace of all the ado. Alone on the one hand the rods alone. A little bent. And alone on the other most alone the nail. Unimpaired. All set to serve again. Like unto its glorious ancestors. At the place of the skull. One April afternoon. Deposition done.

Full glare now on the face present throughout the recent future. As seen ill seen throughout the past neither more nor less. Less! Collated with its cast it lives beyond a doubt. Were it only by virtue of its imperfect pallor. And imperceptible tremor unworthy of true plaster. Heartening on the other hand the eyes persistently closed. No doubt a record in this position. Unobserved at least till now. Suddenly the look. Nothing having stirred. Look? Too weak a word. Too wrong. Its absence? No better. Unspeakable globe. Unbearable.

Ample time none the less a few seconds for the iris to be lacking. Wholly. As if engulfed by the pupil. And for the sclerotic not to say the white to appear reduced by half. Already that much less at least but at what cost. Soon to be foreseen save unforeseen two black blanks. Fit vent-holes of the soul that jakes. Here reappearance of the skylights opaque to no purpose henceforward. Seeing the black night or better blackness pure and simple that limpid they would shed. Blackness in its might at last. Where no more to be seen. Perforce to be seen.

Absence supreme good and yet. Illumination then go again and on return no more trace. On earth's face. Of what was never. And if by mishap some left then go again. For good again. So on. Till no more trace. On earth's face. Instead of always the same place. Slaving away forever in the same place. At this and that trace. And what if the eye could not? No more tear itself away from the remains of trace. Of what was never. Quick say it suddenly can and farewell say say farewell. If only to the face. Of her tenacious trace.

Decision no sooner reached or rather long after than what is the wrong word? For the last time at last for to end yet again what the wrong word? Than revoked. No but slowly dispelled a little very little like the last wisps of day when the curtain closes. Of itself by slow millimetres or drawn by a phantom hand. Farewell to farewell. Then in that perfect dark foreknell darling sound pip for end begun. First last moment. Grant only enough remain to devour all. Moment by glutton moment. Sky earth the whole kit and boodle. Not another crumb of carrion left. Lick chops and basta. No. One moment more. One last. Grace to breathe that void. Know happiness.

Worstward Ho

On. Say on. Be said on. Somehow on. Till nohow on. Said nohow on.

Say for be said. Missaid. From now say for be missaid.

Say a body. Where none. No mind. Where none. That at least. A place. Where none. For the body. To be in. Move in. Out of. Back into. No. No out. No back. Only in. Stay in. On in. Still.

All of old. Nothing else ever. Ever tried. Ever failed. No matter. Try again. Fail again. Fail better.

First the body. No. First the place. No. First both. Now either. Now the other. Sick of the either try the other. Sick of it back sick of the either. So on. Somehow on. Till sick of both. Throw up and go. Where neither. Till sick of there. Throw up and back. The body again. Where none. The place again. Where none. Try again. Fail again. Better again. Or better worse. Fail worse again. Still worse again. Till sick for good. Throw up for good. Go for good. Where neither for good. Good and all.

It stands. What? Yes. Say it stands. Had to up in the end and stand. Say bones. No bones but say bones. Say ground. No ground but say ground. So as to say pain. No mind and pain? Say yes that the bones may pain till no choice but stand. Somehow up and stand. Or better worse remains. Say remains of mind where none to permit of pain. Pain of bones till no choice but up and stand. Somehow up. Somehow stand. Remains of mind where none for the sake of pain. Here of bones. Other examples if needs must. Of pain. Relief from. Change of.

All of old. Nothing else ever. But never so failed. Worse failed. With care never worse failed.

Dim light source unknown. Know minimum. Know nothing no. Too much to hope. At most mere minimum. Mere-most minimum.

No choice but stand. Somehow up and stand. Somehow stand. That or groan. The groan so long on its way. No. No groan. Simply pain. Simply up. A time when try how. Try see. Try say. How first it lay. Then somehow knelt. Bit by bit. Then on from there. Bit by bit. Till up at last. Not now. Fail better worse now.

Another. Say another. Head sunk on crippled hands. Vertex vertical. Eyes clenched. Seat of all. Germ of all.

No future in this. Alas yes.

It stands. See in the dim void how at last it stands. In the dim light source unknown. Before the downcast eyes. Clenched eyes. Staring eyes. Clenched staring eyes.

That shade. Once lying. Now standing. That a body? Yes. Say that a body. Somehow standing. In the dim void.

A place. Where none. A time when try see. Try say. How small. How vast. How if not boundless bounded. Whence the dim. Not now. Know better now. Unknow better now. Know only no out of. No knowing how know only no out of. Into only. Hence another. Another place where none.

Whither once whence no return. No. No place but the one. None but the one where none. Whence never once in. Somehow in. Beyondless. Thenceless there. Thitherless there. Thenceless thitherless there.

Where then but there see—

See for be seen. Misseen. From now see for be misseen.

Where then but there see now—

First back turned the shade astand. In the dim void see first back turned the shade astand. Still.

Where then but there see now another. Bit by bit an old man and child. In the dim void bit by bit an old man and child. Any other would do as ill.

Hand in hand with equal plod they go. In the free hands—no. Free empty hands. Backs turned both bowed with equal plod they go. The child hand raised to reach the holding hand. Hold the old holding hand. Hold and be held. Plod on and never recede. Slowly with never a pause plod on and never recede. Backs turned. Both bowed. Joined by held holding hands. Plod on as one. One shade. Another shade.

Head sunk on crippled hands. Clenched staring eyes. At in the dim void shades. One astand at rest. One old man and child. At rest plodding on. Any others would do as ill. Almost any. Almost as ill.

They fade. Now the one. Now the twain. Now both. Fade back. Now the one. Now the twain. Now both. Fade? No. Sudden go. Sudden back. Now the one. Now the twain. Now both.

Unchanged? Sudden back unchanged? Yes. Say yes. Each time unchanged. Somehow unchanged. Till no. Till say no. Sudden back changed. Somehow changed. Each time somehow changed.

The dim. The void. Gone too? Back too? No. Say no. Never gone. Never back. Till yes. Till say yes. Gone too. Back too. The dim. The void. Now the one. Now the other. Now both. Sudden gone. Sudden back. Unchanged? Sudden back unchanged? Yes. Say yes. Each time unchanged. Somehow unchanged. Till no. Till say no. Sudden back changed. Somehow changed. Each time somehow changed.

First sudden gone the one. First sudden back. Unchanged. Say now unchanged. So far unchanged. Back turned. Head sunk. Vertex vertical in hat. Cocked back of black brim alone. Back of black greatcoat cut off midthigh. Kneeling. Better kneeling. Better worse kneeling. Say now kneeling. From now kneeling. Could rise but to its knees. Sudden gone sudden back unchanged back turned head sunk dark shade on unseen knees. Still.

Next sudden gone the twain. Next sudden back. Unchanged. Say now unchanged. So far unchanged. Backs turned. Heads sunk. Dim hair. Dim white and hair so fair that in that dim light dim white. Black greatcoats to heels. Dim black. Bootheels. Now the two right. Now the two left. As on with equal plod they go. No ground. Plod as on void. Dim hands. Dim white. Two free and two as one. So sudden gone sudden back unchanged as one dark shade plod unreceding on.

The dim. Far and wide the same. High and low. Unchanging. Say now unchanging. Whence no knowing. No saying. Say only such dim light as never. On all. Say a grot in that void. A gulf. Then in that grot or gulf such dimmest light as never. Whence no knowing. No saying.

The void. Unchanging. Say now unchanging. Void were not the one. The twain. So far were not the one and twain. So far.

The void. How try say? How try fail? No try no fail. Say only—

First the bones. On back to them. Preying since first said on foresaid remains. The ground. The pain. No bones. No ground. No pain. Why up unknown. At all costs unknown. If ever down. No choice but up if ever down. Or never down. Forever kneeling. Better forever kneeling. Better worse forever kneeling. Say from now forever kneeling. So far from now forever kneeling. So far.

The void. Before the staring eyes. Stare where they may. Far and wide. High and low. That narrow field. Know no more. See no more. Say no more. That alone. That little much of void alone.

On back to unsay void can go. Void cannot go. Save dim go. Then all go. All not already gone. Till dim back. Then all back. All not still gone. The one can go. The twain can go. Dim can go. Void cannot go. Save dim go. Then all go.

On back better worse to fail the head said seat of all. Germ of all. All? If of all of it too. Where if not there it too? There in the sunken head the sunken head. The hands. The eyes. Shade with the other shades. In the same dim. The same narrow void. Before the staring eyes. Where it too if not there too? Ask not. No. Ask in vain. Better worse so.

The head. Ask not if it can go. Say no. Unasking no. It cannot go. Save dim go. Then all go. Oh dim go. Go for good. All for good. Good and all.

Whose words? Ask in vain. Or not in vain if say no knowing. No saying. No words for him whose words. Him? One. No words for one whose words. One? It. No words for it whose words. Better worse so.

Something not wrong with one. Meaning—meaning!—meaning the kneeling one. From now one for the kneeling one. As from now two for the twain. The as one plodding twain. As from now three for the head. The head as first said missaid. So from now. For to gain time. Time to lose. Gain time to lose. As the soul once. The world once.

Something not wrong with one. Then with two. Then with three. So on. Something not wrong with all. Far from wrong. Far far from wrong.

The words too whosesoever. What room for worse! How almost true they sometimes almost ring! How wanting in inanity! Say the night is young alas and take heart. Or better worse say still a watch of night alas to come. A rest of last watch to come. And take heart.

First one. First try fail better one. Something there badly not wrong. Not that as it is it is not bad. The no face bad. The no hands bad. The no—. Enough. A pox on bad. Mere bad. Way for worse. Pending worse still. First worse. Mere worse. Pending worse still. Add a—. Add? Never. Bow it down. Be it bowed down. Deep down. Head in hat gone. More back gone. Greatcoat cut off higher. Nothing from pelvis down. Nothing but bowed back. Topless baseless hindtrunk. Dim black. On unseen knees. In the dim void. Better worse so. Pending worse still.

Next try fail better two. The twain. Bad as it is as it is. Bad the no—

First back on to three. Not yet to try worsen. Simply be there again. There in that head in that head. Be it again. That head in that head. Clenched eyes clamped to it alone. Alone? No. Too. To it too. The sunken skull. The crippled hands. Clenched staring eyes. Clenched eyes clamped to clenched staring eyes. Be that shade again. In that shade again. With the other shades. Worsening shades. In the dim void.

Next—

First how all at once. In that stare. The worsened one. The worsening two. And what yet to worsen. To try worsen. Itself. The dim. The void. All at once in that stare. Clenched eyes clamped to all.

Next two. From bad to worsen. Try worsen. From merely bad. Add—. Add? Never. The boots. Better worse bootless. Bare heels. Now the two right. Now the two left. Left right left right on. Barefoot unreceding on. Better worse so. A little better worse than nothing so.

Next the so-said seat and germ of all. Those hands! That head! That near true ring! Away. Full face from now. No hands. No face. Skull and stare alone. Scene and seer of all.

On. Stare on. Say on. Be on. Somehow on. Anyhow on. Till dim gone. At long last gone. All at long last gone. For bad and all. For poor best worse and all.

Dim whence unknown. At all costs unknown. Unchanging. Say now unchanging. Far and wide. High and low. Say a pipe in that void. A tube. Sealed. Then in that pipe or tube that selfsame dim. Old dim. When ever what else? Where all always to be seen. Of the nothing to be seen. Dimly seen. Nothing ever unseen. Of the nothing to be seen. Dimly seen. Worsen that?

Next the so-said void. The so-missaid. That narrow field. Rife with shades. Well so-missaid. Shade-ridden void. How better worse so-missay?

Add others. Add? Never. Till if needs must. Nothing to those so far. Dimly so far. Them only lessen. But with them as they lessen others. As they worsen. If needs must. Others to lessen. To worsen. Till dim go. At long last go. For worst and all.

On. Somehow on. Anyhow on. Say all gone. So on. In the skull all gone. All? No. All cannot go. Till dim go. Say then but the two gone. In the skull one and two gone. From the void. From the stare. In the skull all save the skull gone. The stare. Alone in the dim void. Alone to be seen. Dimly seen. In the skull the skull alone to be seen. The staring eyes. Dimly seen. By the staring eyes. The others gone. Long sudden gone. Then sudden back. Unchanged. Say now unchanged. First one. Then two. Or first two. Then one. Or together. Then all again together. The bowed back. The plodding twain. The skull. The stare. All back in the skull together. Unchanged. Stare clamped to all. In the dim void.

The eyes. Time to—

First on back to unsay dim can go. Somehow on back. Dim cannot go. Dim to go must go for good. True then dim can go. If but for good. One can go not for good. Two too. Three no if not for good. With dim gone for good. Void no if not for good. With all gone for good. Dim can worsen. Somehow worsen. Go no. If not for good.

The eyes. Time to try worsen. Somehow try worsen. Unclench. Say staring open. All white and pupil. Dim white. White? No. All pupil. Dim black holes. Unwavering gaping. Be they so said. With worsening words. From now so. Better than nothing so bettered for the worse.

Still dim still on. So long as still dim still somehow on. Anyhow on. With worsening words. Worsening stare. For the nothing to be seen. At the nothing to be seen. Dimly seen. As now by way of somehow on where in the nowhere all together? All three together. Where there all three at last worse seen? Bowed back alone. Barefoot plodding twain. Skull and lidless stare. Where in the narrow vast? Say only vasts apart. In that narrow void vasts of void apart. Worse better later.

What when words gone? None for what then. But say by way of somehow on somehow with sight to do. With less of sight. Still dim and yet—. No. Nohow so on. Say better worse words gone when nohow on. Still dim and nohow on. All seen and nohow on. What words for what then? None for what then. No words for what when words gone. For what when nohow on. Somehow nohow on.

Worsening words whose unknown. Whence unknown. At all costs unknown. Now for to say as worst they may only they only they. Dim void shades all they. Nothing save what they say. Somehow say. Nothing save they. What they say. Whosesoever whencesoever say. As worst they may fail ever worse to say.

Remains of mind then still. Enough still. Somewhose somewhere some-how enough still. No mind and words? Even such words. So enough still. Just enough still to joy. Joy! Just enough still to joy that only they. Only!

Enough still not to know. Not to know what they say. Not to know what it is the words it says say. Says? Secretes. Say better worse secretes. What it is the words it secretes say. What the so-said void. The so-said dim. The so-said shades. The so-said seat and germ of all. Enough to know no know-ing. No knowing what it is the words it secretes say. No saying. No saying what it all is they somehow say.

That said on back to try worse say the plodding twain. Preying since last worse said on foresaid remains. But what not on them preying? What seen? What said? What of all seen and said not on them preying? True. True! And yet say worst perhaps worst of all the old man and child. That shade as last worse seen. Left right left right barefoot unreceding on. They then the words. Back to them now for want of better on and bet-ter fail. Worser fail that perhaps of all the least. Least worse failed of all the worse failed shades. Less worse than the bowed back alone. The skull and lidless stare. Though they too for worse. But what not for worse. True. True! And yet say first the worst perhaps worst of all the old man and child. Worst in need of worse. Worse in—

Blanks for nohow on. How long? Blanks how long till somehow on? Again somehow on. All gone when nohow on. Time gone when nohow on.

Worse less. By no stretch more. Worse for want of better less. Less best. No. Naught best. Best worse. No. Not best worse. Naught not best worse. Less best worse. No. Least. Least best worse. Least never to be naught. Never to naught be brought. Never by naught be nulled. Unnullable least. Say that best worse. With leastening words say least best worse. For want of worser worst. Unlessenable least best worse.

The twain. The hands. Held holding hands. That almost ring! As when first said on crippled hands the head. Crippled hands! They there then the words. Here now held holding. As when first said. Ununsaid when worse said. Away. Held holding hands!

The empty too. Away. No hands in the—. No. Save for worse to say. Somehow worse somehow to say. Say for now still seen. Dimly seen. Dim white. Two dim white empty hands. In the dim void.

So leastward on. So long as dim still. Dim undimmed. Or dimmed to dimmer still. To dimmost dim. Leastmost in dimmost dim. Utmost dim. Leastmost in utmost dim. Unworsenable worst.

What words for what then? How almost they still ring. As somehow from some soft of mind they ooze. From it in it ooze. How all but uninane. To last unlessenable least how loath to leasten. For then in utmost dim to unutter leastmost all.

So little worse the old man and child. Gone held holding hands they plod apart. Left right barefoot unreceding on. Not worsen yet the rift. Save for some after nohow somehow worser on.

On back to unsay clamped to all the stare. No but from now to now this and now that. As now from worsened twain to next for worse alone. To skull and stare alone. Of the two worse in want the skull preying since unsunk. Now say the fore alone. No dome. Temple to temple alone. Clamped to it and stare alone the stare. Bowed back alone and twain blurs in the void. So better than nothing worse shade three from now.

Somehow again on back to the bowed back alone. Nothing to show a woman's and yet a woman's. Oozed from softening soft the word woman's. The words old woman's. The words nothing to show bowed back alone a woman's and yet a woman's. So better worse from now that shade a woman's. An old woman's.

Next fail see say how dim undimmed to worsen. How nohow save to dimmer still. But but a shade so as when after nohow somehow on to dimmer still. Till dimmost dim. Best bad worse of all. Save somehow undimmed worser still.

Ooze on back not to unsay but say again the vasts apart. Say seen again. No worse again. The vasts of void apart. Of all so far missaid the worse missaid. So far. Not till nohow worse missay say worse missaid. Not till for good nohow on poor worst missaid.

Longing the so-said mind long lost to longing. The so-missaid. So far so-missaid. Dint of long longing lost to longing. Long vain longing. And longing still. Faintly longing still. Faintly vainly longing still. For fainter still. For faintest. Faintly vainly longing for the least of longing. Unlessenable least of longing. Unstillable vain last of longing still.

Longing that all go. Dim go. Void go. Longing go. Vain longing that vain longing go.

Said is missaid. Whenever said said said missaid. From now said alone. No more from now now said and now missaid. From now said alone. Said for missaid. For be missaid.

Back is on. Somehow on. From now back alone. No more from now now back and now back on. From now back alone. Back for back on. Back for somehow on.

Back unsay better worse by no stretch more. If more dim less light then better worse more dim. Unsaid then better worse by no stretch more. Better worse may no less than less be more. Better worse what? The say? The said. Same thing. Same nothing. Same all but nothing.

No once. No once in pastless now. No not none. When before worse the shades? The dim before more? When if not once. Onceless alone the void. By no stretch more. By none less. Onceless till no more.

Ooze back try worsen blanks. Those then when nohow on. Unsay then all gone. All not gone. Only nohow on. All not gone and nohow on. All there as now when somehow on. The dim. The void. The shades. Only words gone. Ooze gone. Till ooze again and on. Somehow ooze on.

Preying since last worse the stare. Something there still far so far from wrong. So far far far from wrong. Try better worse another stare when with words than when not. When somehow than when nohow. While all seen the same. No not all seen the same. Seen other. By the same other stare seen other. When with words than when not. When somehow than when nohow. How fail say how other seen?

Less. Less seen. Less seeing. Less seen and seeing when with words than when not. When somehow than when nohow. Stare by words dimmed. Shades dimmed. Void dimmed. Dim dimmed. All there as when no words. As when nohow. Only all dimmed. Till blank again. No words again. Nohow again. Then all undimmed. Stare undimmed. That words had dimmed.

Back unsay shades can go. Go and come again. No. Shades cannot go. Much less come again. Nor bowed old woman's back. Nor old man and child. Nor foreskull and stare. Blur yes. Shades can blur. When stare clamped to one alone. Or somehow words again. Go no nor come again. Till dim if ever go. Never to come again.

Blanks for when words gone. When nohow on. Then all seen as only then. Undimmed. All undimmed that words dim. All so seen unsaid. No ooze then. No trace on soft when from it ooze again. In it ooze again. Ooze alone for seen as seen with ooze. Dimmed. No ooze for seen undimmed. For when nohow on. No ooze for when ooze gone.

Back try worsen twain preying since last worse. Since atwain. Two once so one. From now rift a vast. Vast of void atween. With equal plod still unreceding on. That little better worse. Till words for worser still. Worse words for worser still.

Preying but what not preying? When not preying? Nohow over words again say what then when not preying. Each better worse for naught. No stilling preying. The shades. The dim. The void. All always faintly preying. Worse for naught. Worser for naught. No less than when but bad all always faintly preying. Gnawing.

Gnawing to be gone. Less no good. Worse no good. Only one good. Gone. Gone for good. Till then gnaw on. All gnaw on. To be gone.

All save void. No. Void too. Unworsenable void. Never less. Never more. Never since first said never unsaid never worse said never not gnawing to be gone.

Say child gone. As good as gone. From the void. From the stare. Void then not that much more? Say old man gone. Old woman gone. As good as gone. Void then not that much more again? No. Void most when almost. Worst when almost. Less then? All shades as good as gone. If then not that much more then that much less then? Less worse then? Enough. A pox on void. Unmoreable unlessable unworseable evermost almost void.

Back to once so-said two as one. Preying ever since not long since last failed worse. Ever since vast atween. Say better worse now all gone save trunks from now. Nothing from pelves down. From napes up. Topless baseless hindtrunks. Legless plodding on. Left right unreceding on.

Stare clamped to stare. Bowed backs blurs in stare clamped to stare. Two black holes. Dim black. In through skull to soft. Out from soft through skull. Agape in unseen face. That the flaw? The want of flaw? Try better worse set in skull. Two black holes in foreskull. Or one. Try better still worse one. One dim black hole mid-foreskull. Into the hell of all. Out from the hell of all. So better than nothing worse say stare from now.

Stare outstared away to old man hindtrunk unreceding on. Try better worse kneeling. Legs gone say better worse kneeling. No more if ever on. Say never. Say never on. Ever kneeling. Legs gone from stare say better worse ever kneeling. Stare away to child and worsen same. Vast void apart old man and child dim shades on unseen knees. One blur. One clear. Dim clear. Now the one. Now the other.

Nothing to show a child and yet a child. A man and yet a man. Old and yet old. Nothing but ooze how nothing and yet. One bowed back yet an old man's. The other yet a child's. A small child's.

Somehow again and all in stare again. All at once as once. Better worse all. The three bowed down. The stare. The whole narrow void. No blurs. All clear. Dim clear. Black hole agape on all. Inletting all. Outletting all.

Nothing and yet a woman. Old and yet old. On unseen knees. Stooped as loving memory some old gravestones stoop. In that old graveyard. Names gone and when to when. Stoop mute over the graves of none.

Same stoop for all. Same vasts apart. Such last state. Latest state. Till somehow less in vain. Worse in vain. All gnawing to be naught. Never to be naught.

What were skull to go? As good as go. Into what then black hole? From out what then? What why of all? Better worse so? No. Skull better worse. What left of skull. Of soft. Worst why of all of all. So skull not go. What left of skull not go. Into it still the hole. Into what left of soft. From out what little left.

Enough. Sudden enough. Sudden all far. No move and sudden all far. All least. Three pins. One pinhole. In dimmost dim. Vasts apart. At bounds of boundless void. Whence no farther. Best worse no farther. Nohow less. Nohow worse. Nohow naught. Nohow on.

Said nohow on.

Stirrings Still

For Barney Rosset

1

One night as he sat at his table head on hands he saw him-
self rise and go. One night or day. For when his own light went out he was
not left in the dark. Light of a kind came then from the one high window.
Under it still the stool on which till he could or would no more he used to
mount to see the sky. Why he did not crane out to see what lay beneath was
perhaps because the window was not made to open or because he could
or would not open it. Perhaps he knew only too well what lay beneath and
did not wish to see it again. So he would simply stand there high above
the earth and see through the clouded pane the cloudless sky. Its faint
unchanging light unlike any light he could remember from the days and
nights when day followed hard on night and night on day. This outer
light then when his own went out became his only light till it in its turn
went out and left him in the dark. Till it in its turn went out.

One night or day then as he sat at his table head on hands he saw him-
self rise and go. First rise and stand clinging to the table. Then sit again.
Then rise again and stand clinging to the table again. Then go. Start to
go. On unseen feet start to go. So slow that only change of place to show

he went. As when he disappeared only to reappear later at another place. Then disappeared again only to reappear again later at another place again. So again and again disappeared again only to reappear again later at another place again. Another place in the place where he sat at his table head on hands. The same place and table as when Darly for example died and left him. As when others too in their turn before and since. As when others would too in their turn and leave him till he too in his turn. Head on hands half hoping when he disappeared again that he would not reappear again and half fearing that he would not. Or merely wondering. Or merely waiting. Waiting to see if he would or would not. Leave him or not alone again waiting for nothing again.

Seen always from behind whithersoever he went. Same hat and coat as of old when he walked the roads. The back roads. Now as one in a strange place seeking the way out. In the dark. In a strange place blindly in the dark of night or day seeking the way out. A way out. To the roads. The back roads.

A clock afar struck the hours and half-hours. The same as when among others Darly once died and left him. Strokes now clear as if carried by a wind now faint on the still air. Cries afar now faint now clear. Head on hands half hoping when the hour struck that the half-hour would not and half fearing that it would not. Similarly when the half-hour struck. Similarly when the cries a moment ceased. Or merely wondering. Or merely waiting. Waiting to hear.

There had been a time he would sometimes lift his head enough to see his hands. What of them was to be seen. One laid on the table and the other on the one. At rest after all they did. Lift his past head a moment to see his past hands. Then lay it back on them to rest it too. After all it did.

The same place as when left day after day for the roads. The back roads. Returned to night after night. Paced from wall to wall in the dark. The then fleeting dark of night. Now as if strange to him seen to rise and go. Disappear and reappear at another place. Disappear again and reappear again at another place again. Or at the same. Nothing to show not the same. No wall towards which or from. No table back towards which or further from. In the same place as when paced from wall to wall all places as the same. Or in another. Nothing to show not another. Where never. Rise and go in the same place as ever. Disappear and reappear in another where never. Nothing to show not another where never. Nothing but the strokes. The cries. The same as ever.

Till so many strokes and cries since he was last seen that perhaps he would not be seen again. Then so many cries since the strokes were last heard that perhaps they would not be heard again. Then such silence since the cries were last heard that perhaps even they would not be heard again. Perhaps thus the end. Unless no more than a mere lull. Then all as before. The strokes and cries as before and he as before now there now gone now there again now gone again. Then the lull again. Then all as before again. So again and again. And patience till the one true end to time and grief and self and second self his own.

2

As one in his right mind when at last out again he knew not how he was not long out again when he began to wonder if he was in his right mind. For could one not in his right mind be reasonably said to wonder if he was in his right mind and bring what is more his remains of reason to bear on this perplexity in the way he must be said to do if he is to be said at all? It was therefore in the guise of a more or less reasonable being that he emerged at last he knew not how into the outer world and had not been there for more than six or seven hours by the clock when he could not but begin to wonder if he was in his right mind. By the same clock whose strokes were those heard times without number in his confinement as it struck the hours and half-hours and so in a sense at first a source of reassurance till finally one of alarm as being no clearer now than when in principle muffled by his four walls. Then he sought help in the thought of one hastening westward at sundown to obtain a better view of Venus and found it of none. Of the sole other sound that of cries enlivener of his solitude as lost to suffering he sat at his table head on hands the same was true. Of their whenceabouts that is of clock and cries the same was true that is no more to be determined now than as was only natural then. Bringing to bear on all this his remains of reason he sought help in the thought that his memory of indoors was perhaps at fault and found it of none. Further to his disarray his soundless tread as when barefoot he trod his floor. So all ears from bad to worse till in the end he ceased if not to hear to listen and set out to look about him. Result finally he was in a field of grass which went some way if nothing else to explain his tread and then a little later as if to make up for this some way to increase his trouble. For he could recall no field of grass from even the very heart of which no limit of any kind was to be discovered but always in some quarter or another some end in sight such as a fence or other manner of bourne from which to return. Nor on his looking more closely to make matters worse was this the short green grass he seemed to remember eaten down by flocks and herds but long and light grey in colour verging here and there on white. Then he sought help in the thought that his memory of outdoors was perhaps at fault and found it of none. So all eyes from bad to worse till in the end he ceased if not to see to look (about him or more closely) and set out to take thought. To this end for want of a stone on which to sit like Walther and cross his legs the best he could do was stop dead and stand stock still which after a moment of hesitation he did and of course sink his head as one deep in meditation which after another moment of hesitation he did also. But soon weary of vainly delving in those remains he moved on through the long hoar grass resigned to not knowing where he was or how he got there or where he was going or how to get back to whence he knew not how he came. So on unknowing and no end in sight. Unknowing and what is more no wish to know nor indeed any wish of any kind nor therefore any sorrow save that he would have wished the strokes to cease and the cries for good and was sorry that they did not. The strokes now faint now clear as if carried by the wind but not a breath and the cries now faint now clear.

3

So on till stayed when to his ears from deep within oh how
and here a word he could not catch it were to end where never till then.
Rest then before again from not long to so long that perhaps never again
and then again faint from deep within oh how and here that missing word
again it were to end where never till then. In any case whatever it might
be to end and so on was he not already as he stood there all bowed down
and to his ears faint from deep within again and again oh how something
and so on was he not so far as he could see already there where never till
then? For how could even such a one as he having once found himself in
such a place not shudder to find himself in it again which he had not
done nor having shuddered seek help in vain in the thought so-called
that having somehow got out of it then he could somehow get out of it
again which he had not done either. There then all this time where never
till then and so far as he could see in every direction when he raised his
head and opened his eyes no danger or hope as the case might be of his
ever getting out of it. Was he then now to press on regardless now in one
direction and now in another or on the other hand stir no more as the
case might be that is as that missing word might be which if to warn such
as sad or bad for example then of course in spite of all the one and if the
reverse then of course the other that is stir no more. Such and much
more such the hubbub in his mind so-called till nothing left from deep
within but only ever fainter oh to end. No matter how no matter where.
Time and grief and self so-called. Oh all to end.

CRITICISM

Dante ... Bruno . Vico .. Joyce

The danger is in the neatness of identifications. The conception of Philosophy and Philology as a pair of nigger minstrels out of the Teatro dei Piccoli is soothing, like the contemplation of a carefully folded ham-sandwich. Giambattista Vico himself could not resist the attractiveness of such coincidence of gesture. He insisted on complete identification between the philosophical abstraction and the empirical illustration, thereby annulling the absolutism of each conception—hoisting the real unjustifiably clear of its dimensional limits, temporalizing that which is extratemporal. And now here am I, with my handful of abstractions, among which notably: a mountain, the coincidence of contraries, the inevitability of cyclic evolution, a system of Poetics, and the prospect of self-extension in the world of Mr. Joyce's *Work in Progress*. There is the temptation to treat every concept like "a bass dropt neck fust in till a bung crate," and make a really tidy job of it. Unfortunately such an exactitude of application would imply distortion in one of two directions. Must we wring the neck of a certain system in order to stuff it into a contemporary pigeon-hole, or modify the dimensions of that pigeon-hole for the satisfaction of the analogymongers? Literary criticism is not book-keeping.

. . . .

Giambattista Vico was a practical roundheaded Neapolitan. It pleases Croce to consider him as a mystic, essentially speculative, "*disdegnoso dell' empirismo*." It is a surprising interpretation, seeing that more than three-fifths of his *Scienza Nuova* is concerned with empirical investigation. Croce opposes him to the reformative materialistic school of Ugo Grozio, and absolves him from the utilitarian preoccupations of Hobbes, Spinoza, Locke, Bayle and Machiavelli. All this cannot be swallowed without protest. Vico defines Providence as: "*una mente spesso diversa ed alle volte tutta contraria e sempre superiore ad essi fini particolari che essi uomini si avevano proposti; dei quali fini ristretti fatti mezzi per servire a fini più ampi, gli ha sempre adoperati per conservare l'umana generazione in questa terra.*" What could be more definitely utilitarianism? His treatment of the origin and functions of poetry, language and myth, as will appear later, is as far removed from the mystical as it is possible to imagine. For our immediate purpose, however, it matters little whether we consider him as a mystic or as a scientific investigator; but there are no two ways about considering him as an *innovator*. His division of the development of human society into three ages: Theocratic, Heroic, Human (civilized), with a corresponding classification of language: Hieroglyphic (sacred), Metaphorical (poetic), Philosophical (capable of abstraction and generalization), was by no means new, although it must have appeared so to his contemporaries. He derived this convenient classification from the Egyptians, via Herodotus. At the same time it is impossible to deny the originality with which he applied and developed its implications. His exposition of the ineluctable circular progression of Society was completely new, although the germ of it was contained in Giordano Bruno's treatment of identified contraries. But it is in Book 2, described by himself as "*tutto il corpo . . . la chiave maestra . . . dell' opera,*" that appears the unqualified originality of his mind; here he evolved a theory of the origins of poetry and language, the significance of myth, and the nature of barbaric civilization that must have appeared nothing less than an impertinent outrage against tradition. These two aspects of Vico have their reverberations, their reapplications—without, however, receiving the faintest explicit illustration—in *Work in Progress.*

It is first necessary to condense the thesis of Vico, the scientific historian. In the beginning was the thunder: the thunder set free Religion, in its most objective and unphilosophical form—idolatrous animism: Religion produced Society, and the first social men were the cave-dwellers, taking refuge from a passionate Nature: this primitive family life receives its first impulse towards development from the arrival of terrified vagabonds: admitted, they are the first slaves: growing stronger, they exact agrarian concessions, and a despotism has evolved into a primitive feudalism: the cave becomes a city, and the feudal system a democracy: then an anarchy: this is corrected by a return to monarchy: the last stage is a tendency towards interdestruction: the nations are dispersed, and the Phoenix of Society arises out of their ashes. To this six-termed social progression corresponds a six-termed progression of human motives: necessity, utility, convenience, pleasure, luxury, abuse of luxury: and their incarnate manifestations: Polyphemus, Achilles, Caesar and Alexander, Tiberius, Caligula and Nero. At this point Vico applies Bruno— though he takes very good care not to say so—and proceeds from rather arbitrary data to philosophical abstraction. There is no difference, says Bruno, between the smallest possible chord and the smallest possible arc, no difference between the infinite circle and the straight line. The maxima and minima of particular contraries are one and indifferent. Minimal heat equals minimal cold. Consequently transmutations are circular. The principle (minimum) of one contrary takes its movement from the principle (maximum) of one another. Therefore not only do the minima coincide with the minima, the maxima with the maxima, but the minima with the maxima in the succession of transmutations. Maximal speed is a state of rest. The maximum of corruption and the minimum of generation are identical: in principle, corruption is generation. And all things are ultimately identified with God, the universal monad, Monad of monads. From these considerations Vico evolved a Science and Philosophy of History. It may be an amusing exercise to take an historical figure, such as Scipio, and label him No. 3; it is of no ultimate importance. What is of ultimate importance is the recognition that the passage from Scipio to Caesar is as inevitable as the passage from Caesar to Tiberius, since the flowers of corruption in Scipio and Caesar are the seeds of vitality in Caesar and Tiberius. Thus we have the spectacle of a human progression that depends for its movement on individuals, and which at the same time is independent of individuals in virtue of what appears to be a preordained cyclicism. It follows that History is neither to be considered as a formless structure, due exclusively to the achievements of individual agents, nor as possessing reality apart from and independent of them, accomplished behind their backs in spite of them, the work of some superior force, variously known as Fate, Chance, Fortune, God. Both these views, the materialistic and the transcendental, Vico rejects in favour of the rational. Individuality is the concretion of universality, and every individual action is at the same time superindividual. The individual and the universal cannot be considered as distinct from each other. History, then, is not the result of Fate or Chance—in both cases the individual would be separated from his product—but the result of a Necessity that is not Fate, of a Liberty that is not Chance (compare Dante's "yoke of liberty"). This force he called Divine Providence, with his tongue, one feels, very much in his cheek. And it is to this Providence that we must trace the three institutions common to every society: Church, Marriage, Burial. This is not Bossuet's Providence, transcendental and miraculous, but immanent and the stuff itself of human life, working by natural means. Humanity is its work in itself. God acts on her, but by means of her. Humanity is divine, but no man is divine. This social and historical classification is clearly adapted by Mr. Joyce as a structural convenience—or inconvenience. His position is in no way a philosophical one. It is the detached attitude of Stephen Dedalus in *Portrait of the Artist* . . . who describes Epictetus to the Master of Studies as "an old gentleman who said that the soul is very like a bucketful of water." The lamp is more important than the lamp-lighter. By structural I do not only mean a bold outward division, a bare skeleton for the housing of material. I mean the endless substantial variations on these three beats, and interior intertwining of these three themes into a decoration of arabesques—decoration and more than decoration. Part 1 is a mass of past shadow, corresponding therefore to Vico's first human institution, Religion, or to his Theocratic age, or simply to an abstraction—Birth. Part 2 is the lovegame of the children, corresponding to the second institution, Marriage, or to the Heroic age, or to an abstraction—Maturity. Part 3 is passed in sleep, corresponding to the third institution,

Burial, or to the Human age, or to an abstraction—Corruption. Part 4
is the day beginning again, and corresponds to Vico's Providence, or to
an abstraction—Generation. Mr. Joyce does not take birth for granted,
as Vico seems to have done. So much for the dry bones. The conscious-
ness that there is a great deal of the unborn infant in the lifeless octo-
genarian, and a great deal of both in the man at the apogee of his life's
curve, removes all the stiff interexclusiveness that is often the danger in
neat construction. Corruption is not excluded from Part 1 nor maturity
from Part 3. The four "lovedroyd curdinals" are presented on the same
plane—"his element curdinal numen and his enement curdinal marry-
ing and his epulent curdinal weisswasch and his eminent curdinal Kay o'
Kay!" There are numerous references to Vico's four human institutions—
Providence counting as one! "A good clap, a fore wedding, a bad wake,
tell hell's well": "their weatherings and their marryings and their bury-
ings and their natural selections": "the lightning look, the birding cry,
awe from the grave, ever-flowing on our times": "by four hands of fore-
thought the first babe of reconcilement is laid in its last cradle of hume
sweet hume."

Apart from this emphasis on the tangible conveniences common to
Humanity, we find frequent expressions of Vico's insistence on the inevi-
table character of every progression—or retrogression: "The Vico road
goes round to meet where terms begin. Still onappealed to by the cycles
and onappalled by the recoursers, we feel all serene, never you fret, as
regards our dutyful cask. . . . before there was a man at all in Ireland there
was a lord at Lucan. We only wish everyone was as sure of anything in this
watery world as we are of everything in the newlywet fellow that's bound
to follow. . . ." "The efferfreshpainted livy in beautific repose upon the
silence of the dead from Pharoph the next first down to ramescheckles
the last bust thing." "In fact, under the close eyes of the inspectors the
traits featuring the chiaroscuro coalesce, their contrarieties eliminated,
in one stable somebody similarly as by the providential warring of heart-
shaker with housebreaker and of dramdrinker against freethinker our
social something bowls along bumpily, experiencing a jolting series of
prearranged disappointments, down the long lane of (it's as semper as

oxhousehumper) generations, more generations and still more genera-
tions"—this last a case of Mr. Joyce's rare subjectivism. In a word, here
is all humanity circling with fatal monotony about the Providential ful-
crum—the "convoy wheeling encirculing abound the gigantig's lifetree."
Enough has been said, or at least enough has been suggested, to show
how Vico is substantially present in the *Work in Progress*. Passing to the
Vico of the Poetics we hope to establish an even more striking, if less
direct, relationship.

Vico rejected the three popular interpretations of the poetic spirit,
which considered poetry as either an ingenious popular expression of
philosophical conceptions, or an amusing social diversion, or an exact
science within the research of everyone in possession of the recipe. Poetry,
he says, was born of curiosity, daughter of ignorance. The first men had
to create matter by the force of their imagination, and "poet" means "crea-
tor." Poetry was the first operation of the human mind, and without it
thought could not exist. Barbarians, incapable of analysis and abstraction,
must use their fantasy to explain what their reasons cannot comprehend.
Before articulation comes song; before abstract terms, metaphors. The
figurative character of the oldest poetry must be regarded, not as sophis-
ticated confectionery, but as evidence of a poverty-stricken vocabulary
and of a disability to achieve abstraction. Poetry is essentially the antithe-
sis of Metaphysics: Metaphysics purge the mind of the senses and culti-
vate the disembodiment of the spiritual; Poetry is all passion and feeling
and animates the inanimate; Metaphysics are most perfect when most
concerned with universals; Poetry, when most concerned with particu-
lars. Poets are the sense, philosophers the intelligence of humanity. Con-
sidering the Scholastics' axiom: "*niente è nell'intelletto che prima non sia nel
senso*," it follows that poetry is a prime condition of philosophy and civi-
lization. The primitive animistic movement was a manifestation of the
"*forma poetica dello spirito*."

His treatment of the origin of language proceeds along similar lines.
Here again he rejected the materialistic and transcendental views; the
one declaring that language was nothing but a polite and conventional
symbolism; the other, in desperation, describing it as a gift from the

Gods. As before, Vico is the rationalist, aware of the natural and inevitable growth of language. In its first dumb form, language was gesture. If a man wanted to say "sea," he pointed to the sea. With the spread of animism this gesture was replaced by the word: "Neptune." He directs our attention to the fact that every need of life, natural, moral and economic, has its verbal expression in one or other of the 30,000 Greek divinities. This is Homer's "language of the Gods." Its evolution through poetry to a highly civilized vehicle, rich in abstract and technical terms, was as little fortuitous as the evolution of society itself. Words have their progressions as well as social phases. "Forest-cabin-village-city-academy" is one rough progression. Another: "mountain-plain-riverbank." And every word expands with psychological inevitability. Take the Latin word: "Lex."

1.   Lex = Crop of acorns.
2.   Ilex = Tree that produces acorns.
3. Legere = To gather.
4. Aquilex = He that gathers the waters.
5.   Lex = Gathering together of peoples, public assembly.
6.   Lex = Law.
7. Legere = To gather together letters into a word, to read.

The root of any word whatsoever can be traced back to some prelingual symbol. This early inability to abstract the general from the particular produced the Type-names. It is the child's mind over again. The child extends the names of the first familiar objects to other strange objects in which he is conscious of some analogy. The first men, unable to conceive the abstract idea of "poet" or "hero," named every hero after the first hero, every poet after the first poet. Recognizing this custom of designating a number of individuals by the names of their prototypes, we can explain various classical and mythological mysteries. Hermes is the prototype of the Egyptian inventor: so for Romulus, the great law-giver, and Hercules, the Greek hero: so for Homer. Thus Vico asserts the spontaneity of language and denies the dualism of poetry and language. Similarly, poetry is the foundation of writing. When language consisted of gesture, the spoken and written were identical. Hieroglyphics, or sacred language, as he calls it, were not the invention of philosophers for the mysterious expression of profound thought, but the common necessity of primitive peoples. Convenience only begins to assert itself at a far more advanced stage of civilization, in the form of alphabetism. Here Vico, implicitly at least, distinguishes between writing and direct expression. In such direct expression, form and content are inseparable. Examples are the medals of the Middle Ages, which bore no inscription and were a mute testimony to the feebleness of conventional alphabetic writing: and the flags of our own day. As with Poetry and Language, so with Myth. Myth, according to Vico, is neither an allegorical expression of general philosophical axioms (Conti, Bacon), nor a derivative from particular peoples, as for instance the Hebrews or Egyptians, nor yet the work of isolated poets, but an historical statement of fact, of actual contemporary phenomena, actual in the sense that they were created out of necessity by primitive minds, and firmly believed. Allegory implies a threefold intellectual operation: the construction of a message of general significance, the preparation of a fabulous form, and an exercise of considerable technical difficulty in uniting the two, an operation totally beyond the reach of the primitive mind. Moreover, if we consider the myth as being essentially allegorical, we are not obliged to accept the form in which it is cast as a statement of fact. But we know that the actual creators of these myths gave full credence to their face-value. Jove was no symbol: he was terribly real. It was precisely their superficial metaphorical character that made them intelligible to people incapable of receiving anything more abstract than the plain record of objectivity.

Such is a painful exposition of Vico's dynamic treatment of Language, Poetry and Myth. He may still appear as a mystic to some: if so, a mystic that rejects the transcendental in every shape and form as a factor in human development, and whose Providence is not divine enough to do without the cooperation of Humanity.

On turning to the *Work in Progress* we find that the mirror is not so convex. Here is direct expression—pages and pages of it. And if you don't understand it, Ladies and Gentlemen, it is because you are too decadent to receive it. You are not satisfied unless form is so strictly divorced from content that you can comprehend the one almost without bothering to read the other. The rapid skimming and absorption of the scant cream of sense is made possible by what I may call a continuous process of copious intellectual salivation. The form that is an arbitrary and independent phenomenon can fulfil no higher function than that of stimulus for a tertiary or quartary conditioned reflex of dribbling comprehension. When Miss Rebecca West clears her decks for a sorrowful deprecation of the Narcisstic element in Mr. Joyce by the purchase of 3 hats, one feels that she might very well wear her bib at all her intellectual banquets, or alternatively, assert a more noteworthy control over her salivary glands than is possible for Monsieur Pavlov's unfortunate dogs. The title of this book is a good example of a form carrying a strict inner determination. It should be proof against the usual volley of cerebral sniggers: and it may suggest to some a dozen incredulous Joshuas prowling around the Queen's Hall, springing their tuning-forks lightly against finger-nails that have not yet been refined out of existence. Mr. Joyce has a word to say to you on the subject: "Yet to concentrate solely on the literal sense or even the psychological content of any document to the sore neglect of the enveloping facts themselves circumstantiating it is just as harmful; etc." And another: "Who in his heart doubts either that the facts of feminine clothiering are there all the time or that the feminine fiction, stranger than the facts, is there also at the same time, only a little to the rere? Or that one may be separated from the other? Or that both may be contemplated simultaneously? Or that each may be taken up in turn and considered apart from the other?"

Here form *is* content, content *is* form. You complain that this stuff is not written in English. It is not written at all. It is not to be read—or rather it is not only to be read. It is to be looked at and listened to. His writing is not *about* something; *it is that something itself.* (A fact that has been grasped by an eminent English novelist and historian whose work is in complete opposition to Mr. Joyce's.) When the sense is sleep, the words go to sleep. (See the end of *Anna Livia.*) When the sense is dancing, the words dance. Take the passage at the end of Shaun's pastoral: "To stirr up love's young fizz I tilt with this bridle's cup champagne, dimming douce from her peepair of hide-seeks tight squeezed on my snowybreasted and while my pearlies in their sparkling wisdom are nippling her bubblets I swear (and let you swear) by the bumper round of my poor old snaggletooth's solidbowel I ne'er will prove I'm untrue to (theare!) you liking so long as my hole looks. Down." The language is drunk. The very words are tilted and effervescent. How can we qualify this general esthetic vigilance without which we cannot hope to snare the sense which is for ever rising to the surface of the form and becoming the form itself? St. Augustine puts us on the track of a word with his "*intendere*," Dante has: "*Donne ch'avete intelletto d'amore*," and "*Voi che, intendendo, il terzo ciel movete*"; but his "*intendere*" suggests a strictly intellectual operation. When an Italian says today "*Ho inteso*," he means something between "*Ho udito*" and "*Ho capito*," a sensuous untidy art of intellection. Perhaps "apprehension" is the most satisfactory English word. Stephen says to Lynch: "Temporal or spatial, the esthetic image is first luminously apprehended as self-bounded and selfcontained upon the immeasurable background of space or time which is not it ... You apprehend its wholeness." There is one point to make clear: the Beauty of *Work in Progress* is not presented in space alone, since its adequate apprehension depends as much on its visibility as on its audibility. There is a temporal as well as a spatial unity to be apprehended. Substitute "and" for "or" in the quotation, and it becomes obvious why it is as inadequate to speak of "reading" *Work in Progress* as it would be extravagant to speak of "apprehending" the work of the late Mr. Nat Gould. Mr. Joyce has desophisticated language. And it is worth while remarking that no language is so sophisticated as English. It is abstracted to death. Take the word "doubt": it gives us hardly any sensuous suggestion of hesitancy, of the necessity for choice, of static irresolution. Whereas the German "Zweifel" does, and, in lesser degree, the Italian "dubitare." Mr. Joyce recognizes how inadequate "doubt" is to express a state of extreme uncertainty, and replaces it by "in twosome twiminds." Nor is he by any means the first to recognize the importance of treating words as something more than mere polite symbols. Shakespeare uses fat, greasy words to express corruption: "Duller shouldst thou be than the fat weed that rots itself in death on Lethe wharf." We hear the ooze squelching all through Dickens's description of the Thames in *Great Expectations*. This writing that you find so obscure is a quintessential extraction of language and painting and gesture, with all the inevitable clarity of the old inarticulation. Here is the savage economy of hieroglyphics. Here words are not the polite contortions of 20th century printer's ink. They are alive. They elbow their way on to the page, and glow and blaze and fade and disappear. "Brawn is my name and broad is my nature and I've breit on my brow and all's right with every feature and I'll brune this bird or Brown Bess's bung's gone bandy." This is Brawn blowing with a light gust through the trees or Brawn passing with the sunset. Because the wind in the trees means as little to you as the evening prospect from the Piazzale Michelangiolo—though you accept them both because your non-acceptance would be of no significance, this little adventure of Brawn means nothing to you—and you do not accept it, even though here also your non-acceptance is of no significance. H. C. Earwigger, too, is not content to be mentioned like a shilling-shocker villain, and then dropped until the exigencies of the narrative require that he be again referred to. He continues to suggest himself for a couple of pages, by means of repeated permutations on his "normative letters," as if to say: "This is all about me, H. C. Earwigger: don't forget this is all about me!" This inner elemental vitality and corruption of expression imparts a furious restlessness to the form, which is admirably suited to the purgatorial aspect of the work. There is an endless verbal germination, maturation, putrefaction, the cyclic dynamism of the intermediate. This reduction of various expressive media to their primitive economic directness, and the fusion of these primal essences into an assimilated medium for the exteriorization of thought, is pure Vico, and Vico, applied to the problem of style. But Vico is reflected more explicitly than by a distillation of disparate poetic ingredients into a synthetical syrup. We notice that there is little or no attempt at subjectivism or abstraction, no attempt at metaphysical generalization. We are presented with a statement of the particular. It is the old myth: the girl on the dirt track, the two washerwomen on the banks of the river. And there is considerable animism: the mountain "abhearing," the river puffing her old doudheen. (See the beautiful passage beginning: "First she let her hair fall down and it flussed.") We have Type-names: Isolde—any beautiful girl: Earwigger—Guinness's Brewery, the Wellington monument, the Phoenix Park, anything that occupies an extremely comfortable position between the two stools. Anna Livia herself, mother of Dublin, but no more the only mother than Zoroaster was the only oriental stargazer. "Teems of times and happy returns. The same anew. Ordovico or viricordo. Anna was, Livia is, Plurabelle's to be. Northmen's thing made Southfolk's place, but howmultyplurators made eachone in person." Basta! Vico and Bruno are here, and more substantially than would appear from this swift survey of the question. For the benefit of those who enjoy a parenthetical sneer, we would draw attention to the fact that when Mr. Joyce's early pamphlet *The Day of Rabblement* appeared, the local philosophers were thrown into a state of some bewilderment by a reference in the first line to "The Nolan." They finally succeeded in identifying this mysterious individual with one of the obscurer ancient Irish kings. In the present work he appears frequently as "Browne & Nolan," the name of a very remarkable Dublin Bookseller and Stationer.

To justify our title, we must move North, "*Sovra'l bel fiume d'Arno alla gran villa.*" . . . Between "*colui per lo cui verso—il meonio cantor non è più solo*" and the "still to-day insufficiently malestimated notesnatcher, Shem the Penman," there exists considerable circumstantial similarity. They both saw how worn out and threadbare was the conventional language of cunning literary artificers, both rejected an approximation to a universal language. If English is not yet so definitely a polite necessity as Latin was in the Middle Ages, at least one is justified in declaring that its position in relation to other European languages is to a great extent that of mediaeval Latin to the Italian dialects. Dante did not adopt the vulgar out of any kind of local jingoism nor out of any determination to assert the superiority of Tuscan to all its rivals as a form of spoken Italian. On reading his *De Vulgari Eloquentia* we are struck by his complete freedom from civic intolerance. He attacks the world's Portadownians: "*Nam quicumque tam obscenae rationis est, ut locum suae nationis delitosissimum credat esse sub sole, huic etiam proe cunctis propriam volgare licetur, idest maternam locutionem. Nos autem, cui mundus est patria* . . . etc." When he comes to examine the dialects he finds Tuscan: "*turpissimum . . . fere omnes Tusci in suo turpiloquio obtusi . . . non restat in dubio quin aliud sit vulgare quod quaerimus quam quod attingit populus Tuscanorum.*" His conclusion is that the corruption common to all the dialects makes it impossible to select one rather than another as an adequate literary form, and that he who would write in the vulgar must assemble the purest elements from each dialect and construct a synthetic language that would at least possess more than a circumscribed local interest: which is precisely what he did. He did not write in Florentine any more than in Neapolitan. He wrote a vulgar that *could* have been spoken by an ideal Italian who had assimilated what was best in all the dialects of his country, but which in fact was certainly not spoken nor ever had been. Which disposes of the capital objection that might be made against this attractive parallel between Dante and Mr. Joyce in the question of language, i.e. that at least Dante wrote what was being spoken in the streets of his own town, whereas no creature in heaven or earth ever spoke the language of *Work in Progress*. It is reasonable to admit that an international phenomenon might be capable of speaking it, just as in 1300 none but an inter-regional phenomenon could have spoken the language of the Divine Comedy. We are inclined to forget that Dante's literary public was Latin that the form of his Poem was to be judged by Latin eyes and ears, by a Latin Esthetic intolerant of innovation, and which could hardly fail to be irritated by the substitution of "*Nel mezzo del cammin di nostra vita*" with its "barbarous" directness for the suave elegance of: "*Ultima regna canam, fluido contermina mundo*," just as English eyes and ears prefer: "Smoking his favourite pipe in the sacred presence of ladies" to: "Rauking his flavourite turfco in the smukking precincts of lydias." Boccaccio did not jeer at the "*piedi sozzi*" of the peacock that Signora Alighieri dreamed about.

I find two well made caps in the "*Convivio*," one to fit the collective noodle of the monodialectical arcadians whose fury is precipitated by a failure to discover "innoce-free" in the concise Oxford Dictionary and who qualify as the "ravings of a Bedlamite" the formal structure raised by Mr. Joyce after years of patient and inspired labour: "*Questi sono da*

chiamare pecore e non uomini; chè se una pecora si gittasse da una ripa di mille
passi, tutte l'altre le adrebbono dietro; e se una pecore a per alcuna cagione al pas-
sare d'una strada salta, tutte le altre saltano, eziando nulla veggendo da saltare.
E io ne vidi già molte in un pozzo saltare, per una che dentro vi salto, forse cre-
dendo di saltare un muro." And the other for Mr. Joyce, biologist in words:
"*Questo* (formal innovation) *sarà luce nuova, sole nuovo, il quale sorgerà ore*
l'usato tramonterà e darà luce a coloro che sono in tenebre e in oscurità per lo
usato sole che a loro non luce." And, lest he should pull it down over his eyes
and laugh behind the peak, I translate "*in tenebre e in oscurità*" by "bored
to extinction." (Dante makes a curious mistake speaking of the origin of
language, when he rejects the authority of Genesis that Eve was the first
to speak, when she addressed the Serpent. His incredulity is amusing:
"*inconvenienter putatur tam egregium humani generis actum, vel prius quam a*
viro, foemina profluisse." But before Eve was born, "the animals were given
names by Adam," the man who "first said goo to a goose." Moreover it is
explicitly stated that the choice of names was left entirely to Adam, so
that there is not the slightest Biblical authority for the conception of
language as a direct gift of God, any more than there is any intellectual
authority for conceiving that we are indebted for the "Concert" to the
individual who used to buy paint for Giorgione.)

   We know very little about the immediate reception accorded to
Dante's mighty vindication of the "vulgar," but we can form our own
opinions when, two centuries later, we find Castiglione splitting more
than a few hairs concerning the respective advantages of Latin and Ital-
ian, and Poliziano writing the dullest of dull Latin Elegies to justify his
existence as the author of "*Orfeo*" and the "*Stanze*." We may also compare,
if we think it worth while, the storm of ecclesiastical abuse raised by
Mr. Joyce's work, and the treatment that the Divine Comedy must cer-
tainly have received from the same source. His Contemporary Holiness
might have swallowed the crucifixion of "*lo sommo Giove,*" and all it stood
for, but he could scarcely have looked with favour on the spectacle of
three of his immediate predecessors plunged head-foremost in the fiery
stone of Malebolge, nor yet the identification of the Papacy in the mys-
tical procession of Terrestrial Paradise with a "*puttana sciolta.*" The "*De*

Monarshia" was burnt publicly under Pope Giovanni XXII at the insti-
gation of Cardinal Beltrando and the bones of its author would have
suffered the same fate but for the interference of an influential man of
letters, Pino della Tosa. Another point of comparison is the preoccupa-
tion with the significance of numbers. The death of Beatrice inspired
nothing less than a highly complicated poem dealing with the impor-
tance of the number 3 in her life. Dante never ceased to be obsessed by
this number. Thus the poem is divided into three Cantiche, each com-
posed of 33 Canti, and written in terza rima. Why, Mr. Joyce seems to say,
should there be four legs to a table, and four to a horse, and four seasons
and four Gospels and four Provinces in Ireland? Why twelve Tables of
the Law, and twelve Apostles and twelve months and twelve Napoleonic
marshals and twelve men in Florence called Ottolenghi? Why should the
Armistice be celebrated at the eleventh hour of the eleventh day of the
eleventh month? He cannot tell you because he is not God Almighty, but
in a thousand years he will tell you, and in the meantime must be con-
tent to know why horses have not five legs, nor three. He is conscious
that things with a common numerical characteristic tend towards a very
significant interrelationship. This preoccupation is freely translated in
his present work, see the "Question and Answer" chapter, and the Four
speaking through the child's brain. They are the four winds as much as
the four Provinces, and the four Episcopal Sees as much as either.

A last word about the Purgatories. Dante's is conical and consequently
implies culmination. Mr. Joyce's is spherical and excludes culmination.
In the one there is an ascent from real vegetation—Ante-Purgatory, to
ideal vegetation—Terrestrial Paradise: in the other there is no ascent and
no ideal vegetation. In the one, absolute progression and a guaranteed
consummation: in the other, flux—progression or retrogression, and an
apparent consummation. In the one movement is unidirectional, and
a step forward represents a net advance: in the other movement is non-
directional—or multi-directional, and a step forward is, by definition, a
step back. Dante's Terrestrial Paradise is the carriage entrance to a Par-
adise that is not terrestrial: Mr. Joyce's Terrestrial Paradise is the trades-
men's entrance on to the sea-shore. Sin is an impediment to movement

up the cone, and a condition of movement round the sphere. In what sense, then, is Mr. Joyce's work purgatorial? In the absolute absence of the Absolute. Hell is the static lifelessness of unrelieved viciousness. Paradise the static lifelessness of unrelieved immaculation. Purgatory a flood of movement and vitality released by the conjunction of these two elements. There is a continuous purgatorial process at work, in the sense that the vicious circle of humanity is being achieved, and this achievement depends on the recurrent predomination of one of two broad qualities. No resistance, no eruption, and it is only in Hell and Paradise that there are no eruptions, that there can be none, need be none. On this earth that is Purgatory, Vice and Virtue—which you may take to mean any pair of large contrary human factors—must in turn be purged down to spirits of rebelliousness. Then the dominant crust of the Vicious or Virtuous sets, resistance is provided, the explosion duly takes place and the machine proceeds. And no more than this; neither prize nor penalty; simply a series of stimulants to enable the kitten to catch its tail. And the partially purgatorial agent? The partially purged.

Proust

E fango è il mondo
(LEOPARDI)

Foreword

There is no allusion in this book to the legendary life and death of Marcel
Proust, nor to the garrulous old dowager of the Letters, nor to the poet, nor
to the author of the Essays, nor to the Eau de Selzian correlative of Carlyle's
"beautiful bottle of soda-water." I have preferred to retain the titles in French.
The translations of text are my own. The references are to the abominable
edition of the *Nouvelle Revue Française*, in sixteen volumes.

       The Proustian equation is never simple. The unknown,
choosing its weapons from a hoard of values, is also the unknowable.
And the quality of its action falls under two signatures. In Proust each
spear may be a spear of Telephus. This dualism in multiplicity will be
examined more closely in relation to Proust's "perspectivism." For the
purposes of this synthesis it is convenient to adopt the *inner* chronology
of the Proustian demonstration, and to examine in the first place that
double-headed monster of damnation and salvation—Time.

. . .

The scaffolding of his structure is revealed to the narrator in the library of the Princesse de Guermantes (one-time Mme. Verdurin), and the nature of its materials in the matinée that follows. His book takes form in his mind. He is aware of the many concessions required of the literary artist by the shortcomings of the literary convention. As a writer he is not altogether at liberty to detach effect from cause. It will be necessary, for example, to interrupt (disfigure) the luminous projection of subject desire with the comic relief of features. It will be impossible to prepare the hundreds of masks that rightly belong to the objects of even his most disinterested scrutiny. He accepts regretfully the sacred ruler and compass of literary geometry. But he will refuse to extend his submission to spatial scales, he will refuse to measure the length and weight of man in terms of his body instead of in terms of his years. In the closing words of his book he states his position: "But were I granted time to accomplish my work, I would not fail to stamp it with the seal of that Time, now so forcibly present to my mind, and in it I would describe men, even at the risk of giving them the appearance of monstrous beings, as occupying in Time a much greater place than that so sparingly conceded to them in Space, a place indeed extended beyond measure, because, like giants plunged in the years, they touch at once those periods of their lives—separated by so many days—so far apart in Time."

Proust's creatures, then, are victims of this predominating condition and circumstance—Time; victims as lower organisms, conscious only of two dimensions and suddenly confronted with the mystery of height, are victims: victims and prisoners. There is no escape from the hours and the days. Neither from tomorrow nor from yesterday. There is no escape from yesterday because yesterday has deformed us, or been deformed by us. The mood is of no importance. Deformation has taken place. Yesterday is not a milestone that has been passed, but a daystone on the beaten track of the years, and irremediably part of us, within us, heavy and dangerous. We are not merely more weary because of yesterday, we are other, no longer what we were before the calamity of yesterday. A calamitous day, but calamitous not necessarily in content. The good or evil disposition of the object has neither reality nor significance. The immediate

joys and sorrows of the body and the intelligence are so many super-
foetations. Such as it was, it has been assimilated to the only world that
has reality and significance, the world of our own latent consciousness,
and its cosmography has suffered a dislocation. So that we are rather in
the position of Tantalus, with this difference, that we allow ourselves to
be tantalised. And possibly the perpetuum mobile of our disillusions is
subject to more variety. The aspirations of yesterday were valid for yes-
terday's ego, not for today's. We are disappointed at the nullity of what
we are pleased to call attainment. But what is attainment? The identifi-
cation of the subject with the object of his desire. The subject has died—
and perhaps many times—on the way. For subject B to be disappointed
by the banality of an object chosen by subject A is as illogical as to expect
one's hunger to be dissipated by the spectacle of Uncle eating his dinner.
Even suppose that by one of those rare miracles of coincidence, when
the calendar of facts runs parallel to the calendar of feelings, realization
takes place, that the object of desire (in the strictest sense of that malady)
is achieved by the subject, then the congruence is so perfect, the time-
state of attainment eliminates so accurately the time-state of aspiration,
that the actual seems the inevitable, and, all conscious intellectual effort
to reconstitute the invisible and unthinkable as a reality being fruitless,
we are incapable of appreciating our joy by comparing it with our sor-
row. Voluntary memory (Proust repeats it ad nauseam) is of no value as an
instrument of evocation, and provides an image as far removed from the
real as the myth of our imagination or the caricature furnished by direct
perception. There is only one real impression and one adequate mode of
evocation. Over neither have we the least control. That reality and that
mode will be discussed in their proper place.

But the poisonous ingenuity of Time in the science of affliction is
not limited to its action on the subject, that action, as has been shown,
resulting in an unceasing modification of his personality, whose perma-
nent reality, if any, can only be apprehended as a retrospective hypothesis.
The individual is the seat of a constant process of decantation, decanta-
tion from the vessel containing the fluid of future time, sluggish, pale
and monochrome, to the vessel containing the fluid of past time, agitated

and multicoloured by the phenomena of its hours. Generally speaking, the former is innocuous, amorphous, without character, without any Borgian virtue. Lazily considered in anticipation and in the haze of our smug will to live, of our pernicious and incurable optimism, it seems exempt from the bitterness of fatality: in store for us, not in store in us. On occasions, however, it is capable of supplementing the labours of its colleague. It is only necessary for its surface to be broken by a date, by any temporal specification allowing us to measure the days that separate us from a menace—or a promise. Swann, for example, contemplates with doleful resignation the months that he must spend away from Odette during the summer. One day Odette says: "Forcheville (her lover, and, after the death of Swann, her husband) is going to Egypt at Pentecost." Swann translates: "I am going with Forcheville to Egypt at Pentecost." The fluid of future time freezes, and poor Swann, face to face with the *future* reality of Odette and Forcheville in Egypt, suffers more grievously than even at the misery of his present condition. The narrator's desire to see La Berma in *Phédre* is stimulated more violently by the announcement "Doors closed at two o'clock" than by the mystery of Bergotte's "Jansenist pallor and solar myth." His indifference at parting from Albertine at the end of the day in Balbec is transformed into the most horrible anxiety by a simple remark addressed by her to her aunt or to a friend: "To-morrow, then, at half-past eight." The tacit understanding that the future can be controlled is destroyed. The future event cannot be focussed, its implications cannot be seized, until it is definitely situated and a date assigned to it. When Albertine was his prisoner, the possibility of her escape did not seriously disturb him, because it was indistinct and abstract, like the possibility of death. Whatever opinion we may be pleased to hold on the subject of death, we may be sure that it is meaningless and valueless. Death has not required us to keep a day free. The art of publicity has been revolutionized by a similar consideration. Thus I am exhorted, not merely to try the aperient of the Shepherd, but to try it at seven o'clock.

So far we have considered a mobile subject before an ideal object, immutable and incorruptible. But our vulgar perception is not concerned with other than vulgar phenomena. Exemption from intrinsic flux in a given object does not change the fact that it is the correlative of a subject that does not enjoy such immunity. The observer infects the observed with his own mobility. Moreover, when it is a case of human intercourse, we are faced by the problem of an object whose mobility is not merely a function of the subject's, but independent and personal: two separate and immanent dynamisms related by no system of synchronisation. So that whatever the object, our thirst for possession is, by definition, insatiable. At the best, all that is realized in Time (all Time produce), whether in Art or Life, can only be possessed successively, by a series of partial annexations—and never integrally and at once. The tragedy of the Marcel-Albertine liaison is the type-tragedy of the human relation-ship whose failure is preordained. My analysis of that central catastrophe will clarify this too abstract and arbitrary statement of Proust's pessi-mism. But for every tumour a scalpel and a compress. Memory and Habit are attributes of the Time cancer. They control the most simple Proust-ian episode, and an understanding of their mechanism must precede any particular analysis of their application. They are the flying buttresses of the temple raised to commemorate the wisdom of the architect that is also the wisdom of all the sages, from Brahma to Leopardi, the wisdom that consists not in the satisfaction but in the ablation of desire:

"In noi di cari inganni
non che la speme, il desiderio è spento."

*   *
*

The laws of memory are subject to the more general laws of habit. Habit is a compromise effected between the individual and his environment, or between the individual and his own organic eccentricities, the guaran-tee of a dull inviolability, the lightning-conductor of his existence. Habit is the ballast that chains the dog to his vomit. Breathing is habit. Life is habit. Or rather life is a succession of habits, since the individual is a succession of individuals; the world being a projection of the indi-vidual's consciousness (an objectivation of the individual's will, Schopen-hauer would say), the pact must be continually renewed, the letter of safe-conduct brought up to date. The creation of the world did not take place once and for all time, but takes place every day. Habit then is the generic term for the countless treaties concluded between the countless subjects that constitute the individual and their countless correlative objects. The periods of transition that separate consecutive adaptations (because by no expedient of macabre transubstantiation can the grave-sheets serve as swaddling-clothes) represent the perilous zones in the life of the individual, dangerous, precarious, painful, mysterious and fertile, when for a moment the boredom of living is replaced by the suffering of being. (At this point, and with a heavy heart and for the satisfaction or disgruntlement of Gideans, semi and integral, I am inspired to concede a brief parenthesis to all the analogivorous, who are capable of inter-preting the "Live dangerously," that victorious hiccough in vacuo, as the national anthem of the true ego exiled in habit. The Gideans advocate a habit of living—and look for an epithet. A nonsensical bastard phrase. They imply a hierarchy of habits, as though it were valid to speak of good habits and bad habits. An automatic adjustment of the human organ-ism to the conditions of its existence has as little moral significance as the casting of a clout when May is or is not out; and the exhortation to cultivate a habit as little sense as an exhortation to cultivate a coryza.) The suffering of being: that is, the free play of every faculty. Because the pernicious devotion of habit paralyses our attention, drugs those hand-maidens of perception whose co-operation is not absolutely essential. Habit is like Françoise, the immortal cook of the Proust household, who knows what has to be done, and will slave all day and all night rather than tolerate any redundant activity in the kitchen. But our current habit of living is as incapable of dealing with the mystery of a strange sky or a strange room, with any circumstance unforeseen in her curriculum, as Françoise of conceiving or realizing the full horror of a Duval omelette. Then the atrophied faculties come to the rescue, and the maximum value of our being is restored. But less drastic circumstances may produce this tense and provisional lucidity in the nervous system. Habit may not be dead (or as good as dead, doomed to die) but sleeping. This second and more fugitive experience may or may not be exempt from pain. It does not inaugurate a period of transition. But the first and major mode is inseparable from suffering and anxiety—the suffering of the dying and the jealous anxiety of the ousted. The old ego dies hard. Such as it was, a minister of dullness, it was also an agent of security. When it ceases to perform that second function, when it is opposed by a phenomenon that it cannot reduce to the condition of a comfortable and familiar concept, when, in a word, it betrays its trust as a screen to spare its victim the spectacle of reality, it disappears, and the victim, now an ex-victim, for a moment free, is exposed to that reality—an exposure that has its advantages and its disadvantages. It disappears—with wailing and gnashing of teeth. The mortal microcosm cannot forgive the relative immortality of the macrocosm. The whisky bears a grudge against the decanter. The narrator cannot sleep in a strange room, is tortured by a high ceiling, being used to a low ceiling. What is taking place? The old pact is out of date. It contained no clause treating of high ceilings. The habit of friendship for the low ceiling is ineffectual, must die in order that a habit of friendship for the high ceiling may be born. Between this death and that birth, reality, intolerable, absorbed feverishly by his consciousness at the extreme limit of its intensity, by his total consciousness organized to avert the disaster, to create the new habit that will empty the mystery of its threat—and also of its beauty. "If Habit," writes Proust, "is a second nature, it keeps us in ignorance of the first, and is free of its cruelties and its enchantments." Our first nature, therefore, corresponding, as we shall see later, to a deeper instinct than the mere animal instinct of self-preservation, is laid bare during these periods of abandonment. And its cruelties and enchantments are the cruelties and enchantments of reality. "Enchantments of reality" has the air of a paradox. But when the object is perceived as particular and unique and not merely the member of a family, when it appears independent of any general notion and detached from the sanity of a cause, isolated and inexplicable in the light of ignorance, then and then only may it be a source of enchantment. Unfortunately Habit has laid its veto on this form of perception, its action being precisely to hide the essence—the Idea—of the object in the haze of conception—preconception. Normally we are in the position of the tourist (the traditional specification would constitute a pleonasm), whose aesthetic experience consists in a series of identifications and for whom Baedeker is the end rather than the means. Deprived by nature of the faculty of cognition and by upbringing of any acquaintance with the laws of dynamics, a brief inscription immortalises his emotion. The creature of habit turns aside from the object that cannot be made to correspond with one or other of his intellectual prejudices, that resists the propositions of his team of syntheses, organised by Habit on labour-saving principles.

Examples of these two modes—the death of Habit and the brief suspension of its vigilance—abound in Proust. I will transcribe two incidents in the life of the narrator. Of these the first, illustrative of the pact renewed, is extremely important as preparing a later incident that I will have occasion to discuss in relation to Proustian memory and Proustian revelation. The second exemplifies the pact waived in the interests of the narrator's via dolorosa.

The narrator arrives at Balbec-Plage, a holiday resort in Normandy, for the first time, accompanied by his grandmother. They are staying at the Grand Hotel. He enters his room, feverish and exhausted after his journey. But sleep, in this inferno of unfamiliar objects, is out of the question. All his faculties are on the alert, on the defensive, vigilant and taut, and as painfully incapable of relaxation as the tortured body of La Balue in his cage, where he could neither stand upright nor sit down. There is no room for his body in this vast and hideous apartment, because his attention has peopled it with gigantic furniture, a storm of sound and an agony of colour. Habit has not had time to silence the explosions of the clock, reduce the hostility of the violet curtains, remove the furniture and lower the inaccessible vault of this belvedere. Alone in this room that is not yet a room but a cavern of wild beasts, invested on all sides by the implacable strangers whose privacy he has disturbed, he desires to die. His grandmother comes in, comforts him, checks the stooping gesture that he makes to unbutton his boots, insists on helping him to undress, puts him to bed, and before leaving him makes him promise to knock on the partition that separates her room from his, should he require anything during the night. He knocks, and she comes again to him. But that night and for many nights he suffered. That suffering he interprets as the obscure, organic, humble refusal on the part of those elements that represented all that was best in his life to accept the possibility of a formula in which they would have no part. This reluctance to die, this long and desperate and daily resistance before the perpetual exfoliation of personality, explains also his horror at the idea of ever living without Gilberte Swann, of ever losing his parents, at the idea of his own death. But this terror at the thought of separation—from Gilberte, from his parents, from himself— is dissipated in a greater terror, when he thinks that to the pain of separation will succeed indifference, that the privation will cease to be a privation when the alchemy of Habit has transformed the individual capable of suffering into a stranger for whom the motives of that suffering are an idle tale, when not only the objects of his affection have vanished, but also that affection itself; and he thinks how absurd is our dream of a Paradise with retention of personality, since our life is a succession of Paradises successively denied, that the only true Paradise is the Paradise that has been lost, and that death will cure many of the desire for immortality.

The second episode that I have chosen as an illustration of the pact waived engages the same two characters, the narrator and his grandmother. He has been staying at Doncières with his friend Saint-Loup. He telephones to his grandmother in Paris. (After reading the description of this telephone call and its hardly less powerful corollary, when, years later, he speaks over the telephone with Albertine on returning home late after his first visit to the Princesse de Guermantes, Cocteau's *Voix Humaine* seems not merely a banality but an unnecessary banality.) After the conventional misunderstanding with the Vigilant Virgins (*sic*) of the central exchange, he hears his grandmother's voice, or what he assumes to be her voice, because he hears it now for the first time, in all its purity and reality, so different from the voice that he had been accustomed to follow on the open score of her face that he does not recognize it as hers. It is a grievous voice, its fragility unmitigated and undisguised by the carefully arranged mask of her features, and this strange real voice is the measure of its owner's suffering. He hears it also as the symbol of her isolation, of their separation, as impalpable as a voice from the dead.

The voice stops. His grandmother seems as irretrievably lost as Eurydice among the shades. Alone before the mouthpiece he calls her name in vain. Nothing can persuade him to remain at Doncières. He must see his grandmother. He leaves for Paris. He surprises her reading her beloved Mme. de Sévigné. But he is not there because she does not know that he is there. He is present at his own absence. And, in consequence of his journey and his anxiety, his habit is in abeyance, the habit of his tenderness for his grandmother. His gaze is no longer the necromancy that sees in each precious object a mirror of the past. The notion of what he should see has not had time to interfere its prism between the eye and its object. His eye functions with the cruel precision of a camera; it photographs the reality of his grandmother. And he realizes with horror that his grandmother is dead, long since and many times, that the cherished familiar of his mind, mercifully composed all along the years by the solicitude of habitual memory, exists no longer, that this mad old woman, drowsing over her book, overburdened with years, flushed and coarse and vulgar, is a stranger whom he has never seen.

The respite is brief. "Of all human plants," writes Proust, "Habit requires the least fostering, and is the first to appear on the seeming desolation of the most barren rock." Brief, and dangerously painful. The fundamental duty of Habit, about which it describes the futile and stupefying arabesques of its supererogations, consists in a perpetual adjustment and readjustment of our organic sensibility to the conditions of its worlds. Suffering represents the omission of that duty, whether through negligence or inefficiency, and boredom its adequate performance. The pendulum oscillates between these two terms: Suffering—that opens a window on the real and is the main condition of the artistic experience, and Boredom—with its host of top-hatted and hygienic ministers, Boredom that must be considered as the most tolerable because the most durable of human evils. Considered as a progression, this endless series of renovations leaves us as indifferent as the heterogeneity of any one of its terms, and the inconsequence of any given me disturbs us as little as the comedy of substitution. Indeed, we take as little cognisance of one as of the other, unless, vaguely, after the event, or clearly, when, as in the case of Proust, two birds in the bush are of infinitely greater value than one in the hand, and because—if I may add this nux vomica to an apéritif of metaphors—the heart of the cauliflower or the ideal core of the onion would represent a more appropriate tribute to the labours of poetical excavation than the crown of bay. I draw the conclusion of this matter from Proust's treasury of nutshell phrases: "If there were no such thing as Habit, Life would of necessity appear delicious to all those whom Death would threaten at every moment, that is to say, to all Mankind."

* *
*

Proust had a bad memory—as he had an inefficient habit, because he had an inefficient habit. The man with a good memory does not remember anything because he does not forget anything. His memory is uniform, a creature of routine, at once a condition and function of his impeccable habit, an instrument of reference instead of an instrument of discovery. The paean of his memory: "I remember as well as I remember yester-day . . ." is also its epitaph, and gives the precise expression of its value. He cannot *remember* yesterday any more than he can remember tomorrow. He can contemplate yesterday hung out to dry with the wettest August bank holiday on record a little further down the clothes-line. Because his memory is a clothes-line and the images of his past dirty linen redeemed and the infallibly complacent servants of his reminiscential needs. Memory is obviously conditioned by perception. Curiosity is a non-conditioned reflex, in its most primitive manifestations a reaction before a danger-stimulus, and seldom exempt, even in its superior and apparently most disinterested form, from utilitarian considerations. Curiosity is the hair of our habit tending to stand on end. It rarely happens that our attention is not stained in greater or lesser degree by this animal element. Curiosity is the safeguard, not the death, of the cat, whether in skirts or on all fours. The more interested our interest, the more indelible must be its record of impressions. Its booty will always be available, because its aggression was a form of self-defence, i.e. the function of an invariable. In extreme cases memory is so closely related to habit that its word takes flesh, and is not merely available in cases of urgency, but habitually enforced. Thus absence of mind is fortunately compatible with the active presence of our organs of articulation. I repeat that rememoration, in its highest sense, cannot be applied to these extracts of our anxiety. Strictly speaking, we can only remember what has been registered by our extreme inattention and stored in that ultimate and inaccessible dungeon of our being to which Habit does not possess the key, and does not need to, because it contains none of the hideous and useful paraphernalia of war. But here, in that "gouffre interdit à nos sondes," is stored the essence of ourselves, the best of our many selves and their concretions that simplists call the world, the best because accumulated slyly and painfully and patiently under the nose of our vulgarity, the fine essence of a smothered divinity whose whispered "disfazione" is drowned in the healthy bawling of an all-embracing appetite, the pearl that may give the lie to our carapace of paste and pewter. May—when we escape into the spacious annexe of mental alienation, in sleep or the rare dispensation of waking madness. From this deep source Proust hoisted his world. His work is not an accident, but its salvage is an accident. The conditions of that accident will be revealed at the peak of this prevision. A second-hand climax is better than none. But no purpose can be served by withholding the name of the diver. Proust calls him "involuntary memory." The memory that is not memory, but the application of a concordance to the Old Testament of the individual, he calls "voluntary memory." This is the uniform memory of intelligence; and it can be relied on to reproduce for our gratified inspection those impressions of the past that were consciously and intelligently formed. It has no interest in the mysterious element of inattention that colours our most commonplace experiences. It presents the past in monochrome. The images it chooses are as arbitrary as those chosen by imagination, and are equally remote from reality. Its action has been compared by Proust to that of turning the leaves of an album of photographs. The material that it furnishes contains nothing of the past, merely a blurred and uniform projection once removed of our anxiety and opportunism—that is to say, nothing. There is no great difference, says Proust, between the memory of a dream and the memory of reality. When the sleeper awakes, this emissary of his habit assures him that his "personality" has not disappeared with his fatigue. It is possible (for those that take an interest in such speculations) to consider the resurrection of the soul as a final piece of impertinence from the same source. It insists on that most necessary, wholesome and monotonous plagiarism—the plagiarism of oneself. This thoroughgoing democrat makes no distinction between the "Pensées" of Pascal and a soap advertisement. In fact, if Habit is the Goddess of Dullness, voluntary memory is Shadwell, and of Irish extraction. Involuntary memory is explosive, "an immediate, total and delicious deflagration." It restores, not merely the past object, but the Lazarus that it charmed or tortured, not merely Lazarus and the object, but more because less, more because it abstracts the useful, the opportune, the accidental, because in its flame it has consumed Habit and all its works, and in its brightness revealed what the mock reality of experience never can and never will reveal—the real. But involuntary memory is an unruly magician and will not be importuned. It chooses its own time and place for the performance of its miracle. I do not know how often this miracle recurs in Proust. I think twelve or thirteen times. But the first— the famous episode of the madeleine steeped in tea—would justify the assertion that his entire book is a monument to involuntary memory and the epic of its action. The whole of Proust's world comes out of a teacup, and not merely Combray and his childhood. For Combray brings us to the two "ways" and to Swann, and to Swann may be related every element of the Proustian experience and consequently its climax in revelation. Swann is behind Balbec, and Balbec is Albertine and Saint-Loup. Directly he involves Odette and Gilberte, the Verdurins and their clan, the music of Vinteuil and the magical prose of Bergotte; indirectly (via Balbec and Saint-Loup) the Guermantes, Oriane and the Duke, the Princesse and M. de Charlus. Swann is the corner-stone of the entire structure, and the central figure of the narrator's childhood, a childhood that involuntary memory, stimulated or charmed by the long-forgotten taste of a madeleine steeped in an infusion of tea, conjures in all the relief and colour of its essential significance from the shallow well of a cup's inscrutable banality.

* *
*

From this Janal, trinal, agile monster or Divinity: Time—a condition of resurrection because an instrument of death; Habit—an infliction in so far as it opposes the dangerous exaltation of the one and a blessing in so far as it palliates the cruelty of the other; Memory—a clinical laboratory stocked with poison and remedy, stimulant and sedative: from Him the mind turns to the one compensation and miracle of evasion tolerated by His tyranny and vigilance. This accidental and fugitive salvation in the midst of life may supervene when the action of involuntary memory is stimulated by the negligence or agony of Habit, and under no other circumstances, nor necessarily then. Proust has adopted this mystic experience as the Leitmotiv of his composition. It recurs, like the red phrase of the Vinteuil Septuor, a neuralgia rather than a theme, persistent and monotonous, disappears beneath the surface and emerges a still finer and more nervous structure, enriched with a strange and necessary incrustation of grace-notes, a more confident and essential statement of reality, and climbs through a series of precisions and purifications to the pinnacle from which it commands and clarifies the most humble incident of its ascent and delivers its triumphant ultimatum. It appears for the first time as the episode of the madeleine, and again on at least five capital occasions before its final and multiple investment of the Guermantes Hotel at the opening of the second volume of *Le Temps Retrouvé*, its culminating and integral expression. Thus the germ of the Proustian solution is contained in the statement of the problem itself. The source and point of departure of this "sacred action," the elements of communion, are provided by the physical world, by some immediate and fortuitous act of perception. The process is almost one of intellectualised animism. The following is the list of fetishes:

1. The Madeleine steeped in an infusion of tea.
   (*Du Côté de Chez Swann*, i. 69–73.)
2. The steeples of Martinville, seen from Dr. Percepied's trap.
   (*Ibid.*, 258–262.)
3. A musty smell in a public lavatory in the Champs-Elysées.
   (*A l'Ombre des Jeunes Filles en Fleurs*, i. 90.)

4. The three trees, seen near Balbec from the carriage of Mme. de Villeparisis. (*Ibid.*, ii. 161.)

5. The hedge of hawthorn near Balbec. (*Ibid.*, iii. 215.)

6. He stoops to unbutton his boots on the occasion of his second visit to the Grand Hotel at Balbec. (*Sodome et Gomorrhe*, ii. 176.)

7. Uneven cobbles in the courtyard of the Guermantes Hotel. (*Le Temps Retrouvé*, ii. 7.)

8. The noise of a spoon against a plate. (*Ibid.*, 9.)

9. He wipes his mouth with a napkin. (*Ibid.*, 10.)

10. The noise of water in the pipes. (*Ibid.*, 18.)

11. George Sand's *François le Champi*. (*Ibid.*, 30.)

The list is not complete. I have not included a number of tentative and abortive experiences, no one of which constitutes properly a recurrence of the motif, but rather a premonition of its approach. Of these shadowy, incomplete evocations a certain cluster of three is specially significant (*Côté de Guermantes*, ii. 80–82). He is waiting at home for Mlle. de Stermaria (who might have been the narrator's Albertine if she had not failed him then). He is transported successively to Balbec, Doncières and Combray by the twilight perceived above the curtains of his window, the descent of the stairs side by side with Robert de Saint-Loup who has just arrived, and the dense fog that has settled on the street. These three evocations, although incomplete, are intensely violent, and for a moment he is conscious of the heterogeneous matter and substance of these periods of his past: of the sombre, rugged sandstone of Combray, as opposed to the compact, glittering, translucid, rose-veined alabaster of Rivebelle. But he is not alone, he is interrupted by Saint-Loup, and what might have been the turning-point in his life, the climax that is not to be reached until many years later in the courtyard and library of the Princesse de Guermantes, is nothing more than one of its most fugitive precursors.

The last five visitations—cobbles, spoon and plate, napkin, water in the pipes, and *François le Champi*—may be considered as forming a single annunciation and as providing the key to his life and work. The

sixth capital experience is particularly important (although less famil-
iar than the famous madeleine, which is invariably quoted as the type
of the Proustian revelation) as representing not only a central appear-
ance of the motif but also an application of the erratic machinery of
habit and memory as conceived by Proust. Albertine and the Proustian
Discours de la Méthode having waited so long can wait a little longer, and
the reader is cordially invited to omit this summary analysis of what is
perhaps the greatest passage that Proust ever wrote—*Les Intermittences
du Coeur.*

This incident takes place on the first evening of the narrator's second visit
to Balbec. On this occasion he is with his mother, his grandmother hav-
ing died a year before. But the dead annex the quick as surely as the King-
dom of France annexes the Duchy of Orléans. His mother has become
his grandmother, whether through the suggestion of regret or an idola-
trous cult of the dead or the disintegrating effect of loss that breaks the
chrysalis and hastens the metamorphosis of an atavistic embryon whose
maturation is slow and imperceptible without the stimulus of grief. She
carries her mother's bag and her muff, and is never without a volume
of Mme. de Sévigné. She who formerly chaffed her mother for never
writing a letter without quoting Mme. de Sévigné or Mme. de Beauser-
gent, builds now her own to her son around some phrase from the Let-
ters or the Memoirs. The narrator's motives for this second visit are not
those—furnished by Swann and his fantasy—that granted him no peace
while Balbec had still the mystery and beauty of its name, before reality
had replaced the mirage of imagination by the mirage of memory and
explained away the value of the unknown as Venice will in due course be
explained away and the odyssey of the local "tacot" through a mythical
land by the etymology of Brichot and the appeasing contempt of famil-
iarity. The Persian church with its stained glass "surfed in spray" and
its steeple hewn out of the granite rampart of a Norman cliff has been
replaced by the Giorgionesque chambermaid of Mme. de Putbus.

He arrives tired and ill, as on the former occasion that has been ana-
lysed as an example of the death of Habit. Now, however, the dragon has

been reduced to docility, and the cavern is a room. Habit has been reorganised—an operation described by Proust as "longer and more difficult than the turning inside out of an eyelid, and which consists in the imposition of our own familiar soul on the terrifying soul of our surroundings." He stoops down—cautiously, in the interests of his heart—to unbutton his boots. Suddenly he is filled with a divine familiar presence. Once more he is restored to himself by that being whose tenderness, several years earlier, in a similar moment of distress and fatigue, had brought him a moment's calm, by his grandmother as she had been then, as she had continued to be until that fatal day of her stroke in the Champs-Elysées, after which nothing remained of her but a name, so that her death was of as little consequence to the narrator as the death of a stranger. Now, a year after her burial, thanks to the mysterious action of involuntary memory, he learns that she is dead. At any given moment our total soul, in spite of its rich balance-sheet, has only a fictitious value. Its assets are never completely realizable. But he has not merely extracted from this gesture the lost reality of his grandmother: he has recovered the lost reality of himself, the reality of his lost self. As though the figure of Time could be represented by an endless series of parallels, his life is switched over to another line and proceeds, without any solution of continuity, from that remote moment of his past when his grandmother stooped over his distress. And he is as incapable of visualising the incidents that punctuated that long period of intermittence, the incidents of the past few hours, as in that interval he was inexorably bereft of that precious panel in the tapestry of his days representing his grandmother and his love for her. But this resumption of a past life is poisoned by a cruel anachronism: his grandmother is dead. For the first time since her death, since the Champs-Elysées, he has recovered her living and complete, as she was so many times, at Combray and Paris and Balbec. For the first time since her death he knows that she is dead, he knows *who* is dead. He had to recover her alive and tender before he could admit her dead and for ever incapable of any tenderness. This contradiction between presence and irremediable obliteration is intolerable. Not merely the memory—the experience—of their mutual predestination is retrospectively abolished by the certainty that it is folly to speak in such cases of predestination, that his grandmother was a chance acquaintance and the few years spent with her an accident, that as he meant nothing to her before their meeting, so he can mean nothing to her after her departure. He cannot understand "this dolorous synthesis of survival and annihilation." And he writes: "I did not know whether this painful and for the moment incomprehensible impression would ever yield up any truth. But I knew that if I ever did succeed in extracting some truth from the world, it would be from such an impression and from none other, an impression at once particular and spontaneous, which had neither been formed by my intelligence nor attenuated by my pusillanimity, but whose double and mysterious furrow had been carved, as by a thunderbolt, within me, by the inhuman and supernatural blade of Death, or the revelation of Death." But already will, the will to live, the will not to suffer, Habit, having recovered from its momentary paralysis, has laid the foundations of its evil and necessary structure, and the vision of his grandmother begins to fade and to lose that miraculous relief and clarity that no effort of deliberate rememoration can impart or restore. It is redeemed for a moment by the sight of that party-wall which, like an instrument, had transmitted the faltering statement of his distress, and, some days later, by the drawing of a blind in a railway carriage, when the evocation of his grandmother is so vivid and painful that he is obliged to abandon his visit to Mme. Verdurin and leave the train. But before this new brightness, this old brightness revived and intensified, can be finally extinguished, the Calvary of pity and remorse must be trod. The insistent memory of cruelties to one who is dead is a flagellation, because the dead are only dead in so far as they continue to exist in the heart of the survivor. And pity for what has been suffered is a more cruel and precise expression for that suffering than the conscious estimate of the sufferer, who is spared at least one despair—the despair of the spectator. The narrator recalls an incident that took place during his first stay at Balbec, in the light of which he had considered his grandmother as a frivolous and vain old woman. She had insisted on having her photograph taken by Saint-Loup, so that her beloved grandchild might have at least that poor record of her latter days, a fusillade of syncopes (called "symcopes" by the manager of the Grand Hotel, who now reveals to the narrator this first onslaught of his grandmother's malady and unwittingly provides, in his absurd malapropism, yet another instrument of painful evocation) and strokes having allowed her to see death clearly at last as a coming event. And she had been very particular about her pose and the inclination of her hat, wishing the photograph to be one of a grandmother and not of a disease. All of which precautions the narrator had translated as the futilities of coquetry. So, unlike Miranda, he suffers with her whom he had not seen suffer, as though, for him as for Françoise, whom Giotto's charitable scullion in childbirth and the violent translation of what is fit to live into what is fit to eat leave indifferent, but who cannot restrain her tears when informed that there has been an earthquake in China, pain could only be focussed at a distance.

*　*
*

The Albertine tragedy is prepared during the narrator's first stay at Balbec, involved by their relations in Paris, consolidated during his second stay at Balbec, and consummated by her imprisonment in Paris. She appears to him for the first time, absorbed in the radiance of the "little band" at Balbec, pushing a bicycle, an item in that ineffable and inaccessible procession, winding and unwinding its gracious figures against the sea, and seeming to the envious adoration of the narrator as eternally and hermetically exclusive as a frieze or a frescoed cortège. She has no individuality. She is merely one blossom in this fragile hedge of Pennsylvanian roses breaking the line of the waves, and this original collective mystery of the little band enables him many years later, when Albertine has been detached and made a captive, when the nebulae of this constellation have been synthesized into one single astral obsession, to deny, not merely the objective reality (as was the case with Gilberte) of his love for her, but also its subjective reality, by co-ordinating her with another image. She looks at him one day on the shore (the identification with Albertine is retrospective), and he writes: "I knew that I would not possess this young cyclist if I did not possess what was in her eyes." His imagination weaves its cocoon about this frail and almost abstract chrysalis, this unit in an orgiac band of cycling Bacchantes. He is introduced to her by the painter Elstir, and proceeds to her acquaintance by a series of subtractions, each fragment of his fantasy and desire being replaced by an infinitely less precious notion. Thus her relationship with Mme. Bontemps, her early amiabilities, the effect of a declamatory beauty-spot on her chin, her use of the adverb "perfectly" for "quite," the provisional inflammation of her temple constituting an optical centre of gravity about which the composition of her features is organized, are sufficient taken together to establish an Albertine as remote from the first Albertine, the beach flower, as yet a third aspect, characterised by a pronounced nasal enunciation, a terrifying command of slang, the disappearance of the inflamed temple, and the miraculous transference of the beauty-spot from her chin to her upper lip, is remote from the second. Thus is established the *pictorial* multiplicity of Albertine that will duly evolve into a *plastic* and moral multiplicity, no longer a mere shifting superficies and an effect of the observer's angle of approach rather than the expression of an inward and active variety, but a multiplicity in depth, a turmoil of objective and immanent contradictions over which the subject has no control. Yet already he concludes, before the kaleidoscope of her expressions, before this face that from being all surface, smooth and waxed, passes to an almost fluid state of translucid gaiety, and from the chiselled polish of an opal to the feverish black-red congestion of a cyclamen, that the Name is an example of a barbarous society's primitivism, and as conventionally inadequate as "Homer" or "sea." His first vague gesture of approach is coldly repulsed. He concludes that Albertine is virtuous and that his original hypothesis—that she was possibly the mistress of a racing cyclist or a champion boxer—was not merely incorrect in its specific application but based on an entirely false sense of her character. He concludes that Albertine is virtuous, and his first stay at Balbec closes on that impression.

It is corrected by a visit from Albertine in Paris. To a new vocabulary, garnished with such sophistications as "distinguished," "to my mind," "mousmé," "lapse of time," corresponds a new and sophisticated Albertine, as lavish now of her favours as she was formerly parsimonious. The narrator, while supposing that Albertine has been the object of an initiation, can establish no common measure between these three main aspects of Albertine: the passionate unreal Albertine of the shore, the real and virginal Albertine such as she appeared to him at the end of his stay at Balbec, and now this third Albertine that fulfils the promise of the first in the reality of the second. "My surplus of knowledge ended in a provisional agnosticism. What affirmation was possible when the original hypothesis had first been refuted and then confirmed?" And the pleasure he takes with Albertine is intensified by the reaching out of his spirit towards that immaterial reality that she seems to symbolise, Balbec and its sea—"as though the material possession of an object, residence in a town, were the equivalent of spiritual possession." This compound object of desire—a woman and the sea—is simplified of its second element by the habit of the first. A secondary compound can be formed by jealousy, and the amalgam of human and marine restored, but as a cardiac and no longer as a visual stimulus. But even this new Albertine is multiple, and just as the most modern applications of photography can frame a single church successively in the arcades of all the others and the entire horizon in the arch of a bridge or between two adjacent leaves, thus decomposing the illusion of a solid object into its manifold component aspects, so the short journey of his lips to the cheek of Albertine creates ten Albertines, and transforms a human banality into a many-headed goddess. But the menace of what life with her must be is announced to him more clearly when, after his first visit to the Princesse de Guermantes, he sits alone in his room waiting for Albertine (who, momentarily eclipsed by the mysterious Mlle. de Stermaria, has been absent from his mind all evening), for Albertine who has promised to come and who does not come and whose non-arrival exalts a simple physical irritation into a flame of moral anguish, so that he listens for her step or for the sublime summons of the telephone, not with his ear and mind, but with his heart. For in his anxiety he has added yet another crystal to this branch of Salzburg, the crystal of a need, of that need that tortured him at Combray and that only his mother could allay with the host of her lips. But when she telephones to explain, when he knows that she is on her way, then he wonders how he could have seen in this vulgar Albertine, similar, even inferior, to so many others, a source of comfort and salvation that no miracle could replace. "One only loves that which is not possessed, one only loves that in which one pursues the inaccessible."

The second visit to Balbec, inaugurated by the retrospective loss and mourning of his grandmother, completes the transformation of a creature of surface into a creature of depth—unfathomable, accomplishes the solidification of a profile. From the moment that Dr. Cottard sees Albertine and her friend Andrée (one of the band) dancing together in the Casino at Incarville, and pompously diagnoses a case of sexual perversion, dates the "reciprocal torture" of their relations. From this point lies and counterlies, pursuit and evasion, and on the part of the narrator a love for Albertine whose intensity is related in direct proportion to the success of her prevarications. Because Albertine is not only a liar as all those that believe themselves loved are liars: she is a natural liar. A succession of incidents consolidate the narrator's doubt on the chapter of Albertine, that is to say, exasperate his love for her. She fails to keep an appointment, she lies about an appointment with a mythical friend of her aunt at Infreville, she stares at the reflection in a mirror of Mlle. Bloch and her cousin, two practising Sapphists, and then denies having seen them. Then, the narrator's jealousy and sense of impotence being at their height, there follows a lull, and he is calmed by the docility of an always available Albertine. He becomes indifferent to this new creature who opposes no further resistance. He resolves to break with her, and announces his decision to his mother. Returning one evening with Albertine in the "tacot" from a party at La Raspelière he goes over in his mind the formulae of separation. He happens to mention that he is interested in the music of Vinteuil. Albertine, whose taste in music is as primitive as her appreciation of painting and architecture is developed, hoping to create a favourable impression, declares that she is perfectly familiar with the music of Vinteuil, thanks to her intimacy with Mlle. Vinteuil and her friend, the actress Léa. In a paroxysm of jealousy the narrator is back again at Montjouvain, the horrified spectator of these two Lesbians flavouring their pleasure in a sadistic act of desecration at the expense of M. Vinteuil himself, who has been dead some time.[1] And this vision of Montjouvain seems to come like Orestes to avenge the murder of Agamemnon. And he thinks of his grandmother and of his cruelties towards her. Albertine, so remote and detached from his heart a moment before, is now not merely an obsession, but part of himself, within him, and the movement she makes to descend from the train threatens to tear open his body. He forces her to accompany him to Balbec. The strand and the waves exist no more, the summer is dead. The sea is a veil that cannot hide the horror of Montjouvain, the intolerable vision of sadistic lubricity and a photograph defiled. He sees in Albertine another Rachel and another Odette, and the sterility and mockery of an affection dictated by interest. He sees his life as a succession of joyless dawns, poisoned by the tortures of memory and isolation. The next morning he brings Albertine to Paris and locks her up in his house.

His life in common with Albertine is volcanic, his mind torn by a series of eruptions: Fury, Jealousy, Envy, Curiosity, Suffering, Pride, Honour and Love. The form of this last is pre-established by the arbitrary images of memory and imagination, an artificial fiction to which, and for his suffering, he forces the woman to conform. The person of Albertine counts for nothing. She is not a motive, but a notion, as far removed from reality as the portrait of Odette by Elstir, which is the portrait not of the beloved but of the love that has deformed her, is removed from the real Odette. So that his anxiety cannot be argued from Albertine, but from a whole processus of sufferings and emotions that have been associated with her person and attached to it by habit. His life with Albertine, containing not one single positive advantage, is no more than an appeasement, the token of a monopoly. And not always an appeasement, because the mystery of Albertine persists, the mystery that he sensed in her eyes when they first met before the sea at Balbec, the mystery that charmed him then and that now, because it represents the fragility of his domination, he longs to efface. This last phase of his association with Albertine bears the trace of its inception, its inception in his jealousy and her

---

1. *Du Côté de Chez Swann*, i.

deceitfulness. "How have we the courage to wish to live, how can we make a movement to preserve ourselves from death, in a world where love is provoked by a lie and consists solely in the need of having our sufferings appeased by whatever being has made us suffer?" Surely in the whole of literature there is no study of that desert of loneliness and recrimination that men call love posed and developed with such diabolical unscrupulousness. After this, *Adolphe* is a petulant dribbling, the mock epic of salivary hypersecretion, Mme. de Cambremer (whose name, as Oriane de Guermantes observes to Swann, stops just in time) in tears. Every word and gesture of Albertine are caught up in the vortex of jealousy and suspicion, translated and mistranslated, reapplied and misapplied. Every remembered incident is decomposed in the acid of his mistrust. "My imagination provided equations for the unknown in this algebra of desire." But Albertine is a fugitive, and no expression of her value can be complete unless preceded by some such symbol as that which in physics denotes speed. A static Albertine would soon be conquered, would soon be compared to all the other possible conquests that her possession excludes, and the infinite of what is not and may be preferred to the nullity of what is. Love, he insists, can only coexist with a state of dissatisfaction, whether born of jealousy or its predecessor—desire. It represents our demand for a whole. Its inception and its continuance imply the consciousness that something is lacking. "One only loves that which one does not possess entirely." And until the rupture takes place—(and indeed long after it has taken place, even when the object is dead, thanks to a retrospective jealousy, a "jalousie de l'escalier")—warfare. Albertine mentions casually that she may visit the Verdurins. Anagram: "I may go and see the Verdurins to-morrow. I don't know. I don't particularly want to." Translation: "It is absolutely certain that I will go and see the Verdurins to-morrow. It is of the greatest possible importance." He remembers that Morel has promised to conduct the Vinteuil Septuor for Mme. Verdurin, and concludes that Mlle. Vinteuil and her friend will be among the guests, and that by some infernal stroke of cunning Albertine has made an appointment with them for the following evening. Thus these rare moments of relief that enable him to form the determination to break with Albertine and to put an end to this double slavery that prevents him from going to Venice, prevents him from working, separates him from his friends, and at most and grudgingly affords him the bitter satisfaction of knowing that no rival shall enjoy what he himself cannot enjoy—these rare periods of relative ease are cut short by the intervention of a new motive of jealousy or by the transformation, in the tireless crucible of his mind, of some insignificant detail of their past into a poison for the exasperation of his love or hate or jealousy (interchangeable terms) and the corrosion of his heart. For example, when he is at last resolved on separation, she swears that her aunt has no friend living at Infreville. There is no limit to her deceit and none to his faculty of suffering. And in the midst of this Tolomea he *knows* that this woman has no reality, that "our most exclusive love for a person is always our love for something else," that intrinsically she is less than nothing, but that in her nothingness there is active, mysterious and invisible, a current that forces him to bow down and worship an obscure and implacable Goddess, and to make sacrifices of himself before her. And the Goddess who requires this sacrifice and this humiliation, whose sole condition of patronage is corruptibility, and into whose faith and worship all mankind is born, is the Goddess of Time. No object prolonged in this temporal dimension tolerates possession, meaning by possession total possession, only to be achieved by the complete identification of object and subject. The impenetrability of the most vulgar and insignificant human creature is not merely an illusion of the subject's jealousy (although this impenetrability stands out more clearly under the Röntgen rays of a jealousy so fiercely hypertrophied as was that of the narrator, a jealousy that is doubtless a form of his domination complex and his infantilism, two tendencies highly developed in Proust). All that is active, all that is enveloped in time and space, is endowed with what might be described as an abstract, ideal and absolute impermeability. So that we can understand the position of Proust: "We imagine that the object of our desire is a being that can be laid down before us, enclosed within a body. Alas! it is the extension of that being to all the points of space and time that it has occupied and will occupy. If we do not possess contact with such a place and with such an

hour we do not possess that being. But we cannot touch all these points."
And again: "A being scattered in space and time is no longer a woman but
a series of events on which we can throw no light, a series of problems
that cannot be solved, a sea that, like Xerxes, we thrash with rods in an
absurd desire to punish it for having engulfed our treasure." And he
defines love as: "Time and Space made perceptible to the heart." He per-
suades Albertine to go to a special performance at the Trocadéro instead
of to the Verdurin reception. She consents. The Vinteuil menace having
been averted, he thinks of Albertine as an importunity. He is idly turning
the leaves of the *Figaro* when he is suddenly galvanised by the announce-
ment that Léa is acting at that very gala performance to which he has sent
Albertine. Gala! In a frenzy he sends Françoise to bring her back. She
returns without having been able to speak to Léa. His calm is restored
and again shattered by an allusion made by Albertine to the Buttes-
Chaumont. He suspects Andrée. He sees that there can be no peace and
no rest until Albertine has gone. He will forget her as he forgot Gilberte
Swann and the Duchesse de Guermantes. (But Gilberte is to Albertine
what the Sonata is to the Septuor—an experiment.) And the idea that his
suffering will cease is more unbearable than that suffering itself. "The
lion of my love trembled before the python of forgetfulness." Early one
morning, during a period of calm, he makes up his mind. Albertine must
leave him. He loves her no longer. He will go to Venice and forget her. He
rings for Françoise to send out for a guide and a timetable. He will go to
Venice to his dream of Gothic time on a vernal sea. Enter Françoise. "Mlle.
Albertine left at nine o'clock and gave me this letter for Monsieur." And
like Phèdre, he recognizes the ever-wakeful Gods.

> ". . . ces dieux qui dans mon flanc
> Ont allumé le feu fatal à tout mon sang,
> Ces dieux qui se sont fait une gloire cruelle
> De réduire le coeur d'une faible mortelle."

Shortly afterwards Albertine is killed in Touraine. Her death, her
emancipation from Time, does not calm his jealousy nor accelerate the

extinction of an obsession whose rack and wheel were the days and the hours. They and their love were amphibious, plunged in the past and the present. There is a moral climate and a sentimental calendar, where the instrument of commensuration is not solar but cardiac. To forget Albertine he must—like a man struck down by hemiplegia—forget the seasons, their seasons, and, like a child, learn them anew. "In order to be consoled I would have to forget, not one, but innumerable Albertines." And not only "I," but the many "I"s. For any given Albertine there exists a correlative narrator, and no anachronism can put apart what Time has coupled. He must return and re-enact the stations of a diminishing suffering. Thus his astonishment that Albertine, so alive within him, can be dead—the fact of her life assailed by the notion of her death—gives way to the less painful astonishment that one who is dead can continue to concern him—the fact of her death assailed by the notion of her life. But the stations of this inverted Calvary retain their original dynamism, their crescendo, their tension towards a cross. At each halt he suffers from the hallucination that what has been left behind is still before him. "Such is the cruelty of memory." He describes three of these stages, arranged in descending powers of brutality. The first, a solitary walk in the Bois de Boulogne, when every female figure is an Albertine, the astral synthesis of the bright and riotous band at Balbec paling now and breaking up, with an inverse symmetry, into its nebulae; the second, a conversation with Andrée, who reveals the full treachery and misery of her friend's life; and finally in Venice, when a telegram from Gilberte announcing her engagement to Robert de Saint-Loup is signed "Albertine" through a misreading of Gilberte's vulgar and pretentious handwriting. But this Albertine risen from the dead cannot trouble her real sepulchre, the only inviolate sepulchre, in the unkempt cemetery of the heart. Albertine is the first and the last, the Bacchante of the shore, as seen by the narrator in that pure act of understanding—intuition, and the captive that has recovered liberty and life, possessed of herself among the young laundresses, bathing in the Loire. This final confirmation of the original perspective is typical of Proust's characterisation. Thus there is a suggestion of congruence between the final Duchesse de Guermantes, as she appears at the matinée

of her cousin, and the gently wanton descendant of Geneviève de Bra-
bant, exposed for the first time to the narrator's adoration in the church
of St. Hilaire at Combray, following mass in the chapel of Gilbert the Bad,
her eyes of periwinkle smiling and restless and the colour of the sunlight
filtering through his window or of the girdle of Geneviève herself, and
bathed in the mystery of Merovingian time and the amaranth and leg-
endary radiance of her name. And Gilberte herself emerges from her suc-
cessive transformations, from the Gilberte Swann of the Champs-Elysées,
Mlle. de Forcheville after the death of Swann, Mme. de Saint-Loup, and
finally, by the death of Robert, Duchesse de Guermantes, as first seen at
Tansonville through a trellis of red hawthorn, an impudent nymph lean-
ing on her spade, amidst the jasmine and the copper wallflowers. And he
sees his love for Albertine as a testimony to his original clairvoyance and
an affirmation, in spite of the denegations of his reason, of that vision
of her as a rapacious and elusive gull, hostile and remote against the
sea. "In the midst of the most complete blindness, perspicacity subsists
in the form of tenderness and predilection. So that it is a mistake to
speak of an evil choice in love, since the very fact of there having been a
choice implies that it has been an evil one." And as before, wisdom con-
sists in obliterating the faculty of suffering rather than in a vain attempt
to reduce the stimuli that exasperate that faculty. "Non che la speme, il
desiderio . . ." "One desires to be understood because one desires to be
loved, and one desires to be loved because one loves. We are indifferent to
the understanding of others, and their love is an importunity."

But if love, for Proust, is a function of man's sadness, friendship is a
function of his cowardice; and, if neither can be realized because of the
impenetrability (isolation) of all that is not "cosa mentale," at least the
failure to possess may have the nobility of that which is tragic, whereas
the attempt to communicate where no communication is possible is
merely a simian vulgarity, or horribly comic, like the madness that holds
a conversation with the furniture. Friendship, according to Proust, is
the negation of that irremediable solitude to which every human being is
condemned. Friendship implies an almost piteous acceptance of face val-
ues. Friendship is a social expedient, like upholstery or the distribution

of garbage buckets. It has no spiritual significance. For the artist, who does not deal in surfaces, the rejection of friendship is not only reasonable, but a necessity. Because the only possible spiritual development is in the sense of depth. The artistic tendency is not expansive, but a contraction. And art is the apotheosis of solitude. There is no communication because there are no vehicles of communication. Even on the rare occasions when word and gesture happen to be valid expressions of personality, they lose their significance on their passage through the cataract of the personality that is opposed to them. Either we speak and act for ourselves—in which case speech and action are distorted and emptied of their meaning by an intelligence that is not ours, or else we speak and act for others—in which case we speak and act a lie. "One lies all one's life long," writes Proust, "notably to those that love one, and above all to that stranger whose contempt would cause one most pain—oneself." Yet surely the scorn of half a dozen—or half a million—sincere imbeciles for a man of genius ought to cure us of our absurd puntiglio and our capacity for being affected by that abridged libel that we call an insult.

Proust situates friendship somewhere between fatigue and ennui. He does not agree with the Nietzschean conception that friendship must be based on intellectual sympathy, because he does not see friendship as having the least intellectual significance. "We agree with those whose ideas (non-Platonic) are at the same degree of confusion as our own." For him the exercise of friendship is tantamount to a sacrifice of that only real and incommunicable essence of oneself to the exigencies of a frightened habit whose confidence requires to be restored by a dose of attention. It represents a false movement of the spirit—from within to without, from the spiritual assimilation of the immaterial as provided by the artist, as extracted by him from life, to the abject and indigestible husks of direct contact with the material and concrete, with what we call the material and the concrete. Thus he visits Balbec and Venice, meets Gilberte and the Duchesse de Guermantes and Albertine, attracted not by what they are but impelled by their arbitrary and ideal equivalents. The only fertile research is excavatory, immersive, a contraction of the spirit, a descent. The artist is active, but negatively, shrinking from the nullity of extracircumferential phenomena, drawn in to the core of the eddy. He cannot practise friendship, because friendship is the centrifugal force of self-fear, self-negation. Saint-Loup must be considered as more general than himself, as a product of the oldest French nobility, and the beauty and ease of his tenderness for the narrator—as when, for example, he accomplishes the most delicate and graceful gymnastics in a Paris restaurant so that his friend shall not be disturbed—are appreciated, not as the manifestations of a special and charming personality, but as the inevitable adjuncts of excessively good birth and breeding. "Man," writes Proust, "is not a building that can receive additions to its superficies, but a tree whose stem and leafage are an expression of inward sap." We are alone. We cannot know and we cannot be known. "Man is the creature that cannot come forth from himself, who knows others only in himself, and who, if he asserts the contrary, lies."

Here, as always, Proust is completely detached from all moral considerations. There is no right and wrong in Proust nor in his world. (Except possibly in those passages dealing with the war, when for a space he ceases to be an artist and raises his voice with the plebs, mob, rabble, canaille.) Tragedy is not concerned with human justice. Tragedy is the statement of an expiation, but not the miserable expiation of a codified breach of a local arrangement, organised by the knaves for the fools. The tragic figure represents the expiation of original sin, of the original and eternal sin of him and all his "socii malorum," the sin of having been born.

"Pues el delito mayor
Del hombre es haber nacido."

*   *
*

Driving to the Guermantes Hotel he feels that everything is lost, that his life is a succession of losses, devoid of reality because nothing survives, nothing of his love for Gilberte, for the Duchesse de Guermantes, for his grandmother, and now nothing of his love for Albertine, nothing of Combray and Balbec and Venice except the distorted images of volun-

tary memory, a life all in length, a sequence of dislocations and adjust-
ments, where neither mystery nor beauty is sacred, where all, except the
adamantine columns of his enduring boredom, has been consumed in
the torrential solvent of the years, a life so protracted in the past and so
meaningless in the future, so utterly bereft of any individual and per-
manent necessity, that his death, now or tomorrow or in a year or in
ten, would be a termination but not a conclusion. And he thinks how
empty is Bergotte's phrase: "the joys of the spirit." For art, which he had
so long believed the one ideal and inviolate element in a corruptible
world, seems now, whether because of his incurable lack of talent or its
own inherent artificiality, as unreal and sterile as the constructions of a
demented imagination—"that insane barrel-organ that always plays the
wrong tune"; and the materials of art—Beatrice and Faust and the "azur
du ciel immense et ronde" and the seagirt cities—all the absolute beauty
of a magic world, as vulgar and unworthy in their reality as Rachel and
Cottard, and pale and weary and cruel and inconstant and joyless as
Shelley's moon. So, after years of fruitless solitude, it is without enthu-
siasm that he drags himself back to a society that has long since ceased
to interest him. And now, on the outskirts of this futility, favoured by
the very depression and fatigue that had appeared to his disgust as the
aftermath of a minute and sterile lucidity (favoured, because the preten-
sions of a discouraged memory are for the moment reduced to the most
immediate and utilitarian presentification), he is to receive the oracle
that had invariably been denied to the most exalted tension of his spirit,
which his intelligence had failed to extract from the seismic enigma of
tree and flower and gesture and art, and suffer a religious experience in
the only intelligible sense of that epithet, at once an assumption and an
annunciation, so that at last he will understand the promise of Bergotte
and the achievement of Elstir and the message of Vinteuil from his par-
adise and the dolorous and necessary course of his own life and the infi-
nite futility—for the artist—of all that is not art.

This matinée is divided into two parts. The mystical experience and med-
itation of the narrator in the Cartesian hotcupboard of the Guermantes
library, and the implications of that experience applied to the work of art

that takes shape in his mind in the course of the reception itself. From the victory over Time he passes to the victory of Time, from the negation of Death to its affirmation. Thus, at the end as in the body of his work, Proust respects the dual significance of every condition and circumstance of life. The most ideal tautology presupposes a relation and the affirmation of equality involves only an approximate identification, and by asserting unity denies unity

Crossing the courtyard he stumbles on the cobbles. His surroundings vanish, wattmen, stables, carriages, guests, the entire reality of the place in its hour, his anxiety and doubts as to the reality of life and art disappear, he is stunned by waves of rapture, saturated in that same felicity that had irrigated so sparingly the desolation of his life. Drabness is obliterated in an intolerable brightness. And suddenly Venice emerges from the series of forgotten days, Venice whose radiant essence he had never been able to express because it had been rejected by the imperious vulgarity of a working-day memory, but which this chance reduplication of a precarious equilibrium in the Baptistry of San Marco has lifted from its Adriatic shore and set down, a bright and vehement interloper, in the courtyard of the Princesse de Guermantes. But already the vision has faded and he is free to resume his social functions. He is ushered into the library, because ex-Mme. Verdurin, at once the Norn and Victim of Harmonic Megrims, is enthroned in the midst of her guests, passionately absorbing Rino-Gomenol in the interests of her mucous membrane and suffering the most atrocious ecstasies of Stravinskian neuralgia. While he is waiting alone for the music to be over, the miracle of the courtyard is renewed under four different forms. They have already been referred to. A servant strikes a spoon against a plate, he wipes his mouth with a heavily starched napkin, the water cries like a siren in the pipes, he takes down *François le Champi* from the shelves. And just as the Piazza di San Marco burst its way into the courtyard and there asserted its luminous and fleeting domination, so now the library is successively invaded by a forest, the high tide breaking on the shore at Balbec, the vast dining-room of the Grand Hotel flooded, like an aquarium, with the sunset and the evening sea, and lastly Combray and its "ways" and the deferential transmission of a sour and distinguished prose, shaped and stated by his mother's voice, muted and sweetened almost to a lullaby, unwinding all night long its reassuring foil of sound before a child's insomnia.

The most successful evocative experiment can only project the echo of a past sensation, because, being an act of intellection, it is conditioned by the prejudices of the intelligence which abstracts from any given sensation, as being illogical and insignificant, a discordant and frivolous intruder, whatever word or gesture, sound or perfume, cannot be fitted into the puzzle of a concept. But the essence of any new experience is contained precisely in this mysterious element that the vigilant will rejects as an anachronism. It is the axis about which the sensation pivots, the centre of gravity of its coherence. So that no amount of voluntary manipulation can reconstitute in its integrity an impression that the will has—so to speak—buckled into incoherence. But if, *by accident*, and given favourable circumstances (a relaxation of the subject's habit of thought and a reduction of the radius of his memory, a generally diminished tension of consciousness following upon a phase of extreme discouragement), if by some miracle of analogy the central impression of a past sensation recurs as an immediate stimulus which can be instinctively identified by the subject with the model of duplication (*whose integral purity has been retained because it has been forgotten*), then the total past sensation, not its echo nor its copy, but the sensation itself, annihilating every spatial and temporal restriction, comes in a rush to engulf the subject in all the beauty of its infallible proportion. Thus the sound produced by a spoon struck against a plate is subconsciously identified by the narrator with the sound of a hammer struck by a mechanic against the wheel of a train drawn up before a wood, a sound that his will had rejected as extraneous to its immediate activity. But a subconscious and disinterested act of perception has reduced the object—the wood—to its immaterial and spiritually digestible equivalent, and the record of this pure act of cognition has not merely been associated with this sound of a hammer struck against a wheel, but centralised about it. The mood, as usual, has no importance. The point of departure of the Proustian exposition is not the crystalline agglomeration but its kernel—the crystallised. The most trivial experience—he says in effect—is encrusted with elements that logically are not related to it and have consequently been rejected by our intelligence: it is imprisoned in a vase filled with a certain perfume and a certain colour and raised to a certain temperature. These vases are suspended along the height of our years, and, not being accessible to our intelligent memory, are in a sense immune, the purity of their climatic content is guaranteed by forgetfulness, each one is kept at its distance, at its date. So that when the imprisoned microcosm is besieged in the manner described, we are flooded by a new air and a new perfume (new precisely because already experienced), and we breathe the true air of Paradise, of the only Paradise that is not the dream of a madman, the Paradise that has been lost.

The identification of immediate with past experience, the recurrence of past action or reaction in the present, amounts to a participation between the ideal and the real, imagination and direct apprehension, symbol and substance. Such participation frees the essential reality that is denied to the contemplative as to the active life. What is common to present and past is more essential than either taken separately. Reality, whether approached imaginatively or empirically, remains a surface, hermetic. Imagination, applied—a priori—to what is absent, is exercised in vacuo and cannot tolerate the limits of the real. Nor is any direct and purely experimental contact possible between subject and object, because they are automatically separated by the subject's consciousness of perception, and the object loses its purity and becomes a mere intellectual pretext or motive. But, thanks to this reduplication, the experience is at once imaginative and empirical, at once an evocation and a direct perception, real without being merely actual, ideal without being merely abstract, the ideal real, the essential, the extratemporal. But if this mystical experience communicates an extratemporal essence, it follows that the communicant is for the moment an extratemporal being. Consequently the Proustian solution consists, in so far as it has been examined, in the negation of Time and Death, the negation of Death because the negation of Time. Death is dead because Time is dead. (At this point a brief impertinence, which consists in considering *Le Temps Retrouvé* almost as inappropriate a description of the Proustian solution as *Crime and Punishment* of a masterpiece that contains no allusion to either crime or punishment. Time is not recovered, it is obliterated. Time is recovered, and Death with it, when he leaves the library and joins the guests, perched in precarious decrepitude on the aspiring stilts of the former and preserved from the latter by a miracle of terrified equilibrium. If the title is a good title the scene in the library is an anticlimax.) So now in the exaltation of his brief eternity, having emerged from the darkness of time and habit and passion and intelligence, he understands the necessity of art. For in the brightness of art alone can be deciphered the baffled ecstasy that he had known before the inscrutable superficies of a cloud, a triangle, a spire, a flower, a pebble, when the mystery, the essence, the Idea, imprisoned in matter, had solicited the bounty of a subject passing by within the shell of his impurity, and tendered, like Dante his song to the "ingegni storti e loschi," at least an incorruptible beauty:

"Ponete mente *almen* com'io son bella."

And he understands the meaning of Baudelaire's definition of reality as "the adequate union of subject and object," and more clearly than ever the grotesque fallacy of a realistic art—"the miserable statement of line and surface," and the penny-a-line vulgarity of a literature of notations.

He leaves the library and is confronted by the spectacle of Time made flesh. And whereas a moment ago the bright cymbals of two distant hours, paralysed at arm's length by the rigid spread of intervening years, had obeyed an irresistible impulse of mutual attraction, and clashed, like storm clouds, in a flash and a brazen peal, now the measure of their span from tip to tip is written on the face and frailty of the dying, curved, like Dante's proud, under the load of their years—"unwieldy, slow, heavy and pale as lead."

"e qual più pazienza avea negli atti
    piangendo parea dicer:—Più non posso."

We say farewell to M. de Charlus, the Baron Palamède de Charlus, Duke of Brabant, Squire of Montargis, Prince of Oléron, Carency, Viareggio and the Dunes, the unspeakably insolent Charlus, now a humble and convulsive Lear, crowned by the silver torrent of his hair, Oedipus, senile and annulled, stooped over a missal or scraping and bowing before the astonishment of Mme. de Sainte-Euverte, scorned in the full strength of his terrible pride as the Duchesse de Caca or the Princesse de Pipi, the Archangel Raphael in his latter days, still furtively pursuing all the sons of Toby, escorted by the faithful Jupien, Lord of the Temple of Shamelessness. And the dirge of his sepulchral whisper falls like clay from the spade of a gravedigger. "Hannibal de Bréauté—dead! Antoine de Mouchy—dead! Charles Swann—dead! Adalbert de Montmorency—dead! Baron de Talleyrand—dead! Sosthène de Doudeauville—dead!" The narrator accomplishes a series of identifications, of voluntary and arduous identifications—balancing those of the library, involuntary and spontaneous. From one sniggering and abject puppet, something between a beggarly hawker and a moribund buffoon, he elicits his enemy, M. d'Argencourt, as he knew him, starched and haughty and impeccable: from a stout dowager, whom he takes at first for Mme. de Forcheville, Gilberte herself. So they drift past, Oriane and the Duc de Guermantes, Rachel and Bloch, Legrandin and Odette, and many others, carrying the burden of Saturn towards the light that will rise, towards Uranus, the Sabbath star.

*   *
*

In Time creative and destructive Proust discovers himself as an artist: "I understood the meaning of death, of love and vocation, of the joys of the spirit and the utility of pain." Allusion has been made to his contempt for the literature that "describes," for the realists and naturalists worshipping the offal of experience, prostrate before the epidermis and the swift epilepsy, and content to transcribe the surface, the façade, behind which the Idea is prisoner. Whereas the Proustian procedure is that of Apollo flaying Marsyas and capturing without sentiment the essence, the Phrygian waters. "Chi non ha la forza di uccidere la realtà non ha la forza di crearla." But Proust is too much of an affectivist to be satisfied by the intellectual symbolism of a Baudelaire, abstract and discursive. The Baudelarian unity is a unity "post rem," a unity abstracted from plurality. His "correspondence" is determined by a concept, therefore strictly limited and exhausted by its own definition. Proust does not deal in concepts, he pursues the Idea, the concrete. He admires the frescoes of the Paduan Arena because their symbolism is handled as a reality, special, literal and concrete, and is not merely the pictorial transmission of a notion. Dante, if he can ever be said to have failed, fails with his purely allegorical figures, Lucifer, the Griffin of the Purgatory and the Eagle of the Paradise, whose significance is purely conventional and extrinsic. Here allegory fails as it must always fail in the hands of a poet. Spenser's allegory collapses after a few cantos. Dante, because he was an artist and not a minor prophet, could not prevent his allegory from becoming heated and electrified into anagogy. The *Vision of Mirza* is good allegory because it is flat writing. For Proust the object may be a living symbol, but a symbol of itself. The symbolism of Baudelaire has become the *autosymbolism* of Proust. Proust's point of departure might be situated in Symbolism, or on its outskirts. But he does not proceed pari passu with France, towards an elegant scepticism and the marmorean modes, nor, as we have seen, with Daudet and the Goncourts to the "notes d'après nature," nor, of course, with the Parnassians to the ineffable gutter-snippets of François Coppée. He solicits no facts, and he chisels no Cellinesque pommels. He reacts, but in a different direction. He recedes from the Symbolists—back towards Hugo. And for that reason he is a solitary and independent figure. The only contemporary in whom I can discern something of the same retrogressive tendency is Joris Karl Huysmans. But he loathed it in himself and repressed it. He speaks bitterly of the "ineluctable gangrene of Romanticism," and yet his des Esseintes is a fabulous creature, an Alfred Lord Baudelaire.

We are frequently reminded of this romantic strain in Proust. He is romantic in his substitution of affectivity for intelligence, in his opposition of the particular affective evidential state to all the subtleties of rational cross-reference, in his rejection of the Concept in favour of the Idea, in his scepticism before causality. Thus his purely logical—as

opposed to his intuitive—explanations of a certain effect invariably bris-
tle with alternatives.[1] He is a Romantic in his anxiety to accomplish his
mission, to be a good and faithful servant. He does not seek to evade
the implications of his art such as it has been revealed to him. He will
write as he has lived—in Time. The classical artist assumes omniscience
and omnipotence. He raises himself artificially out of Time in order to
give relief to his chronology and causality to his development. Proust's
chronology is extremely difficult to follow, the succession of events spas-
modic, and his characters and themes, although they seem to obey an
almost insane inward necessity, are presented and developed with a fine
Dostoievskian contempt for the vulgarity of a plausible concatenation.
(Proust's impressionism will bring us back to Dostoievski.) Generally
speaking, the romantic artist is very much concerned with Time and
aware of the importance of memory in inspiration,

> ("c'est toi qui dors dans l'ombre,
> ô sacré souvenir! . . .")

but is inclined to sensationalise what is treated by Proust with pathologi-
cal power and sobriety. With Musset, for example, the interest is more in
a vague extratemporal identification, without any real cohesion or simul-
taneity, between the me and not-me than in the functional evocations
of a specialised memory. But the analogy is too blurred and would lead
nowhere, although Proust quotes Chateaubriand and Amiel as his spiri-
tual ancestors. It is difficult to connect Proust with this pair of melan-
choly Pantheists dancing a fandango of death in the twilight. But Proust
admired the poetry of the Comtesse de Noailles. Saperlipopette!

The narrator had ascribed his "lack of talent" to a lack of observation,
or rather to what he supposed was a non-artistic habit of observation. He
was incapable of recording surface. So that when he reads such brilliant
crowded reporting as the Goncourts' Journal, the only alternative to the

---

1. Cp. for this anti-intellectual tendency: *Swann*, i. 286, ii. 29 and 234; *Guermantes*, i. 162
(Saint-Loup's gesture ex nihilo); *Albertine Disparue*, i. 14 and *passim*.

conclusion that he is entirely wanting in the precious journalistic talent is the supposition that between the banality of life and the magic of literature there is a great gulf fixed. Either he is devoid of talent or art of reality. And he describes the radiographical quality of his observation. The copiable he does not see. He searches for a relation, a common factor, substrata. Thus he is less interested in what is said than in the way in which it is said. Similarly his faculties are more violently activated by intermediate than by terminal—capital—stimuli. We find countless examples of these secondary reflexes. Withdrawn in his cool dark room at Combray he extracts the total essence of a scorching midday from the scarlet stellar blows of a hammer in the street and the chamber-music of flies in the gloom. Lying in bed at dawn, the exact quality of the weather, temperature and visibility, is transmitted to him in terms of sound, in the chimes and the calls of the hawkers. Thus can be explained the primacy of instinctive perception—intuition—in the Proustian world. Because instinct, when not vitiated by Habit, is also a reflex, from the Proustian point of view ideally remote and indirect, a chain-reflex. Now he sees his regretted failure to observe artistically as a series of "inspired omissions" and the work of art as neither created nor chosen, but discovered, uncovered, excavated, pre-existing within the artist, a law of his nature. The only reality is provided by the hieroglyphics traced by inspired perception (identification of subject and object). The conclusions of the intelligence are merely of arbitrary value, potentially valid. "An impression is for the writer what an experiment is for the scientist—with this difference, that in the case of the scientist the action of the intelligence precedes the event and in the case of the writer follows it." Consequently for the artist, the only possible hierarchy in the world of objective phenomena is represented by a table of their respective coefficients of penetration, that is to say, in terms of the subject. (Another sneer at the realists.) The artist has acquired his text: the artisan translates it. "The duty and the task of a writer (not an artist, a writer) are those of a translator." The reality of a cloud reflected in the Vivonne is not expressed by "Zut alors" but by the interpretation of that inspired criticism. The verbal oblique must be restored to the upright: thus "you are charming" equals "it gives me pleasure to embrace you."

Proust's relativism and impressionism are adjuncts of this same anti-intellectual attitude. Curtius speaks of Proust's "perspectivism" and "positive relativism" as opposed to the negative relativism of the late nineteenth century, the scepticism of Renan and France. I think the phrase "positive relativism" is an oxymoron, I am almost sure that it does not apply to Proust, and I know that it came out of the Heidelberg laboratory. We have seen how in the case of Albertine (and Proust extends his experience to all human relations) the multiple aspects (read Blickpunkt for this miserable word) did not bind into any positive synthesis. The object evolves, and by the time the conclusion—if any—is reached, it is already out of date. In a sense Proust is a positivist, but his positivism has nothing to do with his relativism, which is as pessimistic and as negative as that of France, and employed as an element of comedy. The "book," for Proust a literary statement, is for the housekeeper a book of accounts and for Her Highness the visitors' register. Rachel Quand du Seigneur represents for the narrator thirty francs and a bored satisfaction, for Saint-Loup a fortune and unending misery. Similarly when Saint-Loup sees Albertine's photograph he cannot conceal his astonishment that such a vulgar nonentity should have attracted his brilliant and popular friend. The Comte de Crécy carves a turkey and establishes a calendar as surely as the death of Christ or the departure out of Egypt. For the Baron Musset's "infidèle" must be a buttons or a bus-conductor. This relativism is negative and comic. He owes his exaltation on hearing Vinteuil's music to the actress Léa, who alone could decipher the composer's posthumous manuscripts, and to the relations of Charlus with Charlie Morel, the violinist. Proust is positive only in so far as he affirms the value of intuition.

By his impressionism I mean his non-logical statement of phenomena in the order and exactitude of their perception, before they have been distorted into intelligibility in order to be forced into a chain of cause and effect.[1] The painter Elstir is the type of the impressionist, stating what

---

1. Examples: a napkin in the dust taken for a pencil of light, the sound of water in the pipes for a dog barking or the hooting of a siren, the noise of a spring-door closing for the orchestration of the Pilgrim's Chorus.

he sees and not what he knows he ought to see: for example, applying urban terms to the sea and marine terms to the town, so as to transmit his intuition of their homogeneity. And we are reminded of Schopenhauer's definition of the artistic procedure as "the contemplation of the world independently of the principle of reason." In this connexion Proust can be related to Dostoievski, who states his characters without explaining them. It may be objected that Proust does little else but explain his characters. But his explanations are experimental and not demonstrative. He explains them in order that they may appear as they are—inexplicable. He explains them away.[1]

Proust's style was generally resented in French literary circles. But now that he is no longer read, it is generously conceded that he might have written an even worse prose than he did. At the same time, it is difficult to estimate with justice a style of which one can only take cognisance by a process of deduction, in an edition that cannot be said to have transmitted the writings of Proust, but to have betrayed a tendency in that direction. For Proust, as for the painter, style is more a question of vision than of technique. Proust does not share the superstition that form is nothing and content everything, nor that the ideal literary masterpiece could only be communicated in a series of absolute and monosyllabic propositions. For Proust the quality of language is more important than any system of ethics or aesthetics. Indeed he makes no attempt to dissociate form from content. The one is a concretion of the other, the revelation of a world. The Proustian world is expressed metaphorically by the artisan because it is apprehended metaphorically by the artist: the indirect and comparative expression of indirect and comparative perception. The rhetorical equivalent of the Proustian real is the chain-figure of the metaphor. It is a tiring style, but it does not tire the mind. The clarity of the phrase is cumulative and explosive. One's fatigue is a fatigue of the heart, a blood fatigue. One is exhausted and angry after an hour, submerged, dominated by the crest and break of metaphor after

---

1. Cp. analogy between Dostoievski and Mme. de Sévigné: A l'Ombre des Jeunes Filles en Fleurs, ii. 75.

metaphor: but never stupefied. The complaint that it is an involved style, full of periphrasis, obscure and impossible to follow, has no foundation whatsoever.

It is significant that the majority of his images are botanical. He assimilates the human to the vegetal. He is conscious of humanity as flora, never as fauna. (There are no black cats and faithful hounds in Proust.) He deplores "the time one wastes in upholstering one's life with a human and parasitic vegetation." The wife and son of the Sidaner amateur appear to him on the shore at Balbec as two flowering ranunculi. Albertine's laugh has the colour and smell of a geranium. Gilberte and Odette are lilacs, white and violet. He speaks of a scene in *Pelléas et Mélisande* that exasperates his rose-fever and makes him sneeze. This preoccupation accompanies very naturally his complete indifference to moral values and human justices.[1] Flower and plant have no conscious will. They are shameless, exposing their genitals. And so in a sense are Proust's men and women, whose will is blind and hard, but never self-conscious, never abolished in the pure perception of a pure subject. They are victims of their volition, active with a grotesque predetermined activity, within the narrow limits of an impure world. But shameless. There is no question of right and wrong. Homosexuality is never called a vice: it is as devoid of moral implications as the mode of fecundation of the *Primula veris* or the *Lythrum salicoria*. And, like members of the vegetable world, they seem to solicit a pure subject, so that they may pass from a state of blind will to a state of representation. Proust is that pure subject. He is almost exempt from the impurity of will.[2] He deplores his lack of will until he understands that will, being utilitarian, a servant of intelligence and habit, is not a condition of the artistic experience. When the subject is exempt from will the object is exempt from causality (Time and Space taken together). And this human vegetation is purified in the transcendental aperception that can capture the Model, the Idea, the Thing in itself.

---

1. Cp. *La Prisonnière*, ii. 119.

2. Cp. *Swann*, i. 22, 24, 59 and *passim; Guermantes*, i. 63; *Sodome et Gomorrhe*, ii. 2, 188; *Albertine Disparue*, ii. 149 (Paralysed by "O Sole Mio" in Venice).

So that there is no collapse of the will in Proust, as there is for exam-
ple in Spenser and Keats and Giorgione. He sits up all night in Paris, with
a branch of apple-blossom laid beside his lamp, staring at the foam of
the white corollae until the dawn comes to redden them. But this is not
the terrible panic-stricken stasis of Keats, crouched in a mossy thicket,
annulled, like a bee, in sweetness, "drowsed with the fume of poppies"
and watching "the last oozings, hours by hours"; nor yet the remote, still,
almost breathless passion of a Giorgione youth, the spirit shattered in
corruption, damp and rotting, so finely suggested by d'Annunzio in his
description of the Concerto ("ma se io penso alle sue mani nascoste, le
immagino nell'atto di frangere le foglie del lauro per profumarsene le
dita") and so grossly misinterpreted by the same writer when he sees in
the rapt doomed figure of the Tempesta a vulgar Leander resting between
orgasms; nor yet the horrible pomegranates of "Il Fuoco," bursting and
bleeding, dripping the red ooze of their seed, putrid on the putrid water.
The Proustian stasis is contemplative, a pure act of understanding, will-
less, the "amabilis insania" and the "holder Wahnsinn."

A book could be written on the significance of music in the work of
Proust, in particular of the music of Vinteuil: the Sonata and the Septuor.
The influence of Schopenhauer on this aspect of the Proustian demon-
stration is unquestionable. Schopenhauer rejects the Leibnitzian view of
music as "occult arithmetic," and in his aesthetics separates it from the
other arts, which can only produce the Idea with its concomitant phe-
nomena, whereas music is the Idea itself, unaware of the world of phe-
nomena, existing ideally outside the universe, apprehended not in Space
but in Time only, and consequently untouched by the teleological hypoth-
esis. This essential quality of music is distorted by the listener who, being
an impure subject, insists on giving a figure to that which is ideal and
invisible, on incarnating the Idea in what he conceives to be an appropri-
ate paradigm. Thus, by definition, opera is a hideous corruption of this
most immaterial of all the arts: the words of a libretto are to the musical
phrase that they particularize what the Vendôme Column, for example, is
to the ideal perpendicular. From this point of view opera is less complete
than vaudeville, which at least inaugurates the comedy of an exhaustive

enumeration. These considerations explain the beautiful convention of the "da capo" as a testimony to the intimate and ineffable nature of an art that is perfectly intelligible and perfectly inexplicable. Music is the catalytic element in the work of Proust. It asserts to his unbelief the permanence of personality and the reality of art. It synthesises the moments of privilege and runs parallel to them. In one passage he describes the recurrent mystical experience as "a purely musical impression, non-extensive, entirely original, irreducible to any other order of impression, . . . sine materia." The narrator—unlike Swann who identifies the "little phrase" of the Sonata with Odette, spatialises what is extraspatial, establishes it as the national anthem of his love—sees in the red phrase of the Septuor, trumpeting its victory in the last movement like a Mantegna archangel clothed in scarlet, the ideal and immaterial statement of the essence of a unique beauty, a unique world, the invariable world and beauty of Vinteuil, expressed timidly, as a prayer, in the Sonata, imploringly, as an inspiration, in the Septuor, the "invisible reality" that damns the life of the body on earth as a pensum and reveals the meaning of the word: "defunctus."

Three Dialogues
with Georges Duthuit

I Tal Coat

B—Total object, complete with missing parts, instead of partial object. Question of degree.

D—More. The tyranny of the discreet overthrown. The world a flux of movements partaking of living time, that of effort, creation, liberation, the painting, the painter. The fleeting instant of sensation given back, given forth, with context of the continuum it nourished.

B—In any case a thrusting towards a more adequate expression of natural experience, as revealed to the vigilant coenaesthesia. Whether achieved through submission or through mastery, the result is a gain in nature.

D—But that which this painter discovers, orders, transmits, is not in nature. What relation between one of these paintings and a landscape seen at a certain age, a certain season, a certain hour? Are we not on a quite different plane?

B—By nature I mean here, like the naïvest realist, a composite of perceiver and perceived, not a datum, an experience. All I wish to suggest is that the tendency and accomplishment of this painting are fundamentally those of previous painting, straining to enlarge the statement of a compromise.

D—You neglect the immense difference between the significance of perception for Tal Coat and its significance for the great majority of his predecessors, apprehending as artists with the same utilitarian servility as in a traffic-jam and improving the result with a lick of Euclidian geometry. The global perception of Tal Coat is disinterested, committed neither to truth nor to beauty, twin tyrannies of nature. I can see the compromise of past painting, but not that which you deplore in the Matisse of a certain period and in the Tal Coat of today.

B—I do not deplore. I agree that the Matisse in question, as well as the Franciscan orgies of Tal Coat, have prodigious value, but a value cognate with those already accumulated. What we have to consider in the case of Italian painters is not that they surveyed the world with the eyes of building-contractors, a mere means like any other, but that they never stirred from the field of the possible, however much they may have enlarged it. The only thing disturbed by the revolutionaries Matisse and Tal Coat is a certain order on the plane of the feasible.

D—What other plane can there be for the maker?

B—Logically none. Yet I speak of an art turning from it in disgust, weary of puny exploits, weary of pretending to be able, of being able, of doing a little better the same old thing, of going a little further along a dreary road.

D—And preferring what?

B—The expression that there is nothing to express, nothing with which to express, nothing from which to express, no power to express, no desire to express, together with the obligation to express.

D—But that is a violently extreme and personal point of view, of no help to us in the matter of Tal Coat.

B—

D—Perhaps that is enough for today.

II Masson

B—In search of the difficulty rather than in its clutch. The disquiet of him who lacks an adversary.

D—That is perhaps why he speaks so often nowadays of painting the void, "in fear and trembling." His concern was at one time with the creation of a mythology; then with man, not simply in the universe, but in society; and now ... "inner emptiness, the prime condition, according to Chinese esthetics, of the act of painting." It would seem, in effect, that Masson suffers more keenly than any living painter from the need to come to rest, i.e. to establish the data of the problem to be solved, the Problem at last.

B—Though little familiar with the problems he has set himself in the past and which, by the mere fact of their solubility or for any other reason, have lost for him their legitimacy, I feel their presence not far behind these canvases veiled in consternation, and the scars of a competence that must be most painful to him. Two old maladies that should no doubt be considered separately: the malady of wanting to know what to do and the malady of wanting to be able to do it.

D—But Masson's declared purpose is now to reduce these maladies, as you call them, to nothing. He aspires to be rid of the servitude of space, that his eye may "frolic among the focusless fields, tumultuous with incessant creation." At the same time he demands the rehabilitation of the "vaporous." This may seem strange in one more fitted by temperament for fire than for damp. You of course will reply that it is the same thing as before, the same reaching towards succour from without. Opaque or transparent, the object remains sovereign. But how can Masson be expected to paint the void?

B—He is not. What is the good of passing from one untenable position to another, of seeking justification always on the same plane? Here is an artist who seems literally skewered on the ferocious dilemma of expression. Yet he continues to wriggle. The void he speaks of is perhaps simply the obliteration of an unbearable presence, unbearable because neither to be wooed nor to be stormed. If this anguish of helplessness is never stated as such, on its own merits and for its own sake, though perhaps very occasionally admitted as spice to the "exploit" it jeopardised, the reason is doubtless, among others, that it seems to contain in itself the impossibility of statement. Again an exquisitely logical attitude. In any case, it is hardly to be confused with the void.

D—Masson speaks much of transparency—"openings, circulations, communications, unknown penetrations"—where he may frolic at his ease, in freedom. Without renouncing the objects, loathsome or delicious, that are our daily bread and wine and poison, he seeks to break through their partitions to that continuity of being which is absent from the ordinary experience of living. In this he approaches Matisse (of the first period needless to say) and Tal Coat, but with this notable difference, that Masson has to contend with his own technical gifts, which have the richness, the precision, the density and balance of the high classical manner. Or perhaps I should say rather its spirit, for he has shown himself capable, as occasion required, of great technical variety.

B—What you say certainly throws light on the dramatic predicament of this artist. Allow me to note his concern with the amenities of ease and freedom. *The stars are undoubtedly superb*, as Freud remarked on reading Kant's cosmological proof of the existence of God. With such preoccupations it seems to me impossible that he should ever do anything different from that which the best, including himself, have done already. It is perhaps an impertinence to suggest that he wishes to. His so extremely intelligent remarks on space breathe the same possessiveness as the notebooks of Leonardo who, when he speaks of *disfazione*, knows that for him not one fragment will be lost. So forgive me if I relapse, as when we spoke of the so different Tal Coat, into my dream of an art unresentful of its insuperable indigence and too proud for the farce of giving and receiving.

D—Masson himself, having remarked that western perspective is no more than a series of traps for the capture of objects, declares that their possession does not interest him. He congratulates Bonnard for having, in his last works, "gone beyond possessive space in every shape and form, far from surveys and bounds, to the point where all possession is dissolved." I agree that there is a long cry from Bonnard to that impoverished painting, "authentically fruitless, incapable of any image whatsoever," to which you aspire, and towards which too, who knows, unconsciously perhaps, Masson tends. But must we really deplore the painting that admits "the things and creatures of spring, resplendent with desire and affirmation, ephemeral no doubt, but immortally reiterant," not in order to benefit by them, not in order to enjoy them, but in order that what is tolerable and radiant in the world may continue? Are we really to deplore the painting that is a rallying, among the things of time that pass and hurry us away, towards a time that endures and gives increase?

B—(*Exit weeping.*)

III Bram van Velde

B—Frenchman, fire first.

D—Speaking of Tal Coat and Masson you invoked an art of a different order, not only from theirs, but from any achieved up to date. Am I right in thinking that you had van Velde in mind when making this sweeping distinction?

B—Yes. I think he is the first to accept a certain situation and to consent to a certain act.

D—Would it be too much to ask you to state again, as simply as possible, the situation and act that you conceive to be his?

B—The situation is that of him who is helpless, cannot act, in the event cannot paint, since he is obliged to paint. The act is of him who, helpless, unable to act, acts, in the event paints, since he is obliged to paint.

D—Why is he obliged to paint?

B—I don't know.

D—Why is he helpless to paint?

B—Because there is nothing to paint and nothing to paint with.

D—And the result, you say, is art of a new order?

B—Among those whom we call great artists, I can think of none whose concern was not predominantly with his expressive possibilities, those of his vehicle, those of humanity. The assumption underlying all painting is that the domain of the maker is the domain of the feasible. The much to express, the little to express, the ability to express much, the ability to express little, merge in the common anxiety to express as much as possible, or as truly as possible, or as finely as possible, to the best of one's ability. What—

D—One moment. Are you suggesting that the painting of van Velde is inexpressive?

B—(*a fortnight later*) Yes.

D—You realize the absurdity of what you advance?

B—I hope I do.

D—What you say amounts to this: the form of expression known as painting, since for obscure reasons we are obliged to speak of painting, has had to wait for van Velde to be rid of the misapprehension under which it has laboured so long and so bravely, namely, that its function was to express, by means of paint.

B—Others have felt that art is not necessarily expression. But the numerous attempts made to make painting independent of its occasion have only succeeded in enlarging its repertory. I suggest that van Velde is the first whose painting is bereft, rid if you prefer, of occasion in every shape and form, ideal as well as material, and the first whose hands have not been tied by the certitude that expression is an impossible act.

D—But might it not be suggested, even by one tolerant of this fantastic theory, that the occasion of his painting is his predicament, and that it is expressive of the impossibility to express?

B—No more ingenious method could be devised for restoring him, safe and sound, to the bosom of Saint Luke. But let us, for once, be foolish enough not to turn tail. All have turned wisely tail, before the ultimate penury, back to the mere misery where destitute virtuous mothers may steal bread for their starving brats. There is more than a difference of degree between being short, short of the world, short of self, and being without these esteemed commodities. The one is a predicament, the other not.

D—But you have already spoken of the predicament of van Velde.

B—I should not have done so.

D—You prefer the purer view that here at last is a painter who does not paint, does not pretend to paint. Come, come, my dear fellow, make some kind of connected statement and then go away.

B—Would it not be enough if I simply went away?

D—No. You have begun. Finish. Begin again and go on until you have finished. Then go away. Try and bear in mind that the subject under discussion is not yourself, nor the Sufist Al-Haqq, but a particular Dutchman by name van Velde, hitherto erroneously referred to as an *artiste peintre*.

B—How would it be if I first said what I am pleased to fancy he is, fancy he does, and then that it is more than likely that he is and does quite otherwise? Would not that be an excellent issue out of all our afflictions? He happy, you happy, I happy, all three bubbling over with happiness.

D—Do as you please. But get it over.

B—There are many ways in which the thing I am trying in vain to say may be tried in vain to be said. I have experimented, as you know, both in public and in private, under duress, through faintness of heart, through weakness of mind, with two or three hundred. The pathetic antithesis possession-poverty was perhaps not the most tedious. But we begin to weary of it, do we not? The realization that art has always been bourgeois, though it may dull our pain before the achievements of the socially progressive, is finally of scant interest. The analysis of the relation between the artist and his occasion, a relation always regarded as indispensable, does not seem to have been very productive either, the reason being perhaps that it lost its way in disquisitions on the nature of occasion. It is obvious that for the artist obsessed with his expressive vocation, anything and everything is doomed to become occasion, including, as is apparently to some extent the case with Masson, the pursuit of occasion, and the every man his own wife experiments of the spiritual Kandinsky. No painting is more replete than Mondrian's. But if the occasion appears as an unstable term of relation, the artist, who is the other term, is hardly less so, thanks to his warren of modes and attitudes. The objections to this dualist view of the creative process are unconvincing. Two things are established, however precariously: the ailment, from fruits on plates to low mathematics and self-commiseration, and its manner of dispatch. All that should concern us is the acute and increasing anxiety of the relation itself, as though shadowed more and more darkly by a sense of invalidity, of inadequacy, of existence at the expense of all that it excludes, all that it blinds to. The history of painting, here we go again, is the history of its attempts to escape from this sense of failure, by means of more authentic, more ample, less exclusive relations between representer and representee, in a kind of tropism towards a light as to the nature of which the best opinions continue to vary, and with a kind of Pythagorean terror, as though the irrationality of pi were an offence against the deity, not to mention his creature. My case, since I am in the dock, is that van Velde is the first to desist from this estheticised automatism, the first to submit wholly to the incoercible absence of relation, in the absence of terms or, if you like, in the presence of unavailable terms, the first to admit that to be an artist is to fail, as no other dare fail, that failure is his world and the shrink from it desertion, art and craft, good housekeeping, living. No, no, allow me to expire. I know that all that is required now, in order to bring even this horrible matter to an acceptable conclusion, is to make of this submission, this admission, this fidelity to failure, a new occasion, a new term of relation, and of the act which, unable to act, obliged to act, he makes, an expressive act, even if only of itself, of its impossibility, of its obligation. I know that my inability to do so places myself, and perhaps an innocent, in what I think is still called an unenviable situation, familiar to psychiatrists. For what is this coloured plane, that was not there before. I don't know what it is, having never seen anything like it before. It seems to have nothing to do with art, in any case, if my memories are correct. (*Prepares to go.*)

D—Are you not forgetting something?

B—Surely that is enough?

D—I understood your number was to have two parts. The first was to consist in your saying what you—er—thought. This I am prepared to believe you have done. The second—

B—(*remembering, warmly*) Yes, yes, I am mistaken, I am mistaken.

NOTES

POEMS

Whoroscope. Written on June 15, 1930, and submitted to a competition sponsored by Nancy Cunard for the best poem on the subject of time. Beckett won the prize, and in August of the same year *Whoroscope* was published in an edition of 300 copies by the Hours Press. The notes were added at the suggestion of Richard Aldington, the judge of the contest. First publication by Grove in *Poems in English*, 1963.

Home Olga. Appeared in a special James Joyce issue of *Contempo* (Chapel Hill, N.C.) edited by Stuart Gilbert, 1934. First publication by Grove in *Collected Poems*, 1977.

Gnome. *Dublin Magazine*, 1934. First publication by Grove in *Collected Poems*.

The Vulture, Enueg I, Enueg II, Alba, Dortmunder, Sanies I, Sanies II, Serena I, Serena II, Serena III, Malacoda, Da Tagte Es, Echo's Bones. Published collectively in *Echo's Bones and Other Precipitates* by Europa Press (Paris, 1935) in an edition of 327 copies. An earlier version of *Alba* appeared in *Dublin Magazine*, 1931. First publication by Grove in *Poems in English*.

Cascando. *Dublin Magazine*, 1936. First publication by Grove in *Poems in English*.

Ooftish. *transition*, 1938. First publication by Grove in *Collected Poems*.

they come . . . Written in English, 1937. Beckett's French version appeared in *Les Temps modernes*, 1946. First publication by Grove in *Collected Poems*.

Dieppe. Written in French, 1937. Appeared in *Les Temps modernes*, 1946. First publication by Grove in *Poems in English*.

Saint-Lô. The Irish Times, June 24, 1946. First publication by Grove in *Poems in English.*

my way is in the sand . . . Written in French, 1948. Appeared in *transition,* 1948. First publication by Grove in *Poems in English.*

what would I do . . . Written in French, 1948. Appeared in *transition,* 1948. First publication by Grove in *Poems in English.*

I would like . . . Written in French, 1948. Appeared in *transition,* 1948. First publication by Grove in *Poems in English.*

dread nay. Written in English, 1974. First publication by Grove in *Collected Poems.*

Something There. Written in English, 1974. First publication by Grove in *Collected Poems.*

Roundelay. Written in English, 1976. Appeared in Samuel Beckett issue of *Modern Drama* (Toronto), 1976. First publication by Grove in *Collected Poems.*

thither. Written in English, 1976. First publication by Grove in *Collected Poems.*

away dream . . . Written in English, 1981, for an anthology of one-line poems ("Monostiches") commissioned by the French poets Emmanuel Hocquard and Claude Royet-Journoud. Eventually published in 1986 by Flammarion (Paris) in *Orange Export Ltd. 1969–1986,* a collective volume devoted to the publications issued by the small press of that name (edited by Hocquard and Raquel). Other contributors to the one-line poem section include Edmond Jabès, Jacques Derrida (the only poem he ever published), Michel Deguy, Jacques Dupin, as well as a number of Americans: Robert Creeley, John Ashbery (writing in French), William Bronk, Ron Padgett, Michael Palmer, and Paul Auster. This is the first American publication of what is undoubtedly Beckett's shortest work.

What Is the Word. Written in French in late 1988 (*Comment dire*). This translation was Beckett's final literary work before his death in 1989. Published in *As the Story Was Told* (John Calder, London), 1990; hitherto unpublished in the United States.

THREE EARLY STORIES

Assumption. transition, 1929. First publication by Grove in *The Complete Short Prose,* 1995.

Sedendo et Quiescendo. Written 1931. Appeared in *transition,* 1932. The story is a fragment from *Dream of Fair to Middling Women,* published posthumously by the Black Cat Press, Dublin, 1992, and Arcade in association with Riverrun Press, New York, 1993. First publication by Grove in *The Complete Short Prose.*

A Case in a Thousand. The Bookman, 1934. First publication by Grove in *The Complete Short Prose.*

MORE PRICKS THAN KICKS

A collection of ten stories, written between 1931 and 1933, published by Chatto and Windus (London), 1934. "Dante and the Lobster" appeared in *This Quarter,* 1932. First Grove edition, 1972.

STORIES, TEXTS, NOVELLAS

First Love. Written in French, 1946 (*Premier Amour*). As with *Mercier and Camier,* the first of his novels not composed in English, Beckett withheld the story from publication for many years. Finally released by Editions de Minuit (Paris) in 1970. First publication by Grove in *First Love and Other Shorts,* 1974.

The Expelled. Written in French, 1946 (*L'Expulsé*). Appeared in the magazine *Fontaine* (1946) and subsequently included in *Nouvelles et textes pour rien* (Minuit, 1955). The English version, "translated by Richard Seaver in collaboration with the author," appeared in *The Evergreen Review,* 1962. First publication by Grove in *Stories and Texts for Nothing,* 1967.

The Calmative. Written in French, 1946 (*Le Calmant*). Published in *Nouvelles et textes pour rien.* Beckett's English translation appeared in *The Evergreen Review,* 1967. First published by Grove in *Stories and Texts for Nothing.*

The End. Beckett's first work of fiction written in French, 1946 (*La Fin*). The first half of the story appeared in *Les Temps modernes* that same year. Later published in *Nouvelles et textes pour rien.* The English version, "translated by Richard Seaver in collaboration with the author," appeared in the magazine *Merlin*, 1954. A revised translation was published in *The Evergreen Review*, 1960. First publication by Grove in *Stories and Texts for Nothing*.

Texts for Nothing. Thirteen short prose pieces written in French between 1950 and 1952 (*Textes pour rien*). Later published in *Nouvelles et textes pour rien*. Several of Beckett's English translations appeared in magazines and anthologies: Number 1 in *The Evergreen Review*, 1959; Number 3 in *Great French Short Stories*, edited by Germaine Brée (Dell), 1960; Number 6 in *London Magazine*, 1967; Number 12 in *The Transatlantic Review*, 1967. First publication by Grove in *Stories and Texts for Nothing*.

From an Abandoned Work. Written in English, 1954–55. Appeared in *The Evergreen Review*, 1957. First publication by Grove in *First Love and Other Shorts*.

All Strange Away. Written in English, 1964. First publication by Grove in *Rockaby and Other Short Pieces*, 1981.

Imagination Dead Imagine. Written in French in the early sixties (*Imagination mort imaginez*). First published in *Les Lettres nouvelles*, 1965. Beckett's English translation appeared in *The Sunday Times of London*, November 7, 1965, and in *The Evergreen Review*, 1966. Included in the collection *Têtes-mortes* (Minuit) 1967. First Grove publication in *First Love and Other Shorts*.

Enough. Written in French, 1965 (*Assez*). Included in *Têtes-mortes*. Beckett's English translation appeared in *Books and Bookmen*, 1967. First publication by Grove in *First Love and Other Shorts*.

Ping. Written in French, 1966 (*Bing*). Included in *Têtes-mortes*. Beckett's English translation appeared in *Harper's Bazaar*, 1967. First publication by Grove in *First Love and Other Shorts*.

Lessness. Written in French, 1969 (*Sans*). Included in the second edition of *Têtes-mortes* (Minuit) 1972. Beckett's English translation appeared in *The Evergreen Review*, 1970. First publication by Grove in *I Can't Go On, I'll Go On*, edited by Richard Seaver, 1976.

The Lost Ones. Written in French, 1965; the final paragraph was added in 1970 (*Le Dépeupleur*). Minuit, 1970. First Grove edition, 1972.

Fizzles. Eight short prose pieces from the early sixties. Written in French, except for number 7, "Still." Published by Minuit under the title *Pour finir encore et autres foirades*, 1976. First Grove edition, 1976.

One Evening. Written in French, 1979 (*Un Soir*). Beckett's English translation appeared in *The Journal of Beckett Studies*, 1980. First publication by Grove in *The Complete Short Prose*.

As the story was told. Written in English, 1973. Appeared in *The Chicago Review*, 1982. First publication by Grove in *The Complete Short Prose*.

neither. Written in English in 1976 for the American composer Morton Feldman. First publication by Grove in *The Complete Short Prose*.

Company. Written in English in the late seventies. First Grove edition, 1980.

Ill Seen Ill Said. Written in French, 1980–81 (*Mal vu mal dit*). Minuit, 1981. Beckett's English translation was published in *The New Yorker* in October of that year. First Grove edition, 1981.

Worstward Ho. Written in English, 1981–82. First Grove edition, 1983.

Stirrings Still. Written in English between 1983 and 1987. Published in a limited edition by Blue Moon Books (New York), 1989. First publication by Grove in *The Complete Short Prose*.

CRITICISM

Dante . . . Bruno . Vico . . Joyce. Written 1929. Appeared in *transition* June 1929, then revised and reprinted in *Our Exagmination Round his Factification for Incamination of Work in Progress*, which was released by Shakespeare and Company (Paris) that same year. First publication by Grove in *Disjecta*, edited by Ruby Cohn, 1984.

Proust. Written 1930. Published by Chatto and Windus (London), 1931. First Grove edition, 1957.

Three Dialogues. transition, 1949. First publication by Grove in *Disjecta*.

Fizzles. Eight short prose pieces from the early sixties. Written in French, except for number 7, "Still." Published by Minuit under the title *Pour finir encore et autres foirades,* 1976. First Grove edition, 1976.

One Evening. Written in French, 1979 (*Un Soir*). Beckett's English translation appeared in *The Journal of Beckett Studies,* 1980. First publication by Grove in *The Complete Short Prose.*

As the story was told. Written in English, 1973. Appeared in *The Chicago Review,* 1982. First publication by Grove in *The Complete Short Prose.*

neither. Written in English in 1976 for the American composer Morton Feldman. First publication by Grove in *The Complete Short Prose.*

Company. Written in English in the late seventies. First Grove edition, 1980.

Ill Seen Ill Said. Written in French, 1980–81 (*Mal vu mal dit*). Minuit, 1981. Beckett's English translation was published in *The New Yorker* in October of that year. First Grove edition, 1981.

Worstward Ho. Written in English, 1981–82. First Grove edition, 1983.

Stirrings Still. Written in English between 1983 and 1987. Published in a limited edition by Blue Moon Books (New York), 1989. First publication by Grove in *The Complete Short Prose.*

CRITICISM

Dante . . . Bruno . Vico . . Joyce. Written 1929. Appeared in *transition* June 1929, then revised and reprinted in *Our Exagmination Round his Factification for Incamination of Work in Progress,* which was released by Shakespeare and Company (Paris) that same year. First publication by Grove in *Disjecta,* edited by Ruby Cohn, 1984.

Proust. Written 1930. Published by Chatto and Windus (London), 1931. First Grove edition, 1957.

Three Dialogues. transition, 1949. First publication by Grove in *Disjecta.*